FOR PLAY

FOR PLAY

06/15/2010

by

WILL MCMASTERS

This Story is about the sexual revolution and how some real people dealt with it. This story will arouse you, will make you laugh and will teach you things about good sex. This can be a reference book, a joke book, or just a sexy story.
Enjoy.

The Sexiest True Story Ever Written

 www.trafford.com

North America & international
toll-free: 1 888 232 4444 (USA & Canada)
phone: 250 383 6864 ♦ fax: 812 355 4082

TABLE OF CONTENTS

Chapter 1. The Set Up

This is a story about the unusual sexual maturation of three people, two men and a woman; the woman is an ideal happy wife. This summary of experiences should work to motivate lovers to have better sex lives. These experiences would be considered X rated by many people, but this story is meant to present a variety of love making ideas, and such advice would be worthless without explicit details. The details are necessary and we hope this true story will also serve as a learning manual of sexual techniques. We believe true experiences are more helpful than objective surveys. This story covers a 30 year span, and then some, and involves our participation in the sexual revolution and the "Great Pube Wars" that began in the late 1950s.

I want to open people's minds to the possibility that candid sexual discussions between adults do not have a conflict with moral values; in fact open discussions can improve everybody's sex life. Mature married couples can morally do anything they want to please each other, but how much can be done or discussed with close friends for the purpose of growing relationships is a major point for this discussion. Married couples discussing sexual techniques is a great idea; Ego problems? Probably.

Discussing intimacies with people outside a marriage may be more dependent on the level of sophistication of the people involved. Married couples may be more experienced? Don't be so sure. We are not suggesting any physical sexual practices between couples just informative motivational dialogue. Disclosure and discussion between adults for the purpose of enhancing relationships is important. However, we do find some sexual practices to be perverted, even for discussion, and they are not discussed or experienced in this story. For reporting these true experiences boundaries were established that should reflect good taste. In this case, the stories will offer suggestions for great lovers, married or not. As a reader warning, this book is erotic and may not be appropriate for immature children.

A sense of humor regarding sex is necessary because humor can help overcome inhibitions. Humor is a big part of the lives of happy people. My personal writing style is to narrate this story, which, as I said is a true story. So, I tried to recapture some original humor whenever possible. These experiences offer factual details that actually happened, but obviously we changed the names and sometimes the chronology to protect the guilty, or innocent, depending on your point of view. I hope to present this as an erotic non-fiction novel combined with motivational, yet with sex manual type instructions. We also feature our psychology and philosophy as well read and experienced men and women. I want our readers to understand that we are amateurs when it comes to reporting, but sincere. I hope you appreciate the humor along with these fascinating personal observations.

I had the privilege of spending the past fifty years with a close friend that sexually attracted women like no other person I ever even heard of. I have named him Jack Callahan. Jack was not out to "bed" or to conquer women, he was respectful and straightforward about his intentions, yet many beautiful women pursued him. This is something all men wish they had to deal with. I will repeat Jack's qualifications as they apply to this series of events are spread over 30 years. Our attitudes also evolved as we became more experienced.

Jack and I both believe that most people repress their sexual desires and we call those repressions "inhibitions." Our social values and our up bringing established our moral codes, which have always been in conflict with our natural desires, more so for all preteen men. All lovers want to have confidence and desires that build their own self-esteem. Doing so without experience is the challenge of youth. We all hope to exude sex appeal and a lack of experience contradicts that desire. Performing sexually, or discussing sex early in the sexual revolution was either embarrassing or perhaps even considered immoral, but much less so today. All experiences should be learning experiences and dealing with negatives or rejection is the hard part of the "Pube Wars." We often refer to the early stages of the sexual revolution as "The Great Pube Wars." These repressed or undeveloped natural urges are the root cause of sexual inadequacies and discussing them or in the case of this story, relating them as sexy events that could easily explain one's inhibitions as being superfluous, or more harmful than beneficial. Read on!

So, please indulge me and allow me to tell this story in a personal narrative format. I feel like a good friend confiding in you, the reader; think of me as a new intimate friend wanting to share some amazing experiences that if properly told will enhance your love life regardless of your gender. To reiterate, this is not a series of sex exploits based on some machismo need for two guys to count their conquests. It was never like that. The two of us were so fascinated by women, almost to a fault because we seem to have dedicated our lives to learning how to please women.

The reciprocity received from women in the form of pleasure was more than we expected. And all of these relationships were left in good stead. No one's feelings were hurt and all experiences were discussed with all participants in an adult and respectful manner. No one caught any diseases or had unwanted babies as a result of our experiences, and I assure you no one's feelings were hurt. We burned no bridges. It turns out to have been a fun project for all involved. We are not scientists; just a couple of accomplished basketball players that roomed together in college and unknowingly agreed to a long term plan to better learn how to treat women.

What really makes for great sex is passion. Passionate people are always referred to as "great lays." The opposite of passion would be "mechanical sex." Pornography is mechanical and must dub in fake passion. We have touched on passionless sex as part of some of our internal scientific tests, which while mechanical at the outset, always eventually turned passionate. Perhaps you will learn more about passion from our experiences; we did.

Lovers should always express themselves verbally during sex because that increases passion as well as pleasure. We should at least make noises of satisfaction, moaning, purring, grunts and anything that comes to mind, and actually that is normal and should not be restrained. Even if you have to fake pleasure, learn to do it; that will make you sexy as well as enhancing your partner's sexual pleasures. Men seldom make noises during sex and why that is, is perhaps another research project meant for the more professional scientists. Is it considered less macho to be silent? When someone calls another a great sex partner it usually means that partner was vocal during sex. Think about that. Isn't that what you remember most?

I suppose there is some danger for "screamers," and we deal with that issue. The sounds of sex may attract unwanted attention from those not involved. We relate some of those noisy experiences in this story. Keep in mind that vocalization will always turn a partner on to higher levels of pleasure. To reiterate, such traits are not as prevalent with men. Men tend to be restrained, but passionate reactions to sexual behavior works two ways. It can enhance both partners pleasure, while less passionate reactions can lead to routine sex. Such rationalization is complicated, but again relates to inhibitions and repressed desires and may restrain the urge to try creative sexual adventures.

Sexual adventure has always been a difficult rationalization for adults because we all mature at different paces and general rules may not apply to everybody. Imaginary adventures are the grounds for fantasies. Young children are born with fewer inhibitions and probably no fantasies and they spend the rest of their lives trying to repress or perhaps reduce their inhibitions brought on by adulthood.

Children growing through puberty need codes and rules to contain permissiveness. Young people need to mature gradually and in spite of social limitations will grow into healthier sex lives if excluded from too much regulation. Guilt and excessive inhibitions need to eventually be curtailed or eliminated. The answer is solid subjective sex education programs. Children need not rush their sexual development; that can be counterproductive. Sexual development is quite a conundrum.

Today, children grow up too fast. Their lives are inundated with sex on TV and in movies. Even Illustrator drawn bra advertisements were taboo when we were growing up. There definitely has been a twentieth century sexual revolution, which my age group participated therein. That also makes this story less unusual. The way we talk and explain our views may seem out of date for some younger readers, but we are sure you will get the meanings.

Passion may not be teachable, but it can be suggested. We can learn passion by example. We will plant some seeds of passion in this story, or, increase the power of suggestion. It is entirely possible to become more passionate and learn passion from the examples of others, especially from these true experiences if we can write them with passion. This story should "turn you on."

There is an ongoing controversy regarding what is acceptable to religion or what might be attributed to plain human sexual drives blamed on "mother nature." The evolution of sexual attitudes is what the sequence of events in this story is meant to illustrate. The purpose is to show married couples that being creative and working on new foreplay techniques, and talking about sex can enhance married life. Of course, to reiterate, the new ideas and explanations will make great lovers out of anybody.

I remind you that this story actually happened, however, the names, places and sequences may be fictionalized. I also have taken the liberty of embellishing the details of each experience to increase there "learn ability." The personalities described herein may be combinations of more than one person's personality. These experiences were selected because of their potential to give you some good ideas, or teach you something. We eliminated many experiences in order to condense the more meaningful events.

I want to begin with the sexualization of this featured very moral wife, and then follow up with the lessons, which should benefit all the people who read this philosophical sexually explicit story. You might say that we are examining the psychology of sexual behavior. The lead female character is Cynthia, and I apologize if I make all the readers named Cynthia blush. A woman named Carol Mason is our best example of a sexy woman whose experience teaches and Cynthia absorbs, grows and evolves.

Young men, beginning with puberty, are primarily driven by the physical desires for sex. After reaching puberty, we supposedly think about sex every twenty seconds. I can't confirm that. Actually nobody can, but we believe most men are naturally horny; we are born with "little heads" that are destined to control our lives. Is this some sort of cruel trick from God to inhibit men's maturity? Men's emotional side is developed later and at too slow a pace that never catches up with the more mature sexual emotions of women. In other words, sex is more emotional for women and more physical for men, and when will the two meet? It will forever never be beyond the personal level for women to pursue sex for their own benefit. But, isn't that what the sexual revolution was all about? Women, maybe pursuing sex for their own personal benefit? At first, the majority of women seem to view sex with potential negative repercussions or too much guilt. Maybe I can open some doors for you if you can open your mind.

Women at puberty start emotional developments that never cease. Emotional development continues for women during their entire lifetimes. They can waiver or increase, or decrease without warning. Maturing must be more difficult for women. They have more water in their bodies and their physical sexual make up is far more complicated than men. Women are generally more sensitive, thank goodness. The conflict between the two sexes commences during what we call the "Great Pube Wars." (ages 11 to 21 or often times longer) Some studies show that only 20% of women have more advanced physical urges. And about 80% of men run those urges off the charts. After this story, I conclude that women have greater sex drives than reported or polled, certainly more than 20%.

The sex drive of men is derived from their God given allocation of hormones determined by their DNA. The same holds true for women, but women seem to have more control over their urges and that can be a social reaction as to how they are raised. After all, where would society be if women were equally as aggressive and horny as men? Statistics reflect that it takes women, on an average twenty minutes to become aroused and men can do the same almost instantly, but probably an average of half as much time.

It is significant to note that women with college degrees are less apt to get divorced today and that college women tend to marry at a later age, and women initiate two thirds of all divorces. In 1960, the average age for women to marry was 20. Today the average age for a woman's first marriage is 26. Women who marry later tend to have fewer children. Yesterday's "loose" women are today's "liberated" women. Today women can explore their sexuality without being punished for their libido. No fault divorces have greatly increased the divorce rate in the US. Our initial entry into the sexual revolution began in the late 1950's before women were armed with pills and men were poorly armed with condoms. Ahh, the Great Pube Wars, what excitement, join with us.

I'm going to begin by telling you about a true, particularly fascinating spectacular week of adult sexual growth and enlightenment. Then, I will flashback to college and our initiation to sex. You might call it a personal moral revolution, which may not seem normal to everybody, and that is certainly debatable. We think our experiences are exceptional while normal. Then there is always that controversy as to how sinners rationalize their actions. I don't know who supports our activity and who is morally opposed; please keep an open mind. You can make your own judgment.

My name is Will McMasters and this story involves me, my wife Cynthia, and my best friend Jack Callahan. We were all 45 years old at the time of this story. We will flashback after the first stories and explain how we developed to this first point. Cynthia and I had been happily married for 21 years, and have three children. Jack and Angela had been married for ten years. Angela had had two small children and had grown cool and disinterested in sex. That's another story for later. To repeat, I want to narrate this story as explicitly as I can and I hope no one is offended. But I do hope you will be pleasantly shocked.

Jack and I were college teammates and roommates both standing 6'5" having played on a major winning college basketball team. Jack became a successful stockbroker and I am a successful lawyer. We were, and are both in great physical conditions at just over 200 lbs. Jack was considered better looking than me, but both of us are classified as "tall, dark and handsome." We both had well defined muscles having lifted weights all of our lives, but not heavy stuff. We were so similar in size that we could have traded clothes.

Jack Callahan is a rare blue-eyed dark haired man of Irish heritage. Jack was the better basketball player and his "movie star" image was greatly enhanced by his admiration and respect for women. Actually he had several real life movie parts and was a member of the screen actor's guild. Together we developed this fascination of women into a science, research based on true experiences while always trying to learn better ways to treat women. It was an unplanned scientific effort based on respect, admiration and an overwhelming awe. It just sort of happened.

There are many famous names of scientists who studied and wrote volumes of pages about sex. The Kinsey report, Sigmund Freud, Dr Helen O'Connell, Anne Hooper, Dr. Grafenberg, (the guy who supposedly discovered the "G" spot) "The Joy of Sex," and many, many more scientists who arrived at conclusions from interviews and even to the extreme of conducting tests on cadavers. (yuk). The problem with their conclusions is that they were "second hand." The experiences in this book are revealed from "hands on," "mouth on," and "penis in" experiences. All of our female subjects were real women and although they had no idea they were being tested, or better said, so fondly remembered, their contributions were far more meaningful than ours. Their reactions were uninhibited and naturally passionate, and they were all willing to talk about their reactions. Our contributions by women are real and probably not adjusted for pollsters. That adds reality to the experiences rather than interpretations by scientists. But we promoted and instigated discussions at the time these events occurred and there was no faking. The women's verbal input was extensive, but were not aware they would be remembered, nor were Jack and I taking notes. These women were special in their ability to communicate about sex, and we take credit for getting them to expound.

However, many of the ladies did get to comment on how they felt and what could be done to improve sex at the time. We asked many questions and once intimate with women, and with due respect, you'd be surprised what can be discussed and learned. If properly approached with respect, many women would also divulge sexual experiences and feelings in a scientific manner. They were not aware that their opinions would be made public so they were more willing to talk about sex, but then their identities are protected and their views were never discussed with others at the time. Neither did Jack or I realize at the time of these sexual experiences that we would be writing this book.

To summarize: as a result of confidential exchanges of information between two good friends and college teammates, and many trusted intimate women friends, we hoped to improve our love making abilities to provide women pleasure not realizing that we would write this book. This book is both objective and subjective.

We think our more intimate experiences are more meaningful than scientific surveys.

The Characters.

Jack had the personality, good looks and physical build that attracted all women. He had broad shoulders and a flat stomach that rippled with muscle. Actually, so did I, but I didn't have the charm Jack had. I was basically shy. Regarding Jack's personality, he could do a stand-up comedy act in any group exemplifying an obvious comedic sense of humor and quick wit that could bring spontaneous enjoyment and laughter to any group, men or women. Jack was also a great dancer and loved to dance.

Jack was strong and tough; he grew up in a big city as a tough street fighter, never a bully, always relying on his charm to make life easy. He had no fears. He had a vertical leap allowing him to "slam dunk" a basketball with two hands from a standing start. Jack was an all around great athlete. I am also a talented athlete, but I am also an honor student. My sense of humor was not as obvious as Jack, but I was classified as charming and somewhat "laid back."

We played for a major State school with a national reputation. During one big basketball game, an opponent took Jack's legs out from under him after he stole the ball and was up in the air for an easy lay-up. Jack fell hard in a sitting position, a drop that would break most people's backs. Jack rolled over to his knees and after catching his breath, jumped up and punched Gordon Rollins in the nose. The foul had already been called on Gordon. The benches emptied; a lot of scuffling, calm prevailed and Jack got his free throws. Jack and Gordon were both ejected from the game.

We won and the ejections were late in the game. After the game we all showed up at the same restaurant for a joint team dinner after this Saturday road game. Our team arrived by bus whereas our opponents arrived individually. Gordon was sitting at a table right inside the dining room with two good-looking co-eds. Gordon was an arrogant bachelor bastard and with a smirk greeted us with, "Hey Jack how's your ass?"

Jack quickly replied, "Its fine how's your tongue?"

That is the kind of retort that is considered fast and witty and very insulting. Jack walked toward Gordon hoping to kick his ass, when Gordon took one girl by the hand and quickly exited amid the resounding group laughter resulting from Jack's comment. Gordon, already sporting a black eye, wanted no part of Jack. Nobody in their right mind would pick a fight with Jack. I stepped in and restrained Jack to keep the peace. That is but one illustration of this exceptionally witty talented good-looking man. All women loved him, and all men respected him. Back in college, Jack was extremely popular. I'll get to some of his relevant experiences later. I must get on with this story. Jack reminded many of a taller, better built, better looking James Garner, of TV and movie fame.

Jack and I have forever discussed the most intimate details about sex with each other. We talked about our relationships with women purposely to share knowledge and experience, never to be discussed with others. No macho bragging allowed, but pure motivational research directed at improving our abilities to satisfy women. As I said, women fascinated us, we idolized them, they seemed smarter than us and always more mature sexually. They just didn't fully realize their potential and that frustrated us. You might say we were obsessed with women, but with all due respect. Our sex drives were, well, we were two constantly horny guys. We were always alert to any passing female with outstanding qualities. We considered ourselves critics that lived in a live art gallery of beautiful women.

We also discussed Religion, politics, philosophy, history, psychology, and science. Jack specifically had an interest in Civil War history. We also followed most sports and would often bet with each other. We never bet large sums of money, mostly lunches and beers and just enough to keep a competitive interest in sports.

Our sex experiences began in college; we roomed together, traveled with the team as roommates and were forced to be in the same room for some sexual adventures with women. Privacy was a difficult accommodation so we had to work together with trust and secrecy. Many times I stayed late at the school library, or I had to pretend to be asleep while I listened to all those delightful sounds emanating from good sex. Too often I had to get a hold of myself. What happened to Jack and I in college is significant to our sexual development and to this story. We had the most unusual experience in college with one woman that set the stage, and raised the bar for all later adventures. I, first, must fast forward to this big eventful week that occurred when we were both 45 years old. I will come back to those years in college, which will also blow your mind.

Cynthia, my wife and my high school sweetheart, was aware of the long close friendship and intimate revelations between Jack and me. She was slowly developing into a confidential teammate, so to speak, and for over 25 years, a close confidant in our little intimate threesome that enjoyed talking about sex. It was good clean adult fun and names or dates were seldom mentioned. Relating these experiences was as much of a learning experience for Cynthia as they were subliminally arousing all of us. We were not really sure of Cynthia's deepest feelings because she had so many moral conflicts even being an avid listener.

Cynthia enjoyed limited sharing of experiences at first, but would never contribute any of her own. To my knowledge, Cynthia did not have any experiences whatsoever outside of her marriage. We were only separated for a few years in college. She went to a private girl's college many miles away from our State school earning a teaching degree. Cynthia and I corresponded regularly knowing that someday we would get together. She didn't have any experiences with other men in college or she would have told me. Cynthia might be considered "old fashion," but wanted so much to be close to Jack and me as a team. When growing up, she harbored "little girl" thoughts about saving herself for her husband, raising a family and living happily after. And that was very good.

She was a sort of a prude, but as she matured, that was to prove to be a "projected image." Women don't normally want to be recognized as "horny." They dream about being desired, loved, with security and being in control of relationships. Helping her sexual maturation without being offensive to her was the real challenge. She loved pretending to be sophisticated even though we had to explain much to her. She did not get many sexual jokes or understand the long list of sexual slang. She thought "fuck" was a nasty swear word and never to be spoken in good company.

In my opinion, she was naïve, sweet and innocent. Her upbringing was strict, never wandering far from her parental oversight. I think, buried inside her libido, was a strong desire to be sexy, however subtle, but never showy and always restrained by her peers and family. She demanded respect and her moral judgments of others were important not to be heard, but kept private between her husband and only the closest of friends, especially Jack Callahan. Cynthia was one of those well trained "neat freak" homemakers that when I went to the bathroom in the middle of the night, I would return to find my side of the bed made and my wife asleep. (I'm kidding).

Cynthia was not a big prude about the basics of marital sex. To her sex was a private function not to be discussed with others. Much of her resistance to spontaneous marital sex was her fear of continual unplanned pregnancies. She was very inhibited and always blushing at the idea of "dirty sex talk." Her evolving attitude and conversion to a mature and adult understanding of foreplay and sexual adventure within a marriage was the goal of these related intimate stories. She didn't think of them as Jack bragging about his conquests, nor did he act that way. Sometimes, Cynthia did not want to hear stories of Jack's adulterous adventures; it may have been a mood swing. I did not discuss any of my previous sexual experiences. There was nothing to be gained by doing so. Discussing Jack's sex life was acceptable and accomplished the same thing. What transpired over the many years prior to the coming story of the "big week," were discussions about what Jack should do and was allowed to do because of his wife's lack of interest in him, or sex. It was Jack telling an amusing sexual incident that triggered this big week of attitude change.

Scatophilia is deriving sexual satisfaction from talking naughty or about obscene matters with strangers, or in fact just being aroused from talking about sex. This book might be considered a "Scatophilic book.

Cynthia was "my" virgin when we married. She loved sex and it would be difficult to find fault with her present attitude. What I confessed to Jack was that I wished she was more passionate, or maybe more vocal, or more expressive as our marriage grew. She was a silent lover with little body language. We often exchanged words of love, usually after sex. She never declined an opportunity to make love and even enjoyed performing full fellatio during her menstrual periods. Fellatio was a regular part of our foreplay as was cunnilingus. I had no reason not to discuss this with Jack, but I feared our sex life was getting routine and Cynthia was all about being in love and nothing else was important. No complaints about that. I was hoping for some stimulus from Jack's experiences to motivate Cynthia to new techniques. We had a plan.

Cynthia might even be considered sexually aggressive in her own conservative way. I said she never had a "headache" and never said no even to therapeutic quickies. Her rather cute term to suggest having sex was, "I sure feel like getting chummy tonight." Or, "I hope we can cuddle naked for a while." I had insisted that Cynthia sleep in the nude, which she was always reluctant to do. She kept a robe close at hand in case she had to get up to check on the kids or cover herself on a short trip to the bathroom. Her body was always covered except in the dark and under the sheets. What a shame, she had a perfect body.

Wow! What a great wife I had. And Jack was full of envy as we discussed her sexual skills over the years, which were directly related to her exceptional beauty and sexy body. She had the natural ability to swing her hips and every step she took reeked of sex appeal. Every movement of each body part was perfectly orchestrated yet natural to her. She was actually quite naïve about her sexuality. I was keeping Jack informed on her ability to perform fellatio so readily, to excel without any self-commendation. Her ability to perform fellatio so well and so naturally was inexplicable. But underneath all this talk was our mutual ever lasting and growing admiration of Cynthia. Jack was all envy and often told me so. She was so sexy and beautiful and it was frustrating that she did not realize her potential.

Jack would often share his sexual adventures with Cynthia and me, and I would use her arousals to take advantage of her new excitement later those evenings at bedtime. Our sex life was wonderful in spite of her lack of body language during sex. It was an interesting ongoing learning experience for all three of us. My wife appreciated my enthusiasm, but never said much about it. I am a vocal lover. I thought I deserved compliments, or at least a more passionate reaction. Cynthia was just too "reserved."

All of my friends admired Cynthia for her beauty and grace, even the ladies. My conversations with Jack about his sexual adventures contributed evermore to my own appreciation of my wife. Jack being so envious was actually appreciated as a guy thing. He claimed he fostered fantasies about Cynthia and that was OK. All he had to do was look at Cynthia and think about things I had revealed to him. I think sharing these things with the three of us also drove Jack on to new heights with his own sex life. There were occasions where I would brag about Cynthia in front of Cynthia. Cynthia appropriately blushed, but never talked about what she thought about our marital sex.

There are three kinds of sex. There is making love, there is therapeutic sex, which relaxes or relieves stress, and finally there is sport sex, which should consist of adventures and variety, but ideally within a marriage. Group sex was a horrible idea because it implied sharing no more than a physical commodity, which was degrading to most women. The acceptance of the three modes of sex is an adult interpretation. All three modes should involve foreplay, but perhaps with less reciprocity in the case of therapeutic sex.

Therapeutic sex is a very unselfish act, but unfortunately, most people are not sufficiently skilled in any kind of foreplay. Foreplay is the single most important ingredient in love and sex. Why not open discussions between partners that might also be considered as foreplay. That worked for Cynthia. Soon after hearing a good story, she seemed to enjoy sex more. The explicit sex stories became a subtle form of foreplay. Actually, it is all a matter of better communication between partners. Men unfortunately are not great communicators once he gets "her" in bed. There is little intimate discussion of the merits of love making techniques for fear of hurting someone's ego.

One must be extra careful in screening women who might enter into adult conversations about sex. That conversation may only work with more sophisticated people, or possibly with sophisticated groups of good friends. Such "one on one" discussions can be a fun way to get to know someone because you can measure their level of sophistication. I wonder if such conversations take place with how many other people. In our case the main ingredient, that we seemed to emit, was trust. We were sure we had earned a person's trust before engaging in sexy conversations. This often worked for us because we had a knack for when to bring such discussions to the table.

Once Jack and I got to be more familiar with women, we were very good at judging their level of interest and how and when to tactfully proceed. Men have the difficult task of being aggressors, which always requires the utmost of tact and diplomacy. Women are easily offended when allowing a fast approach reflects on their reputation. Men need a sixth sense to know when they can advance a relationship. The worst example I ever heard was ex-President Clinton entering a hotel room with an unsuspecting and shocked Paula Jones watching him expose himself thinking he had so much sex appeal he didn't need tact. She eventually won that lawsuit after being smeared for being offended by Bill's low class proposition. You get the idea here regarding the tact necessary for successful seductions? Good!

My Cynthia was a physical marvel. Cynthia resembles a taller Sandra Bullock, the movie star, but with short black thick wavy hair and bigger breasts than Sandra. She had retained her high school figure and had been voted beauty Queens in both High school and college. Cynthia was 5'8" about 130 lbs and even in her late 40's, and after three kids, was a superb physical "Playboy type" specimen. She had perfect leg definition with calf muscles that flexed when she walked, yet tapered perfectly. Her thighs were also perfectly honed (no flab) and her smooth spotless skin was like slightly tanned pearls. Her dark black curly hair was always worn short because it would have been a big job keeping it in place if longer. Her hair was thick and of strong fiber, always neat and every wave in perfect place.

Instead of combing her hair she could shake her head and all of her hair fell back into place. Her hair needed little care other than daily shampooing and monthly cutting. Her pubic hair was the same texture and she had pubic hair borders as if she had shaved the little triangle. She didn't have to shave her pubic hairs; the shape was natural. Her upper pubic hairline stopped naturally and reflected a perfect triangle. I don't understand why it never changed. After all, she had to have regular beauty parlor haircuts and I'm pretty sure she didn't get her pubic hair shaved.

Here is a major piece of advice for all lovers: every time when she showered, Cynthia applied commercial "hair conditioner" to her pubic hair. Every woman should know of that treatment because that fresh odor lasted a long time, and if done by all women would greatly increase any man's natural desire to spend facial time between a woman's legs. A fresh smelling pubic area was like inhaling honey and we bees were lost in a paradise of olfactory heaven. Take note, ladies, let the conditioner hold in place during the shower, the last to be rinsed. This also works for guys. What have you guys got to lose with sweet smelling pubic hair? You never know when you might get lucky. Remember that old line? "I suppose a blow job would be out of order?"

Women cannot adequately describe that first warm feeling of a flat hot tongue lying on their clitoris, and what technique a man applies next is part of what this book is about. What do you do with your tongue? The many techniques depends on the outcome of highly stimulated test runs knowing none can really fail, but learning how to drive a woman to a climax, or extend their pleasure. There is a major art form on purposely interrupting cunnilingus and fellatio with a series of teasing. It may be called stalling. It frustrates the drive to orgasm, but extends the pleasure. Many such techniques are revealed in this book.

Cynthia had medium sized breasts; they were "perky" and pointed straight ahead. She never acquired wrinkles or stretch marks and her waist tapered gradually to her hip line. Her ass was firm and did not jiggle. Her hip swing was natural, but was accentuated when wearing high heels. Her ass had that special curve that never went unnoticed. She turned many a head. She had what some thought an athletic build, with beautifully shaped broad shoulders and no body fat. There was nothing that could be done to improve this gorgeous woman. She was always classy, statuesque, and well groomed. She was always clean and had perfect manners, conducting herself with the stature of well-bred royalty. She was somewhat aloof and her English heritage reflected conservatism coupled with her strict protestant upbringing. She was hot, didn't realize it and wouldn't admit it, but liked being told about it.

Now Cynthia simply could not have a complete orgasm during sexual intercourse, and that is not uncommon for women. But cunnilingus (Oral stimulation of the female genitals) is or should be a common practice in every successful sexual encounter. It arouses a fire in any woman and is not easily doused. When the sex act begins with cunnilingus, the results guarantee greater pleasure to the male. If a woman climaxes prior to intercourse, she is hot, wet and tight. How can a pussy be hot, wet and tight? That sounds like an oxymoron of conflicting attributes. Let me confirm that both tight and wet are possible. Cynthia loved cunnilingus; it always gave her an orgasm.

A man's reward is considerably more gratifying with the right sexual techniques. A woman's reaction comes from how the man reacts since a man's recognition or understanding of inter vaginal nerves are rare. (The "G" spot comes to mind). A passionate man forces a woman's reaction. And cunnilingus is an easy price to pay for excellence. The problem is the lack of male/female communication that is necessary to promote mutual orgasms. Most men lack the ability or desire to learn or improve upon that skill necessary to make a woman climax. Too many couples consider such foreplay talk as counterproductive because it reflects on the woman having too much experience or a man not having enough experience and either might be damaging or embarrassing.

The clitoris contains more than 8000 nerve endings, twice the amount found in an inflated penis. These minute strands of sensitive tissue are concentrated into a smaller area than the male penis, and the clitoris gets "engorged" or inflated like a penis, only on a smaller scale. When engorged the clitoris can become overly sensitive and each woman will have differing levels of sensitivity. Again, each individual is unique and his or her DNAs have different balances of hormones. Perhaps people should have printed copies of their hormone tests for comparative purposes. That is unlikely, but with the new age of medical records on computers, why not? Men might think twice about courting a woman with low testosterone, or maybe too much. Wait until you read about Carol Mason.

Cynthia's clitoris was very sensitive. When engorged it resembled a "bean." Clitorises vary in size from a small pea to a large lima bean. At first, her orgasms only came with oral sex being performed on her. Her intensity consisted of a few minutes of building pleasure ending with a short gasp. That's a pretty short orgasm. The immediate result was her clitoris became too sensitive for continued contact. I would blow gently on the risen little head, which always seemed to be begging for more action. She had to cool down her clitoris for a moment, but she was always appreciative, even though the moment seemed too brief. It was obvious with her wetness and anxiety she was anxious to proceed to intercourse. Most humans are disappointed at the length of time they enjoy orgasms, which makes a strong case for prolonging anybody's orgasm with a more teasing and an artful stalling technique of foreplay.

I wonder why God put the clitoris so far away from the vagina. Is it supposed to cause a woman to reach for better clitoral contact during intercourse with a wiggle, or move her hips hoping for more contact? I think the full thrusting penis is supposed to tap or lightly "flatten" a raised clitoris when the penis is driven into the vagina to the hilt. The constant tapping should build to an orgasm. Not easy to do. Maybe that means accelerating strokes to a mutual peak; each couple differs. Practice makes perfect!

I remember the old saying that if the clitoris was the width of a man's thumb away from the vagina she would have more and better orgasms. "The closer the thumbs, the better she comes." The objective of a woman's sexual movement was to get in a better position to feel the rapid repetition of the base of the penis, or even a man's pelvic bone, tapping or slapping gradually against the clitoris working toward an orgasm. I imagine the strokes are to be gradually increased until she reaches a peak, if a man can keep the pace without firing prematurely. There is also a prevalent theory that short strokes, say an inch or two at a rapid pace will better cause a woman to climax. I think the multitude of techniques will differ with each individual and part of sexual development is to strive to find the right technique. This is another recommendation for better communication.

What is supposed to happen is that as the penis moves inward it pulls the woman's skin pulling the clitoris closer to the thrusting penis. When a woman is too wet, the skin under the labia does not move. Her pussy may be too slippery to pull the clitoris into the action.

This act of foreplay coordination unfortunately is seldom discussed between couples. Again, it may cause ego damage. I will never understand why the ego is so important; worrying about an ego is considered a selfish feeling. Does an ego have to relate to durability? It often does for men performing sexually. For women, lasting a long time can be counterproductive to them if not working toward an orgasm.

Most women can enjoy some unlimited thrusting if wet and sufficiently aroused. But clitorises are very sensitive delicate instruments. An engorged clitoris may even try to recede to protect itself from too much rubbing. Or, it may become more aroused from the frustration of lack of contact. It is a cause of wonder why women don't climax more often. All of these conditions must be just right and yet they are different for each individual. The answer is different for each woman, but wetness is always a positive sign even if counterproductive to intercourse from a woman's point of clitoral contact. So, wet is good, and an aroused clitoris is good. The solution is in the foreplay and performing cunnilingus is the most important strategy. How much guilt should men bear for a lack of a woman's climax? All of the guilt? Perhaps.

Why don't young women condition their genitals by self-stimulation and hands on practice? Society has too many restrictions on the lack of self-esteem that reflects on masturbation. We don't even talk about it enough, especially back in the late fifties when we were growing up. Can you imagine sex education promoting masturbation for young girls when it was considered a normal thing for young men? For young men it was a matter of applying guilt to perhaps curtail masturbation. More on that later. Boys were always told that "jacking off" was bad for you. I didn't believe it.

Remember the story of the preteen boy who's Mother caught him masturbating and she told him excessive playing with one's self could result in blindness. The young man responded and asked if he could keep doing it until he needed glasses.

Cynthia loved the concept of oral sex and enjoyed the feelings created by my tongue. I think she looked forward to oral sex as much as intercourse. Cunnilingus did effectively prepare her mood more than any other technique, but I think she was disappointed that she didn't get more out of sexual intercourse, (no orgasms) or even having cunnilingus last longer. (Always with quick orgasms in her case) She never said a word about such things. I think Women's orgasm problems stem from a lack of pubescent self-stimulation, which usually was considered "disgusting?" At least that might be considered the case for my generation. Intercourse always felt good for Cynthia anyway.

Cynthia seemed to enjoy performing full fellatio (Fellatio to orgasm) especially during her menstrual cycles and she did not have to be asked. She began the practice during pregnancies, but always as reciprocal for my providing oral sex during pregnancies and being careful with sexual intercourse at late stages of pregnancy. She felt fellatio was an act of love that was supposed to help poor needy husbands release the tensions of life when sexual intercourse was not convenient or maybe messy. How necessary should it be for a man to have to get aroused with fellatio as foreplay? Is discussing such things going to hurt feelings or suggest inadequacies? That's another subject for later.

Cynthia readily absorbed my teaching her what felt best and how to improve her fellatio techniques. I taught her how to use her tongue, when to blow and cool the area and how to time swallowing with the ejaculation by pulling and stretching skin, and keeping it warm as it softens. The trial and error was a minimum effort, and she really learned fast with no objections. She was really good at it. She was especially cooperative over the years, but she never raved about how she looked forward to it, or how enjoyable if was for her. I'm not sure any woman rave about that and maybe it was not to be expected. It was just something that I would have appreciated. Is that the male ego problem, or the beginning of a lowering of self-esteem without rewards? From a heterosexual point of view it did seem like a messy and unpleasant process to the cocksucker, but then many women think eating pussy might be messy or unpleasant for men. We all have many adjustments to make regarding good sex. I'll never understand a man that doesn't like licking pussy. And every woman deserves a good licking now and then. The world has much to learn.

Sometimes I felt that my constructive comments to Cynthia were interpreted as a form of criticism and that she needed to do more to please me. Eventually after this coming event, I did ask and she said she never felt like I was complaining. Perhaps that was another problem in communication? Did I lack the communicative skills to make that delicate point back then? I often told her she was superb even though she was not emotional during the performance. But, sex was becoming too routine; it was like she was performing a service albeit for mutual pleasure. Obviously, her act was purely one of love and her desire to please her husband. Hey, that ain't all so bad! In fact she loved making love, never said no, but I didn't think she was vocal enough. How selfish of me!

Many people enjoy sex in silence not realizing that vocalizing and expressing joy would encourage their partner and increase each partner's enjoyment. I harbored this growing fear that sex might become routine and that the urges might fade with age. I believe that is bound to happen in spite of how deeply people love each other. Do we have to let it happen? Of course not!

Cynthia was conservative, yet so beautiful and a cooperative sex partner that criticizing her lack of exhibiting passion would have been out of order. This coming lesson was to hopefully accomplish the bursting out of her cocoon and raising her to full butterfly status. Little did she realize the upcoming events that would forever raise her conservative libido.

So, follow us into the sexual revolution and please know that the feminist's movement is primarily designed to eliminate the double standards that stand in the way of female sexual freedom.

Chapter 2. The VW Bed

Our dialogue became more specific when Jack had finally convinced Cynthia that he was entitled to sexual adventures out of marriage as long as he harmed no one and his partners were screened and qualified and thoroughly enjoyed what was going on. Jack actually had a knack for knowing how to stay out of trouble and not get caught. He was truthful in his propositions. He convinced Cynthia that Angela wouldn't care if she found out as long as she could concentrate on her kids. It made me wonder how Jack ever ended up with Angela.

A major start of this sexual awakening of Cynthia began when the three of us were having lunch on a nice summer day, and Jack was reminiscing about a girl named Sue. This initial meeting between Jack and Sue occurred the previous winter, but came to mind when we were inquiring about how that clandestine relationship was coming along.

Jack and Sue met and had a few drinks last year at a company due diligence meeting. Sue worked at Jack's company as a trainee. Using our special old movie star identification code, Sue resembled Kim Bassinger. Sorry if we reflect on older movie stars from our past. Jack and I played this silly movie star game our whole lives thinking we could better describe the events with some relative recognition. Remember, I never met some of these women. We are trying to accomplish the same recognition techniques using examples, but certainly with no reason to disrespect any movie stars. My wife thinks I resemble a much bigger Gregory Peck, who at this writing has died. I wonder if she thinks I look like a dead person, nah, just kidding. You have to play this movie star "identification game" with us to get the most out of these stories.

At company parties Jack and Sue were flirting, occasionally smooching, and getting turned on passing in corridors and having quick meetings in dark corners. It was advanced flirting with "come on" sayings and challenges about what could happen. The excitement builds as the partners use their body language to build tension, or build foreplay. Many people play these games just for fun and never go so far as to get involved sexually. Flirting is a common game people play. Eventual sex is a more serious game.

Sue was married and claimed her husband was a workaholic who wasn't servicing her account properly. Teasing each other was a more sophisticated form of flirting and both Jack and Sue knew what they were doing and thoroughly enjoyed the game. Sue was tall and blond and well equipped with a very sexy personality to compliment her sex appeal. You might say she was a very horny mother. Sue demanded confidentiality, something Jack also demanded. They were both excited at the newness of their meeting and the exchange of confidences. It was a smooth proposition on both their parts.

You often see in movies where people get so anxious to have passionate sex that they tear off each other's clothing, snap bras, pop buttons and rip panties to shreds. This anxiety is actually foreplay and sometimes occurs with first time encounters. This experience with Jack and Sue is an example of how that anxiety causes people to take risks, risks of getting caught. The entire scene becomes one where passion overcomes reason, and that is exciting. It's funny how we seldom get to witness such activity except in movies. Remember, the uncontrolled anxiety becomes uncontrolled passion. The greater the risk of getting caught and the need to get started creates more pleasure.

At this particular company party, Jack had playfully touched her body in sensitive places after having playfully tugged at her panties in a clothes closet. That preliminary game was too dangerous for comfort and was short-lived. The circumstances of being overheard were too dangerous. Sue reacted by more teasing and flirting and body language making Jack pursue her "goodies." She would grab Jack's crotch when she was sure no one was looking, and then move away as a further tease. The office ass grabbing was dangerous but exciting. The game was getting serious. It had reached the point where a hard penis seeks hot pussy was a passionate goal. They acted like two cats in heat.

This first time they had sex was on a snowy night with those big wet snowflakes falling, and it had snowed at least six inches by early evening. Another corporation was sponsoring this office party to promote their stock. Jack and Sue had been flirting for weeks and this party was another stage of building sexual tension. They continued to discreetly rub against each other or sneak "feels."

When they could take no more frustration at that evening due diligence party, they sneaked outside into the dark of night. The outdoor parking lot was full of cars and there were no people in sight. The parking lot was well lit, but the falling snow blurred everything. It appeared quite foggy. Jack and Sue were almost frantic after hours of party type foreplay and there was little time to waste searching for privacy. Their excitement had reached great proportions; this was to be their first time and they knew they were going to fuck no matter what the odds. All that was desperately needed was both privacy (hah, that was a joke) and a compromising somewhat comfortable place to have sex, a quickie if you will.

As previously disclosed, during one heated moment behind a closed office door at that meeting, Jack had tugged at Sue's panties thinking they might achieve a quick stand up fuck, that plan was aborted as too dangerous. Besides, stand up sex is never that good because it limits penetration and pumping room. Also, the door might have rattled.

Besides, Jack was too tall for stand up sex. He would have to keep her lifted off the floor during sex and that may weaken the outcome.

Once outside, they surveyed the inconvenient circumstances and surveyed the crowded outdoor parking lot. It was very quiet and peaceful. The scene resembled a Christmas postcard. They both wore long winter coats. Sue, being creative and equally anxious, climbed onto the hood of a nearby Volkswagen "bug" and laid her head against the windshield. The front bumper supported her. Her long coat served as a blanket underneath her body so she was not lying against the cold steel. She lifted her dress removed her panties, and exposed her bare legs and pussy and exclaimed how good the falling snow felt on both. Jack took his cock out and opened his pants, but not dropping them. His heavy coat covered his ass.

Jack climbed on to the VW and hooked his feet on the front bumper and fell forward into her snow flaky bare-legged spread. Sue released her feet from the bumper and slid up on the VW hood with her bare legs in the air. She guided herself back down to meet his cock and it slipped right in, sword in sheath, so to speak. The shape of the VW was a perfect sexual intercourse accommodation. The windshield served as a pillow of sorts and tipped her head forward.

All that was exposed were Sue's long extended legs, while her coat served as a blanket against the cold steel VW. Her spreading legs seemed to be trying to kick off the heavy cool wet snow. Again, Jack's coat covered his ass, which was not bared even under his long winter coat. The temperature extremes between their moving parts, as Jack described to Cynthia and me, (in detail) from the cold wet snow to the extreme heat of her warm hot pussy was sensational and they found that feeling to be an unexpected stimulant. This hot to cool switching was the theme for relating this experience. The temperature changes greatly enhanced their pleasure to their surprise, and Cynthia was surprised just hearing about it. Cynthia seemed more attentive than usual. Jack and Sue had to be quick for fearing of being caught, but as everyone knows, sex with fear of exposure has a special "rush." So Jack pumped hard hoping to complete the mission before the possibility of getting caught. The sounds of their sex were like on a sound stage with Sue's exclamations and Jack's pounding against the VW hood. The VW was making a "tin can" popping sound. Jack and Sue were oblivious to their surroundings. Nothing would have been worse than "coitus interruptus." That fear also enhanced the pleasure. You might call the event, "fast and furious."

Sue was very vocal and that made the experience even more exciting. It was Jack's description of Sue's vocal reaction that we wanted Cynthia to pick up on, so Jack made a good case about how turned on her reaction was to him. After quick mutual orgasms Jack, when withdrawing, lost his balance with his feet caught on the front bumper and fell over backwards lying in the snow with only his moist warm steaming "flagpole" extended into the wet falling snow.

Remember the famous quote from Dr.Kellogg's health clinic at the turn of the twentieth century. "An erection is a flagpole on a man's grave." Dr. Kellogg, later known for his invention of cornflakes, offered health advice that sex was debilitating and bad for one's health. He was also a vegetarian and espoused the evils of "Onanism." (Male masturbation). The movie about Dr. Kellogg was a hilarious comedy and featured the exposure of sexual paraphernalia and women riding bicycles for sexual pleasure. Married couples were separated and slept in separate rooms for health reasons, to abstain from sex. The movie was called, "The Road to Wellsville."

Back to the VW. Sue thought that Jack's bare exposure to the cold elements was funny, so she climbed off the VW and acted like she would pull Jack upright by holding his penis with two hands. They were laughing and playing a humorous "gotcha" game. They heard someone coming (no pun intended) and pulled themselves together quickly. Sue was still bare legged with her skirt up facing Jack and was commenting how cool it was that Jack's semen was running down her leg and freezing. She was still pulling on Jack's cock like she would use his cock to help him stand up while he was trying pull on his zipper. Good luck with that thought. Sue thought that was funny and wanted Jack to clean her up before his semen froze on her leg. Jack grabbed a handful of snow and was about to wash her bare legs when they thought they heard someone coming.

As Jack was trying to stand up in the snow and zipping his fly, they noticed that Sue's ass had made a slight indentation in the VW hood and that Jack had bent the front bumper while pushing ahead with his strokes. They were both adjusting their clothing as a couple approached them; the humor was even more exciting as they laughed heartily while this unsuspecting couple passed them on the way to their car. The strange couple eyed them with suspicion wondering what was so funny. They did not notice the ass shaped dent in the VW hood. Jack and Sue got away with a spectacular quickie by minutes; not bad. It was a funny story, but also pure excitement to relate. The snow and Sue's vocalization emphasized our point, and Cynthia seemed quite interested in our focus on sexual noises. Jack suggested to Sue they leave a note on the windshield of the VW explaining how they got the fucking dent. Didn't happen!

Well, Cynthia and I laughed at Jack's description of this very exciting sexual adventure, which he preferred to call it. Jack's retelling was more humorous than the actual event. Jack and Sue had a long affair after that initial encounter and it was to be very rewarding with no harm done. Sue was on the pill and that made things easier. Cynthia was turned on, but subtle about it, pretending to be more amused than aroused. Jack would later tell us of some of the more exciting things he and Sue did. Their long term affair is worth noting because it was exciting and rewarding and they never got caught over a twenty year span. We have too many such stories to include all experiences. That affair was a good thing regardless of how one would pass judgment on it. Actually they did not meet that often, perhaps monthly and as they got older they became very good friends with less sex.

This story reminded us of that joke where a man and a woman flirted all evening at a hotel party. Sex was on both their minds, but the man was shy. The sexy aggressive woman appeared at his hotel room door and opened her robe and she was stark naked. She was gorgeous and reeked of sex. The guy was stunned and while he hesitated,

She said, "You better ask me in I think I hear someone coming."

She stepped into his room and he said, "Wow! You have the greatest ears. When you heard someone coming, that was me."

There were other stories and jokes that enlivened our lunch meetings and Cynthia often reacted by being sexually aggressive that night in our own bed. I had had a vasectomy years earlier and her interest grew thereafter, but not her expressions of joy. It could have been my imagination, but I was hoping for emissions of pleasure like grunting or "yumming," or some vocalization instead of the conservative protective emotions as if her feelings of pleasure were always to be private and contained. I suspect that noises of pleasure become naturally subdued after years of marital sex. It is not meant to become routine, it often does. I'm sure you have heard stories where some women can scratch deep scars in a man's back or maybe some heavy pounding. That didn't happen to us. Many lovers are silent because they are focusing on the pleasure.

In fact, most lovers experiencing sexual pleasure at first do concentrate on the feelings. When the feelings of pleasure are so new, the focus is more fascinating and people don't react with vocal expressions as they are in a trance with the newness. When lovers become more experienced they are more likely to express themselves. Men, perhaps, take longer because their pleasure is more immediate whereas a woman has to build up to orgasms and are more often the buildup is interrupted. Actually lovers can interrupt each other's orgasms, especially women are more easily distracted by a man's physical energy. Women can feel more like an accessory to a man's pleasure and men need to recognize this. A man needs to concentrate on her pleasure. The rewards will be much greater working as a team.

The lesson was that sometimes a quickie creates the mood and accounts for the passionate drive, which can be considered foreplay. Anxiety is often considered essential to foreplay. Quickies, when there is adequate time and privacy, are a different matter. A man seeking a quickie without foreplay may be considered selfish. Again the individual circumstances may differ and prevent judgments. Women are not usually into quickies unless preceded by a lot of body language foreplay. Often women will allow quickies knowing that being so willing the guy will reciprocate with foreplay on the next round of sex. Dancing qualifies as body language foreplay. Today young people dance as if simulating sex acts and having grown up in a different environment, I find that hard to cope with, especially those of us raising daughters. Dancing must be great for condom sales.

Quickies are also a great confidence builder. Curiosity plays a role here, and sometimes humor. Quickies are more often defined as sport sex. It is fun if there are no consequences and too often the repercussions are not thought out in advance.

Chapter 3. Boy Oh Voyeur

This week of sexual education continued this same July during the summer following the "snow fuck" winter. The luncheon disclosing the VW quickie came first, and then this "Sheila incident." I realize quickies like the snow fuck are often degraded, because of the lack of foreplay, but the key is that the foreplay in a quickie is in the anticipation of the possibility of accomplishing the act. To reiterate, this excitement builds during the search for privacy or lesser degrees of comfort and surely, quickies are often quick hoping to succeed before getting caught. That can be very exciting. Quickies between married couples are usually done because the parties may be tired or whatever. Marital quickies usually fall into the category of "therapeutic sex." The goal still should be to ignore making sex routine.

Cynthia and I were temporarily living in an apartment, while our new home was being finished. In the apartment next to us was another temporary guest, Sheila, who spent a few afternoons sunning poolside with Cynthia. Our children were visiting grandparents at their cottage on a lake.

After much poolside girl talk, Sheila, a single woman neighbor confided in Cynthia that she was moving to Phoenix to get away from

Denver and a bad situation. Sheila moved to our same apartments as a temporary situation. It seems her former roommate confessed to being a Lesbian and began forcing herself on Sheila and was stalking her while sharing living quarters. Sheila was not aware of her roommate's deviation when she first moved in, which were for economic reasons. She had actually fought off several attacks while rooming with the Lesbian, which makes no sense if one is simply not interested. Her roommate would not listen to reason. Sheila was simply not interested in another woman. Sex is only real when both partners are willing to play. Forced sex is a crime. If a woman is not open to same sex sex, then it will not be sex; why bother?

I think homosexuals have this feeling that no one would refuse them if they would give their sex a try. It doesn't work that way. Sexuality is based on each individual's hormone balance. That balance was determined in one's DNA and persuasion will not alter that hormone imbalance. There are some people born on the fence with equal hormonal balances and they tend to be bisexual. This theory does not preclude individuals experimenting with same sex sex. However, our experiences are limited regarding such abnormal categories. We simply didn't meet any homosexuals that we were aware of or had to deal with.

Homosexuality is not a part of this story. Jack and I ignored "Gays" because it was none of our business unless that view was being forced on us. Perhaps Gay's should not try to promote their hormone imbalance as normal and just stay out of other people's way. Perhaps homosexuals should keep their sex lives to themselves and not promote it as something special. People would leave each other alone as a sense of fair play. Nobody can alter another's sexuality by force. Unusual sexual practices should be kept private and as long as they don't intrude on others. If Gay people want relationships, so be it, as long as it isn't forced on my sex life or the subject enforced on my children. I'll do the explaining to my kids.

Sheila was terrified. Sheila also confessed that she never had a good experience with men. Based on her past experiences men were lousy lovers who treated her with no respect and used her body for their selfish motives. Sheila claimed to have never had an orgasm. She said the men in her limited experience could not even spell foreplay. Sheila was really depressed. Sheila was attractive and very sexy and had a big smile in spite of her dilemma. Using our theme of identifying characters with their resemblance to movie stars, Sheila resembled Julia Ormond.

Cynthia began giving Sheila positive advice using Jack and I as examples of men who knew how to treat women. She began with comments on the joys of cunnilingus. Sheila said she had never experienced such pleasure. Cynthia related the exciting example of Jack's VW adventure. Sheila enjoyed the confidential discussion and she loosened up as Cynthia began advising her on how to qualify and communicate with men, how to be demanding; it was like a "women's rights commercial." In my opinion, it was like the blind leading the blind, but with the best intentions. Cynthia had no idea how she could have been a great sexual advisor and she would never have considered doing what she was suggesting for Sheila. It simply was not proper.

Cynthia told Sheila that she could arrange for Jack to give her a lesson that would introduce her to oral sex and foreplay and teach her how to reciprocate. Sheila could not believe what she heard.

"You mean that you are suggesting that I have sex with your husband's married friend to experience the true value of sex?"

"Yes," was Cynthia's reply.

The rest of the discussion was about reducing the shock level. Somehow to our amazement, Cynthia must have been very convincing. Sheila agreed to allow Cynthia to ask Jack if he would perform the service, but promising nothing. Sheila could withdraw anytime with no hard feelings. Cynthia called Jack at his office and Jack thought it was a practical joke that I might be promoting. Nevertheless, Cynthia's request was a shocker to Jack. He listened to Cynthia explain the whole situation by phone and then called me to question if I knew what the hell was going on. I had not talked to Cynthia and I agreed it was most unusual. I was shocked that Cynthia would conjure up such a thing considering her conservative attitude. Although it pleased me that she thought Jack and I treated women right. I was becoming more aware of this exciting wife, whose attitude had been buried in the elite version of what was proper or acceptable by the up-tight elite. There is an old saying that those who don't get enough sex make the rules. Is that supposed to normalize their own inadequacies?

This conversation between Sheila and Cynthia raises another interesting thought. I wonder about the ability of women who just met to discuss such details. Guys can talk about sex, but probably not so respectful to women. Would guys suggest trying cunnilingus techniques on women with guys they just met? Male conversations are usually more machismo and a showy thing. Women however, would be more sympathetic and concerned. Such discussions between men and women, is a whole different "ball game."

I called Cynthia and she explained poor Sheila's plight. The deal was on! That night we drove Sheila to pick up Jack, whose wife was visiting parents and had their kids with her. In the car, I reaffirmed the benefits of this plan and I assured Sheila she could cancel at any time. I told Sheila that Jack was a perfect gentleman and that we were along to establish communications and to talk about the situation openly. Sheila seemed anxious to meet Jack and when he approached my car, she exclaimed, "Wow, he is good looking."

The ride to the restaurant was very charming and we all bonded nicely. Our conversations were mostly about sex and attitudes. After dinner, Sheila and Jack began to kiss in the back seat and we could not make out the whispers, but Sheila was obviously intrigued and anxious. You can always feel sexual tension when people become aroused. It was about 9:00 pm and Jack and Sheila were engaged in a "hot" embrace and kissing rather passionately. I guess that is understandable when people realize they will probably have sex. Keep in mind that Jack is very smooth with women and his respect for women is always obvious.

When we arrived at Jack's house, Jack and Sheila were very cozy. I told them to get a room or we would turn the hose on them. They laughed and when I suggested they go the bedroom, they almost ran. Cynthia and I agreed we would find something to do to each other on the couch, play some music, fool around, and for them to take their time.

Then I had a sneaky idea, I pulled Cynthia to the short stairway leading to Jack's bedroom and we laid down on the carpeted stairs with our heads on the top step. What we had was a perfect side view of the bed and we watched silently as Jack undressed Sheila. They were standing. The inevitable naked hug was very lovely. They kissed for a few moments while their bodies were firm against each other. Voyeurism with two first timers can be a once in a lifetime experience, especially when they don't know they are being watched. It seemed sinful to Cynthia, but she was not about to move. First time sex is usually hotter and the sounds and smells are beautiful. Viewing this experience seldom and almost never reoccurs and is true serendipity.

Jack's compliments and his preliminary foreplay was expert. He constantly caressed Sheila with his hands and whispered compliments that instilled confidence in her. Jack laid her on the bed very gently and after kissing her breasts moved his head between her legs, and he was whispering something we couldn't hear. Sheila rose up on her elbows to watch Jack, but she also soon fell into a stage of pure excitement. She was very vocal, but inaudible. It was like a person talking in their sleep. When Sheila appeared to have an orgasm with Jack's tongue she alternately pushed on Jack's shoulders and stamped her bare feet on the bed. That was interesting.

Jack took his time and the secondary effect on Cynthia watching was sensational. She was obviously new to voyeurism. Jack and Sheila did everything; they licked and sucked and caressed and eventually changed fucking positions a few times. Jack directed Sheila on top of him and guided her through various moves. He tried a rear entrance, but was brief because he knew he would lose her eye contact. On the final act Jack was on top and they had moved about so much that they ended up with Sheila's head hanging over the bed and rocking in pleasure. Her nice breasts were rocking in unison. That moves some blood to the head and makes for hotter sex. Sheila could not see us, but her mouth was wide open as she moaned in ecstasy. She was being thoroughly fucked.

So Cynthia and I watched in silence as two hot lovers experienced their first sexual intercourse. The show seemed to last the length of a full time movie. The room reeked of the arousing smell of good sex and while we were as quiet as we could be I noticed that Cynthia had her left hand between her legs and I sensed movement. She was masturbating, something I had never witnessed before. I dropped down to the lowest step. I lifted her summer full cotton dress and pulled off her silk panties. I took off my pants and underwear and had to kneel on steps just below Cynthia's bottom. Cynthia was not completely aware of my actions because she was fascinated and distracted by the sex show. I raised Cynthia's beautiful bared bottom and I gently mounted her from behind so my head was upright, but out of sight from the bedroom. I held her hips and stroked quietly and gently while we watched with delight and enjoyed this dual sexual experience.

Our own pleasure was special and you have to imagine the variety of emotions we were experiencing. The view was the highest form of foreplay and our simultaneous sexual pleasure was heightened. It was the sexiest scene I had ever seen, or done. Cynthia had never seen another couple make love, not even a porno movie and as I stroked her gently with my penis she did something unusual. Her fingers were feeling my penis as it moved in and out of her. I think she was both masturbating and simultaneously feeling my cock. We had a history of trying multiple positions and I had never before felt her hand monitoring the thrusting action. She was really turned on but her intense focus was on the scene. Cynthia was breathing fast, but quietly. I had a great quiet orgasm, and stayed inside her remaining still, but "uptight." She kept her finger caressing her clitoris and I could feel her movements against my penis, which actually never softened. She continued to rub her clitoris during the entire event.

Jack and Sheila made a lot of sexy noises, and hearing that, I believe, was also a first for Cynthia. It may have been a subliminal input, but she was in shock. Remember, my lone concern for Cynthia was that she was not vocal enough during sex.

Jack and Sheila finally rolled over on their backs and began whispering. Cynthia and I took that as a signal to sneak away. I pulled out and I was still erect. We scrambled on our hands and knees to around the corner and hurriedly dressed. Cynthia went into the guest bathroom and fixed herself up, but she could not hide the fact that she looked like she had just been laid. She had that flushed sexually satisfied look. Sheila and Jack came down from the bedroom and they, too, had that satisfied look. Sheila hugged Cynthia, hugged me and expressed her gratitude verbally. The three of us moved to my car. It was a beautiful summer night and the three of us were more appreciative of the good life than any time before. The ride home consisted of a higher than a kite Sheila raving about what just happened to her. Sheila was never aware of our voyeurism. Little did she know that Cynthia enjoyed getting laid as much as Sheila.

The next day we had lunch with Jack and told him that we watched everything. Jack loved the idea and asked Cynthia what she thought. Cynthia had many questions, like what specifically were you doing with your tongue to cause such a reaction and how did you know when to stop. Did she come? How could you tell? How long did her orgasm last? Did she come during intercourse?

I told Jack that it was Cynthia's first time viewing hot real sex and that she had never seen a porno movie. We asked Cynthia about watching oral sex. Cynthia said that she couldn't see Sheila suck on Jack's cock because Sheila's ass was in the way. She felt watching another woman receiving oral sex was the biggest turn on of the evening. Her curiosity was definitely at a high. Cynthia had many questions, and Jack responded in detail as much as he could and that really accentuated Cynthia's interest. Jack explained how he felt with each position and why he changed positions. He was determined to show Sheila as much as possible per our instructions. It was as if Cynthia had also experienced a new awakening. Cynthia had been completely focused on every stroke and every reaction by both partners and she remembered it all very well. It was if she was feeling the sex while only watching. Such visuals are equally as passionate as any kind of foreplay. Voyeurs long for the feelings, which again remind us that our brains are our biggest sex organ. Viewing is one thing, but the sounds and smells are also major contributors. For Cynthia, the newness of everything she was experiencing could have been an overdose, if there is such a thing. Cynthia was definitely hyped up to a very intense sexual level. Imagine a semi-innocent getting so much stimulation at one time and for the first time. She was being fucked, was masturbating and watching very hot sex at the same time. She could smell and hear the sex. Cynthia was really turned on! And this a conservative rather prudish wife?

At first during the sexual revolution, cunnilingus was seldom discussed, or for that matter may not have been a common practice except among the more advanced lovers. Coming from a small town may have kept me in the "licking dark" also. I can remember in high school that someone would use eating pussy as a weak insult. "So and so eats it or so and so is a cocksucker" were derogatory terms. I'm not sure what "eating it" meant. We boys dreamed the term cocksucker was meant for the girls and we knew they were inexperienced and probably unapproachable. We wondered how much foreplay was to be learned and how much came naturally. If we did not understand cunnilingus, how would we expect the girls to know what to do putting penises in their mouths? Jack was more experienced because in high school his older experienced girlfriend taught him all about oral sex. That relationship was secret and involved an older brother's ex-girlfriend. Jack began college with more sexual experience than most people.

Cynthia claimed she had never seen another man's penis. She claimed she never saw Jack's penis because it was always buried somewhere. I explained Jack was never circumcised and we had to explain the difference. Cynthia seemed to become obsessed with penis curiosity. The conversations were hot and getting hotter. It was to continue.

Chapter 4. Yo ho, Blow the Man Down

The next day the three of us accepted an invitation to a small cocktail party and since Jack was still home alone, he offered to pick us up. Once in Jack's car, Cynthia was in the front seat and I sat sideways behind her. In the car we continued the voyeurism discussion. Cynthia was raving about how sexy the whole scene was to her. Cynthia reiterated that was her first time seeing another couple have sex and she still had never seen another man's erection. Voyeurism and having simultaneous sex was her most exciting moment and she was extremely "high" on sex. She said she thought if she saw a sexy man with a "hard on" she would not be able to control herself; she would have an uncontrollable urge to suck on his penis. It was a very good tease because I never heard her say that before. She was definitely teasing us, but was not overly confident in that contribution to our sex talks.

When Jack heard Cynthia say that she would like to suck on a hard cock, he frantically began to unbuckle his pants while driving. I grabbed his arm slapped his head and told him to get control of himself. We wrestled briefly in fun and the car swerved a bit. Cynthia laughed heartily that she had caused the ruckus. After we settled down, she said she was only kidding, but could she at least see Jack's penis. She said she didn't know what a circumcised man looked like.

Jack said, "And you will never see mine."

"What?" said Cynthia? "Why not?"

Jack continued, "Because it's not physically possible for someone as sexy as you to view a "softee." The penis will rise in wild anticipation and beat you to the showing. A good cock would not want to be seen with his pants down; he wants to be seen in his full glory. You, Cynthia, could raise an erection on a dead man by merely walking up to his coffin."

Cynthia grinned at the compliment.

"Thanks, so can I still see it? I still have never even seen another man's penis," repeated Cynthia. "Come on, you guys said I was an equal member of this sexual research team."

"Hey," I said, "where were you during our voyeurism experience?"

"I never got a good look at his penis because his big fanny was in the way, besides I was concentrating on the beauty of the big picture. I was so moved by the movements and grace of the whole scene; the sounds and smells. I admit it was the biggest turn on I ever imagined. I feel like someone else, and I don't know who." Sighed Cynthia. There was a wistful pause as no one spoke.

"Hey," I said, "Do you remember my fucking you from behind while you were watching Jack? I mean, you kept feeling my cock stroking you."

"Oh Honey, don't be ridiculous, of course I felt your cock in me and yes it made the whole experience more fantastic, but can't I still be curious about what Long John looks like?"

"Hey, wait a minute, you guys didn't tell me you were fucking while I was fucking."

"So, now you know, can I get still get a look? I am still curious," said Cynthia. "You guys said I could be one of the guys when it comes to learning more about sex, what happened to that idea?"

Cynthia looked at me for approval. I said she could look, but to please dig it out herself because Jack was driving. It was incomprehensible to see my staid conservative proper wife with such a curious request and apparently willing to pursue the adventure. That voyeurism must have really gotten to her.

She said, "OK then" and began to unbuckle Jack's pants. Jack pretended not to react and kept his eyes on the road. Cynthia was very slow and deliberate, she carefully unzipped Jack's zipper and spread his pants open like a picnic blanket. She had to feel around in his underwear for the object of the search and she found it quickly. It was hiding in his underwear. She pulled his penis out very carefully like she was unwrapping a present, which obviously aroused Jack even more; he was rapidly getting erect. She pulled it out with two hands and it sort of "unbended" as if it had come from a tucked position, which it had. She tucked his underwear under his testicles. Jack was immediately erect. Cynthia then held Jack's erect penis in her left hand; she was left-handed. She was amazed to watch it finish growing so fast in her hand. It grew so fast she did not get to see the circumcised look. Her mouth widened and her eyes glistened, as she never lost her focus. She did not see the helmet rise from its collar. She held the hard shank with her left hand and stared intently, moving her finger and thumb gently up and down the shaft without pulling any foreskin. Jack told Cynthia that he had affectionately named his penis "Long John Silver," and, Cynthia knew that; when Cynthia heard that comment she exclaimed,

"You know it is kind of silvery. Is that different?"

She leaned forward and examined "Long John" more closely and commented about the different smoothness and that Long John's helmet was on straighter than mine. She gently tested the firmness and said,

"They must all be this hard otherwise they wouldn't work, would they," observed Cynthia. We had no explanation for that.

"Soft cocks can't fuck," I explained.

Cynthia asked if there was an explanation for the little "fireman's helmet." We had never heard that expression before, and that was unusual. That was Cynthia's original expression and we were both fascinated by the term. Actually penis heads do look like firemen's helmets.

"Well," I explained, "the helmet as you call it, is of a tougher skin and thicker. I suspect it may be intended to protect that valuable sensitive nerve on the bottom there, which is the center of a man's pleasure, it's like a control panel; the nerve is the main trigger, but then, you know that, don't you?"

"Ummm," Cynthia added, "I suppose then you could relate it to a football helmet designed to ram into the defensive line. Do women's holes really have to be opened by ramming?"

"Not now honey, that's a different story and I'll tell you later. What do you think about Long John? How many cocks do you want to see?"

Cynthia ignored that comment.

"He seems the same size as yours, but his helmet is definitely on straighter; how did ours get tilted?" Cynthia asked me.

I said, "Mine is a vision of a man tipping his hat to a woman, an old custom from the old West. I don't know; I was born with a tilted helmet. It is not hard to believe, but no two penises are the same, maybe similar. Some point to the left, some to the right, some sag, and some are harder than others, some longer, some fatter and so on. I read that, by the way, because I had never seen another man's erection except Jack, either." I was hoping that comment went unnoticed since I would have to explain when I had seen Jack hard before. Cynthia did not notice that comment. Cynthia only knew about larger than average penises. She had never seen a smaller cock except on a baby.

Jack drove on as if nothing was happening. He was trying to be nonchalant regarding her comments. He did appear to be exceptionally aroused based on his breathing and somewhat lack of concentration on his driving. Cynthia was caressing his penis while we talked. However, Jack appeared to be watching the road.

I was fascinated by my wife's inquiry. "This is amazing," she repeated several times. Cynthia `spoke quite seriously as she were a Doctor conducting a physical exam. She pulled his foreskin gently over his little helmet, released it and exclaimed, "I think it's still growing."

Jack laughed and said, "She could pick her size by pumping the pump to the desired size, a proprietary feature."

She said, "Thank you, I wouldn't know about your mechanics, sounds like a lot of BS to me, but then, what would I know about that. My knowledge is now limited to two hard cocks." Cynthia pulled Jack's foreskin over his helmet and pulled it back twice while she studied the flexibility of foreskin.

I said, "Hey, the pump story is an old joke."

"What joke?" said Cynthia.

I explained about the magic penis that grew to the appropriate size on request by being pumped, but it's a long joke resulting is a reversal that was not funny and not timely. Cynthia was softly rubbing Jack's penis while she kept talking. Her eyes were focused on Long John Silver.

"Maybe I should do something to stop it from growing so we don't get hurt here." Cynthia purred. "If it goes off, will the wet stuff hit the ceiling? Should I pump it?"

(FYI, semen, once shot is believed to travel at an average speed of 28 mph.) After some silence and more starring at the firm element, Cynthia broke her concentration and looked at me and said, "Should I?"

"Should you what," I asked.

"You know," she half whispered.

I said, "Well, go for it, maybe we can show off your magnificent expertise that we have bragged about so often."

She squeezed long John again as if she were testing a ripe tomato. Cynthia then did the expected, she looked me in the eye and said, "Are you sure this is OK with you?"

I said, "Go ahead and see what happens."

Cynthia leaned over and put her mouth gently on Jack's penis and gave a little hum sound, sort of a "yum yum" purring noise.

Jack flinched. I'm not sure he was expecting oral contact, maybe some hand caresses; he was startled. Jack had to pull over to the curb for safety reasons and he was pleasantly shocked and surprised that this friend's very proper wife was about to, maybe, give him a blowjob. We both watched intently. I leaned over and had the better view from the backseat. She licked and flicked her tongue on his exposed nerve. She began with the tease of light tongue touches. I was very aroused watching Cynthia. When she performed on me, my view angle was different.

She kissed and flicked her tongue on Long John's main nerve, licked his penis like an ice cream cone, and after a few twitches on Jack's part she moved to the sucking position. She then took about half of Jack's penis in her mouth and sucked gently; she began a slight bob and held the gentle pull pressure constant. Jack said he could feel the warmth and wetness in her mouth, and it felt better than any pussy. Cynthia knew just how much saliva it took to warm and lubricate a shaft. She had a knack for making the texture equal to her pussy, but no pussy could ever do what a great blowjob can do. Pussy's don't have tongues and they don't suck, imagine what the world would be like if they did? Intercourse would not last very long. A correct blowjob requires a tongue to be flat against the main male nerve, but not possible in a car or from that angle. No matter, the inside of her cheek worked as well, it just took more skill. Tongue and skin texture against the penis is important.

With the next series of bobs, she began to work his foreskin with her hand. She pulled the foreskin back and forth, with an occasional twisting action in coordination with her bobbing head. Jack's sensitive nerve was being caressed by the inside of Cynthia's cheek. She was alternately caressing his shaft with her left hand. She caressed his testicles with her right hand and pulled them out from underneath the action. She caressed his testicles gently with her right hand. Cynthia definitely knew how to suck cock and she was totally into it, especially feeling Jack's passion. Jack's reaction increased her enthusiasm. Jack was clutching the steering wheel and was trying to move his hips a little. All he could see was the back of her head. The suction has to be like a gentle tug that simulates tightness. It has to be just right. I noticed that a few times Cynthia would only take the helmet in her mouth and suck on it ever so gently and then drop down fast. The plunges were infrequent. She knew that changing the technique prolonged and enhanced the climax. A woman does not simply masturbate a man into her mouth. Blowjobs are an art form.

Jack exclaimed how wonderful it was and that it may be too good and he could not prevent an explosion. Jack began to raise his hips off the seat and began moving his hips. Cynthia knew he was about to come; Woman seem to have a natural reaction to a man coming, especially with the excitement of the newness of long John silver. My God Cynthia looked good. I could actually imagine her on my own cock. She was good, and the excitement of Jack's reaction increased her pleasure. Jack was pounding the steering wheel. Love had nothing to do with this act. It was purely physical for both of them. It was very sexy for me and I wondered how I would feel about this later.

Her years of personal training kicked in, as became appropriate, she sucked, pulled the skin up and down in perfect rhythm with his hip movements. She swallowed in perfect rhythm with his bursts of semen. Jack had about four major pushes and grunts, the usual sequence of ejaculating. He was very, very, vocal, which greatly excited Cynthia. Her hand on his shaft protected her from having an out of control penis rammed into her mouth. She bobbed with his undulating and then held her position motionless. Cynthia had about half of Jack's cock in her mouth and she gave a few more gentle sucks. We were both about an even seven inches, not too big, not too small, but physically right for big guys. We were bigger around than most men so we were told when we were younger. Cynthia kept control and hummed a bit.

Me? I was fascinated. I was in a stupor and I was really turned on. My cock was throbbing and hard as a rock from watching. I noticed a few things that added pleasure in my own voyeurism. As soon as she felt the first burst of semen, she made a humming sound. She clenched his stomach skin and squeezed it. Just prior to his second burst she sucked so that her cheeks were indented creating dimples like someone sucking a thick milkshake through a small straw. That pressure made Jack twitch in ecstasy and Cynthia swallowed the second load in perfect timing. She then sucked and with each subsequent weaker ejaculation she instinctively pulled his foreskin forward. You could see her sexy swallowing muscles. It was like a ballet in slow motion and my mind had slowed down to focus on this amazing blowjob. Cynthia added a few small sucks while pulling Jack's foreskin as if to complete the ejaculation with some extra pumps. She then pumped his foreskin a bit faster after she felt he had completed ejaculation and carefully watched to see if her pumping would produce more semen. Yet her reaction was so gentle; she treated Long John like he was a fragile instrument. Cynthia finally warmed Long John as deep in her mouth as she could holding him motionless and kept a slight sucking pressure constant.

Jack was very vocal expressing his pleasure; Jack finally settled down and moaned a big sigh, Cynthia kept long John warm and held her position, Jack did not move. She finally withdrew, checked the smiling penis mouth for any late drops, licked the helmet, and made a few gentle pulls on Jack's shaft while she blew on it. She was checking for any leftovers. She blew and cooled the warmness of where her hand was holding it and went down for a final mouth-hold, a final suck while listening to Jack's ravings and compliments. Cynthia appeared relaxed, but she was obviously very excited. She was as excited as we were. She kept it warm for a few moments, pulled off, gave Long John a sweet kiss on his helmet, then she sat up, smiled at both of us and said, "how was I?"

Jack could not speak. He looked like he had fainted with his eyes open. My erection was about to burst through my pants.

"My God, whispered Cynthia, "I really enjoyed that. I think I had an orgasm."

"Cynthia, that was unbelievable. I am about to have an orgasm myself. I never imagined how sexy you could be watching you perform. I had not imagined you were so sexy doing that. You have got to help me here, I'm about to burst."

Having said that I unbuckled my pants and dropped them down to my thighs. I was half kneeling on the floor with one leg stuck behind the seat. I was cramped between the seats and my erect penis was sticking out between the seat backs. I was out of control.

"Yummy yummy." Said Cynthia, "I understand." and she turned and quickly took my penis in her mouth. Jack sat erect and drew closer so he could see her action better. Now his viewing angle was perfect; Cynthia's tongue lay flat on my goody nerve and she began to hum and stroke my foreskin while she sucked vigorously. I lost control and began to move my hips. I could not control my pumping, but Cynthia had her hand on the base of my clock and protected herself from my wild fucking. I began to come instantly and I felt my cum fly into her sucking mouth. It took less than one minute. I was hoping I was not too rough. Cynthia was humming louder exhibiting her own version of uncontrolled body language. Cynthia was now squeezing my thigh with her right hand. She appeared extremely passionate. She acted like she was being fucked. She moved her shoulders and upper body like she was having an orgasm. She repeated her sucking and swallowing technique while exclaiming moans with her mouth full being pumped with my cock. So much for the gentle treatment Jack had felt. Cynthia also began to clench my thigh as if she were squeezing the juice out of me. Our moment of passion was completely out of control. After I had this forceful orgasm, I fell back against the back seat and I was still oozing semen. I could not hold my kneeling position in such a small car.

"Are you Ok?" Cynthia blurted. She seemed concerned at my exhaustion.

There was silence and very heaving breathing by two guys who had just been smitten by a momentary pleasure force greater than life itself. It was amazing how such a simple experiment got out of hand and much to our surprise Cynthia reeked with satisfaction.

"Wow, that was really something. I can't believe I did that." Cynthia smiled and wiped her mouth. "I really enjoyed that. I actually ate two cocks. Delicious, would that be two scoops of warm cream?"

"I think you single handedly slew two dragons. I mean we are put down and I am so light headed I can't see straight." Said Jack.

"I guess I now realize how important orgasms are for you guys, and you sure are easy to please. I am so envious that you can enjoy so much pleasure so easily. I wish I could come like that. Will, honey, I know how much longer it takes to get me that high, but I really appreciate a good licking even more and I imagined myself having sexual intercourse with you even though my mouth was getting the action. I sure could feel what goes on down there with you guys. I got some real satisfaction doing you both. Thank you both." It is important to know that Jack and I always use pubic hair conditioner and smell good.

I could not believe what she just said. My conservative wife taking reacting like that, wow, was I satisfied even though I could not control my quick orgasm. That oral voyeurism was more than I could handle. I was so impressed and I realized in retrospect how lucky I was to have personal access to such perfection in a love relationship. I can't imagine a more perfect example of good oral sex. I had just showed off to my best friend what a great sex partner I married and loved. I also recognized that I had her taught her well and demonstrating that to Jack made me proud. Her sudden change of attitude is what was most amazing. When we arrived at the party, Cynthia acted as if nothing had happened. She was her usual "bubbly" self and conversed with everybody, smiling and cheerful. On the way home Jack again raved about how good she was and how lucky I was.

Jack asked," Did you really satisfy Will that way during your periods?"

"That's where I learned how to do it and yes, I really enjoy doing that to Will. He taught me early in our marriage and I got to the point where I really get into what I do because I feel a little orgasm myself when I feel him coming. I try to reciprocate for what he does to me and we have lost count as to who owes who good oral sex. Every time I put Will in my mouth it makes me think about receiving oral sex and I get more turned on. I have to admit, I like sucking cock. And I admit I felt pleasure during your climax, Jack."

Jack was stunned, "Do you realize how unusual that is? I never heard of a woman enjoying cocksucking that much. Angela would never even try oral sex."

I could not get that whole experience out of my mind and I was most anxious to make love to my wife and could hardly wait until we got home. I knew I had it so good. Cynthia and I had a great night of good old-fashioned missionary position sexual intercourse. When spent we clung to each other until we fell asleep. (I rolled over with Cynthia on top and I was still inside her, great afterglow!)

There is much to contemplate here. There is the conflict between sex and love. This raises the issue of whether blowjobs are really sex. Obviously they are, but are they to be acceptable as just giving pleasure to dear friends. It would never work that way for cunnilingus because the act is far more intimate and it would take a very uninhibited woman to allow such pleasure so casually. Are blowjobs that easy for women to perform? It looks easy from a guy's point of view, but only real sexy women will accept the swallowing technique as a good thing. It seems more like a distasteful sacrifice, but I will assure you women readers that the skill of giving a good blowjob will forever be appreciated and will enhance your reputation as a great sex partner. Cocksucking is the best foreplay and does not have to end with an orgasm. I would hope that trading oral sex will help screen guys that know how to reciprocate. If the act continues to be one sided, I would move on unless an unfinished blowjob leads to better intercourse. Semen is definitely "food for thought." By the way, there is about ten calories in a load of semen.

Chapter 5. To Bare Witness

We both felt sad for Jack because of his own disappointing marriage, but Cynthia and I also knew that Jack had a sex life that exceeded any male's wildest dreams. It meant more than Cynthia could know when he said he had never experienced such pleasure in his entire life than the surprise blowjob. I sometimes wonder why they call oral sex done to a man a "blow job?" There is very little blowing; in fact oral sex on a woman should have its own name. Jack and I made up names back in college. We called women who know how to perform oral sex "peniticians." And we named men who knew how to perform cunnilingus, "Gyneseurs." We thought we were clever, but the names never caught on. They weren't slang enough.

The drive home from the slow moving party was quiet, but Jack again reassured Cynthia that that experience was meant for only the best of friends and that he did not expect any further treatments. Remember, the blowjob occurred on the way to the party. However Jack did hint at an opportunity to reciprocate and give Cynthia a good licking, with my supervision, of course. Cynthia said she didn't think she could handle that experiment alluding again to her old shy self.

There is no doubt in my mind that my wife's experience with the blowjob was a carry forward from the voyeuristic high we experienced together. Cynthia was so motivated and passionate that a new interest in eroticism was a natural result. She showed no guilt and her enthusiasm for sex reflected no let up. She was turned on to cocks and she now admitted as much.

The next day, the three of us had lunch again, which was now a daily event while Angela was on vacation; and with the new exciting activities fresh on everybody's mind, we were more focused. We were still living in the temporary apartment with our kids on vacation with their Grandparents.

Jack jokingly said we still owed him the chance to watch us have sex. Cynthia reiterated she couldn't do that because that was her most private act, and she felt the blowjob squared us for having watched Jack have sex with Sheila. By the way, Sheila did enjoy a few more sessions with Jack before leaving town. She had written Cynthia a nice intimate letter making Cynthia feel like a sex therapist.

Cynthia was really proud of her spontaneous moment and when we labeled her a true Penitician; she pretended she did not get it. I worried what her reaction would be after she blew Long John Silver down. That act was no longer a "bone of contention." She only brought it up in the scientific sense always welcoming compliments. She never mentioned the moral challenge. I think she knew and trusted the relationship between Jack and me, and knew that she was close enough to be in our inner circle of uninhibited experiences. Her enthusiastic oral sex performance and especially her mature attitude gave her credibility and advanced stature in our private club. For now, I decided to let her have her moment of glory and I acted proud. God, she was sexy, and she continued this attitude and retained her enthusiasm for performing on me. I assure you that is exactly what happened and her enthusiasm for all kinds of oral sex increased after this week. She acted like she always needed a good licking and she was enjoying it ever more. And all future sex between us was an attempt to better any previous activity, and we talked about how to improve techniques. That was fun because talking about our new experiences also enhanced sexier foreplay.

Both Jack and I would often take a lunch break from the stock market and my law practice. I specialized in estate planning. And, Jack and I looked for every opportunity to do business together. Jack loved telling broker stories with his fictional investors, Ben and Eileen Dover. He loved telling us how stupid most investors are by buying high and selling low. Jack's client base as it grew provided many opportunities for sexual adventures. Jack did not hustle women clients, they too often hustled him and he had many tactful policies as to how to deal with the temptations. Jack Callahan probably turned away more pussy than most men get in a lifetime. His adventures with us motivated him on to bigger and better things.

The mutual interest in revamping my conservative wife's sexual transformation had advanced well beyond her being considered prudish. Cynthia was thrilled to be privy to hearing about Jack's new or old experiences. She was reconfirmed being on the inner circle of a couple of good looking Jocks. All of Jack's experiences excited her and I think made her a more "horny" wife. I was the lucky recipient of her growing interest in something other than routine lovemaking. We seemed to be making love more frequently and with more emotion and only a few days had passed. We even had a few before dinner sexual snacks with each other. Sex was every night and every morning and with good foreplay. I'm talking longer timed sessions both evening and morning here. And our three kids were out of town. That was great and, Jack too, was happy for me. Jack was really envious and both Cynthia and I liked that. We were on a roll.

That day we began to advance the idea of all going to bed together with limited fooling around. That, again, raised many moral issues. Jack simply asked if he could watch us make love since he wanted to see Cynthia's perfect sexy body in action. He said he was willing to come in his pants and stay at arm's length if she agreed. Jack even agreed to masturbate while we had sex and Cynthia could watch him.

That thought made her look like she was interested. But, Cynthia thought she would be too distracted even with Jack watching or her watching Jack. But she admitted she was greedy for any new experience that would turn her on. She insisted on absolute control of any possible situation. And Cynthia was adamant about not screwing two men at one session, or maybe even in her lifetime. She felt it was immoral, and compromised her marriage vows. She was not about to play slut and let us screw her for comparative reasons. She said she couldn't deal with it emotionally.

If she agreed to any adventure, it was to be a onetime only session including discussion and learning about foreplay techniques. I believe Cynthia harbored a secret desire to have Jack reciprocate by going down on her as reciprocity for putting Long John Silver in his place; submission! I think she was hoping to find something different that she could pass on to improve my skills, if that were possible.

But she would not admit any such thing. After all, we did enjoy an exceptional ability to communicate and we were both open to trying something new. I was always willing to try something new. She hinted that she wanted the potential threesome to be scientific and more like a classroom session with questions and answers. She didn't want to get involved with what resembled group sex or anything even close to it. This was to be a delicate situation and Cynthia was protecting her moral code. What was each of us to gain, and what might be the risks? Cynthia wanted to discuss those thoughts openly before we did anything.

So we modified the proposed presentation into a single lesson on oral sexual techniques and that if we agreed to a single experiment and discussed it scientifically, she could call the shots, make requests and end it at her discretion. Jack admitted that his purpose was that he desperately wanted to see Cynthia naked. He felt he deserved that pleasure since we watched him fuck Sheila without permission. The idea that he was watched was a phony concern; he loved the fact that we watched. I also think Cynthia was faking embarrassment about our joint voyeurism. Why was she also putting on an act? Acting prudish no longer seemed acceptable and she wasn't worried about her reputation. She knew we would never disclose anything we did to anybody. I think she may have had nightmares that her Mother would confront her about her sins. Her Mother was a sanctimonious old woman that probably didn't have any more sex after she bore four children and her duty was complete. But then those were the prevailing pre-world war two social attitudes.

I then suggested limited participation on Jack's part, no intercourse between Cynthia and me, but we could lay around naked and touch and talk and see what we could learn. Jack going down on Cynthia was discussed and Cynthia seemed very interested in that, but acted like she had to think it over. How could any women refuse an orgasm with a new tongue? We could compare licking techniques. I did want to show off my beautiful wife to my closest friend and confidant. It was going to be an adult adventure between three best friends. Although scientific in purpose, we all agreed that some passion would be inevitable. Think about this; a new face in a woman's genitals is awful intimate.

That old question always comes up; is oral sex really sex? I mean could Cynthia allow Jack's face between her legs and not get turned on? It was simply a matter of overcoming her inhibitions. Sex and inhibitions have always been the prevailing problem, but oral sex is hard to justify as not being sex yet requires losing all inhibitions. An interesting question!

Jack and I argued it was not to be considered cheating if supervised by a husband and Jack vowed to never bring up the idea of getting together unless we did. Cynthia, I concluded, was secretly interested in showing off her well-toned body. Why not? She was ready to show off a little more than her skills and she had already made that point with Long John Silver, who was always treated as a third uninvolved person, or a simple sex object. Long John was now an easily acceptable topic of conversation.

Jack then told Cynthia that she did not realize what a perfect body she had and that her modesty was frustrating. She should learn to "strut her stuff" a little more. He said she should reward the whole world and exhibit her beauty like any great work of art. Sometimes flattery can be too powerful. During a conversation in the car, Jack asked if he could just see Cynthia's legs. She lifted her skirt to her panty line and gave him a quick shot. That was a valid request and I agreed that I was proud, but how willing was I to share this fine work of art. Jack was agreeable, but I wondered if Playboy magazine would pay us enough. (Just kidding) Nah, Cynthia would never go that far. Her exposure limit to date was to wear a two-piece bathing suit in public. And, I think she knew she looked good in a two-piece suit.

One time when we took our kids to a public pool, some college guys were hitting on her big time. She flirted and teased them in her own way because she was in control. I sense that she walked with a little added swing. That scene was spoiled when one of our grown children approached her and called her, "mom." Another time when sunning at the community pool I caught her staring at a handsome college dude sleeping on his back with a bulging crotch. She was starring at his crotch through sunglasses, but I knew. She could have been fantasizing. I think all women would do stuff like that if they thought nobody else was watching them.

There is that adage that if a person were traveling alone and met another attractive member of the opposite gender and both were attracted to each other and both had everything to lose, would they make out if they were absolutely sure they would never get caught? Suppose a good-looking housewife roomed next to Cary Grant and they agreed to an adventure never to be revealed because they both had reputations to protect. It would be an easy answer if a handsome married man met Sophia Loren and she flirted and propositioned him and no would ever know. Celebrities often get frustrated and can't have sexual adventures like non-celebrities. It is important to them if they can be assured of confidentiality.

How does one measure temptation? Everyone wants to be reassured about his or her sex appeal. That and plain curiosity are the main reasons people often fantasize about sex with an attractive stranger. Especially if they think they will never be caught. Then

57

again there is the excitement of the newness and adventure of the "forbidden fruit" theory. I suspect all sexual adventures have everything to do with how discreet the conditions might be. I think everybody has fantasies. I wonder how many people would deny themselves secret sexual adventures if they were sure no one would ever know about it.

We were in Las Vegas once and a "B" movie star hit on Cynthia. It was harmless, but food for thought. When he saw me approach and saw my size, he smiled and moved on. Cynthia forever teased me and would not reveal how much cash she was offered. She probably did not get an offer, but she had fun teasing me. I was now up to 230 pounds from some part time weight lifting. It made me a little more intimidating at courtroom appearances. I could easily bench press 300 lbs. I know Cynthia was equally proud of my body and looks. I suspect she liked showing me off, too.

Cynthia was warming to the threesome idea because she really was curious as to what would happen, or if she really could learn something, or feel some new pleasures. We suggested two exposed erections at the same time. That perked up her interest. She was adamant that she did not want to have sexual intercourse with two men. She later confided that oral sex would be interesting, but she still insisted on calling the shots. The voyeurism she experienced was still foremost in her mind.

Jack and I often wondered if women thought penises were attractive; Cynthia said she thought they were magnificent, but she could have been just telling us what we wanted o hear. Man to man, cocks are ugly, but a pussy is beautiful. Lips are sexy and a pussy has lips. Pussies are meant to be kissed. The pussy is like another mouth, but probably cleaner. A pussy is designed by God to be tempting, inviting and knowing what the rewards will be is spectacular. It drives men insane. Pussy's taste good, smell good and feel good, and we think that is normal and wonderful. If a man has any hesitation about agreeing, then his attitude is abnormal, or he has some serious hormonal imbalances.

The three of us finally came to an understanding. Cynthia was seriously thinking about it and every time Jack told a sexy story, or suggested oral sex you could tell she was opening up her mind. Jack told Cynthia that he wanted to taste her and that she looked so delicious. That compliment really turned her on. We told her we would never stop licking until told to do so. Jack's stories were mostly about why passion and enthusiasm and verbalization made for better oral sex. Jack was telling us of a few examples where noise got out of hand. Cynthia's curiosity was gaining. I reminded her about Sheila's reaction to being licked for the first time. Sheila really lost it with pleasure. How could Cynthia resist these conversations? And the week without children was soon coming to a close.

I knew Cynthia was proud of her body and inherently all women are exhibitionists if properly adored. I think Cynthia's curiosity was growing and at least she was willing to talk about it. She kept repeating that she had to be in charge and she could request anything she wanted that she thought would enhance her knowledge about sex. We had to promise to play the role of sex slaves. Our primary understanding was a matter of trusting your partners. Besides she loved the compliments, and was anxious to hear about what Jack had to say after seeing her naked body. Cynthia finally admitted she would show off for Jack with confidence. She said she could pose with confidence. This was to be the week that was!

This big week was winding down. Saturday was soon upon us. We had just enjoyed the experience of hot original voyeurism watching two passionate beautiful people have "hot" sex for the first time. We watched a woman go crazy getting her pussy licked. Cynthia and I enjoyed the pleasure of the extended visual effects in the heat of silence while we made love, and Cynthia subsequently reciprocated by putting Long John Silver in his place a few days later while she was still turned on about the voyeurism. We had both experienced powerful spontaneous oral sex that was almost too good to talk about without getting aroused again. Everything we had just done was discussed at the next two private luncheons, and we were now venturing into another planned experience. The excitement was building. The important thing to note is that none of us ever

59

really "came down" from the heights of the new found passion of sexual adventurism. It wasn't going to be an obsession, just some lip smacking mouth-watering fun. We proceeded "lickedly split."

Cynthia and I were driving to pick up Jack in our big Cadillac sedan not realizing the potential for the blue leather backdrop. We couldn't meet at Jack's house for fear of neighbors coming over thinking there was a party and they felt they were always welcome if they brought their own booze, especially with Angela out of town visiting her parents with their two kids. We were going to my younger brother's condo. My brother was a tennis and golf pro and was off playing in a California tournament. His very secluded condo was at a private country club.

Jack climbed into the back seat with some nice greetings meant to relax us all, yet he could not hide his enthusiasm. He was about to see Cynthia unveiled, a pleasure that had been festering in his dreams for many years. We repeated the rules. Cynthia was to enjoy the pleasures of two male sex slaves. We had promised her a full body tongue massage and a sound dual licking. She agreed to strip naked and show off her body with confidence. She was comfortable because Jack was our closest friend and trustworthy. The trust between the three of us was built on years of confiding and sharing the most intimate of sexual details. We could always communicate intimately, especially after the two preceding events, which had left Cynthia in a curious state of "high alert" for pleasure.

We followed Cynthia up a flight of steps at the condo and after all these years of being madly in love with her I still found myself watching her hips swing with each step. Her legs flexed as if sculptured by Michelangelo himself. She stepped aside and I unlocked the door. Jack had brought two big vanilla candles and went directly into the bedroom. Vanilla smell is supposed to be an aphrodisiac. We followed Jack. We lit a candle on each side of the bed on the matching little tables. Cynthia stood silently and nodded her approval of the setting. The room was cool.

We stood at the foot of the bed and made a sandwich with Cynthia between us with Jack kissing her first while we gave her the first dual hug. They had kissed many times, but this was the first kiss that signaled impending pleasure. They usually just sort of pecked each other on the lips in a brotherly sisterly manner. They lingered slightly more this time. I turned Cynthia around and collected my preliminary "sandwich" kiss, which was also more passionate than usual. I collected a little tongue and never knew whether Jack had the same tease or not. And I wasn't concerned. A woman's tongue penetrating a man's mouth was always suggestive. It usually means it is an invitation.

I was the preliminary choreographer here, so I told Jack to step back about six feet and perform a strip tease while Cynthia and I hummed "Night Train." He was magnificent and added a little tap dancing humor, a little shuffle with each gyration. Cynthia watched gleefully and began to loosen up and relax. When we first entered the Condo she was as nervous and tense as I had ever seen her in spite of our careful psychological preparation. Whatever fear she had was leaving her body and her body language began to fall in stride with the game. She was swaying her hips a little with our humming "Night Train," the standard stripper's melody. She even clapped her hands a little.

When Jack was fully naked, Cynthia noticed and commented that Long John Silver looked a little embarrassed. His little helmet was partially tucked in and he was sticking out, as we say, "half cocked," at about half-length. Jack was fondling Long John as if his penis was doing the dance. That action caused Cynthia to focus more on his cock than his dance. Long John was growing before her very eyes and that slight distant vision with Jack was new to her. Jack joked that Long John was in shock with wild anticipation. While Jack was dancing in the single spot, I had disrobed while behind Cynthia, and my penis was lying on the small of Cynthia's back. I had my hands on her hips. She reached back and gave me a comforting pat as Jack continued to dance. The purpose of Jack making a fool of himself was to make Cynthia relax. The humor is always relaxing when building sexual tension.

Cynthia watched long John closely, watching him grow because of her presence. I began to unbutton her white short-sleeved blouse. Jack was now focusing on Cynthia's buttons, Cynthia was watching Jack as he was slowly stroking Long John; he was pulling his foreskin over his helmet so Cynthia could imagine the stroking during sex. We were sort of giggling a relaxed giggle. We were all swaying with the imaginary music. I pulled Cynthia's blouse off of her shoulders and she drew her shoulders back subconsciously showing off her perfectly shaped covered breasts. It was to be one step at a time. Cynthia was now watching Jack's eyes. I then unzipped Cynthia's full skirt and it dropped to the floor. She stepped out of it not losing her concentration on Jack's eyes. Cynthia was standing in high heels, panties and bra, and what a sight to behold as she swayed her hips to our humming.

"Look he's waving at me," grinned Cynthia, glancing down at Long John.

Jack caused his penis to flex and it seemed to stretch with no hands; he again pulled back his foreskin and pulled on Long John as if he were masturbating. Jack showed her a few fast strokes. Long John was not new to Cynthia, but the view was more full length than her previous close up, and Jack stroking himself was new and definitely arousing her. Long John was now at full mast. I undid Cynthia's bra and she helped by shaking her shoulders the way strippers do and voila! Both breasts were spectacular, a matching pair as they always are, both firm, erect, and pointing at Jack. It was Jack's first full unobstructed view, and he drank in her beauty. I could see him "gulp." Long John bobbed and bowed untouched. Cynthia was now watching Jack's eyes and she smiled. Sandra Bullock never looked this good.

I then turned Cynthia away from Jack and, bent her over and helped her out of her panties. The idea was to show Jack her magnificent ass. Cynthia caught on to what I was doing and gave Jack and Long John a little sideways wiggle before straightening up. Her high heels played an important role here; they accentuated her beautiful long legs. Her breasts moved ever so delicately as she swayed.

I turned her toward Jack and I pushed her forward for a second "sandwich" hug and kiss, now a naked kiss. We pressed ourselves against Cynthia from both sides. I cupped her breasts from behind while Jack kissed her on the mouth. Cynthia found long John with both hands and caressed him gently. I turned her toward me again and Jack cupped her breasts and I gained a few two handed caresses on my totally erect penis with no name. Cynthia later thought mine should have a name and suggested I name my penis "Winston." Cynthia turned around again facing Jack. Jack kissed her on the mouth and cupped Cynthia's ass while facing her. I was massaging her breasts, but not pressed against Cynthia. Cynthia carefully backed off and watched Jack's face while he felt her ass. It was a strange exchange. Long John was snug up against Cynthia's chest, just under her breasts because of our 6'5" bodies sandwiching her. I stepped back and saw that Cynthia was feeling Jack's ass as we separated. We were totally into the moment at the start, so we all separated and moved to the bed.

"Cynthia, you are incredible. What a great ass and your breasts are exquisite, better than my wildest dreams." said Jack. "It is so exceptional for you to be in such good shape after having three kids; I mean your skin is so tight and smooth. And your breasts don't sag, how do you manage?"

"Well, thank you" she blushed. "I really appreciate what you are saying, coming from you with all the women you have seen, that's quite a compliment." replied Cynthia. She kept her shoulders back.

I led Cynthia the short distance to the side of the bed, while Jack was pulling down the bed spread revealing clean white sheets illuminated by candle light. The "roomglow" was perfect and the candlelight seemed to accentuate Cynthia's beauty. She glowed a golden glow as she lay back on the bed with her black hair, perfectly in place, framed by the silky white pillow. What a sight to behold. I couldn't tell if she was blushing or just glowing. She subconsciously seemed to be posing with one leg folded and that foot flat on the bed. Her other leg was extended and her legs held in a closed position. Her arms were at her side. She looked like a classy naked beach postcard. I had removed her high heels. Cynthia could not help but observe two very present erections pointing at her as Jack and I kneeled on each side of her. She appeared fascinated. She reached out and held both of our cocks for a few moments as if she were weighing them. Our penises were at her shoulders.

Jack and I crawled up beside her, I on her left side and Jack on her right. Before we got started, Cynthia sat up, reached down and grabbed both of our penises and for the second time and caressed them both simultaneously. She acted like she should perform oral sex on us alternately, but I stopped her and reminded her that this was her moment and to enjoy herself. She gave each of us a full length "Popsicle" lick before reclining. She let go of our cocks and again reclined with a really big smile.

We simultaneously kissed her on each assigned cheek. She alternately watched us and stroked both of our heads. She kissed me on the mouth and Jack started caressing her right breast, a gentle movement that pushed her full breast upward and then around in a circular stroke. Her hands kept stroking our heads. Jack then kissed her on the mouth and we worked our hands on both breasts. We stayed with this caressing until Cynthia appeared impatient for extended caressing. We alternated kissing her mouth. She began to move her body to express with body language that we move on. Her body language seemed to suggest some pussy licking as her legs parted. Her nipples were hard.

We were too tall for her to touch our cocks as we moved down her body. It was her body language that urged us on because she spoke not a word. She was moving her hips slightly and lifting her ass off of the bed dropping back with a quiet grunt. Cynthia was now breathing heavily and there were increasing signs of sweeter louder moans. Her eyes seemed opened extra wide and she watched our every move. She seemed to be in an enchanted trance. She never closed her eyes. She carefully observed everything that was happening to her, even kept her eyes open while being kissed. She watched Jack more intently and that was normal, and she was still stroking my head.

When we alternately kissed and gently sucked our assigned nipples we both began to massage her stomach and sides gradually moving our hands to her inner thighs. I looked up at Cynthia without taking my mouth off her breast and she was breathing heavily through her mouth and beginning to make some more very sweet louder sounds. Jack and I each were massaging an inner thigh while tonguing her breasts and that combination was very effective. Cynthia's sounds were natural and I think uncontrolled. That too was a very good sign. Jack and I began alternately kissing her stomach or a breast, even some intermittent skin licking along the way. Cynthia smelled and tasted great. There was to be no more talking, just feelings. She kept parting her legs and slightly raising her knees as if becoming more frustrated. Jack and I were sort of cupping her pussy with passing caresses. Her leg spread was a natural invitation to fuck and she seemed not to be able to control the urges. She kept her legs apart, but not quite raised off of the bed as Jack and I concentrated on caressing her inner thighs, touching her labia while kissing breasts and skin. We licked her skin watching each other to make sure we didn't cross over into each other's territories. Stomach kisses are very effective to a naked woman. It reflects special tingles while not ticklish. We took our time and Cynthia's reaction was one of frustration. Frustrated because we weren't getting to the cunnilingus licking part, I guessed.

So much for the objective scientific approach; there were no questions or answers.

I grabbed the other big pillow and began to place it under her hips when she arched her back to assist me and as I settled with my face between her legs, she then spread her legs and pulled her knees higher in that most welcoming position making easy access to her sweet wet pussy, the real good stuff of life. I took my time and licked her labia as if I were searching for their parting. I laid my face in the most appealing spread at the gateway of heaven while Jack moved up and kissed her mouth and alternated between her breasts and lips. There is no sexier view than a beautiful woman with her legs spread. It is the most wonderful of invitations, especially when you are so close.

Jack was massaging her stomach skin very lightly; almost tickling her while I did what I was really good at, licking pussy. Her body began to react. A woman's skin is a major sex organ and her breathing was getting harder. Her body began to move slightly lifting her hips just a little as if she were slowly fucking while creating a more obvious "welcome mat" for my tongue. Her hands were on Jack's shoulders. Cynthia was "moaning, eowing and ahhing" with increased passion.

Cynthia later quipped that being kissed and having her pussy licked at the same time was a most unusual sexy experience. She was being kissed on the mouth, with one breast being massaged by one man, her belly being caressed while I was licking her pussy with my right hand massaging her open breast. I guess you could call that "full court coverage." We kept that up as long as we could knowing her pleasure was building by leaps and bounds. Cynthia was breathing through a wide-open mouth emitting alternate "hums" and "oohs." I'm sure you ladies can identify with her arousal.

Knowing from experience with Cynthia, I had mastered her climatic buildup by teasing with one rhythm and when I felt her buildup I would purposely switch techniques to prolong her pleasure. Reaching a climax for Cynthia was now like climbing a ladder and each rung is a new level of pleasure. My tongue would make her drop down a few rungs and start climbing through the same pleasure zones a second time. That is a good analogy of building toward a climax. The frustration greatly increased her climax. I again use the other analogy of packing more gunpowder behind the bullet with each stall technique. When it fires, it has more force behind it. The concept certainly works for men too, except we often cannot control or stop our premature firing.

I would push the skin surrounding her clitoris upwards with full long upward tongue strokes. I would stop, hesitate, and give a few gentle sucks forming a small circle with my lips as if her clitoris was a miniature erected penis. That always caused her hips to move as if she was doing the fucking and my sucking mouth was a vagina. When sucking, there was no direct contact with the clitoris, so the sensitivity level was not increased, just the pleasure. I could feel and measure her clitoris grow in my mouth, and as it expanded it usually became more sensitive. At that most sensitive moment I could sense when to retreat to flicking my tongue sideways just underneath her clitoris not making direct contact. This caused her hips to move more as if her body was reaching for that regular consistent contact that she knew would cause her to burst with pleasure.

She eventually could no longer hold back her urges and reached a super climax without the direct pressure. The flicking underneath her clitoris definitely prolonged her orgasm. She was very vocal exclaiming "yes, yes, that is so good, yes, yes." I believe it was her best orgasm ever and she seemed to hold the higher pleasure level longer. She was clenching Jack's shoulders, almost pinching him, which had to be an unusual feeling while climaxing. Have you heard the expression that an orgasm is so intense that it blows the wax out of both ears? (It is an old joke.) Cynthia's entire body rocked and twitched with her orgasm. It had to be her best ever with the double attention.

I blew gently on her clitoris and slowly rose up to kiss her left breast. I dragged my tongue over her entire body as I climbed upwards. Jack held his position for a few minutes, which seemed like a long time to Cynthia, we seemed to be in slow motion. The pause gave Cynthia a chance to catch her breath, but just enough to not lose her "high."

Jack then licked his way down between her legs. I moved to her face and left breast. Her tongue went wild in my mouth. Jack put a hand on each thigh while slowly caressing them as he assumed his "face in" position. He was checking out and admiring the long legged gateway and was rubbing his cheeks against Cynthia's thighs. Cynthia did something unexpected, she rose up on her elbows to watch Jack, rather than lie back and enjoy the feelings. I tried to kiss her so she could again experience the French kissing accompanied by the pussy licking. She was too intent on watching Jack to pay me any heed. She sort of pushed me out of the way of her view of being eaten by another man. Her eyes were glazed over as if she was in another world. Her mouth was wide open and she was intently fixated on Jack as if she were stretching to see the impossible "to see action."

I had thoroughly briefed Jack on the sensitivities of Cynthia's pussy. We had shared so may experiences years ago that we knew instinctively that no two women were alike. Their sensitivities varied with no logical explanation. Some clitoris' you could actually bite and they never became overly sensitized. But that stuff is for later discussions.

Jack teased and sucked and licked and flicked in perfect rhythm. Cynthia was destined to come again fast. She could not handle the newness and the constant intensity. Multiple orgasms in rapid succession were inevitable and an exceptional treat for Cynthia. It was obviously a result of the newness of the circumstances. Remember, first time experiences are unique, and the pleasure is always accentuated. It was as if this whole extreme event started with her pussy being licked with different styles and with different lickers. The experience for Cynthia was one gigantic continuous orgasm. She never came down from the high. She was totally in a different world and she was not herself. She was birthing another personality that seemed to be trapped inside her. Jack blew and cooled her periodically and she seemed to have experienced a series of huge orgasms. She had been more vocal than ever, even grunting slightly during her "uums and oohs." I found myself almost holding her down during her second violent orgasm. She told later she had a series of great orgasms and the gaps closed into a continuous long orgasm.

Cynthia was breathing very hard. She reached down and gently pushed Jack's shoulders away as she whispered, "enough, enough."

Jack raised himself up on his haunches with his knees under Cynthia's thighs. He laid his penis across her pubic hair with his now bulging main nerve resting on her soft belly. His testicles were up tight against her hot wet pussy. Jack began a slow stroking motion dragging his balls over her clitoris thinking she would like to witness his ejaculation onto her belly. Cynthia rose up a bit and put her left hand on top of Jack's sliding penis and he stopped the sliding motion. She pushed his penis down between her legs. To our utter amazement and a complete violation of the pre-game rules, Cynthia whispered, "put it in me, put it in me."

Jack did not hesitate. He slowly stroked her labia with the head of his cock a few times thus rubbing their most sensitive nerves together. The old expression is "plowing a furrow." Jack slowly and gently entered paradise. Cynthia was still in a trance and her eyes were fixated on the new penis going in and out of her pussy. She remained on her raised elbows. It was if she was a different person in a different world. Jack was more up on his knees than laying on her. He was poised on his outstretched arms. The only contact they had was his penis and her vagina. Jack was also fixated on their combined genitals. I don't recall if she ever watched herself getting fucked before. Maybe she was becoming too uninhibited. They both were focused on the "in and outs" of fucking. Cynthia's knees were raised to a high level. I never imagined how good that scene was because I could never have had this view.

Can you imagine the reaction if I would have stopped the procedure right then. It really didn't cross my mind, but the cruelty of separating them seemed immature. After all, did I really expect her to stop the act? Actually I forgot who I was and I was turned on by the view. I was having an out of body experience, which I will refer to several times. The candlelight and the sweet smell of sex is wonderful and I was caught up in the moment the same as Cynthia. I was vicariously experiencing her pleasure. I thought I was watching myself making love to my wife. It was a vision no man can imagine. I alternated between watching their strokes and Cynthia's eyes. Her eyes fascinated me. They were ablaze!

The strokes were slow and soothing at first. Jack picked up the pace and began to hit the end stroke a little harder, which did gently flatten her clitoris. Obviously I couldn't see what was happening at the point of contact with each stroke, but I instinctively knew. She began to grunt more loudly with each stroke. Jack accelerated his strokes to almost a frenzied pace. It was wild and Cynthia was almost shouting how good she felt. She even used God's name. I couldn't count the strokes, but there were many, perhaps a hundred. They both reached an orgasm at the same time, although I think Cynthia was in a constant state of "high orgasmic" pleasure. Jack was very vocal, almost shouting. I think Jack was exaggerating his role to encourage her passion and show his appreciation. And all during that wondrous event, she never took her eyes off of the stroking penis and was clutching Jack's extended flexed arms. She appeared to be pushing and pulling on Jack's arms with the rhythm of the act. She was absolutely fascinated by witnessing herself getting fucked. She was fixated on her own genitals as if she were having an "out of body experience."Jack's vocalization heightened the moment to the point where I almost came.

As I said, for me it was an "out of body experience," but I was watching her eyes more than the full picture. I guess I too was hypnotized by the event. I was never aware of Jack's presence during the fucking. I only saw myself fucking my wife, but from a different view. I was most captivated by Cynthia's eyes. I later wondered why I watched her eyes so intently. I did glance at the stroking a few times, but I was more interested in her facial and vocal reactions. They seemed to have bolts of lightning flashing from her dark brown eyes. They glowed a golden brown in the flickering candlelight. And Cynthia was beaded with perspiration causing even a greater glow. What a turn on!

They stopped moving and starred at each other for a moment. Jack did not move. Cynthia watched Jack slowly withdraw and she starred at his "spent," but fully erect penis. It was like she wanted to verify what had happened. Long John had served her well. She dropped back off her elbows and reached to kiss me on the mouth. She was still panting heavily. (Finally) Quickly and anxiously she pushed my shoulders down and guided me between her legs. She pulled my cock into her in a most demanding manner. Her anxiety to keep fucking was unbelievable. She acted like she couldn't wait to get me inside her. She was still in a state of "shock and awe" and was equally focused on my getting on with her pleasure while she was still "hot to trot, so to speak.

I entered her immediately with my knees under her thighs. I stated pumping before I got in her; don't know why. We were fucking harder and faster than usual. The sexaction was to be continued without further interruption. Cynthia's hands were clenching my biceps. Our chests were not touching, but our bellies were sliding against each other fast and wet with perspiration. Her breasts were rocking hard with the fucking. I never noticed her breasts when Jack was pumping. We performed as if Jack and I were a single non-stop fuck. I was way too high to concentrate on making this ride last. So was Cynthia. We were watching each other's eyes for the eye action that accompanies our orgasms. I know she had another orgasm. It was if she had never stopped coming, a constant long lasting continuous orgasm that began with the oral sex. Such a feat was incredible and I believe resulted from this concerted effort to raise her level of enjoyment because of the newness of the first time threesome. I hoped she would stay at this level using only my foreplay techniques. Could this experience improve an already perfect relationship? I was hoping we would never again require any outside physical stimulus. Cynthia later claimed she reached another orgasm with my faster strokes. My rapid shorter strokes slapped her clitoris at just the right speed.

Cynthia had thrown her arms around me and was still watching my eyes. She was watching my pleasure level build in my face and she was very vocal. She was whispering words of love and how good I felt and I stroked hard and fast knowing I was about to burst with ecstasy. I had a "blow out" orgasm that shook every bone in my body. Cynthia tried to move her hips as if to better facilitate my pleasure. We were frantic and both perspiring heavily. I was obviously caught up in the most passionate moment of my life. I had enjoyed watching my wife fuck another man as if she were fucking me. As I said, it was to be an only "out of body" experience I would ever have. I had created a worthy visual work of art. My wife had been lit like a stick of dynamite, now exploding.

I collapsed; we were both perspiring and breathing heavily. I withdrew slowly and Cynthia watched me do so. She smiled at my erect spent very wet penis, looked at Jack's erect very wet spent penis, smiled again. We lay together in complete exhaustion and cooled down. No one spoke. Jack was as quiet as I have ever seen him. I believe he was in shock watching Cynthia and I perform so passionately.

Cynthia rolled on top of me and kissed me on the neck. As she cuddled, she looked back at Jack and seemed amused that Jack was still stroking his second hard-on. She watched him play with himself. Apparently, she too thought watching us fuck was more than Jack could handle. Cynthia was lying on her stomach over me with one knee slightly raised over my legs. I could feel her heart pounding against my chest and her breathing was still fast. We were trying to relax. Jack was massaging her lower back and gradually, in an act of admiration, began to rub her buttocks. As a reflex, she raised her ass higher creating a more convenient angle for the massages. Jack's hand passed over her labia and he grooved her labia with his index finger between her cheeks. Cynthia twitched and parted her legs a bit more to accommodate Jack's inner thigh massage and gentle fingering. He made a few more slow passes at her pussy. She was again experiencing ecstasy. Then Cynthia abruptly got on her knees, straddled me, and moved her fanny facing Jack. It was as though she had reached a tolerance level of too much additional stimulation. She lowered her head into my chest raising her ass as high as she could. She sort of waved her ass like a cat in heat and flexed her buttocks; she reached under herself and began stroking her labia watching Jack's moves under herself.

Jack rose on his knees and entered her vagina from behind. Cynthia carefully watched Jack and backed into him and grunted at his sudden entry. She then put my penis in her mouth and timed her mouth strokes with Jack' gentle strokes in her vagina. Then,

Jack held Cynthia's hips and began a hard faster stroking as if he was madly driven and had no choice. Cynthia adjusted to the faster strokes, released my penis and just looked at me. She really wasn't seeing me, but the look on her face was fascinating. I thought she was trying to kiss me, but she was rocking too hard and she was gasping with each stroke. My penis lay between her breasts and I could feel the sliding motion. Cynthia was obviously concentrating on feeling the harder fast strokes. I put my hands on her shoulders and pushed. It took only about thirty hard strokes and Jack clutched her hips and allowed his cumlite ejaculation while holding steady. Cynthia was focused on my eyes. Jack's eyes were fixated on her ass and he groaned in ecstasy. He was mesmerized. Cynthia was held motionless. The desire to hold a sexy woman's ass is inexplicable. We are almost hypnotized by a female ass, we male weaklings. We held that position while Cynthia kissed me and Jack continued to stroke slowly after he came still admiring the view.

Cynthia later told me she was looking at me and was imagining I was fucking her from behind. She did not understand how I was performing such a trick while facing me, but she felt the sex was just between the two of us. She said the feeling of having her ass slapped so hard was wonderful. When Jack had reached an orgasm she said she could feel him pulsating and Jack then held her ass very tight. It was during that stillness that she kissed me. In her mind she thought I was coming. I asked her what she was thinking when she was watching Jack's eyes while I was fucking her from behind. She said she still knew it was me doing it because Jack was watching her ass getting pounded and was focused on her curves and her ass. Jack never looked at her face. She said that gave her some extra satisfaction. She was arousing everybody in sight, including herself, and that gave her a thrill.

Studies show that rear entry sex better stimulates a woman because she cannot see who is doing her, so she therefore concentrates more on the action and what she feels. A "G" spot orgasm is more like a rumble or a "thumping" felt through her whole body whereas a clitoral orgasm is more like electrical shock or electronic vibrations concentrated on the 8000 nerves in the vaginal complex. An orgasm is a sustained tremble and the "G" spot has an entirely different feeling. A woman prefers the clitoral climax, but the "G" spot offers an unusual feeling probably a feeling having been evolved from cavemen days. Rear entry sex for a woman is curious at first, and yet always feels good. She is forced to refocus her vibes. Women are often compelled to watch themselves with such 'rear ending." It is very sexy.

During this threesome Cynthia was a sight to behold; she appeared to be posing. Her back curved like a beautiful statue while her ass was being "flapped," or spanked as she grunted with each plunge. Cynthia had raised her ass higher and spread her knees. She had tempted and had teased Jack to use his new erection, and he could not resist. Cynthia had held steady while Jack entered her from behind and she seemed to be reveling in her ass being irresistible. But from the male view, holding her hips and "slapping" against an ass was also extra stimulating. Cynthia seemed hotter with desire upon feeling the hard strokes. She obviously seemed wetter than usual but that served to make us pound harder.

To repeat, after Jack came, he held his position tight inside her not moving and she began to kiss me on the mouth. Jack gave her a few very gentle strokes so Cynthia could feel the hard cock inside her while she kissed me facing me. She was in obvious ecstasy and when Jack withdrew she quickly moved and crossed her knee over me so her ass was in my face. She looked under herself at me, and again waved and patted her ass while she rubbed her clitoris. I got on my knees and plunged in for another wild ride. No one spoke and Cynthia looked at Jack's face as I worked toward my second orgasm. Jack was watching her ass and curves getting poked and he was in a trance. Jack pushed against her when I came and tried to caress her hanging breasts. She turned her head and watched me have an orgasm as best she could. This was a most unusual three way act and we would spend many hours reviewing this spectacular event. We had exhibited two basic sex positions and Cynthia was higher than a kite on sexual pleasure. "G" spot? Definitely!

I think the urge to fuck a woman from behind is uncontrollable when offered. I was fascinated as she pushed off of Jack's chest while I got to admire the curves of her stretched body. Cynthia knew she was showing off her ass, but maybe did not realize she had lost all semblance of self control. She had begged me to fuck hard and fast and we were stunned at her endurance. I, too, came hard and fast, and not delivering much fluid. My balls ached from so much stroking, but I could not resist the fast climax. I came and we held our positions as if we were locked together like two spent dogs. The three of us were breathing so hard we sounded like approaching hurricanes. Cynthia had laid her head on Jack's chest and watched me over her shoulder as I gradually withdrew. I had stayed in her for several minutes as we all came down a bit. She then rolled over and smiled at me so sweetly like she had delivered more pleasure than she imagined, not mentioning what she had received. It was as though Cynthia had to feel every sexual position and analyze every feeling while the opportunity existed. Was she testing her ability to entice men to fuck her? It was like we were back in cavemen times. She held her hand over her crotch tightly and relaxed for a few moments staring at the ceiling. Jack and I were in a trance.

Then Cynthia heaved a big sigh and slid down the bed, bounced onto the floor and headed for the bathroom holding her hand under her pussy. Jack and I looked at each other and rolled our eyes and gave each other the "thumbs up." Jack was very emotional and actually thanked me and told me how much he appreciated our close relationship. We had enjoyed a lifetime of sharing excitement both on and off the basketball court and in and out of bedrooms. He said this was the most exciting thing that ever happened to him and I said the same thing. Jack said I should probably write a book. Hmmm, there was a pregnant thought.

We got up and entered the bathroom. Cynthia was just rising from the toilet and exclaimed,

"Wow, I have never imagined so much love juice coming out of me. I expected the "cum" to squirt out of my ears at the end there. It looked like I was filled to the brim and it even felt good releasing all that good stuff. Are you guys OK?" She asked. "I thank you both for that spectacular time. Wow!"

I think we were a bit more wobbly than Cynthia, and we exaggerated our staggering as if she had done us in while she was still refreshed. We peed as she went to the shower. She giggled at the display of weakness on our part. And she did glow with an aura of freshness as if she had slain a couple of giants. Do you realize how much women really control our sex lives yet make it seem like it was our idea? Cynthia was totally satisfied, yet she had to eventually rationalize the event from a moral standpoint. Men? That should not be the case. Moral judgments were already dead.

Showering as a threesome was also a new treat. Cynthia soaped down both cocks and washed herself. She showed no signs of being sore or worn out. The stay power of women is seldom recognized for its true value. They are blessed with so many good feelings. How could she get sore, she was as wet as I had ever imagined, yet tight. We washed her breasts and made the mistake of allowing water spray to wet her head. She was not upset; nothing would upset her this day. Cynthia looked even more beautiful with her wet hair tight against her head and her face was indeed flush. We dried and dressed and made some preliminary comments about how good the event felt. There was neither embarrassment nor any comments about Cynthia losing control and allowing Jack to fuck her. She had made a big "no no" about that before hand, but totally ignored mentioning it. We kept quiet about that, too. I was preparing a rationalization in my mind for later use. I understood that her reaction was only human and no one could have resisted the moment. Especially knowing Jack and I were sterile.

I was wondering how Cynthia and I would reconcile the moral issues. I guess the matter would only be a problem if it was to become a frequent event and I didn't think that would ever happen. After all, Jack had an exciting sex life and did not need to involve complications with us as his best friends. The mutual motivation to explore and discuss sex was still our goal. That served as foreplay for everybody's sex life. Perhaps you readers can see the advantage of that adult level of communications. I think it is possible to accomplish the same thing without sharing intercourse. It was simply too hot at the time and rationalizing our actions would be a discussion point for years to come.

What we had endured was a "fucking frenzy." Can you imagine how fired up people can get? It was like sharks smelling blood except Cynthia was another shark. The sexual motivation grew with each orgasm. Why wasn't the excessive satisfaction sufficient? And, there is so much inexplicable excessive desire for a man to mount a woman from behind. It is so "animalistic." It feels so good to hold a woman's hips and take that plunge. Smacking against buttocks is an inexplicable urge. Why are their asses so sexy? Why men are so compelled to fuck a sexy ass is unimaginable. Everything about a woman's body is designed to arouse us. Spreading legs or waving buttocks, what's a poor guy to do?

But what about Cynthia? How can we explain her explosion of sexual desire? It is like multiple orgasms begetting more orgasms? People should tire more after so much sex, but first time encounters have a special adrenalin rush that enhances sexual behavior. I cannot describe our pleasure level. A woman can usually make a man reach a climax whenever she desires it. Women are usually in control of a man's orgasms, but maybe not so aware of their female power. These new circumstances were rapidly rising from the exciting voyeurism, the curious blowjob; the sexual frenzy all beginning with the past barrage of stimulating sexy stories told by Jack Callahan. Our unspoken goal was to arouse some extra passion in my wife and behold, the results blew up in our face. There were no moral repercussions, but we all knew that a continued threesome relationship would have ruined our lives. We knew it was a one-time event. Can you imagine yourself reaching such an intense pleasure level?

What about me? What about my enjoying watching my wife fuck another man? It is called "troilism" when a man enjoys imagining, or actually watching his wife performing so well on another. Was being proud wrong or immoral? It never happened again, but I have to admit I played it in my mind many times and it always served to arouse me. I felt no guilt, jealousy or embarrassment. I doubt I will ever understand it, but I know it was thrilling. Go figure!

What is the deal with Cynthia's ass flashing? What kind of test was that? Men's lust and understanding their temptations is something that has evolved way before the "Great Pube Wars." In the beginning, teenage boys were curious about breasts. It took great efforts to get to feel them, eventually getting to touch bare breasts. Unbeknown to us was that only one percent of women can achieve an orgasm by having their breasts massaged. We had an inexplicable urge to rub our faces on bare breasts. What was that all about? Then we used to admire girls legs being totally curious as to what was between them.

Our observations were innocent and our hormones forcefully drove us onward. As we became more sophisticated we began to admire sections and parts of females. Later we observed eyes, smiles, faces, and subliminally personalities as they were connected to flirting. We gradually became aware of skin and curves as girls matured. What force obsessed us? Why us and not them? But, the grand finale was to admire and evaluate asses. Why the animalistic urge to poke an ass? Did their buttocks move separately or in unison? Were they soft or hard? Would they flex during sex? What was the great mystery that drove us mad with whatever was between their legs? Crazy things entered our young minds. We eventually were taught the fundamentals in boy's gym class, but the not the reasons for our urges. The urges are inexplicable and we are destined to be fools about our urges.

What role did hips and hip swings play in arousing us men? As men grew older we fell back to the fundamentals of checking out "T and A." (Tits and Ass) Now perhaps, the most senior evaluation is strictly asses and why that arousal grows to override all else is inexplicable. Older men have an urge to grab or pat female asses. Whenever a man has a chance, he observes a woman walking away from him and he checks out asses first and legs when available. Admiring sexuality is like observing art and fundamentally not crude, so they say. I think Jack and I can read female asses like palm readers read palms. That's probably wishful thinking?

Women, during the "Great Pube Wars" are innocent of their sex appeal and they too mature with little sophistication. They begin to experiment with featuring their body parts as they mature. (Bras, tight clothes, flashes of skin etc) That process fuels the Pube Wars. They watch their breasts grow and are not aware of the potential using their asses until older. Then women begin to sense they are arousing men in many different ways and the Pube Wars are raised to another level. The need for education and communication lags the maturation process thus creating the problems that follow with adult sexuality. Women wear makeup and dress to attract men, yet are always prepared to reject some admiration. Go figure! The subject of sex appeal is addressed frequently while revealing some of these stories. Many people have sex without love to reaffirm their appeal and that is another psychological issue. Many times people engage and experiment with sex out of curiosity. According to sexual surveys both men and women, as adults naturally desire to have sex four times a week. The average time to complete sexual intercourse is seven minutes. These many urges are repeatedly discussed herein.

The record shows that the second most frequent place to having sex is in automobiles. And the average time for mutual foreplay is ten to twelve minutes. This threesome session just completed must have been setting records. I wonder about that learning practice of interrupting foreplay and stopping at some agreed to point. We didn't discuss the stopping point that much, but it seemed to be mutually understood. The sexual revolution has so many rules that were either controlled by guilt or some set of unwritten rules set up by girl's parents. They must have been thoroughly indoctrinated. Young men are left hanging out there simply making mistakes and being rejected with little explanation. It is little wonder that the sexual revolution was so difficult. There was no "Geneva Conventions" for the Great Pube Wars.

In my opinion Cynthia endured an overdose of sexual stimulation and exploded with sexual energy trying to do all that had been stored up in her conservative sexual upbringing. She had watched Jack mount Sheila from behind and that was her first time vision. It was as though she had unleashed a monster within herself, but wait a minute, did she not unleash the same monsters out of Jack and me? I asked her if she would try and explain all her reactions some day. She said, "No! I should withhold some mystery, shouldn't I?" (Darn it, beaten again)

Chapter 6. WHOSE TOES ROSE?

We walked to the car in the darkness of a cool summer night. We walked in a satisfied silence. The mountain breezes were so comforting and we all had red flushed complexions, the usual obvious flushness of face that reflects on people who just had a lot of sex. More people can tell when you have just had sex than people realize. It is a hard social cover up, when necessary. I had mentioned that we lowered all the car windows and that natural breeze was wonderful considering how hot we had been. It had been an awesome night!

Jack opened the rear driver's door and Cynthia climbed in with Jack right behind her. Jack and I seemed a bit wobbly, and Cynthia definitely had a stronger step. She actually strode with some new-found authority, and that natural hip swing in high heels seemed even more beautiful and accentuated. I was driving. So Jack and Cynthia got into the back seat rather than walk around the car. This was my Blue Cadillac sedan with blue leather seats. (Neat car). Jack asked Cynthia if she could openly talk about what just happened to her and what her most intimate reactions were. She was willing to talk and was very excited; she had not come down from the highest pleasure level she ever had. She later admitted that she tingled for days after so much excitement and so many orgasms. She said she was still feeling the full effects of such intense orgasms for months to follow. Her desire for sex had increased exponentially.

"Listen," I said, before we start talking, I have a request. Cynthia, why can't you ever say fuck or pussy, or use some term other than medical terms like, "nice penis, or how is my vagina?" You are one of us now and in our private conversations you have advanced into a world of new exploration and newly discovered skills, but you would be even sexier if you could talk the sexy talk now that you walked the sexy walk."

"Well, OK, fuck, fucking, fucked, my pussy got licked and fucked and my pussy still tingles and I loved getting fucked and I had uncountable multiple orgasms and I really enjoyed having an orgasm each time I got fucked. Did you like fucking my ass? There, does that make you feel better?" She blurted.

"Whoa, do I sense some hostility here?" I asked.

"I don't know, you tell me, am I a slut or a better educated wife? Am I now a flagrant adulteress, or what, what do you think? Oh what the hell, it's done, water under the bridge, I did it and I have to admit it was the most sensational experience I will ever have. I hope my Mother never finds out." Cynthia blushed and frowned.

"Take it easy," Jack said, we'll tell you our reactions in every detail, which I think was the purpose of this meeting." We will have many great discussions for many years to come, believe it!"

"Do you remember my saying that I would not have sexual intercourse with you Jack?" I wonder what my husband thinks now that I didn't even hesitate to let you inside me. I practically begged you to fuck me. I was totally out of control and I would never have tried to prevent anything, it was so wonderful, yet where was my guilt? What happened to my morals? I wasn't deceived, I knew what I was doing and I was supposed to be in charge. My body took charge over my brain and, I was controlled by my "little head," my little lovable "bean," like a guy. What is my clitoris, a "bean head?"

I never thought I could come so many times and I don't feel guilty about the orgasms, but should I? And what was I doing begging to get fucked from behind? It felt like I was being spanked, but ooh so good. What the hell was I doing? If I have a "G" spot that sure hit the spot. Keep talking, and convince me my soul will still be saved." Cynthia begged.

Cynthia turned her back to the side rear door and crossed her arms, still frowning.

Jack began: "I thought watching you and Will making love was like a sexy ballet, a great beautiful work of art. You both were so graceful. Your body languages were like you were ballet dancers. I watched your legs the most, Cynthia, and I cannot begin to tell you how perfectly flexed they were. It was almost like you were posing for an artist. Your legs were spread like they were an invitation to a great hall of pleasure, the gateway to paradise. You truly opened up that gate and I am so grateful for the privilege. As for the ass fucking, it was beautiful and sexy. No man could resist you Cynthia, ever, I couldn't stop myself."

Cynthia nodded, covered her eyes for a moment and looked at me to see if I reacted to Jack's compliment.

Jack continued, "I noticed the most subtle yet interesting thing, your toes arched and pulled back when you had an orgasm and even more interesting, your toes flexed as if they knew exactly when Will was coming. Actually your toes were flexed to an extreme almost the whole time. I read where the vagina, I mean pussy, does not feel much internally, but your toes acted independently like, how did your toes know Will was climaxing? Your legs pulled back about four inches and you rocked with each apparent ejaculation, oops I mean each squirt of cum." You didn't rock during fucking, because I think Will's strokes were faster than you could wave your legs, but you rocked with Will's final strokes. Were you aware of that?"

A stunned silence ensued!

"Are you kidding me, are you making that up? That is so weird and I find that hard to believe. You mean my body did things on its own? That is scary. Did you know that would happen? Have you read about the toe thing or did you make that up?" asked Cynthia.

Jack replied, "Yes, I did read that toe reflex action years ago, but obviously I've never witnessed it before; I forget to look at toes while I'm fucking, OK? I read that women flex their toes when they climax, but I never read why. Women's toes rise almost like erections when they climax."

"OK, OK," said Cynthia, "tell me more, this is really interesting, better yet show me what I did. How did I move my legs and show me what my toes did."

With her back against the rear door, Cynthia kicked off her high heels and raised her legs and pushed bare feet against Jack's chest. Jack had turned to face Cynthia. Her loose full white skirt fell back to her panty line exposing her long sexy legs. Jack took the flats of her feet, spread her legs about two feet and bent her knees back and asked her to hold that position. Then he took her toes and bent them back. With Jack holding her toes arched firmly, Cynthia began to rock her legs gently about six inches slowly back and forth.

"There is nothing sexier than when a woman spreads and lifts her legs. I have never seen statues of that scene, but then such beauty, unfortunately is called pornography," I observed.

"And I don't even own a pornograph," laughed Jack.

"Another bad old joke," I grunted.

"Hey guys, remember me, I'm spreading here." Cynthia quipped. "Are my sex slaves distracted by some dumb guy thing?"

Cynthia, put her hand over her mouth as a modesty reflex, and lifted her dress now bunched up to her waist. She covered her crotch and that delicate part of her fine white silk panties with her left hand. She was obviously still very wet and her love juice was showing through her silks. She had noticeably spread her legs further apart. That was real sexy and I think the "new" Cynthia knew what she was doing. I think she wanted more than to explore the toe story. It was if she were trying to test the bent toe theory while touching her clitoris.

Jack jokingly stuck her left big toe in his mouth. I glanced back and told Jack that I had read that some women like to have their toes sucked.

Cynthia said, "That's not necessary, just keep showing me how my toes bend and how I moved. This is fascinating and actually feels good. I'm not sure what I'm supposed to feel in my toes. Or maybe my pussy is supposed to feel the toe thing."

Jack said, "You know, we men are the real slaves, a wet pussy smells so good that mother nature compels us to be slaves to women. That olfactory factor is a big stimulant in the animal world. Male animals can smell a female in heat from miles away."

"Really," said Cynthia, That's good information; I just need to figure out how to use that information," she quipped, "Right, Will? If I dip my finger in my pussy and put a whiff under your nose does that mean you will immediately take out the garbage?"

"Stop it you two, stop it, we are having a serious discussion here about fucking, Are you with me or not?" Said Jack. The car did smell sexy.

Silence! No time for humor, Jack was right, we were interrupting the mood.

Jack gently bent all of Cynthia's toes and began to rock her legs back rhythmically and gently. It was about a six-inch variation and he continued to hold her toes rigid during each movement. I noticed Cynthia was rubbing her clitoris in rhythm with her legs rocking,(her little bean was obviously still hard) but probably not so conscious of what she was doing. She was concentrating on any possible feeling between her pussy and flexed toes.

"Well, I don't feel any need to bend my toes, maybe because I'm still so damn turned on from this whole evening, but I am curious. I don't know if this is a fair test since I'm still so turned on. I wonder if my clitoris will ever soften back to normal." Cynthia said.

Jack kept moving her legs and holding her toes erect.

I noticed that Cynthia was continuing to rub herself in rhythm with the leg rocking and she exclaimed, "You know, I am still horny, but I'm not sure bending my toes is doing it. How can I be so wet, so horny, yet completely satisfied? I'm wondering if I have become permanently horny, which puts some new pressure on my husband, right?" Cynthia gently kicked my head and then quickly assumed the sexy spread.

Jack moved her extended spread legs and she rested her legs on the front seat back and her left leg on the back shelf. Jack took her hand off her pussy and put the two knuckles of his right hand against her wet spot and said,

"Wow, you really are wet. Who says your toes didn't open some valves somewhere. Maybe your toes are some sort of faucet for pussy juice. How can you still be so horny after all we did?" Jack observed. Cynthia looked at Jack's knuckles on her pantied pussy and grinned.

Cynthia said nothing, but her eyes were beginning to glaze over as Jack massaged her silky wet panty cover with the back of his knuckles. She looked at me and again grinned. Cynthia raised her legs and slowly began the six-inch rocking motion unassisted, without saying a word. She grabbed her toes and pulled them back with both hands as if she was testing a new feeling. Jack was accommodating the test by rubbing her pussy in rhythm with her rocking motion, and the mood was certainly losing the scientific moment. She tilted her head back and closed her eyes. She looked like she was going to have another orgasm when suddenly she interrupted the probable orgasm.

Cynthia straightened both legs, accidentally kicking Jack in the back of the head. She put her knees together, lifted her hips off the seat and slid her panties off. She put her right leg on the back of the passenger seat, kicked me gently on the side of my head and said,

"Don't look, no, watch my feet."

She placed her left leg on the back shelf and her right leg behind the driver. The glow of her bare legs against the blue leather was a view to behold. Cynthia looked like a Playboy centerfold with the blue leather backdrop. She was exploding with sex appeal and I pulled the car over to the curb. I wanted to see what she was going to do. I was growing a new erection just watching after just having had my brains fucked out. My erection was a little painful. How come? I wondered.

Of course I looked and I tried to watch her feet. Cynthia then beckoned Jack with her right finger and pointed to her exposed pussy with her left hand. Cynthia was spreading her labia, stretching her clitoris to make it more receptive to a tongue. I suspect that was a newly acquired tact. It was not suggested, just a natural uninhibited act that she was unaware of or more anxious than concerned. It was like Cynthia had become an out of control sex addict.

"Start licking me you sex slave," she exclaimed.

Jack dove right in and started licking her pussy as she grabbed his head with her right hand and held on to it tightly should he would try to escape. She kept her left hand stretching her labia to push her erect clitoris toward Jack. That was certainly uninhibited. She had clasped Jack's hair; he wasn't going anywhere. Jack was a sex slave caught in a delicious trap, much like those flowers that close on their prey. I could hear the moist licking. I could actually hear more slurping and it was sexy, but consisted of a steady rhythm that I was all too familiar with. I imagined I was where Jack was. Cynthia laid her head back against the open rear window. Jack was giving her a steady "doggy lick," straight up resulting in pushing the skin toward her clitoris, which was very effective. It wasn't necessary to change techniques or stall an orgasm, Cynthia was already on her way to a climax and the steady licking was most effective. She closed her eyes and began to moan a delicious response. Yes, I noticed her toes flexed. Cynthia was rocking her legs in a gentle motion. She grabbed her toes and arched them while she rocked her spread legs in unison with Jack's tongue. She commenced another orgasm, eyes closed and a sweet expression. It was a quiet orgasm. She sighed a sweet slow moan.

She came quickly, exclaimed how good it felt, then she pushed Jack's head back and said, "stop, stop, that's enough. That was too good. I came again, it was delicious. Can you believe this?"

Jack sat up, Cynthia pulled her legs off the shelf and sat back and accidentally kicked Jack in the head again. Jack was in shock; he didn't feel a thing.

Cynthia closed her legs and said, "You know this whole evening has been a fantastic experience, you both have made me feel better than I have ever felt in my life, but you know, it has been all about me. I have been fucked and licked like an all day sucker and until I'm satisfied beyond recognition, but what I miss now is the chance to reciprocate. I don't want to stop feeling this pleasure. I just learned that after every orgasm with a tongue, I crave having a fat cock in my pussy. You have both been my sex slaves and I appreciate it so much. After all, that is the reaction you guys wanted isn't it? I want to try some different action here; I want to do something that I have never done. I want to do whatever I want to do to you guys. Yes, I want to sit on and fuck a fat cock! I want to be in charge of the fucking. I want to ride a fat cock, I want to fuck some more! Jack, take out your cock!"

Jack dropped his pants to the floor and yes he was erect and throbbing. I pushed the front seats as far forward as it would go making extra room in the back seat. I was stunned at what she had just said. Why was I being so aroused? Cynthia bent over and took Long John in her mouth, gave it a few pulls, kissed his little helmet, and then to our surprise, lifted up her dress and threw her right leg over Jack, he adjusted and slumped slightly using the extra knee room. She took Long John in her hand with his helmet protruding from her left wrist. She had control; she stroked the groove between her labia with the head of his penis about five times like she was plowing her own furrow. Her eyes rolled in ecstasy. She tipped to the left, found the opening to her own pussy and slowly mounted him settling down on Long John. She brought her knees up on the seat as Jack slumped more. Her skirt covered her ass. I lifted her skirt so I could see the action. What a wonderful view. Her ass was flexing.

I had pulled the car to the curb again, and had turned around not wanting to miss this passionate activity. Cynthia was not talking; she was focusing on being in charge and being the "fucker" instead of the "fuckee." I kneeled on the front seat and faced them. I cupped her breasts hoping to participate. She didn't react. I unbuttoned her blouse, unhooked her bra and pulled the bra up exposing her breasts while she was rocking back and forth riding the base of Jack's cock. She was undulating not bobbing. I don't think she was even aware of my presence. Cynthia was focused on her own movement. As she was undulating back and forth, Jack tried to bounce. I think Jack wanted the up and down bob because that feels better to a guy, but Cynthia was persistent, she was getting the rub she desired and she ignored Jack. She had discovered a good rub against the base of Jack's cock and was working toward a "fucking" climax. This undulating action rubs the penis against the rear wall of the vagina. They are short strokes, but very effective for an aroused male. A man doesn't get to regulate the action; he just hangs on and tries not to climax too soon. Jack and I were again both erect, but Jack's third orgasm would be more difficult, or, better said, longer lasting. And a man's third climax will be short on fluids.

It was like Cynthia had discovered a new position not caring what the penis wanted. Obviously her animal instincts took charge and I wondered how she would handle the rationalization of these new purposeful acts. She was just beginning to give in to the uncontrolled urges when she invited Jack to enter her when back at the condo. Both of her hands were clutching Jack's shoulders.

Cynthia was breathing hard in short snappy bursts of air, almost a breathy series of loud gasps like panting. She was panting with each of her strokes. These were sounds I had never heard before. Jack was in that sexual shock when you know you cannot hold back the climax. It looked like he was getting close because she was obviously climaxing and her pleasure seemed to be growing with each of her strokes. She was undulating like a stripper doing bumps. It may have been my imagination, but these short fast strokes could have been a hundred and Cynthia was concentrating on her point of contact. Because she was so wet, she had to rub harder. Cynthia was perspiring from her forehead and breasts.

To my surprise, her animal instincts became more verbal than I had ever heard in our long relationship. Cynthia shouted, "give it to me, give it to me, I want to feel you come, let it go, come on, fire that gun, I'm coming, come with me."

Jack shot on command, and I almost fired mine just watching. Cynthia threw her head back and repeated, "I did it, I did it, I could feel him coming, my clitoris was tight against his cock and we both came at the same time. I think I'm still coming. I don't think I will ever stop. Oh God, thank you, thank you."

That was strange, was it just an athletic event, a rubbing contest searching for the right feeling?

Jack had "held her ass tight as he came, so as not to slip out with her gyrations. She was like riding a bucking bronco. I was holding her breasts firmly. Cynthia relaxed a bit while breathing hard and finally looked at me, looked at my hands on her breasts, and bent back and kissed me on the mouth and began giving me a lot of tongue. She had never kissed Jack during the entire fuck. She had done her own thing. I pulled back and whispered in her ear that I had to have her right now and that I was turned on beyond control. I said if she didn't fuck me immediately I would come in my pants.

Cynthia said, "absolutely, I'm ready for you Will, get back here, hurry, I'm still coming."

Cynthia dismounted Jack and fell against the back car door holding her crotch and asking for my handkerchief. She tapped the hanky against her very wet pussy and seemed to enjoy rubbing the "cummy" new texture against her very wet clitoris. She told us later that that test of smoothness and the enhanced slippery change in her lubricant was a very significant experience. She concluded she was less apt to get sore from the more aggressive rubbing with "mancum" spilling from her pussy. Our supply of semen was not up to par. We were both producing "cumlite." There was not time to build a new supply, but we can still feel orgasms, even if a bit painful.

A man's second orgasm has a smaller supply of semen, obviously. We call that second shot, "cumlite." It still feels good. If you men have the ability to go for a third orgasm, it may be void of semen and we call that, "cumair." A man also may feel an aching in his testicles; we call that, "blueballs." There are other examples of cumlite in this book.

Jack pulled his pants up, we checked the street for people, and it was dark and lonely. We changed positions and I climbed into the back seat and dropped my pants to my ankles. Man was I hard. I slumped for a better angle and there was my hard erection already in her hand. Cynthia kissed my little helmet, checked the hardness and concluded I was ready. She repeated the procedure of rubbing my cock against her clitoris and up and down her labia. Cynthia's labia were a bit longer than our other experiences. I'd guess they were extended about a half an inch and did tend to cling to whatever was between them. I believe the larger labia better kept the "furrow" wet and warm.

She again tipped to the left found my penis with her pussy and with more familiarity took me in to the hilt. She started undulating immediately and was hanging on to my neck with both hands. She moved with the same rocking rhythm probably even harder because of the newly acquired lube job. She said she never stopped coming and rode me a little harder. This time she was watching my face and eyes and not the action. But she knew she was having a "good rub." She had learned what was to become a valuable lesson in the art of reaching orgasms on cue.

She repeated her begging and said, "Come on honey I know you're going to give it to me, I want all of you, gimmee that good cream, give it all to me, come on. Let me feel you come, come on let it go, I want you and I want all that cum."

Talk about hoping for a change in my wife's vocalism. I was so excited at this new aggressiveness and the sexy sayings were exciting. Was this a different woman? Had we created a monster? I hoped so. I also was aware that Cynthia was drooling a little bit. It was like she forgot to swallow. She was working short fast strokes, undulating so I felt constant action against my cock.

I fired! I bobbed and grunted with ecstasy. She had ridden this stallion before and she knew how to hold on. She pushed her left hand against the car ceiling to brace herself and kept me tight inside her. A man has to pump somehow and having her on top was no obstacle with a strong ejaculation.

She began to laugh. I held her ass tight and Jack was watching her ass move and trying to cup her breasts. She ignored the breast holder as before. She was focusing on her contact with the base of my cock. She stayed on me and rested. Her breathing slowed, she smiled with a look of complete dominance over everybody's male pleasure. Cynthia kept kissing me on the mouth. We all cooled down together, although Jack and I were in another unexpected state of shock. It took a few minutes to gather our thoughts as regarding Cynthia's aggressive eruption.

Cynthia began, "I'm sorry, if I was out of character, but I just had to fuck some more and do it my way. I wanted to be in charge and it really felt good. I just had to do the fucking, and I had to rub myself against a hard cock. That was fantastic. Was that selfish? I wanted to find the right rub with no concern for your cocks. I was rubbing on the base of each cock and I controlled the pressure against my clitoris, that was really wonderful. Actually, I think I have been in a constant state of orgasm and I never really came down from that first wonderful climax hours ago. I may never come down. Is this going to be permanent? Have I become a nymphomaniac? What happened, will you forgive me? Will, I'll fuck you into a coma if you will let me. You may have created a monster and I will be your sex slave. Please forgive me for my actions today, I promise I will be the best fuck you will ever have every time. Please forgive me if I have overstepped my moral boundaries."

Jack began to clap. Cynthia dismounted and fell back against the back of the rear door and exclaimed the most surprising shocking remark I could ever imagine. She looked out the open window facing the cool breeze; her forehead and breasts were beaming with perspiration. Her legs were spread slightly with her left leg on the back shelf. She was holding her left hand over her bare pussy. She said in a clear voice into the dark night . . . . . . "next?"

Jack and I began to laugh at her new sense of humor and we all laughed uncontrollably while we dressed. Cynthia tucked my hanky nicely in her panties, which was also a sexy display. There was no end to her enticing natural movements. Every move was now stimulating. The car reeked of sex. That odor is an aphrodisiac come lately. It would forever make my Cadillac a sex symbol. Jack drove the rest of the way to his house and we began to exchange reactions to the entire evening. This discussion was to last for years, the sex was never to happen again, but let me tell you some reactions while they are fresh in my mind. This saga continues with the next adventure.

We dropped Jack off at his house and he pretended to stagger to his back door as if he were drunk, feigning being worn out after a strenuous basketball game look. Cynthia laughed at Jack's antics and after we left him she went into a deep trance starring ahead.

I asked, "Are you OK?"

"What have I done?" she whispered, "What have I done, what did I do, Oh my God (getting louder), who am I? I think I threw a sexual fit; I went into a rage of orgasms. My God, what happened?"

"Cynthia, stop it, you just got so turned on you lost control. Imagine the good that you can get from this evening." I argued. A first time can only happen once and that blew your mind. All you have to do now is think about how we can continue our heightened lovemaking, not that it needed improvement. Honey, I was equally turned on watching you and I have learned some valuable things that I will never forget. Whenever I think about tonight, I will become motivated, now that I know what stirs your feelings. To me, it was an out of body experience. I never saw Jack, I only saw me doing what Jack did and I know what we look like and it was a beautiful sight. Jack is not competition for us; he is a friend that we invited to share in our most intimate acts. Don't think for one moment that Jack didn't reach his highest level of passion in spite of his many more experiences. He will never match or surpass what we just shared with him."

"Well," Cynthia said, "You'll have to keep convincing me and reassuring me, and by the way, what is your explanation to God? I may have some major guilt to deal with. Should I go to a shrink? Am I now a nymphomaniac? Will I become a hooker and sell myself for $100 a load of cum?"

"Cynthia, stop it, stop that kind of thinking, you lost control over your sexual urges, you were led into it by me and Jack. If you have to blame anybody, blame me, because I can absolutely guarantee you that I love you more than ever and this evening made me appreciate what a wonderful wife I have. Love and Trust were behind everything we did. It will always be private and now we have something special to talk about for the rest of our lives. We are not joining any group sex parties; they are beneath our status. We are advanced lovers with rare abilities to communicate. Imagine what we have done to the perfect rapport we had before this night?" I kept talking. I wonder if Cynthia realized she had just had passionate sex in the three basic positions with two men at the same session. Hmmm

When we got home we showered and fell into bed and a fast sleep. When we awoke next morning we were spooned and as a natural act we began a slow soothing sideways "cuddle" fuck. I came and we nodded off again and awoke stuck together. We arose, showered again together and dressed. We went to church that morning as though we had never sinned.

Chapter 7. How High The Moan

I told Cynthia one of my goals was to try to stimulate some more vocal reaction from her. The heightened motivation from the recent experiences seemed to have done the job. Cynthia was to be congratulated for becoming so uninhibited. We gave her a PHD in sex appeal and a master's degree in "Penitology," or on how to please men. The compliments offset my criticism of her not being expressive enough. Cynthia said she was not aware of her previous lack of expression but she did realize the advantage of expressing passion. She was sorry it did not come naturally, but she agreed she felt very uninhibited after her new experiences. She also assured me she was not faking any pleasurable sounds. She claimed she was truly less inhibited now and understood the lesson. She said I could be assured that I gave her immense pleasure with love.

Cynthia later told us that she could better feel her clitoris expand and with practice and with her new experiences it did not become overly sensitive thus enabling better climaxes. She definitely felt her orgasms were now lasting longer and hoped the heightened sensations would continue for the rest of her life. (Which it did) She learned that when riding on top of my cock, she could find the right rub and that is why she was appreciative of her aggressive experience, she learned to take charge of the action. It did not previously occur to her to search for that "right rub." We explained that with her increasing enthusiasm during sex I could not hold back coming with her.

As foreplay to her "riding a cock horse," I had a special request that if she could squat on the flat of her feet in bed and sort of do deep knee bends on my cock; my visual experience along with the tightened muscle action would greatly increase my pleasure. I had to advise her that it felt so good that she would have to be careful not to fire my gun too soon. Cynthia subsequently tried and mastered that move. She was so good that during my learning stages, I sometimes could not hold back my orgasms. Watching a woman squat on the tip of your hard cock is a real treat. Actually, it feels too good. The pussy seems tighter and the visual angle is too exciting for a man; it is almost impossible to restrain the urge to come. Cynthia also learned to look down at the action while squatting. She said it was a big turn on for her, too. This position worked better with my midsection elevated a bit, like allowing Cynthia to straddle a small footstool with my head in a chair. Jack began to try the same squat action with his own partners and we again enjoyed the comparative dialogue. We actually taught Jack something new to try. There wasn't anything we couldn't talk about. The talking contributed much to our fantastic sex lives.

A few weeks had passed and one menstrual cycle later Cynthia and I were still sexually higher than kites. My "menstrual cycle" oral sex was longer lasting and more enjoyable than ever before. It was like the big week of sex was affecting Cynthia permanently and cock sucking was elevated to a level I never knew existed. We decided to make the best of that wonderful week. We weren't able to perform every night, but our sex life increased and had very few letdowns. Routine had disappeared.

We also agreed that we did not need to do anything again that involved Jack directly. We told him that and he agreed that he too could not handle that much intensity again. To reiterate, we agreed to continue the intimate dialogue whenever possible and Cynthia was willing to hear any new "Jack" adventure so we could stimulate some marital projects of our own. And finally Cynthia could contribute to the conversations with techniques and new marital experiences of her own, or which she might imagine. You might say she was better at stimulating us than we were for her. She disagreed with that theory. Cynthia was now qualified to discuss the most intimate details of every sex act. She would occasionally tell Jack to try something on his next partner and report back to us the results.

This next event was a cool fall evening with no snow. Our skiing club scheduled a picnic in the mountains. The campground was a small valley surrounded by hills and big pine trees. The campfire site accommodated a large fire and had a cement patio around the pit. There were about twenty couples and when the festivities began, committees were formed. Cynthia and I were assigned to find some firewood along with several other couples. The firewood teams started off in different directions and Cynthia and I climbed the steepest hill and walked through a beautiful pine forest. I examined the trees and thought to myself how easy they would be to climb. The limbs were spaced like steps. I suggested we climb a tree and fool around for fun. Cynthia, cautious and skeptical reluctantly considered the adventure, and she was wearing a full blue denim skirt, which made her "goodies" more accessible for fooling around.

I was conjuring up a new sexy idea. I hinted that if she "depanted" she might get a "good licking" enhanced by the nice cool breeze hidden by some green branches. It involved a climb into a tree, and the sweet smell of fresh pine. There weren't many bushes or ground cover and the pine tree looked awful private. I again, asked Cynthia to remove her panties, which she did quickly. Anytime I suggested licking her pussy, she was instantly agreeable. I liked that trait because she was equally willing to perform on me. I put her panties in the back pocket of my blue jeans.

She whispered, "Are you out of your mind, because I know you think getting fucked high up in a tree would be exciting, but I think it's too dangerous."

I said, "sweetie, we'll climb out of sight, and if someone comes buy we can be quiet. Most woodsy picnickers don't look in treetops. It wouldn't take too long to fuck and I'll give you a good licking and we can take advantage of this breeze. I think a cool breeze wafting through your pussy would give you a great orgasm."

"You won't have to take off any more clothes." I continued, "Come on, where is that new adventuress attitude?"

"You talked me into it, you smooth talking devil," she said.

We were wearing sneakers and light denim jackets. The climb was easy, the big branches were aligned like steps and the tree was about two feet in diameter, just about the limit for me to hug a tree. As we climbed, Cynthia's sexy ass was in my face and knowing it was bare under the denim, I teasingly gave her a little bite.

She jumped and said, "watch it there big guy." Damn, she had a sexy ass and the swing movement while climbing was exciting. I did have further intentions, but first things first.

I, again bit her through the denim and said I was hoping for a bigger piece of ass, perhaps a bigger piece than a mouthful. We laughed.

"This isn't a case of you getting lucky, I am a sure thing, but I think you better be extra careful, this tree may be moving already. I don't want to fall and be discovered in some uncompromising position. The ride to a hospital stuck together would be hard to explain," she whispered. Now there is a humorous thought.

"Let's play it by ear," I said. We can always give up.

"By ear or by ass," she retorted."

My, my, were we getting to be a witty couple. It was great fun and we loved spicy dialogue. It was finally happening after years of evolving sex talk.

About 30 feet off the ground the big tree branches were getting smaller. The trunk was about a foot in diameter and the branches were solid and perfectly spaced for climbing without hugging the tree. She stopped at my command and I told her where to put her feet, but she had to turn around and face me. About a foot above her head was a branch that she could hold with both hands. I then placed her foot on a sideways protruding branch and another to my right that was about six inches higher. Cynthia was squatting and facing me with her back rigid against the tree. Her feet were extended about a foot out on the solid branches. That position made for a perfect spread. I "bunched" her full denim skirt and tucked it behind her waist and she backed up against the tree with her denim skirt clumped behind her back. She was exposing an ideal spread for eating pussy. Damn that view was sexy and coupled with that breeze, wow.

I had hugged the tree with my left arm. Thank God for my long arms, and my right hand was free to touch those great thighs. I let my tongue find the crease and worked it into that flat "start" position. Cynthia had sexy labia and they served her well by keeping her pussy wet and ready. I began to massage her clitoris area with a circular motion keeping the flat of my tongue flat against her clitoris. I intermittently licked and that allowed for more cool air contact. What you guys have to understand here is that you must next lick from under the clitoris and begin to push skin toward the clitoris. It is almost like a "gathering" process. It's like raking leaves into a pile. As the clitoris gathers substance it becomes easier to work with.

Next, and just as necessary, I formed a small circle with my lips and applied a gentle sucking directly on her clitoris. The sucking resembles fucking only the clitoris swells making a tiny penis and my mouth might resemble a small tight fitting pussy. That sucking motions technically helps to engorge the clitoris. It swells just like a miniature penis and becomes very sensitive. Cynthia was not free to move her hips as she would have liked. That increased the passion.

With the extra breeze, I often pulled back and spread her labia with my hand allowing the cool breeze to stimulate her. My breath was obviously hot, so there was an alternating current wafting about her engorged clitoris. The fact that Cynthia could not move freely made our experience a bit like bondage. She also had to be quiet.

Now, after much experience with my wife, I knew that direct contact with the flicking was too much too fast, so I developed a technique that only works for my wife. I flick my tongue just under the clitoris and I can flick my tongue sideways with as much pressure as I need. I can change directions and withdraw just enough to flick the top of her clitoris.

OK, this is more information than I need to tell you. I'll frequently revisit pussy eating techniques in this book.

Cynthia was experiencing pure ecstasy. I couldn't see her face, but she was making the sweetest of sounds, but barely above a whisper. In about a few minutes, which is good timing for a woman to reach a climax, she whispered, "You can stop, That was so wonderful, I'm so satisfied." I blew gently on her pussy and she did twitch a few times.

I climbed up a few feet so my midsection was just under her very inviting pussy. We could now see each other's faces. I took my cock out through my fly and rose up to get inside her. I was a few inches too short. I asked her not to move. I rose up on my toes and I could barely enter her, only about an inch, and that was stretching it. I had one arm wrapped around the tree and one hand to guide my cock. There were no other support branches available. I could insert my penis helmet, maybe another inch. Her pussy was a bit dry from the breeze, but immediate inside her she was wet. The outer dryness gives a pussy a slight tugging action with each little thrust. I moved my free hand and grabbed the same branch that extended over Cynthia's head. Cynthia could now dip her pussy an inch or two to meet me part way.

What Cynthia did then is what many men will claim is a spectacular grip. Cynthia lowered herself while in the squat position so with a slight deep knee bend could bounce on just the top two inches of my penis. It was very precarious because all she had to hold was the branch over her head. She gripped that branch with both hands leaving her pussy on its own. Once I was in that first inch, her pussy never let it go. We didn't need our hands for the sex. Her squatting action flexed her thigh muscles even more and seemed to tighten her pussy. I had leaned back so I could better facilitate thrusting, which could not be done anyway. She was doing all the stroking, with a slight bounce on just the tip of my cock.

Our treed predicament was frustrating, and that was good. The temperature change between her warm pussy and the mountain breeze and the fact that each bob was 'reopening" her tight pussy was wonderful. I could feel the cool air on the exposed base of my shaft. I held fast without moving and I was stretched and flexed to my limit. This position really provided for extreme sensuous action. My wife had already mastered this position in a bed, but the tree suspension made her flex her muscles even more. Her pussy was having a slight sucking effect as if her pussy was trying to pull me in and stop me from falling, and that cool breeze, wow, what great feelings. There is no adequate description to have a cool breeze wafting around a hot pussy while you are being sucked therein. The concept of ejaculating without moving is in itself unusual. It heightens the sensation.

We heard a noise, people passing below, we froze. I looked at Cynthia and she released one hand and put her finger over her lips to shush me. She kept squatting and bobbing about two inches. I simply couldn't hold it, I began to ejaculate and she knew. I was only inside her by an inch or so. I felt like my whole body was throbbing. Every muscle in my body was working together to fire without pumping. She looked at me and smiled and enjoyed the tension of my climax. She stopped bobbing and was holding the end of my cock in her pussy keeping it hot. We looked into each other's eyes. We both held our breath and that too accentuated the orgasm. Cynthia could feel my release and my extra pleasure. We were both silently holding our flexed positions. We were pulsating as if we were one body. Another firewood couple passed underneath. I'm sure the passing couple noticed nothing. We were locked together and our position was frozen like an ice statue.

After the couple passed us by, Cynthia whispered, "I could feel every pulsation, every squirt. I think the opening to my vagina does have some muscle pull. I felt I was trying to stop you from falling. I know I couldn't, but I became very sensitive to your orgasm. My pussy tingled because of the circumstances and yes, that breeze is a treat."

The breeze was drying the exposed part of my shaft. I held myself upright until my toes could take it no more. I said, "I'm falling out of you." I relaxed and released the tension and settled back on my branches. I carefully re-zipped my fly. I was oozing a little.

Her legs were apart and stretched on branches of different heights, and Cynthia said she could not hold the position much longer either. I helped her move her legs to a central branch and helped her stand up and turn around. I had used the same branches and began lowering myself very carefully with her covered fanny in my face again.

About half way down, Cynthia said, "oh oowe, I'm in big trouble here. I have to pee so badly and you know how I hate peeing outside."

"Why not pee from up here? I'll get on the other side of the tree and hold your skirt out of the way. From this height you cannot possible get splashed, in fact the circumstances could not be better. You have the breeze and sticking your ass out by hanging on to this branch over your head will work. Look, put your feet on these two branches and that will spread your legs just right, hold your ass as far out as you can, squat and let er rip."

"Oh God, I can't do this, what if someone comes by now? Cynthia blurted. "I'm in real pain here."

I came around beside her because her skirt was too full for me to reach her behind. I held on the tree trunk with my left hand and tucked her skirt both front and back by sort of "bunching" her skirt into my right hand and holding it away from her ass. Her head was now on the other side of the tree trunk so her ass was higher. She was sticking her ass out from the tree trunk; she was poised like a statue and a beautifully carved ass, sort of hanging out to dry. Cynthia closed her eyes and I said, "no, no, don't close your eyes, watch what you are doing."

Cynthia said, "Like I can steer? I can't see, are their branches in the way, what if I splash on me, or the next branch, do I have a clear shot?"

I replied, "Listen, if you do a good job, I'll let you write your initials in yellow in the snow with my instrument sometime."

"Ok! That's the just the incentive I needed." She grinned.

"Damn it Cyn, just do it, the coast is clear, get on with it. You won't hit anything but the ground." I advised her.

She let loose, and whether you believe me or not it was a beautiful sight. I saw a "golden rope drop from her sweet ass and by the time the first drop hit the ground, in a wavering line, the flow shut off like a turned off faucet. There was a breeze, and it guided her stream away from the tree. I watched the golden rope fall into the ground and then disappear. Cynthia paused as if she was again enjoying the breeze flowing under her. I helped Cynthia to my side of the tree and we climbed down giggling. I gave her my ever handy hanky and her panties. She pulled up her panties, tucked the hanky between her legs, looked at me, smiled and said, you know, "I must really be good, I don't know if you noticed, but I never dropped a drop of cum." Have I got a tight pussy or what?"

Speaking of tight pussies, according to the Guinness book of records a Russian Mom, Tatiata Klozhevnikova, plugged her vagina with a tube attached to a hook and using her vaginal muscles lifted a 31 pound glass ball. Now that is tight! There are exercises women can do to tighten their pussies. We are not knowledgeable in those details.

As we smugly walked away, we glanced back at the site and the ground was steaming. I thought a good idea for naming that event was, "A steamy good time." Nobody missed us at the picnic, we mingled and had a good time, but knowing that we pulled off a special exciting tree top sex and pee event fit right into our program for original sexy experiences. We met some old friends and they said, (Hi) "High, what's up? We were so smug. Cynthia and I are frequent huggers. True, now tree huggers, but we were always very affectionate in public. We always had an arm around each other.

Several months had now passed and Cynthia and I decided that our new attitudes were worth it and that we would create the sexiest marriage ever. After the "tree top" experience we became even more motivated. Obviously we could not keep up the creative pace, but we vowed to make it a project and see how much we could do about forever improving our sex life. It was to be a lifetime fun project.

And, yes, we told Jack about our "tree top tall" experience and challenged him to try it. Isn't that a song title? (Tree Top Tall?) You might consider any sexual event that includes breezes and temperature changes.

Chapter 8. Hallowed Weenie

We were invited to a big Halloween party at some friends that lived in a big mansion. This event occurred the Halloween of the same year of the "week that was," the week that changed our sex lives. Cynthia was equally determined to be creative with her newfound sexuality. I know she thought out this Halloween event in detail, but I never saw her practice the tuxedo dance nor did I ever see the rented tuxedo until Halloween.

At the Halloween party there were fun and games, lots of contests and it was a costumed event. We participated in an apple relay, passing an apple from person to person without using hands. Silly stuff, but always fun if all adults play. I was going to the party wearing just a Frankenstein mask. No matter what I wore, all would recognize me or Jack, who was bringing Angela. We both stand out in any crowd.

As I was getting dressed Cynthia came out of the bathroom wearing an old fashion garter belt with the thigh length dark nylons, the garter belt clips mid thigh, classy black high heels, and a black bow tie around her bare neck. Her hair, the tie, her top hat, her shoes and her pubic hair all matched. She was bare breasted and was wearing a black "top hat" like in the movies, but the shock was that she wore no panties. The garter belt was it. Cynthia looked fantastic.

"What the hell are you doing?" I asked.

"What, you don't like my costume?" Cynthia asked.

"We'll be arrested for sure and make all the news shows and that won't help my business. I can see the headlines, Lawyer's wife exposes bare ass at Halloween party." I said.

"Listen silly, this is for you, this goes under my costume, and when we get home, I have a special event planned for you and this is just a preview. I'm going to do a strip tease from my tuxedo costume and fuck your brains out wearing just this. This will be a hallowed event for your weenie. Now what do you have to say?" She gloated.

I tried to grab her for a quickie, but she ran into the bathroom, yelling for me to wait, it would be a spectacular promise of excitement. She came out of the bathroom wearing a short knee length tight black skirt, a white fluffy pleated shirt with the black bow tie in perfect place. False white cuffs were attached to the tuxedo coat; the blouse was sleeveless. She had a small waist length tuxedo jacket with short split tails behind. The tails were split at her waistline. The coat was open in the front showing her nipples pushing against the one size too small ruffled rented shirt. She wore the top hat that I was hoping to keep on her head for that elusive "quickie." To my wondering eyes did appear, a "fall," an attached long matching hairpiece that when in place did not resemble my wife. No one had ever seen her with long hair and I doubt any at the party would recognize her.

"You dance with me and keep thinking what's under my costume. You can use the whole evening as foreplay just thinking about my tight wet . . . . demands." She said in a lilting voice.

She was bedazzling, and oh yeah, sexy original and classy. At the party she stole the show with the best most original costume. No one recognized Cynthia with long hair. She added the "lone ranger" mask for the party. There were cocktails and dancing and we danced. Jack and Angela were there and I told Jack what was under that sexy skirt. He begged for a quick look. Cynthia said, sure, why not. A look, but no touching by either of us, we agreed. Angela was distracted and could never keep track of Jack at parties. So we sneaked into the fancy guest bedroom reserved for guest's coats, which was one entrance to a very fancy bathroom. The bathroom was between two luxury bedrooms, and we locked both doors.

We had some unexpected mirror exposure and a lighting rheostat turned down low. I began to hum the theme from "Night Train." "Da bump, da bump da bump da bump . . . . da boom bang, boom bang." (You get the idea.) Cynthia never intended to take off her clothes. She flirted by lifting up her skirt slowly revealing the matching black bare pussy with the matching black bow tie. She pulled the long false hair over her masked eyes and face to make sexy peeks through the mask. All that showed was the whites of her eyes. The garter belt was the only article of clothing under her skirt. She danced to the imaginary "Night Train" slowly turned around and did some bumps and grinds to my beat. She had her hands on her hips to keep the dress up. She strutted like a model, bent over, wiggled her ass, kinda hula like, and turned a few circles, a very little sexy dance ending with a big circular grind and for a finale a quick snappy bump. The tails covered her ass, but when moving provided short glimpses of her curves. Jack obviously was getting an erection. I was almost there, especially knowing I was to get the full dance routine later at home. Cynthia faced us, held her skirt for an additional flash look, and looked at Jack's crotch checking the results of her first quickie exhibition.

Cynthia said, "is that rise in your levies my compliment or are you carrying a gun?"

I was stunned and Jack was speechless. Then, someone knocked on the door and asked to use the rest room. Cynthia quickly pulled her skirt down. Jack said, "I'll be right out."

Cynthia and I left by the other door and Jack exited toward the male guest. No one saw us. Cynthia had a few drinks and was giggly, but surprised herself at her spontaneous act. I feel the exposure tease for Jack was for my benefit as well as showing off. It was foreplay aimed at me.

It proved to me that if Cynthia could do that then all women harbored a secret desire to exhibit themselves. Do all well toned women have a secret desire to strip in public? I don't know that, but I'd like to think that any women with that much self confidence maybe knowing they could not be identified, or maybe wearing a mask, might try crazy things like that quickie tease. Obviously the face mask was not sufficient coverage to provoke a public dance. I wonder if Cynthia would have stripped in a neutral environment, like a strip bar on the other side of the country. Wouldn't that act build self esteem? On second thought, would men want to strip for women? You don't hear much about male stripping except as a novelty act at some women's parties. Are there many strip joints that cater only to women? I understand there are some strip joints for women.

Jack and I knew of a very conservative girl with nice tits that was very shy. She told us that one time when she was in college, she was out of town with some girlfriends at a bar that promoted an amateur strip show for $100. This girl had a few drinks and on a dare entered the strip contest. She explained that once she got started she could not stop with all the cheering from an audience hidden behind bright lights. She said she stripped bare like a pro, won the $100, and then didn't believe her friends when they told her what she did. The moral of the story is; what women would surprise you if they could perform that way knowing they would not be recognized. The idea that many women would show off if they could remain anonymous is an interesting concept. An interesting poll question, no?

We laughed and giggled having made Jack suffer a bit from only a quick look at a "gartered" pussy. We were standing at the hors' d'oeu'ves table and Jack asked Cynthia if she was enjoying her new-found sexuality.

She replied, "Absolutely, and I can climax like a trooper, actually I come quite often and I love fancy balls. I am having a ball, er lots of fun. No pun intended, of course. I'm sorry about that tease back there. My husband made me do it."

Cynthia lifted the mask and winked another newly developing gesture. Winks are so sexy. Perhaps winking is another sexual gesture that should be further developed by many people.

Jack replied, "Who was that masked woman in the bathroom? Was that you? It went too fast, but I did get a few admiring peeks, this chick was sexy beyond description. I am pleasantly surprised at your exploding sexuality and as your good friend and mentor, I am proud of your development. You have a great ass. You have become a phantom icon. You are so sexy and I am so happy for you and Will. And you have also improved my sex life with our private tales of your ever evolving talents, and little sexy exposures like your garter belt. But I don't think Angela would ever do a dance like that, and she would think the garter belt out of style."

Actually garter belts were a nuisance for most women; little did they realize what sex appeal they were losing with the advent of panty hose. In sexual encounters, removing panty hose causes unnecessary delays. Removing gartered stockings was a sex act in itself, even better when fucking with the stockings in place. As women get older, gartered stockings can hide wrinkles and such. But maybe the time it takes to take panty hose off increases desire. I have not read about any such study. Perhaps Playboy Magazine should conduct such a survey.

A woman's genitals need to "breath" and nylon panty hose originally caused a loss of circulation. I read where panty hose can cause itching with so much nylon contact, thus the little cotton patch was invented, now a necessary part of panty hoses.

I imagine the guy, or woman that invented the cotton crotch patch made a fortune. That is an example of those little known inventions created by necessity that goes unrecognized. I think that inventor should get a "Noble Piece" prize. I wish I had thought of that. (Back to the party.)

"Have you ever asked Angela to do a strip for you?" Cynthia inquired. "Angela has a good figure."

"But she doesn't have the personality nor the inclination, or interest." Jack moaned.

Jack and I both paid Cynthia our compliments regarding the quickie tease dance and I told Jack in front of Cynthia what was going to happen to me when we got home. Cynthia certainly had found some confidence. She beamed and glowed. I was really proud. Jack joked about the price of admission if he could watch that dance. Cynthia told him he couldn't handle the view at any price. Those were fighting words and they left Jack speechless.

Jack asked Cynthia if there was anything he could do to reciprocate for the quick view.

"Well," said Cynthia, there is something I would like to see. I'd like to watch a man jack off so I can see how the cum flies and see the quantity. You want to meet me in the bathroom?"

What the hell just came out of her mouth? Wow, always a surprise. Did Cynthia develop a new hidden second personality? Perhaps a mild form of schizophrenia? That can't be because schizophrenia is a disease of the mind and Cynthia was actually enhancing her personality opening her mind up to process new internal sexual feelings. The creativity and the willingness to try something new is an extremely healthy thing to do. It may be that she was fast becoming aware of her sexuality and had some catching up to do. Would I complain? Hah! Never!

Jack said, "No way, I can't afford to waste a bullet, but Will ought to do that for you on his own. You'll have to think of something else. You saw me fuck Sheila, so I think you still owe me some more voyeurism."

"Jack, I love you, you have made a big difference in my life, but our deal was no more group anything." Cynthia said. "And you did fuck me and you got to watch me getting fucked, have you forgotten already?"

"I'll never forget anything that involves you. I was just grasping for straws, wishful thinking if you please. Cynthia, I am envious of you and Will, and I really appreciate our close relationship. The tables have turned on me because I am always thinking about what I can do to change Angela. If she knew what we did, or how we talk, she would file for divorce. I have a very difficult situation and I'm afraid I'm stuck."

"But, Jack, you have a great secret sex life and I believe exceptions should be made for you. I would never violate our confidence and I would never talk to Angela about sex. Please know that." Cynthia opined.

Cynthia and I said we would work out a plan where we would conduct our own scientific studies. We were going to focus on orgasms, foreplay, and ideas for unusual adventures. We were to consider sport sex as a part of marital sex. We agreed to share our results with Jack and he agreed to contribute his experiences. Jack's sex life was most unusual. He attracted women and he respected them making him an ideal candidate for experimentation.

We were determined to be as scientific as possible. This began the next stage of our mutual scientific interest in sex.

"I'll think this evening will be both fun and interesting." Cynthia said with her new confidence. I was most anxious to see what she planned when we got home.

We sat down to snack with Jack and Angela for "kid talks" when Angela excused herself and went to the rest room. Jack tried to stand up and knocked his knuckle on the bottom of the table as if he had struck an erection on the underside of the table. That's an old trick I'd seen before and it always raised concern, especially among the more gullible women. We laughed except Cynthia thought he really hit his penis on the underside of the table. Well. I told Cynthia it was an old joke just to get sympathy.

Cynthia reached under the table and squeezed Jack's pants and said, "Let this be our first experiment, and yes, it's semi-hard, so that blow didn't break his helmet, did it? Isn't that what the helmet is for? Now see what you can do with Angela. Has Angela ever seen that trick? There's an opening for you, Jack, you need to work on her. I find it hard to believe that she can't be more aroused."

Cynthia and I danced and she could feel my being aroused on every slow dance. I think I am setting a record for consecutive erections that go unused. That's always a disadvantage for men when dancing aroused. It's hard to hide those feelings. In high school, it was particularly embarrassing. Women seem to enjoy the "dance floor tease." I think dancing is a form of group foreplay like the old rituals used by ancient tribes. Dancing as a sexual tease comes natural to women. It is in their DNA.

On the ride home, Cynthia was again fired up in her experimental tease mode. She lifted her skirt up to reveal the bare skin just above the garter belt clips. I reached over to touch and she slapped my hand, so we played that "who can be the quickest" slap game, always a handicap for the driver. Then she put her hand between her legs and pretended to rub herself, pretending to enjoy herself while watching my reaction.

"Honey, I am so wet and ready, I can barely wait to get you inside me." she whispered.

I think that kind of foreplay is cheating.

"How about a few licks on the driver?" I begged.

She laughed and teased on denying me any touches. I was at a disadvantage because I had to drive, but the 25-minute drive tease was fun. As we grew older, Cynthia, when we were alone, would tease me even giving a few blow-jobs while the two of us drove on long trips, especially coming home in the dark from skiing trips. I actually looked forward to being teased and the circumstances made me think about reciprocity. Yes, life is good.

I tell you, by the time we got home, I was really turned on, and the best was yet to come. Imagine a wife making such an effort when in reality she had no professional strip tease dancing experience. We made a quick trip to the basement recreational room where our kids were having their own party chaperoned by our oldest son home from college. Our master bedroom was very private and at the other end of the house from the guest rooms. We have our own stereo system and a nice master bathroom complete with hot tub and Sauna. I am a successful lawyer.

I stripped down to my underwear while Cynthia put the well used collector's recording "Night Train" tape into the player. She had the kicks and the night-stick twirling down just like in the movies although she could not kick as high with the tight skirt. Cynthia had to lift her skirt for each kick. No matter. She kept the top hat on and took off the tux coat and skirt while she stripped off the shirt. She had been braless. Then she replaced the tuxedo top-coat leaving her bare breasts partly exposed under the coat, which was split in the back and gathered at her waist like a vest. Her navel was revealed. When she turned, the split coat offered a tease look at her lovely ass.

Here's the picture; a black top hat, coat parted revealing perky straight pointed breasts, bare midriff, navel exposed, the black silk garter belt, a black patch of pubic hair matching the bow tie and top hat, the tie was still around her bare neck with no jewelry, and long hair falling from her head. I almost thought she was a stranger. I wondered what other things she could do with a blond wig. White cuffs were attached to the coat sleeves. The nylon stockings held firmly at mid thigh and the black high heels accentuated her naturally long legs. When she bent over the tux coat split revealed glimpses of her sexy bottom and the rear view of the stockings. The long hair, long legged look and the formal tuxedo touch made a great scene for any dance no matter how talented the dancer. Cynthia was a winner if she did nothing but strip. I could not take my eyes off of her midsection except when she turned and her lovely ass was featured. She occasionally lifted the tux coat to expose her ass, which was framed by the back of the belt. Her amateurish attempts at bumps and grinds were effective; man was I turned on. She would tip her hat responding to my compliments. The only thing that was weird was she still wore the "lone ranger" mask.

Cynthia had me stand up, pulled down my underwear and she sat on the bed to take my erection in her mouth "hands free." She was swaying her shoulders with her hands on her hips moving with the beat of the music. The top hat, long hair and mask display was an unusual view for "hands free" cock-sucking. She then stood, pushed me down on the bed and crawled up my body while dragging her breasts over me. She stopped and gently sat on my chest. Actually she was sitting on my face, but weightless. She tapped my head with the baton in rhythm with the music and I complied by leaning into my tongue action. It was a difficult task, but I loved it. It was too difficult a position for an orgasm; it was just a pussy tease.

Next, she turned around so she was lying on top of me with her ass in my face and my cock in her mouth. For a few moments we licked each other. I had a hard time concentrating on this position as do most people because it is hard to concentrate on licking while being licked. It is still a sexy position and works better with each partner lying on their sides. Mutual orgasms while lying 69 is a nice treat on occasion.

She took in a few moments of pleasure and slid down to my cock, and while using no hands she wiggled and mounted me with her chin on my chest and tipped her hat at having taken me inside her unassisted and hands free. She made a "tent" with the long black hairpiece and that was a sexy first. Then she engaged in a very formal top riding dance to the music. Cynthia parted the coat exposing full breasts that now moved with the music and her dance, now confined to riding my cock. The garter belt and stockings were still in place and I fit nicely in her pussy under the "black" belt. I wondered if she thought of herself as having earned that 'fucking black belt."

Next she got up, blew gently on my cock, like it needed cooling, tipped her hat and danced across the room to a stool, sat on the stool and spread her legs exposing the long legs with the clipped stockings. She never took off her high heels. She did a few kicks with music and beckoned me kneel in front of her. I got in a few more good licks while she lightly tapped the beat on my head with the fancy cane. Her silk stockings rubbing against my cheeks was a new sensation. She pushed me away with the night stick and while I was kneeling, she had me put my hands behind my back challenging my penis to find its own way into her pussy. She watched my penis, even guided it in with the baton; she moved her pussy just enough to cooperate with my "loose cannon" and that was really sexy.

Cynthia slowed her beat down so my helmet could better find its way inside paradise. She sat and had me fuck her slowly with short strokes while she kicked a little dance and watched the genital action. Cynthia was still wearing the high heels and the view of the stockings, high heels, legs spread, mask, top hat, long hair and that bow tie was better than any sex scene I could imagine. She had to bend her knees because the legs extended required too much energy on the small footstool. The bent knee spread was natural. She began tapping me on my ass with the baton to regulate my strokes. She balanced herself with one hand on the chair that matched the footstool. She took off the tux coat with one hand while I was stroking and suddenly pushed me out with the cane in my stomach.

I withdrew into the cool air and she strutted back to bed looking back at me over her shoulder through the long locks of hair and beckoned me to follow her. She was now naked except for the top hat, bow tie, mask, garter belt and high heels. She was flashing her uncovered ass using an exaggerated hip swing. She threw herself on the bed, spread her legs, high heels up in the air, and beckoned with her cane pointing to and gently tapping her pussy. The music had started over. I put a pillow under her and mounted her with my knees under her legs. She raised herself up on her elbows and watched me fuck her. I kept my focus on her eyes, which glowed behind the mask. Cynthia then sort of gently paddled me with the dancer's stick on my ass building up our pace. When I neared orgasm she was hitting me harder with the stick demanding faster action.

"Come on Cowboy, ride me harder, come on giddy up, come on Honey, fuck me faster."

Cynthia was very vocal and full of sexy comments during the entire experience. She revisited the "give it to me" repetition.

"Come on Baby, I want to feel you come, I want you to keep fucking me when you fire, tell me when you come, too."

I cannot tell you how grand that orgasm felt. I did have a red butt from the stick, but it was worth it. Did she fake her fucking orgasms? It didn't make any difference because I know she had multiple orgasms during the cunnilingus. I'll never know and I don't care. The event was spectacular.

We stayed in a clinch while kissing, eyes open, mask discarded, allowing me to soften and slowly fall out. That moment of tenderness was our usual finale. We kissed and purred until I fell out. Cynthia always tried to tighten her vaginal muscles to hold my penis until the last moment. She tipped her hat a final time and threw it to a chair. I helped undress her removing the silk stockings, and we fell asleep like spoons. When we awoke, she was still wearing the strapped black bow tie and the false hair. It was truly a Happy Halloween.

I think that evening reflects another example of the continuing success of the sexualization of Cynthia. She was totally uninhibited and I could certainly see her change of confidence. She had become determined to keep her husband interested in her and maybe less interested in Jack's stories. Cynthia enjoyed listening to my recapping the dance fuck to Jack. She was thrilled at the retelling of her new skills. That luncheon was weeks later, but my Halloween memory never faded. To this day, many years later, I can recall any of the many experiences we had over a life-time of a successful marriage.

The videotapes are permanently embedded in my memory player. The aftermath of that exciting dance lasted for years. I tried my hand at stripping, but it was not the same. Does this example not open up ideas for wives wearing wigs, or masks, and different costumes, or negligees? There are many articles written about couples doing role-playing games. We could write a book about such new ideas, but choose to show you real examples.

Chapter 9. Full Dis-Clothes Her

The next few weeks after Halloween we talked about Cynthia's desire to witness ejaculation, and even go so far as to see if she could watch my tongue action on her clitoris. Cynthia wanted to know more about what was happening to our bodies. She hoped to maybe even request certain tongue movements by name, but we had to identify them first. Remember, here are two 45-year-old partners renewing sexual desires and studying them after years of good sex. We never felt our sex had become too routine, but that did not mean we couldn't seek new stimulation. I put together a script for a semi-scientific study and we discussed the strategy. I say "semi" because we decided that we would get too turned on to try and do both a scientific study and not make it sexy. We decided to try and do both. During the planning stage we suggested body positions and angles that gave us insight into the various techniques. We started with a fresh dual shower.

First, there was the equipment and setting the stage for multiple tests. We wanted to do all the tests and have some passionate sexual fun while we were at it. We set up a small three-foot step-ladder and a plain armless chair in our private master suite bathroom. There was a giant mirror built into the wall over the dual sinks. The giant tub was opposite the sinks. The tub was equipped with massage jets. The toilet and bidet were behind a private door to the right of the shower stall, which was opposite the entrance to the bathroom. This is a big bathroom. The shower stall or the tub could easily accommodate two people and the shower was equipped with inside benches and had several adjustable water jets. Oral sex foreplay in a shower with benches and cascading waves of water is real sexy. I had no guilt, even though these were things I learned in college, which you will soon discover. We often enjoyed using the shower for advanced foreplay before adjourning to the bed. The bathroom door had a full-length mirror attached on the bathroom side. There was another full-length mirror on the entry side of the bathroom door.

We placed the back of the armless chair up against the tub so the back of the chair was snug against the tub side. The small step-ladder was locked open and was snug against the front of the chair. To test the view, Cynthia stood on the bottom step, bent over and steadied herself holding on to the back of the chair. Her bare breasts dropped over the empty chair space. She was not kneeling, but the set-up raised her bare ass to the perfect height for my eventual standing rear entry sex act. We were naked, of course, while setting the stage. Cynthia leaned over the chair standing on the bottom rung of the small ladder, bracing herself with her hands on the back of the chair. I then went to the bathroom door and adjusted the full-length mirror on the back of the door so Cynthia could watch the future sex act with my penis moving in and out of her ass. We noted the required door position.

Once we felt the angle was right, we changed the stage for the first act. We moved the chair over close to the mirror on the back of the door, facing the mirror at an angle that allowed me to kneel in front of Cynthia using a folded towel as a soft floor mat to protect my knees from the tile floor. We adjusted the chair to the mirror angle, which was only a few feet away so she could see her own pussy. We put the small ladder to the right of the door on the hinged side so Cynthia could hold her legs apart. Her left leg was to go on the corner of the sink to the left of the door, which had to be closed for the correct viewing angle. Her right leg was raised to the top of the small ladder on the right of the mirror. With her foot on the ladder, she could spread her legs in comfort with her knees raised. We arranged everything, marked the positions of the props and then went back to the bathtub to carefully plan the sequence. We were going to accomplish several tests in sequence. The first act is to try and see how my tongue looks and works when kneeling using the full-length mirror. Cynthia had a small magnified hand mirror that turned out to be less useful as we became passionate.

The plan was to finish that cunnilingus test with her having an orgasm. The orgasm was to wet her pussy for act two, which was a side view of the two of us fucking doggy style, but with me standing. This rear entry sex was a temporary act and I was to withhold ejaculation. Follow along here, because I doubt any reader has tried this and you may learn something. Learning about what we look like when performing should be a fruitful lesson.

There are actually clubs where women meet with a counselor and learn what their bottoms look like. They bring magnified mirrors to the meetings, so I read. They study and discuss group therapy for sexual problems. By way of interest, in the 1880's clinics were started, and vibrators invented to use sexually stimulating vibrators to relieve women, or treat them for hysteria, tension, and degrees of irritability using orgasms induced by electrically powered vibrators as treatment. Then during the sexual revolution vibrators used away from such clinics were considered masturbation. A fine line for such definitions?

Women cannot possibly view their own pussies without mirrored help. And with a husband, or anybody else watching would take a serious loss of inhibitions. But this was very private session between husband and wife, and we were determined to make this experience sexy. We had to keep the lighting bright if we were to see anything and that was a bit hard to deal with, but we were determined.

You see, Cynthia wanted to see as much as possible as to what I did with my tongue. So, we began the big test. She put her right leg on the small ladder, which was positioned like behind the door. Her left leg was on the corner of the long sink. She pulled her labia apart with both her hands stretching her skin ever so carefully. We examined her equipment together with me pointing out what I was about to do. Clitorises range in size from a pinhead to the end of a thumb. Cynthia's clitoris when erect would rise about a quarter of an inch, slightly smaller around than the end of her little finger. In our humble opinion most clitorises would double in size when erect or engorged. The skin under a clitoris, the side toward the vagina was slightly less sensitive as was the skin collected on the topside. That allows for more direct contact during orgasm and once a woman reaches that point a man should switch his licking to a sideways flick under the clitoris. Obviously techniques differ between women, but a gentle sucking on an erect clitoris is usually effective in prolonging orgasm. The clitoris becomes a small penis and the man's mouth becomes a tight sucking pussy. We are only talking seconds here for orgasms and that is too bad. Orgasms for people just don't last long enough. However, to repeat, the beneficial emphasis belongs in the foreplay.

I demonstrated the basic tongue up swing using my index finger. I used my finger to explain the different tongue strokes. I explained how I was trying to "gather skin" like I was making a pile of skin on her clitoris. I then explained about the gentle sucking action using my fingertips. Fingers can be too rough, so Cynthia was more curious than aroused. When I put my head between her legs, my head blocked her view from the "mouth on" techniques, but I could demonstrate some tongue flicking action. The hand mirror was helpful for this close contact, more so than the mirrored door. At each tested tongue movement I asked if something felt better than the other. Cynthia stated that the changing of techniques was just as effective as any continuous action.

There is no more sensitive organ on the human body than the tongue. We can eat and talk at the same time and the tongue stays out of harm's way. The tongue can be used more delicately than anything else. The tongue can touch anything more lightly or more gently than a finger. I told her I would use my tongue and pull back to describe what I just did. The mirrors would work for some shots. We would see what happens.

I began by flicking my tongue across her pussy, which was stretched thus causing her clitoris to stand up a little and more quickly. Then I would pull back and show her what I did, but using my finger. We repeated this process followed with each explanation and some questions. She focused on the mirror and I gave her a great show, in spite of the bright lights.

I demonstrated other beginning moves by removing her hands and gently touching my tongue around the labia. I ran my tongue over her closed "crease" as lightly as I could as if her labia would open voluntarily. I had read where that could happen. But the male tongue initialing parting the labia is very stimulating. The first tongue contact should be from the top down opening the tongue into a flat position so the first feeling she gets is the warm flat tongue on her clitoris.

Some women can be ticklish when working the tongue towards the labia. Jack and I never experienced that. Women's inner thighs are a real turn on for men. Caressing inner thighs with tongue and cheek is a good technique. "Tongue and cheek is a good technique" could be a nice mantra? (get serious man!) A woman's thighs are often gently perfumed and when spread can be one of man's biggest turn ons. Imagine yourself smelling the flowers leading to the gates of paradise as you slide your cheeks along life's sweetest highway. Kissing your way there makes for these techniques that always work in your favor.

Cynthia could for sure decide which movement felt best, but she lost count. She finally asked me to stop the lesson and get on with the good feelings. What has to happen next is a man tries different strokes and when he finds a stroke that gets the best reaction, he remembers that move. But changing modes stalls a climax and increases her pleasure. Gentlemen, this is an "art form," and you can be a great artist. Good cunnilingus is like a reverse blowjob. Imagine how it would feel if the same licks were done to you. Cunnilingus, in my opinion, is meant to stimulate a man almost as much as his partner.

Changing techniques may be frustrating, but it is good to tease and hopefully will, in a friendly way, frustrate a clitoris. An analogy is that teasing resembles packing gun-powder into a small pistol and every time you tease you pack in more explosives resulting in a greater explosion when somebody fires their gun of pleasure. The ending climax will always be greater.

I explained this to Cynthia telling her to enjoy the teasing because it would result in a stronger climax. The teasing and changing techniques also prolongs orgasms in women extending the pleasure build-up, which can be just as intense as the climax.

The experiment itself was now frustrating Cynthia and even though she wanted to see whatever she could see during the "parting of the seas." She could no longer concentrate on the test. I turned my head a little to the side hoping she could see some action and proceed to go for the big bang and I stopped talking. She caught on and had the same goal, and although she seemed to try and see what was happening as her intensity towards an orgasm grew and her eyes were becoming glazed. A guy should try and sneak a peek at a woman's face during cunnilingus. There are many hidden rewards that often go unused.

Cynthia definitely could not stay focused. And she claims her vision went blank at the climax. Hmm, interesting. She said she did learn a lot and that in the future when I was eating her she would tell me to not change the licks because she had her "bell" rung. I was being well trained. But I was also in control of her pleasure because I could extend the pleasure even if it frustrated her more immediate goal of reaching for the orgasm.

I had read that men see a white flash when they reach an orgasm. We supposedly go blind for a moment. Ask yourself that question.

After Cynthia caught her breath, we then moved the chair and ladder to the doggy style event and angled the door mirror so she could watch our next beautiful intercourse. She loved this test because she already had an orgasm and her pussy was wet and ready. The objective of this doggy style fucking was for me not to come. When I was close we were to advance to the next step. Cynthia's focus was glued to the mirror. To her, it was a fascinating sight and I performed with longer slower strokes. I picked up the pace only briefly slapping myself against her ass causing her breasts to swing with the same motion. Any breast movement adds to good sex. I enjoyed watching me fuck her sexy nicely curved ass. She exclaimed how sexy her view was. I believe Cynthia was still trying to figure out how she lost control with the double fanny fucking she had experienced. She was beginning to talk about that more, but was still fascinated by how and why it felt good and why she wanted to view the action. It would be difficult to interrupt coitus with such a sexy view, but I did.

She was very wet and the rear pussy entrance always seemed a little tighter. I can prove that visual stimulation works. At just the right moment, I pulled out and faced the wall behind the tub, my erection throbbing. The big guy was really frustrated at being taken from a warm pussy and thrust out into the cold air.

Cynthia quickly moved the ladder out of the way and sat in the chair facing me at an angle that allowed both a frontal and side view of my soon to erupt penis. There was no mirror for this experiment. Her face was about two feet away from my wet cock and well situated for this event.

Cynthia was about to witness a man's ejaculation. I began to pump my cock hard with my hand to get any distance. I was too close to coming to do slow strokes and I needed the bigger bang, so to speak. I didn't want to spill or drool it out. And when a man pumps fast and hard it does enhance the thrill. The pressure builds as if we are firing our much larger cannons stuffed with bigger measurements of the heavily packed "gun powder" derived from teasing and frustration. The hand firing is much more violent and would provide Cynthia with good visual fireworks. I fired round one, which flew across the narrow side of the tub and some cum even made it to the tile wall. I may have mentioned that semen travels at 28 mph and the total quantity is about two teaspoons. I couldn't help but notice that when I first came she opened her mouth. It was like a mother's reflex when feeding a small child. Mother's open their mouths to mimic the baby's mouth. Of course, she was way out of range for the missiles.

The second burst was shorter and landed in the dry tub. The next two were sort of short-range missiles that fell on the inside tub wall. I turned towards Cynthia as I was in labor and she quickly put her mouth on the end of my cock and replaced my hand with hers and gave me a few gentle squeezes. She kept it warm for a few moments and then looked to see if there were any leftovers, a small drop appeared, she gently sucked my cock while I ended my twitching. She made a "yummy noise."

Cynthia then kneeled on a towel reached into the tub and took some fresh semen between her thumb and forefinger and rubbed them together. She exclaimed,

"This is so neat, such nice stuff. It feels so "oily." She smelled it and touched her tongue to her fingertips. Semen has a slight bleach odor, which depends on a man's diet. "It has such an interesting texture; it reminds me of cooked okra."

Okra is used as a gel, kind of like a coagulant used to hold some soups together, specifically "gumbo." I'm not sure I liked that analogy, but "sticky" is also sometimes descriptive. I believe semen has a clinging ability to keep its place on vaginal walls. Semen requires more of an acquired taste than pussy. That is my personal opinion and I have never tasted semen. Sexual excitement most often overrides tasting anything negative related to sex.

Cynthia then rubbed the fresh semen against the tub bottom as she continued to test the texture. She was fascinated at the texture and quantity and noted the "splash" effect pattern, which frankly doesn't mean anything. How else would a woman know how much juice she was taking in if she couldn't once witness ejaculation? She was somewhat familiar with quantity from giving me blow jobs, but couldn't obviously see what was "incoming."

Cynthia explained that the first shot of semen always hit the back of her throat and the swallow was a reflex. She said she didn't have time to analyze semen taste because she had to concentrate on the next burst. She said she always concentrated on the timing as I had taught her. Good timing prevented the possibility of choking, although choking was thought to be a negative excuse to avoid swallowing.

I asked Cynthia about the taste and she replied that it reminded her of her first taste of caviar. She felt that tasting me was a loving act. She then asked about the taste of her pussy. The fluids emanating from the vagina is similar to that woman's saliva, except far less bacteria. There is a salty taste, but ever so slight after a female orgasm. There are some theories that female lubrication is a form of ejaculate.

God has provided vaginas with a taste and odor that causes men to be aroused. It is like an addictive drug. I believe I mentioned the olfactory factor with the animal kingdom to attract males when the female is fertile. I can only speak here from experience. The only pussy that I ever thought was a turn-off was probably not bathed often enough. That was somebody else and a long time ago. I repeat and I know for a fact that commercial hair conditioner arouses me. I'm not so sure that when motivated knowing my efforts will be greatly rewarded, that I cannot, I repeat, I cannot find fault with any hot wet pussy taste. I sometimes wish I could get my face in far enough to cover my ears with that good stuff and hope I can hold the smell intact on my cheeks for as long as possible. I remember when I was a high school kid, if I ever got a finger dipped in that good stuff, I would try and preserve it and smell it for days. I do not, I repeat, do not think that is weird. Come on guys admit it.

While we were talking Cynthia turned on the tub water and gently swished the semen down the tub drain. She was surprised at the seemingly lack of solubility. Semen seems to hold together in or on water in clumps. It is like semen struggles for survival against all odds knowing its purpose in life. If semen does have a mind of its own, it probably is part of the ejaculating male's personality. I think we are beginning to fantasize here and not going anywhere.

Cynthia then took her hand mirror, squatted with her ass against the cool tile over the faucet and began to urinate in the tub. This was also part of the plan and we turned on the cold-water faucet. The hand mirror was magnified and Cynthia could see for the very first time how her clitoris parted and the urine swished under the pressure of such small outlets. The clitoris, or maybe an area proximate to the small head, forms two small "nostrils" and each side is under tremendous pressure with more urine emanating from nozzles that are too small.

The two streams joined forces immediately. We watched until she finished. She watched with a magnified hand mirror and I watched "live." I noticed that when she stopped peeing it was an immediate finish, like a turned off faucet. Women usually dry the spot with a quick padding of toilet paper. She didn't take that action because the TP was not handy. Cynthia used the faucet and splashed cool water on her clitoris. I asked if there was a sexual thrill when peeing after sex. She said yes, because obviously her little head was still engorged. Did it always feel sexy to pee? I wonder if women would answer that question truthfully.

Cynthia thought about that and concluded there was always a slight thrill because of where it flowed from. Having a relaxing pee was more fun than the hurried pressure to release when the need to pee is urgent. After all, a woman's urinary tract is only about an inch long and the bladder sits right on top of the little tube. Men have a longer tube resulting in more feeling, but that little clitoris can serve a double pleasurable use, while men cannot pee with a hard-on. Our pleasure center is not in direct contact with peeing. Nor can we get erect while peeing. Our valve system has a conflict. Does peeing have a sex thrill for a man? Only if outdoors in the wind or with a female witness.

When I was in high school the guys used to play a game where we would all pee in front of the car and the first one done could turn on the headlights shining on the late finishers. It was a dumb game, but what the heck, boys will be boys. It would have been more fun if some girls would play that game. It never happened, nor was it ever suggested.

Actually the whole experience with my wife turned out to be more of a sexual turn on than a scientific experiment, but we did engage in many interesting discussions in interpreting the feelings from that experiment. The discussions lasted a lifetime when relevant.

Cynthia asked if I could describe in detail how my orgasm felt. "A penis operates much like a submarine with valves that open and close for different functions." As I said, "you can't pee through an erect penis."

"Is that not too much information? I'll remember that on my next submarine ride. And that's something that never comes to mind," said Cynthia.

I explained the prostate gland works like a squeezing a "gravy baster." A muscle squeezes the prostate gland at the first moment of climax. The first trigger is very forceful and makes the heart even more aerobic. Actually the heart becomes aerobic for both partners beginning with foreplay. Our entire body reacts, every body organ is stimulated and our eyes supposedly do flash for a moment of blindness. The squeezing muscle twitches during sex and builds up pleasure pressure with the stimulation. Sex feels so good that a man should prolong the climax as long as possible by concentrating on the build up and his partner's needs.

When the first prostate squeeze takes place there is a burst of the larger quantity of semen. The quantity affects the pleasure, as does the pressure working against the release. The narrow tube in the penis offers just enough resistance to increase the thrill. The internal valves open, but not wide enough so there is a force that wants to stem the flow thus creating necessary resistance. That resistance is necessary so the testicles can "dump" sperm into the passing stream. First the Prostate gland, then the testicles, then the length of the penis and then the load escapes with a bang. The stream of semen rushes by the testicles, which are now up tight on each side of the base of the penis. In my case the semen valve is closed because of my vasectomy. The weight of the sperm is insignificant compared the quantity and weight of semen. The little swimmers are supposed to go with the flow until scattered within the vagina.

As the first load of semen rushes up the penis, or down whatever the case may be, it causes the walls to swell as if too much fluid is being forced through the narrow passageway. Imagine running by a picket fence with a stick and clap each board. Another analogy I imagine about a male orgasm is like strumming a guitar and every nerve ending is a guitar string. Each ejaculation load of semen represents a series of giant strums and the guitar strings vibrate in unison. The semen rushes through the penis and seems to flick or pluck a thousand nerve endings (about 4000 goody nerves) that will send volumes of built up energy rushing by that picket fence; or, another analogy is each slab or guitar string resembles individual "goody" nerves when vibrating. The tingles hit every pleasure nerve in a man's body, from head to toe. The brain is rattled and shuts down to protect itself from the shock. The semen bursts out of the penis and floods the vagina with warm fluids that are essentially "basic" as if measured on a litmus scale. A woman's mouth and her vagina have the same Litmus "PH reading" as does her saliva. The mouth and vaginal fluids are compatible and the seminal fluid is at home in the vagina. It is warm and protected to allow the little swimmers to find that reward at the end of the rainbow of pleasure.

A man's thrill is amplified by how fast the rushing semen can pluck each string or slat, actually each nerve ending in the passageway. The quantity of the first blast enhances the pleasure, but successive blasts sort of reap the trembling passage left by the first ejaculation load. You might think of a young man clipping a card on the spokes of his bicycle and feel the flaps flicking against the spokes. You need 4000 flicks to get the picture, and all within seconds.

"Do you get the analysis," I asked. "Aren't I poetic?"

"Yes you are, my dear, and I'm sure those clinical experts like Dr. Kinsey would be amused." Mused Cynthia. "If you talk like that enough I'm gonna slap your slats, baby."

"As soon as the first burst is shot, the prostate gland sort of inhales and tries another squeeze to clear out the stuff left behind. The process is repeated with each reflex shooting a smaller load. But the picket fence still gets "flicked with the stick" because the nerves haven't recovered from the initial burst. The squeezing process repeats itself a few more times and then twitches to a soothing halt. Unfortunately a man's orgasm does not last long enough, but the stroking during fucking makes for a prolonged build-up that feels so good. Men are too often in a rush to shoot their cannons and should learn to take more time being aroused. After the climax, the valve system changes and the penis begins to soften."

"Wow," said Cynthia, "you are so articulate; where in the hell did you learn that?"

"Yes, I have read about the subject, but I think my analogy is original. Now, you tell me how it feels when my penis fires in your mouth," I asked.

"OK, I can feel you are about to fire and after all the practice you gave me during my past menstrual cycles I knew exactly what the rhythm was to be. It is "suck, pull, and swallow in succession until the pulsations cease. The first burst is really satisfying to me; it hits the back of my throat and actually makes my pussy tingle. My mouth identifies with my pussy; I try to make my mouth into a pussy. My mouth feels all the thrills my pussy can't feel. But I have more feeling as to the pleasure I am giving rather than what I am feeling. Your pleasure flows through my system giving me much satisfaction because I have pleased you." Said Cynthia.

"My God, your description is even arousing me. You said that very well." I said.

131

Cynthia continued, "After about the third burst I start to taste the salty flavor and it again, reminds me of when I tasted caviar. Food for royalty, right? And I can feel the rhythm of each drop coming; I believe it is a natural instinct, and I purposely make each pull of the foreskin more gentle. Stretching foreskin during a blowjob is something a pussy can't do and I think concentrating of the big nerve is an art form. I concentrate on the flat of my tongue gently caressing your main nerve, or depending on the angle, the insides of my cheeks are just as effective. I think I suck a little harder with each subsequent blast. You told me a gentle sucking makes it feel tighter. I don't know if sucking helps the first semen burst. I think it has much force whether I suck or not, but the secondary bursts seem to need a little help."

"You know, that is accurate. The slight sucking after the first shot does feel better and I can tell because I can feel the "little tugging." I interrupted.

Cynthia continued again, "You are right and I can identify that with my engorged clitoris. As I said, my clitoris reacts to your orgasms. It is a pleasant tingling. I sometimes will touch my clitoris during fellatio with my other hand. I doubt you ever noticed that. I always check your smiling helmeted little head and if there is a drop hanging there, I lick it with pleasure as if my challenge is not to let any "little yous'" escape. Then I keep my mouth on your penis to keep it warm while you come down from that ecstatic high. Then I check for leaks, blow gently where I was gripping the staff, kiss the head, look at you and smile like a puppy looking for a reward. Right?"

She continued, "Your response has always been sensational, and now that I can picture that long picket fence I'll enjoy myself even more. I think I can slap every picket fence slat nary missing a one, all 4000 of them. That is the power of a woman's mind. I can simulate my pussy with my mouth. If I could only make my pussy do what my mouth can do. Such a challenge! After all, you take care of my personal penis and I shall forever strive to nurture and care for it too. I read once that women can train their pussy's to grip and grab and even suck a little. I hear that some women can pick up objects with their pussies."

"Good grief woman where did you learn all that?" "Do women talk about that stuff?" I asked.

"No, I heard most of that stuff from you and Jack. Remember, I will do anything to please you because I love you. I would do anything to bring you pleasure." Cynthia gloated.

"Wow! Cynthia, I can't begin to tell you how much I love you and I will never cease to be amazed at the pleasure you give me. I will have to work even harder to reciprocate and see what we can bring to each other." I said.

"I am really getting a lot out of this experience. I wonder why it took us so many years to reach this level of communication."

Cynthia added, "I think your vasectomy played a major part. I was always worried about unplanned pregnancies, and I thought my level of satisfaction had reached a peak. And raising kids is always a distraction from sex. How wrong was I? My goodness, can we ever learn enough about each other, and can you imagine all the married couples that never learn to communicate?"

Cynthia went on, "you know, I have to admit I was also fascinated seeing how urination works with my indoor plumbing. I couldn't tell much, though."

"I was also fascinated and it was my first close look at female urination. Could you see how the clitoris parted like two tiny nostrils? You were holding your labia out of the way and I hope the mirror worked for you," I continued.

"Well," Cynthia said, "the urine came in such a rush that I couldn't tell, but your angle was better than mine. Oh yeah, peeing after sex feels good."

That statement came from a woman whose ass has never touched a public toilet seat. Cynthia tried never to have to use a public restroom and now we were discussing the most intimate life processes. I wondered if our discussions had to go this far, but now that we started, I felt it most rewarding. What a turnaround of discussions. Who cares about the weather reports or other trivial social discourse when people can discuss intimate pleasures? Should all adults advance to such objectivity? Would not everybody's sex lives be more progressive and to everybody's advantage with communication on the most intimate details of our bodies?

Back to the pee pee test; "triggering the start of the hard squishing spray is similar to the initial prostate squeeze, I continued. "The rush of urine turns to a spray first and then forms a stream. Did that feel sexual?"

"Yes, big time. As I just said, it always feels good when a woman pees after sex. There is a tingling that vibrates the clitoris as it performs a dual function. As a matter of fact, I think peeing anytime feels a little bit sexually gratifying. After all, we pee through a pleasure center. Does it work the same for men?" Cynthia asked.

"Not in my opinion, but peeing is always a welcome relief. The only time it might feel sexual is peeing outdoors with a rewarding breeze, or a woman watching. I agreed to let you handle me and try to write in the snow with my big pen." I said.

"Let's put that on our list of new things to try," Cynthia smiled. "Should I wear protective clothing?"

"I figured you would want a plastic gown. Have you ever heard of urolagnia?" I laughed.

"Oh oh! Do I need this information?" She questioned.

"Jack told me about this chick that had a craving for peeing together. Jack said she had him kneel in front of the toilet after sex, but it didn't have to be after sex; she spread her legs sitting on the toilet seat and took his penis and held it like a small garden hose. His instructions were to hold off the start until she began and then she held his flowing penis about a half-inch from her parted clitoris so that Jack's hot stream reflected off her clitoris forming a single clean stream of urine. But for the duration of the act of dual peeing, she had a special kind of orgasm with her clitoris spread, tightened and reacting to the pressure of Jack's hot stream. She said the orgasm was completely different and similar to a prolonged release of pleasure." I said.

There are many examples of Urolagnia (sexual pleasure from urination). A few women are known to masturbate and time urination with their orgasm. The urination when climaxing adds significant pleasure. So they wash their hands when done? Big deal. We didn't feel that male participation in female urination was a necessary turn on except for the mutual release of urine after sex, or peeing together anytime. We say do what ever pleases them, no big deal.

"Hmm, it sounds messy to me. Well if you ever want to try it I'll accommodate you, but I have already turned into a sex monster and I'm not sure I want to give up the privacy of a good pee." Said Cynthia. "Can I first write my name in the snow with your big pen?

"Yeah, right, that will be a real treat." I said.

"Yeah, right, hey, that's a double positive as opposed to double negative. Well, I see sex brings out the philology in you. Yeah? So fuck me," teased Cynthia. "You said I should use that "F" word more, did you like that? Do you like me saying, fuck me?" Need I say more; we went to bed for seconds. I didn't have time to demonstrate or explain "cumlite." Cynthia kept saying over and over, ever so quietly, "fuck me, fuck me," while I was doing it.

And, Cynthia must have whispered "fuck me" five times as we moved to our bed. Yeah, that turned me on.

Gee, only ten calories in a load of semen. As for pussy, who cares about calories!

Chapter 10, The Great Pube Wars

You must be wondering why Will and Jack acquired so much sexual knowledge at ages 45. This chapter may be the best time to explain how we began to acquire so much sophistication. These experiences were rare based what our friends were doing or learning. It was also difficult to separate reality from fiction during the "Great Pube Wars." High school guys never admitted to weaknesses in groups and often bragged about fictional things. Our experiences of substance began when Jack and I met in college. I'll skip over the high school stuff quickly for now and come back later.

I had mentioned that Dr. Kinsey had interviewed thousands of subjects who remained anonymous. Heck, they could say anything that the Doctor wanted to hear. How are we to know or learn from those interviews? They certainly weren't inspirational. Inspiration, motivation, or good old "turned on" passion might have been a better goal for these studies than reporting statistical evidence that may or may not be accurate. I don't think sexual lessons should be so objective.

How did Jack and I come about so much "hands" on experience? That's what this book is all about. I think my memories of real happenings are more meaningful than the professional science reports regarding sex. These science book interviews that I read seemed cold to me. It's like reading that sex is about putting tab "A" into slot "B." I never saw any information on foreplay, or the art of performing sex. It left too many unanswered questions for the young men I grew up with. All the information presented to us was what we shouldn't do, or should restrain from doing. There were religious and moral codes that were in force. I had read the Kinsey report while in high school. How did that happen? Let's go back to my high school for a moment.

My closest friend in high school consisted of a football player, whose father was a physician and had a complete home library on all medical subjects, especially sex books explaining what was normal and what was not, but they were also formal and objective. Yes, we saw all the gory photos of diseased victims of sexual overkill. They were disgusting, but I have to admit, they played a role in keeping us young studs in an unwanted stage of abstinence. And that was good for teenagers in the late 50s. Sexual education consisted mostly of showing scarred syphilis victims in movies to the boy's gym class. That "scare" technique worked.

We didn't think our classmates had sexual diseases, but the movies forced us to focus on fighting the "Great Pube Wars" more gradually, at a normal development pace with our "goody girl classmates," with no allowances to seek outside professionals, like a young whore. We were also living in a restricted small town environment that recommended condoms, but they were not easily available. No one wanted to ruin their college careers with unplanned marriages, and if you couldn't get condoms, you abstained from sexual intercourse. More fodder for the "Great Pube Wars." Jack Callahan grew up in a big city and his experiences were more advanced.

Teenagers acquiring condoms was not easy in my youth. Our attempts were made into the humorous scenes of many teen-age romantic comedy movies. Imagine standing before a druggist and have them ask you for your name and phone number so they can call your parents or your teacher for condom approval. It also reminds me of that great comedic TV scene where the four elderly

"Golden Girls," are standing at the checkout counter in a crowded drugstore, and the clerk asks over the sound system for a price check on condoms.

However, the Doctor's home library did create some exceptional interest on the normalcy of fellatio and cunnilingus. The books were not written as a motivational discourse, but certainly aroused more than just our curiosity. Cunnilingus seemed unnatural for us at this stage of maturity, but subliminally, our curiosity won. Our very small group of close friends (Guys) talked about these things in high school and I am convinced we were ahead of our time. Our conversations were about,

"What the hell are they suggesting?" Put my mouth where? Were these normal things to apply to their "private bathroom body parts?" You can imagine our initial shock reaction, which was soon overcome by an interest in possible results.

Getting high school girls in the early fifties to cooperate on advanced sexual techniques considering our lack of communicative skills was unlikely. I believe there was also a stronger religious presence. In our day it was a major accomplishment just to cop a feel of a covered breast. No one could imagine suggesting cunnilingus to such well morally governed classmates, especially not knowing how to perform if we were given the go ahead to try something so kinky. Further sexual advances from touching bare breasts, or touching any bare skin took most of our high school years. It was our belief that few classmates went "all the way." If they did, they were certainly discreet about it. That was a sign of the times. Everything changed with the advent of the birth control pill and the social movement toward women's sexual liberalization. Later came the famous Playboy Magazine and their movement to promote explicit sexual articles supported by sexy pictures. However, we had a growing concern about our lack of useful sexual education and all of these new social advances seemed to leave us further behind. We became determined to learn and explore sex at an early age.

Comparing experiences started with my two close high school buddies. We developed an early advanced curiosity along with mutual trust. However, our communications with young girls did not exist. My first look at a girl's "privates" was when I was eleven years old. One summer night I was sitting on the bottom step of a back porch with three 14-year-old girls that I believe set me up because I was so easily embarrassed. The girl on the top step was not wearing panties and kept her legs apart so I could see under her skirt. When they caught me looking Connie exclaimed,

"Will, what are you looking at? Do you like what you see and would you like to see more?"

I was terrified and mumbled something about "I dunno," and tried to look away when the flasher opened up the view. So I stared at "it." The three girls asked if I would show them mine and I said nothing. I was confused because I was so damn curious, but two embarrassed to do anything. So they teased me and said someday I would wish I had done more. I was big for my age, but I had no pubic hair and I just learned that little girls had some.

I agreed to stay while the two other girls left and this over developed girl with tits took me inside the screened porch and lifted her dress up so I could see better in the porch light. I was fascinated and she rubbed herself a few times and asked if I wanted to touch her. She guided my hand to a wet spot and I reacted by pulling back. She unbuckled my belt and my pants dropped to the floor. She pulled down my underwear and there was my hairless erection. She jacked me off with her forefinger and thumb; I ran home and never told anybody nor did I return to the scene. Her big thrill, I guess, was watching me ejaculate, which felt pretty damn good to me. I mean, who would ever bring up the two fingered thing. I was too embarrassed to revisit her for more experience, but I have great recall for that first glimpse of the mystery target of a man's life. My penis grew as I matured.

The length of a soft penis has no correlation to how much it grows. The average size of soft penises is three to four inches and erect penises from five to seven inches. You could be a "two incher" and grow to eight, size changes are not related to each other, hard or soft.

You can see why I had an early start being "overly" interested in sex. I didn't know what to expect and I was basically shy. In High School I was focused on a college scholarship for basketball, and I had many offers. I don't think my obsession about sex was any more than normal.

Going off to college is the most exciting think that happens to young adults. The new freedom and living away from parents was the second official step in reaching adulthood. The first step towards adulthood was getting your driver's license. That license certified that you were smarter than your parents. And my parents were never a problem. Nor was I. We were a close family and we were well-behaved children. We were relatively poor being supported by my father, a world war two veteran turned machinist making $65 a week, while my Mother worked as a waitress. They pooled their income and we were a very frugal family. Both my brother and I were fortunate to be so athletic. Truth be known, my brother and I got our exceptional athletic ability from our Mother. I doubt our parents could have afforded college educations for us. But we could have worked our way through because both my younger brother and I were excellent students. We both had many athletic scholarship offers.

Jack Callahan and I met the first day at college. We were both on scholarships and destined to be stars. We were assigned to be roommates for our entire college careers. We could have changed roommates, but we got along famously from the first day. Being the same size we could work out "one on one" at basketball and as a result we put in more practice time than our teammates. We were so enthused about basketball that we began working out the first day and frequently thereafter. That self motivation may well explain why we were both exceptional players and why we were in better physical condition than our teammates.

Our college dorm room consisted of two beds, two desks, one closet and bathroom with a single sink, toilet and a big curtained shower stall, no tub. Jocks took showers, not baths. There was about ten feet between our beds. Our freshman year disallowed girls in the men's dormitories. Later during our sophomore year, and from that day forward, girls were allowed in the guy's rooms for joint studying, yeah, right. "joint studies, get it." Commingling students at college dormitories was another sign of steps towards women's liberation.

The major impact on the close macho relationship between Jack and I came during our junior year. Jack and I had already pledged our code of confidentiality. We discussed intimate details, which consisted mostly of Jack sharing details with me for my learning curve. Jack trusted me and on occasion needed me to cover for him when absent without leave from certain college events. We never discussed sex with other guys. Nothing irked us more then to hear male counterparts bragging about sexual conquests and dropping names, especially in locker rooms. This offended us greatly and every time we heard anything disrespectful about women acquaintances we would threaten the loud mouth and degrade him for his had taste. It got to the point where we were such "big" jocks that no one challenged us. Jack was known for his abilities with fists, so that quietly ruled our locker rooms. We were the stars of a successful basketball team. We were gentlemen; we never used bad language. We played on a team that won the conference championship our last two years. I'd say we were more civilized than most guys.

Jack had many sexual experiences in high school. He even had older girls proposition him. Once when out with his older brothers, they got drunk and Jack at 15 had to drive them home. When Jack was dropping off his older brother's date, she screwed him in the back seat and had her own condom. Jack did not resist and never told his brother. He continued to have sex with this older girl all through high school. After she graduated, she worked as a waitress in Jack's old neighborhood. She gave Jack some valuable experience. Later in high school, Jack had several sexual relationships with classmates because he could get condoms from his brothers. Perhaps that was the advantage in growing up in a larger city. I was curious about his sex life and began to ask questions so I could learn something.

Jack had even experienced being "blown" by this older girl and I thought about it but had not gone so far. I wondered if we were normal horny or elevated because of our early discussions. Jack had performed cunnilingus, or was so taught by the girl three years older who dated others, but kept her relationship with Jack secret. She kept her own supply of condoms. When Jack first described eating pussy I was surprised but easily aroused to the possibility of doing it.

Jack and I began our discussions on what made women so attractive and how could we learn to be great lovers. Remember, we were driven. Our first rule of thumb was that a woman was sexy as long as the distance between her waist and the ground was greater than the distance between her head and her waistline. Does that make sense? That simply relates to long legs and why women do everything they can to look long legged. My Dad's advice to me was, "never mess with an ass wider than your own." But, sexy asses were a first observation for both of us. And Jack and I felt that a woman's attitude about sex was a primary concern. That means personalities have to be sexy. I think all women would agree with that evaluation. A woman has a difficult task to come across as liking sex but not about offering sexual participation without relationships. Remember, when the wars began, little did we realize that the average number of sex partners for men and women in a lifetime was eleven. Ahh, the "Great Pube Wars continue at the college level. Eleven? Wow, that seems like a lot to me. Cynthia only had two. Most people don't count and certainly Jack is above average. Eleven partners per person? Hmmm!

Chapter 11. What Ever Floats Your Boat.

Our sophomore year had been rather uneventful, however, Jack always had women chasing him and coeds were no exception. They flirted with Jack and if I was with him I was ignored, but to a lesser degree and I would kid Jack that I enjoyed flirting with his "leftovers." I was shy, but learning.

The basketball season was exceptional in that we were two sophomores that earned starting positions. During the season we worked hard and concentrated on our studies. The result was that we developed good study habits. The teams had to meet at the library after lunch for monitored study sessions. I was actually Jack's tutor. Not officially, but I gave him my good study habits and we often discussed our class subjects with exceptional interest. The theory was that studying after rigorous basketball sessions was not conducive to promoting concentrated study time. The pre workout study time worked for us because we acquired the habit and discipline to do our homework before basketball practice and we were always prepared for morning classes.

Our classes were coeducational, so young students were growing in an environment that included men and women. College time is a great environment for young people to mature without parental guidance. Our newfound independence either makes you a better adult, or you can fall into the party group that stalls maturity. The sports programs at some colleges are disciplined programs thanks to NCAA supervision. Women's sports were just beginning to develop. And in our case the cheerleaders were more like acrobatic teams or dancers than just yelling and leading cheers. Our school spirit was exceptional.

St Patrick 's Day became a special event for us because of Jack's Irish heritage. We always celebrated that holiday with Jack having a few green beers in the company of many other celebrants and since I drank little, I would act as Jack's guiding leprechaun. I had to wear a green sport coat, a green bowler hat and a big button that said, "World's Largest Leprechaun." At one campus green beer joint Jack was dancing with all comers and not paying much attention to whom he was dancing with. He unexpectedly was dancing with an old woman that had to be close to seventy years old. Jack was wearing a big button that said, "Kiss me I'm Irish."

First, a beautiful coed had planted a big wet kiss on Jack and when he came up for air, this seventy year old lady caught Jack off guard and kissed him with tongue like it was her last kiss before dying. She clung to Jack like she was having an orgasm. I think she was. The on-looking coeds were laughing. Jack gave the old lady her money's worth and treated her like a coed. He treated her like she was Miss America. Fortunately another coed was waiting and was next in line and the elderly lady had to move on. The ladies lined up to kiss Jack and it was good clean fun. Jack was never drunk and always in control.

What we didn't notice was the old lady sneaked up on Jack and handcuffed herself to his right hand. She laughed and told Jack the keys were back at her place and he would have to take her home to get free. The crowd thought that was a great prank and wondered how Jack would handle that emergency tactfully. He did kiss a few more coeds and the elderly lady allowed the kisses, but used the opportunity to feel Jack's ass. This was one very drunk horny old lady. And the crowd thought this a great comedy act.

When you drink a lot of green beer, guess what, a guy has to pee, and pee plenty. Jack called the old woman, "Darling" and explained he had to go to the men's room. Now this was to be quite a scene. There was a big line in the men's room at the urinals. Jack waited his turn with the woman handcuffed to him and the men's room crowd loved teasing the old woman. She was beginning to get embarrassed not expecting the attention and all the young college cocks peeing, shaking their cocks to flip off that last drop and then being zipped up. One guy removed the old lady's sunglasses, which she was hiding behind.

Jack took out long John and with his shackled hand held steady while he peed. It looked like the old lady was holding Jack's cock to steady his aim. When finished, he gave Long John a few extra shakes, which included her left hand contributing to the action. She was finally blushing out of control realizing she bit off more than she expected. Jack exited the men's room and kept his hand at his fly so it looked like the woman would not let go. She was so embarrassed she took the keys out of her purse, unshackled Jack, kissed him goodbye, bowed to the crowd and left with her dignity only slightly damaged. Jack did not hurt her feelings and the humor of the situation won out.

"I'll see you later honey," Jack shouted.

That incident was talked about all around the campus and Jack's reputation for being a "stand up guy," spread further. Some coeds would even flash handcuffs at him from a safe distance. One drunk coed asked Jack if she brought her own handcuffs would Jack fuck her. Jack turned away more pussy than most guys get.

The point I'm making is that an objective of not hurting a girl's feelings and using humor as a way out is most tactful. Sexy women in particular are hit on by countless men who too often lack tact. A woman needs to develop policy that is tactful or humorous. This is an acquired skill. I think the perfect denial for a woman when propositioned is to say, "I like you, but I have to tell you that I am involved and in love with someone else and I want to be faithful to my relationship. Shouldn't that be true for both of us?" That statement challenges a man's character.

I once heard Jack get propositioned on the phone by an anonymous female caller. She said she heard he was a great fuck and wanted him to meet her. Jack's response was,

"Mom, I don't need the confidence builder, I'm doing fine, now stop embarrassing me." I thought that was witty.

I heard a woman approach Jack, hug him from behind and say, "Umm, you smell so good, what is it you have on?" Jack's reply was, "I have a hard on but I didn't think you could smell it."

These typical college events continued into our junior year except the sexual encounters increased. Condoms and birth control pills made the start of the sexual revolution boom. We were caught up in women's liberation at the outset. I think college coeds played a bigger role because they were the first to be free from parental control. They were becoming more adventurous and aggressive. This liberation of women would gain power for the next fifty years. Today women make up half of the work force. Is it still a man's world?

During football season of our junior year the basketball team sponsored a "float" in the homecoming parade. We recruited a dozen or so cheerleaders to dress up in football uniforms supplied by a local grade school team. The small uniforms fit snuggly on the girls and Jack and I were charged with handing out and fitting the small football uniforms on the girls. This was an unexpected "hand rubbing" experience. I think the girls stripped down to their underwear in our presence knowing I was shy and Jack was known as a really nice guy that respected women while being classified as a real "hunk." Yeah, there was a lot of good flirting and kidding going on.

Women loved Jack and he was always charming. Jack's sense of humor loosened up the ladies, but they seemed to lack modesty anyway, and all were in a hurry. The occasion left no room for "hanky panky" other than our personal viewing privileges. Many of the girls wore "T" shirts over their bras and it was the small shoulder pads that created most of the problems. We saw quite a few nice legs. The few bras fitting under the shoulder pads were the most fun to watch. They required our expertise regarding uniforms and pressure points. The girls outnumbered us and were gleeful in their requests for advice on how to tie the shoulder pads or how to take the unnecessary pads out of the pants. There were too many women shuffling in and out of clothes to get any more than glimpses of white panties and some skin, mostly legs and bras going into football uniforms. This was really unusual, yet fun for Jack and me. It was a group flirtation thing for the cheerleaders. And it was our pleasure being in the ladies locker room. These were examples of the boldness of the new sexual revolution.

After a lot of female giggling, we exited the classroom designated as the "equipment room" and ushered the football uniformed girls to the float chassis for their football positions. One girl pretended to throw a pass to another while the other girls were to dance about as if they were trying to intercept a pass. The float was covered with artificial turf resembling a football field. Our emphasis was on the female form, mostly bust lines. It was crude, but effective because the girls looked sexy in the tight uniforms. Football players with shoulder pads and nice breasts were a rarity. I know Jack and I were more pleased to have been in the locker room than coaching the all girl team.

The girls felt liberated because of their numbers. They outnumbered us and they seemed to enjoy the flirting game more so because I was so bashful. This was part of the early stages of the sexual revolution when women were first getting their confidence. After all this analysis, the one thing I wish I had known more about would be, how to get those young girls to an orgasm. Now that I know how they masturbate I think what I could have achieved with two wet fingers gently stroking labia during the Great Pube Wars. Males performing "hand jobs" were more subject to exploring and finger poking vaginas. It was good but think how much better we could have been had we known what to do. I think we may have "rubbed them the wrong way."

Chapter 12. The Professional Dresser

Now comes the phenomenon of all cheerleaders, Carol Mason, lead cheerleader. She was late and claimed she had trouble finding a parking place for her Cadillac convertible. Carol's parents owned several auto dealerships including Cadillac; we learned later. I had to take Carol back to the equipment room and fit her by myself. Sound's good right? Carol was not a shy girl. She was 5'4" and stocky. Carol had striking green eyes. Believe it or not, that was the first thing men noticed about her. She was all muscle, very tan and had breasts that were too large for her cheerleading image. Carol could do back flips, front flips and could land doing the splits. She could almost be considered a contortionist because she could bend over backwards and grab her own ankles. She could walk on her hands and do the splits simultaneously. She had a small waist and was very sexy in an athletic way. Her leg muscles looked like they could strangle a man. (The male term of the day was to refer to firm legs as great "wrap-a rounds") She carried herself with body language that reeked of sex appeal. Her tanned body had no sign of flab. Her arms were muscled, but feminine, but no one noticed because of those magnificent breasts. She had slightly larger hips for such a small waistline. She was curvy, but the big surprise was her large bust line. I'd say her breasts were grapefruit size, but packed solidly so they did not move during her gymnastics. Her hair was a dark blond, almost light brown.

I would like to make a comment here about green-eyed women, in case I forget to bring it up later. We have no scientific data to draw any conclusions, so let's just say that in our opinion, green-eyed women seemed to have greater sex drives and a higher libido. And as for our movie star comparison technique, Carol Mason resembles Scarlett Johansson, and built a bit like Scarlett only better defined muscles. I don't know what color Scarlett's eyes are. Between Carol and the movie star, their face, lips and hair were very similar.

Carol and I were in a hurry; we were late. I found the right size football pants while she disrobed right in front of me. Wow! She sensed my shyness and I had to gawk at her bust line. They were text book shaped and pointed straight ahead like head lights. Naturally, her bra might have centered them. They were tightly packed. She had natural cleavage. She watched my eyes.

"Take a good look," she said, "you will never see a better pair of tits."

I actually blushed. I didn't know women talked like that, at least not from the girls I grew up with. I think she sensed my shyness. I wouldn't call her brazen just yet, but the idea of meeting a woman with so little fear of men was shocking to me. She seemed overly confident. I suspected she might be into kickboxing or something like that. I never asked. She was definitely a superb athlete.

Now the tricky part, getting those nice "white pantied" hips into the small football pants. I held up the pants while she sort of bounced her way into them. I was bent over with my arms around her while behind her, her ass was up against my crotch and my hands were grabbing the hip line of the uniform. My forearms seemed to be pushing her breasts inward. I was making more cleavage! Her breasts didn't seem to bounce at all, they were firm and I noticed that her rib cage had no flab. Her stomach was flat and looked hard. We made it! I got her into her pants. Hmmm. Why did those boobies not bounce? They were a natural set, I was sure. And what was I doing trying to get her into her pants instead of out of her pants. I was an oxymoron, no doubt.

"Thanks," she said, after just getting the pants on her. "I may need you as a professional dresser someday when I start my show business career."

Carol turned and faced me. She had a straddle stance with her hands on her hips; the tight bra held firm waiting for me to apply the shoulder pads. I laughed, blushed, and said thanks for the career offer while I laced the pads. The pads did not close over her breasts and she looked uncomfortable. I then held out the largest small sized numbered shirt. The shirt was number 69. She looked at the number, smiled and winked at me.

"Nice number, did you pick it out for me? What position should I be playing?"

I blushed again and said nothing. Once she got her head and ponytail through the neck I had to help her pull the shirt over the breasts and the shoulder pads. The shoulder pads were necessary to illustrate the football equipment. The football jersey looked like an impossible fit; it was funny. Her breasts were obviously going to protrude further than the shoulder pad harness. We laughed while we surveyed the situation. Here I was touching her breasts freely as I tried to tuck loose clothing inwards, but only as a professional dresser, of course. I felt obligated to keep the shoulder pads from pinching her breasts. I caught myself holding one breast while smoothing out wrinkles on the tight jersey. There were four hands on her breasts, hers and mine all reining in those big "hummers." Her mid section was bare and the jersey simply did not fit over her tits.

I studied her; she looked at me and said, "What do you think?" I shrugged my shoulders.

"Well, it will have to do. Are you OK with this? I don't know what to do about flattening your breasts a little. Those shoulder pads and bra seems awfully tight," I said. "It seems a downright shame to flatten those babies out. You have such nice shapes, I hate to hide them."

I noticed I was still holding a breast pushing it against the other, why, I don't know. Carol paid no attention to my hand. She was studying the problem.

"I have an idea," she said. And she pulled off the jersey first, then the shoulder pads and with much huffing and puffing. And we worked so hard to get them on. That effort on her part was a most stimulating strip tease show. Then what to my wondrous eyes should appear? She took off her bra. Her breasts still never moved. I promise you those babies were real, too.

She said, "Are you going to help me or do you think you can make my tits smaller by staring at them?" I blushed again. I just wasn't used to such a bold controlling woman.

I helped pull the jersey down over the shoulder pads and her bare breasts, and the jersey did flatten them but not enough to hide them. There was no way those breasts could be hidden, and the pads seemed to be pinching her breasts. I did get to handle those bare biggies some more, and she, again, pretended not to notice. My assistance was only business. You know, that view of her breasts and nipples sticking out of a football jersey would never go unnoticed. I worried about the shoulder pads rubbing against her skin under the jersey. Football players wear T-shirts.

I then had a brainstorm. I took off my sweater and stripped down to my bare chest and handed her my T shirt. I think she liked my bare chest and she touched my chest and said, "Nice breasts."

So, Carol again disrobed and pulled my T-shirt over her head. I helped her tuck my long shirt into her football pants. I was tucking in the rear and found myself feeling her buttocks while pushing my shirt downwards. We then loosely laced up the shoulder pads and pulled the football jersey over her head and breasts. This was a tough job. My T-shirt stopped the pads from possible chaffing, but even the double layer of shirts did not hide her breasts or her nipples; they still were most obvious, and she looked very sexy. I only hoped the parade was sufficiently darkly lit to shadow those beautiful boobs. However, it was obvious she wasn't wearing a bra, and she seemed rather proud. The point being, her breasts did not sag; they were firm and hard as though, if she decided to do so, she could go without a bra. I put my sweater and my letter jacket back on.

Her nipples were prominent, so be it. She smiled, thanked me, adjusted herself and we moved out to the float. I helped her on the float just as the parade began. I found myself pushing her ass onto the float with both hands. Another glorious moment! I felt like I had just made out.

Breasts, boobs, tits, whatever they are called are an enigma to men. Whether we were breast-fed or not, we are compelled to strive for breast contact. I wonder if there are more stimulating ways to caress breasts. Should we maul each unit, tickle or lick them? Men have to ask what feels best. I don't think breast size makes any difference to the "feelee." Women with small breasts may be more sensitive to the touch. Some say more than a mouthful is a waste anyway. It is a fact that caressing breasts stimulates a woman. I think the consensus is that the feeler must be gentle and not maul breasts, yet in the heat of passion women may want their breasts mauled.

Back to the future, Cynthia was most affected with a gentle massaging and lots of mouthing, but when aroused was more anxious to get my face between her legs. Breast manipulation does not usually provide orgasms. Why breast caressing contributes to a woman's desire to feel a cock in her pussy is an individual thing. Perhaps the height of the stimulation is the deciding factor as to what to do next. I would always ask. OK, Back to the past.

Chapter 13. A One Night Sit

When the parade was over, Carol was flirting with me big time at the float. I guess we had become bosom buddies, or I had passed the test as an official dresser. I asked about her breasts and the shoulder pads and she seemed rather casual about the whole experience. She did ask if I thought her nipples were too obvious and I again blushed and I said I thought they were perfect. I felt like I was being treated like one of the cheerleaders. Carol seemed to enjoy my leering at her boobs and made me blush every time she caught me. When she caught me she would throw her shoulders back.

"Remember what I told you in the locker room, that you will never see a nicer pair of tits? I guess based on our experience, you and I are good friends you having felt my breasts, right? I assume you will not be spreading any stories." She said. "You practically gave me a complete physical exam tonight and I'd like to keep that private."

"Carol, please know I'm not that type of guy that kisses and tells. I feel privileged that you allowed me to get so close to you and I have to tell you, your breasts really felt wonderful, so I am guilty of enjoying the moments." I hope you don't hold that against me."

"Will, I'll hold them against you anytime you want," Carol replied with a big grin.

I again blushed. "OK," I said meekly.

"Look, you just said the right thing and thank you for the compliments. I know you are a nice guy and I apologize if I came off a little aggressive back there." Actually your shyness is a rare blessing, I like that." She added.

I told her I loved every minute of our dressing experience. We hung out at the float for about a half hour while Jack opened the equipment room and supervised the changing of the guard, so to speak. Carol and I were examining the float as if we knew what we were looking at, so we had a reason to keep talking. I knew Carol was purposely stalling and was enjoying my shyness, which I was exaggerating. I knew I was going to undress her and get my T-shirt back and that was why she was stalling. She wanted to keep our exchange of nakedness between just the two of us.

She asked if I was going with anybody. I told her that basketball practice and that rigorous game schedule kept me off the dating market, and that I really missed the social scene. I wasn't really lying because I worked hard at both basketball and studying, and my commitment to my high school girlfriend was not firm. She said she heard I was a genius; I blushed again. Well, that wasn't true, I was in the top 1% academically and I did spend time studying. She asked if she could study with me sometime and I said sure, anytime. I jumped off of the float and held my arms out to assist her. She fell into my arms gave me a big kiss on my lips. I held on thinking she might flip me or something. Carol had a strong grip. I was thinking she probably could have done a front flip off the float landing with the splits, but was faking the needy feminine role for assistance. I set her down on the ground and again felt her firm body against me. We walked back to the equipment room.

She proceeded to tell me how much she enjoyed cheering at the basketball games. I told her I was aware of her gymnastics ability, but I was never in a position to watch, being distracted by the game and the timeout coaching. She complimented my athletic skills and then told me she thought I was sexy and had a nice build. Why did I blush? I was still unsuspecting, that's why. I was modest compared to her, and you might say I was protecting myself, but underneath everything, I was really aroused. I was looking forward to being her professional dresser; after all, I was more familiar with football uniforms.

Carol asked me to join her for a "soda" break at the student union so we could talk some more and I agreed.

When we got to the equipment room, or unused classroom, Jack was leaving with his arm around another cheerleader and he threw me the keys. I unlocked the door and the football uniforms were in neat piles and Carol's clothes were hanging on the last hanger.

"Come on, big boy, now that you have dressed me I think you know what to do about getting me out of this stuff." She winked at me. I thought her winks were like green flashes of light.

So, I began the unwrapping of this fabulous female athlete. Taking the jersey off over her head was the most fun because I had a private view of her bare breasts protruding from my white T-shirt, and untying those shoulder pads could be tricky with my knuckles against her breasts. Her eyes were covered momentarily under the jersey, so I was in complete charge of protecting her bare breasts from rough edges. I removed my undershirt from her again exposing bare breasts while her eyes were covered. When I took off my jersey; she did nothing to assist me. She motioned for me to take off the football pants like she was directing a professional dresser. Kneeling down with my face at panty level was also a major turn on and a necessary step to pulling the football pants over her hips. My forehead was against her stomach for leverage and my face was too close to her panties for my comfort. She smelled wonderful. She was purposely letting me do most of the work. When she was bare breasted and only wearing panties, I stood and stepped back and feasted on what I saw. I was staring at her panties. I had a hard on that was pushing to escape and Carol noticed and smiled at my bulge. She obviously loved being in control, she took my hand, dragged a chair with her and walked me to the door swinging her hips with a bit extra swing. She took the keys from me and locked the door and began to undress me.

"You have been dressing and undressing me, now it's my turn. I want to see your gorgeous body," she said.

I allowed her to do all the work.

She sat down on the chair, her face at my belt level and pulled my pants down; I stepped out of them. She surprised me by going right at my underwear not giving me a chance to react. She pulled my shorts off and was face to face with my erection. She looked up at me and smiled and put her mouth over my cock and began sucking, licking and gently stroking the underside of my testicles. She watched my eyes and I watched her mouth. You might say I was paralyzed. She sure seemed to know what she was doing. I thought I had died and gone to heaven and earned 72 virginal cheerleaders. We were both hot and breathing hard. I was weak kneed and holding on to the wall behind her to steady myself. Carol pushed me back seemingly admiring the results of her good work, stood up, sat me down on the chair, and gracefully removed her panties. Carol gently straddled and mounted me. She held my cock in one hand while guiding me into paradise. She actually did a deep knee bend using the floor as a base. Actually, she was doing chair level deep knee bends on my cock, with regular rises on to her toes.

The first thought that crossed my mind was, wait a minute, no condom?

"You are wonderful," I moaned, "but are we safe?"

"Don't worry about it I'm on the pill and I started taking the pill this year. You are so sexy and I can't tell you how much I want to fuck you, I am so turned on now I have to fuck you," she moaned.

What could I do? I don't think I would be classified as the fucker. I was the fuckee. And, there was nothing in the room more comfortable than being straddled on that armless chair, so we stayed with it. There was nothing I could do but enjoy myself. This was too good to be true. I did get to kiss her breasts during the act and she would bend backwards resting her hands on my knees to allow me a better position for kissing and caressing her breasts, which were extra prominent and stretched out because of her arched back. She would rise and push her breasts into my face. I loved it. And, yes, she could really bend backwards. For one moment I thought she was going to put her hands on the floor over her head. It didn't happen, but I'll bet she could have. What was really sexy was Carol doing deep knee bends while pushing off the floor, which was very athletic. With each "dip" she would fall forward on the way down. I was most conscious of this unusual very athletic action. She alternated hitting my face with her breasts and kissing me. Then she would rise up and continued that rising and falling motion never changing the pace. It sure worked for me. Getting seduced and fucked like this was a first time for me and I was thrilled.

I came; we kept on kissing for a few moments. She knew I had an orgasm; she stopped moving and allowed me to ejaculate not wanting to interrupt the throbbing with more action. How very considerate. She kept kissing my face and telling me how good I felt. We relaxed and stayed connected for a few minutes. Then she stood up very slowly, pulled me out of the chair, hugged me and said.

"This is kind of a reverse date here, we had sex and now we go for the drinks. We still have a date don't we?" She asked.

This was also a first for me. I was engaging in a standing full frontal hug with her breasts against my cock.

"Absolutely, and what a wonderful start." I said. "You are really something, forgive my state of shock, but you are a wonderful surprise. I hope you're not going to treat me like a one night sit." (I thought that was witty.)

Carol said, "If I never see you again, you will never know what you missed. I can't imagine you not coming again." (She thought that was witty).

From that day forward, I had the best sex life imaginable. We had sex about six times a week. We tried every new position and every type of advanced foreplay.

We studied together and cuddled and fucked like minks. Life was good. We went to movies and became movie critics. If we met after basketball practice and if I was too tired, I'd get a nice blow-job. But, what was important for this book is that I developed the habit of always eating pussy. When Carol climaxed before we had sex, sex was very good. Carol was always exceptionally clean. Her attitude was very objective and more in a sporting sense than a love affair. She acted like a close intimate friend, sometimes like a nurse. Carol considered herself a teammate, even though limited to cheerleading. She was never embarrassed if Jack overheard us or even caught her running to our shower naked. Jack gave us the necessary privacy. If Jack had a bed guest, we did not know who was there and didn't care as long as we were quiet. Carol was an amazing woman because she was so athletic. We often tried sex moves and positions that most women could never do. More on that subject later.

Our communications were exceptional and I have to give Carol most of the credit for this bonding achievement. She actually told me what to do with my tongue and my rewards were a feast of reciprocity. I had no idea how many times we kissed and touched; I could not count the new pleasures. When she was on top she was almost too considerate and she claimed to have an orgasm each time I ate her or she rode me. The rule was that she needed an oral climax before I got on top. There was a big difference in our orgasms when foreplay was emphasized. How can anyone describe such a glorious experience? Love was never mentioned. That was strange.

Chapter 14. Who was that woman?

We found her Cadillac convertible and she began to explain.

"My daddy owns a dealership, so I get new cars every 90 days or sooner. I don't want you to think I sleep around. I don't have a boyfriend and I don't want a love relationship. I have a theatrical agent and I am exploring several offers to dance on Broadway, or maybe even Hollywood. I don't want children or a husband to get in my way. I'll get married when I'm older if I decide to do so. I started taking the pill hoping I would find someone like you. I hear you have a high school sweetheart and that's OK. What I want is a "fuck buddy," somebody exclusive to me and somebody I know isn't sleeping around."

"How does that sound to you?" She asked.

I agreed and told her that the basketball team had a difficult schedule and if we find time for sex, I would consider myself the luckiest man alive. I told her I liked movies and that we could get together for lots of dating activities. I told her she was more sophisticated than I and that she was so sexy that I would trust her completely and she could trust me. I did tell her that I wanted to confide in Jack and I told her about the understanding and secrecy pact between Jack and me. That was OK with her.

We agreed that meeting in my room was better than her place because she had several roommates, which were not to know about us. I suggested she come on occasion to study with us jocks and that the curtain that Jack and I had rigged between our beds would suffice for privacy. Carol stated she would never spend the night because the bed was too small and she didn't want to be a "no show" at her room, the less gossip, the better.

Carol continued. "Well, I have had a lot of experience for my age, but with only one guy. When I was in high school I had this older boyfriend that my parents didn't approve of. I dated other guys, but never divulged my secret lover. That made our sex better. I think, I was under age and our sex life would be considered illegal, but we trusted each other. He had his own place, and he knew how to fuck. I never was in love with him; in fact he was stupid and had no future to provide for any woman. He was just a fuck machine with an endless supply of condoms that was better than my vibrator. I admit I am a horny woman. He liked licking me and that was becoming more important as I grew into sexual maturity."

She continued, "After high school he went on to his career as a truck driver. I never saw him again and I assume he found someone else. I worked at our country club every summer as a lifeguard. I also play tennis and golf and I have had dancing lessons since I was six years old. I have studied ballet, tap dancing and Jazz, I can also sing a little, so I am a serious contender for a show business career. As I said I already have offers and I will graduate this year and probably go to New York City."

"I am so impressed with you; I don't know what to say. I do agree on our secret pact and I assure you I will enjoy a relationship that allows me to make love to such a beautiful woman." I reconfirmed our pact.

It was getting late and the student union was closed, so Carol dropped me off at my dorm. We had a prolonged kiss in the car. I caressed her breasts and noticed that she was not wearing a bra. I must have missed that. Carol touched my cock inside my pants as if confirming our intimate rights. It was as if the mutual touching was the same as shaking hands. When inside, Jack appeared to be asleep, so I shut the bathroom door and showered. I couldn't help but notice the new carton of condoms opened on the sink counter. I was extra quiet and sure enough, Jack was asleep with his arms around a blond head, also sound asleep. I heard her leave later. Jack would have to wait to hear about my finding the "mother lode."

When I told Jack what happened to me, we engaged in one of many conversations evaluating women. I asked Jack how a person like him, who so many women find attractive, decides on which one to pursue. The key response is "attitude." What is the difference between attitude and personality? One's personality is distinctive characteristics or qualities that individualize us. Attitude is a settled way of thinking, which surely contributes to one's behavior. Attitude has to do with tolerance, perhaps tolerance of another's personality. Remember the phrase that opposites attract? But attitudes have levels of sophistication. Some people accept others more readily without forming judgments. And women with great attitudes usually have a better sense of humor. Perhaps being clever is part of an attitude. But reactions to dealing with what others say and do is at the core of personality development.

Before one judges another, one should evaluate another's attitude. How Carol Mason reacts to my inexperience is how she judges me and I liked her attitude, her way of evaluating the immediate circumstances. More fun than fear? Curiosity? Confidence rather than insecurity? Adventurous personalities are a sign of a settled way of thinking and much confidence. A woman's initial reaction to what you first say to her and her evaluation of the first thing that a man says creates an attitude. This reaction sets the stage for what could happen.

The next phrase that is often used is, "an attitude adjustment." That is the ability to change one's attitude. We call that maturation and when all this relates to sex, you must have the ability to discern between attitudes and personalities. Doesn't the "Golden Rule" play a role here? Do unto others what you would have them do to you? The same rule applies to sex and that includes consideration for others and an attitude that wants to investigate another's personality based on the first meeting. The attitude defines what will happen.

Jack's attitude was sophisticated. He was "joyful," he was respectful to all women and he was considerate from the start. Jack reacted to women's attitudes and how they reacted to him is what moved a relationship forward. If a woman is offended by a man's initial approach then they both need attitude adjustments. My attitude toward women just had a major adjustment. I was thrilled to meet a woman who was attracted to me and her attitude would affect my personality forever.

Naturally the basic requirement of attraction is physical. Sex appeal is a combination of attitude and physical attraction. Sex is primed by physical attraction, but mutual enjoyment is an attitude thing. Jack just happens to begin a relationship with attitude because all involved are attractive sexually. The rest of us simply go for it without thinking. We are ruled by our "little heads" and that also goes for women. A woman's attitude evolves around her admission that she has a little head.

For the most part, women's initial reactions to men are cautious. They are "on guard" as they try to judge just how much to allow you into their lives. A guy doesn't really know if he appeals to a women. There are exceptions, but women in general do not want to appear aggressive. They have to let you think you are advancing and those signals are often too subtle. If a guy moves to close for that first kiss, he better be pretty sure of himself. Many times he will be eliminated, or maybe get right to the point. There is nothing worse from a man's point of view than to have a woman show interest in him just to be polite. It's like hearing, "can we just be friends?' Yeah right, a guy is horny, gets wasted erections about a woman who will never allow him intimacy. It's supposed to be a man's world. I don't think so. It can be a cruel world.

Chapter 15. Sex, Lies and Hot Air Stories

The incident that moved Jack and I closer to our sexual education project occurred late one Friday during a relaxing evening at the student union recreational center frequented by students. Jack, Julie, Carol and I were having a few sodas and trying to have an intimate conversation without being overheard. Julie was the other small blond cheerleader, who had a crush on Jack. Julie was shy, but sexy. Finally, the ultimate group question of intimacy testing was asked.

"What's the sexiest experience you have ever had" Jack asked Julie. Our ears perked up because Julie was a shy quiet mystery. She reminded me of myself because of her frequent blushing. I'm not sure whether Julie was aware of my relationship with Carol. I'm sure she suspected we were lovers and that was about to be confirmed as a secret, and Jack advised her to never discuss anything that was discussed at our double dates. Julie was not that close to other cheerleaders and I think Carol explained something to Julie separately however limited. We had agreed in unison that we would not talk about whatever we discussed with others.

Julie responded with a big flushed look and said, "I'm not sure what you mean, why doesn't someone else talk first?"

Carol and I nodded agreeing to follow suit as a comfort to Julie. It was most appropriate that Jack should begin. These conversations between Jack and me and future encounters with women was to become extremely significant.

Jack told us that last summer he went to a hot air balloon festival with a date. The two of them went up what seemed like a few hundred yards with the balloon tethered to the ground. It was the girl's father's balloon. Jack and his date had control of eventually lowering the balloon basket and since it was late afternoon they were up in the air and started fooling around. Jack embellished the breeze factor and the view and the privacy. After some passionate kisses, they took off all their clothes from the waist down. There wasn't enough room to lie down. Jack continued that when they leaned over the side at the same time the basket tipped rather dangerously and they had the feeling of falling, like when you look out a window from a tall building. Of, course there was no glass. They were fooling around while ducking below the basket line and this date helped Jack get erect by caressing his cock. Jack said that she anxiously watched him fumble with the condom. I often wondered how many women would agree to sex if they knew ahead of time that you had a condom. This girl thought the hot air experience would be fun and unusual. She was game.

"I stacked our jeans under her feet so her ass was higher. My height was a distinct advantage because I could lift and hold her with ease. I had a difficult time entering her while her breasts were pressed against the basket side. We had removed her bra, but replaced her jacket should anybody on the ground have binoculars. I could feel her bare breasts with my hands under her coat. We moved close to a tie line and I mounted her from behind and the basket tipped slightly I could place my head next to hers, sort of cheek to cheek. I had to lift her up and that was a bit treacherous, yet exciting. I pressed her steady against the side of the basket with my arms wrapped around her waist." Jack continued.

"We felt like we were fucking suspended in the air. We could only see the ground and there was a cool breeze. I couldn't stroke fast, but that was good, sex lasted longer and was more sensuous. I had braced both of us against the side of the basket. I had taken a wide stance so I was lower against her. Both of my arms were wrapped around her waist and hips. I had to squat to get the right angle and we were "spooned." It was a gentle experience, and the only sounds were our heavy breathing and sex sounds. She did grunt with each stroke. It was an unusual feeling of ecstasy. The thrill of being suspended in the open air was most stimulating. We imagined we were two birds having sex in flight because our faces were outside the basket as we leaned over the side. When I came I was thrusting harder and there was the sensation that with each thrust we would fall from the basket. So, the danger factor I believe increases sexual pleasure. I believe the quietness, the wind, and the danger made that an unusual experience." Jack concluded.

I don't know who was going to top that story. I believe it was a lesson in sensuousness. We all looked at each other waiting for someone to break the silence and speak. I think we were all imaging or fantasizing as if we were doing it. Keep in mind the strategy underlying these conversations is to keep the sex at an objective level hoping to increase the requirement of bonding for love relationships. I was amazed that these things were happening to Jack so often. Actually, they weren't that often, but when hearing them at one session, one would get the feeling that Jack lived a "Hollywood" style sex life. That was not the truth. When they occurred, they were unusual. Do you know how unusual these sexual experiences are? If one couple experienced any single such experience we have reported it would be extremely unusual. Most couples go a lifetime and never do anything that exciting, or that far out. Perhaps it would be better said if we acknowledged that we have no idea what kind of sexual experiences other people have. Therefore, we can only assume that some of these unusual experiences reported in this book are rare. No matter whether they are rare to you or not, we still maintain that our conclusions are based on our actual experiences regardless of conflicts with the more scientific journals. I believe we can teach you something that is not just a lot of hot air. Read on.

Chapter 16. Hot To Trot?

Carol. Beamed, "Hell, I can top that. Is there going to be a prize here?"

"The prize is to see who can think of some new experience that we might consider sharing as a means of stimulation, or just some new ideas. In a subtle way we are being scientific, although Will here is the brain and someday maybe he can write a book and draw some conclusions that may be as entertaining as they are scientific." Jack said. (Hmmm)

Carol continued, "Well, I'd sure like to read that book since I am on the inner circle here. I will add what I think is unusual and exciting, but, you guys have to know there is a double standard for women. What we girls do cannot be evaluated by the same standards, because it's a man's world. Guys can be macho studs and notch their guns with trophies of conquest. But, if a woman tries some adventure she is at the mercy of men. Women with experience can only be whores or sluts. I think you guys will never get real stories from other women because they will not trust the promised confidentiality. Women dare not brag about their seductions. I trust you guys and I assure you we girls will not be discussing our adventures with other men. Our peers would label us as sluts and some men will then assume you are an easy mark and not be so tactful in hoping to get laid. Anyway let me tell my story since I am one of the guys now. I may be missing the balls, but I can accomplish the same thing using tits. Never underestimate the power of tits."

Well, our balls were not as big as Carol's tits, but we admired the metaphor.

"My weird summer experience was after my freshman year in college, and I was taking horseback riding lessons at our country club from this older German "green cardie" guy. One day, we had an unusual opportunity to witness a stallion being bred with a worthy mare. Let me tell you, there is nothing sexier than watching two horses fuck, my God the size of that horses cock was a sight to see. As a result we enjoyed a barnyard quickie shortly thereafter, a secluded roll in the hay, which I regret, but I was easily seduced after a long dry spell and after watching the stallion fuck. I'm never dry. But, knowing Wolfgang would use a condom was too tempting even though I did not want a relationship with this guy, which proves that the old proverb about a "roll in the hay" is not what it is built up to be. This guy was only satisfying himself. And sex in a haystack can be tricky and itchy. I thought "Wolfgang" was an arrogant ass, but it was my only summer experience and at the time I was horny. Did I have an Orgasm? No. Thank God for my two regular sex partners, "Black and Decker."

At the mention of a Black and Decker, Julie looked shocked and blushed like she didn't get it. I wonder how many women have their private sessions with vibrators. If it is a common practice, then women would have better sex lives and more orgasms. Julie just shrugged her shoulders and blushed looking at Jack.

Carol continued, "This was really a wild sex idea, and I believe an original idea. It was evening prior to sunset and the wooded horse trails were pretty much empty. There were lots of trees and green coverage. I had suggested this unusual fuck to macho Nazi Wolfgang and he was most anxious to try it. He had a nice hard cock and that was all that was important to me at the time. We rode double to a secluded spot and we dismounted and took off our riding pants. Wolfgang was so meticulous, and he acted like he was doing me a big favor. He was folding his riding pants so they wouldn't show any wrinkles. Nobody about to get laid should be so meticulous or presumptuous; it is a turn off. When I suggested I ride his cock while we rode the horse, he said, "Yah yah." He was a German horseman in his mid twenties and had an accent. I subconsciously resented his superior Nazi attitude. He climbed on the horse bare from the waist down. His riding pleated jacket was very neat, and he was wearing one of those black bowler hats with a visor. I stood on the ground and had to stretch to arm his cock with a condom while wetting my own pussy with my fingers. He was of no help; he was posing like a Nazi general." And his cock was, "Achtung."

"I had to grab the horse's mane and jump up on to the horse facing Wolfgang. I mounted his erection by hanging on to his neck with one hand and fumbling his cock to the right place. Again he was of no help. It was quite an athletic feat, if I do say so. Not every girl could do this trick because when fucking I had only my legs dangling and had to hold on to his neck with both hands suspended on his cock. I'm talking the guy's neck, not the horse. I was a free falling weight on his cock. He then kicked the horse that went into a trot causing me to bounce uncontrollably. Do you all know what posting is? Well, I couldn't post with my legs dangling. Wolfgang had to hold his body away from the saddle to protect his balls. His ass never touched the saddle. The horse was actually doing all the fucking work. Nobody could speak while the horse was bouncing, just some loud grunting. I even thought I heard the horse grunting. It was probably my imagination because there was some serious thrusting going on. That hard bouncing fuck really felt good to me; Wolfgang? I wasn't so sure about him. I had a great quick orgasm, something I don't often feel. I felt like I was getting fucked by a machine gun."

I felt my testicles tremble. Men's "little heads," penises, actually do have their own thinking process and individual personalities. This story was affecting us guys and not favorably. Ouch!

"After I came, and I'm sure he did too because I yelled at him when I was coming and that usually will get a guy off. His cock fell out of me while he was trying to rein in the horse. I crushed his "weenie" against the English saddle with my ass. He was not a happy camper. He yelled in pain and cursed me while reining in his horse and grabbed his slippery, now soft rubber covered cock with one hand. When the horse stopped, he bounced even harder, the horse, not Wolfgang. Wolfgang dropped the condom and was trying to hold his wounded pecker with one hand with the reins in the other. He was still standing in the stirrups. I'm sure that hard reining made the horse bounce even more.

I stretched back over the horses' neck and flipped my leg over his head and accidentally kicked his head knocking his hat askew. I fell to the ground bare ass and landed on both feet. My boobs also took quite a bouncing, but not hurting. Actually I think my breasts enjoyed the ride even covered with my riding coat because my nipples were rubbing against the inside of my coat. I felt like I was a gymnast that had just dismounted from parallel bars. He dismounted, gave me a dirty look, and untied our riding pants off the back of the saddle. We got dressed and rode back to the stable with me on his back and him complaining about how inconsiderate I was. I suspected he wanted me to get on my knees and kiss his sore cock. Hah! Not this day. Like, I could do anything about the horse's gait. I should be the captain of the "pussy roughriders." I'm telling you that horse really bounced hard and I was able to pull his neck down, not the horse, Wolfgang's neck, to ease some of the hard bounce after I came. I suppose I could have broken his neck, or at least given him some whiplash. Wolfgang! Not the horse. I guess that was a sexy experience for me and not for Wolfgang because I "killed" his golden staff. I still giggle about our indignant break up, which suited me fine."

Carol added, "Most of all, I still remember the fucking horses more than Wolfgang. Talk about panting, grunting and pissing. They had this old beat up stallion covered with worn out leather vests, who supposedly allowed the female to kick the shit out of the old horse so the featured stallion would not risk injury. After the female was worn out, they dragged the old stallion out and brought in the fresh breeding horse, who got erect watching the old horse trying to mount his mare. Two big animals fucking is quite a sight and a real turn on. I'll never forget it."

Jack and I were stunned hearing a woman talk like this. We liked her attitude.

"During one beginner's grooming lesson I had to learn about cleaning horses," Carol continued, "I did get to wash the penis of a big stallion. That really felt weird, I mean it was big and getting hard, like holding a baseball bat. I felt weird because I was arousing this huge cock. Actually I was embarrassed, but no one saw me. I gave up riding lessons after that. But I still get aroused when I see the Budweiser stallions. I love watching those commercials." She laughed.

"I kept hearing about why women liked straddling a horse while on a saddle, or that riding a bicycle gave them a sexual thrill," quipped Jack.

"Nah, it didn't work that way, at least not for me. I just think horses are magnificent animals and having that big animal between my legs might have a sexual power play for some women, but commanding that big stallion gave me a simple power play. I also learned that animals have strange sexual foreplay, their foreplay is more like rituals. The female horse pees all over the male while he tries to mount her and the stallion has this beat up look in his eyes like he is a slave to mounting her. The mare's eyes look like fucking feels good. Dogs also have these pathetic looks while fucking and I wonder why they can't act like they are having fun. Dogs should wag their tales while mating rather than hang them like they are being beaten. I wonder how humans evolved from the cave man dragging a woman into a cave, or only entering women from behind. The word is countenance; isn't that an overall body language thing? Actually, I think females are responsible for the development of foreplay. Same with animals. I can make a great argument for that theory. Speaking of countenance, I have to admit Will is a great lover because he wants to be good, "he shines his countenance upon me."

Everybody looked at me for some reaction. If that didn't sound like one of the guys, nothing would. We were aghast, especially Julie. Jack kidded me in front of Carol that she might be dangerous, but during the recovery period from that story, Carol hugged me reassuring me that she would never take me horseback riding. Jack and I both felt the "ouch" sympathy male reaction of any guy getting his pecker crushed. Carol sure sounded like one of the guys. We suggested she open a cock washing service to raise money for the cheerleaders.

"Hmm, maybe for the right price I could get a few sorority girls to raise charitable money like they ask us to do for car washes." She grinned.

I confessed that I had no sexier experience than when I first met Carol. That pleased her immensely, and I had promised not to reveal the details. But, Carol proceeded to tell everybody how bold she was about mounting poor innocent me. And how much fun she had embarrassing me. She said it was a real turn on and that maybe meeting shy men might be more rare as we grow older. I then looked to Julie, who said,

"I just don't have anything to say. I guess I'm kind of a novice at this stuff." I just haven't done anything that exciting, but after listening to you guys, I wish I had. Maybe I'm not courageous enough."

Jack reassured Julie and gave her a hug and told her they would try and create their own adventures, but no horses. Julie giggled at that. The bottom line is that I was amazed at the boldness of Carol. Carol was in a class by herself and Julie in her lifetime would never be able to match Carol's attitude when it came to sexual experiences. I believe Julie represented the majority of women. They held back on their feelings hoping never to be classified as too experienced. Carol, on the other hand sure seemed to be goal oriented. Her attitude was very feminist, yet, in fact, she was just like one of the guys. I think Carol liked this image. It brought to my young mind that women were entering a new phase of sexuality. I suppose it was related to the birth control pill, but obviously women were raising what feminist's called, "the glass ceiling," or better said, "the mirrored ceiling." It wasn't a matter of women's rights as much as women wanting to have equal standards when it came to sexual judgments. Jack once told me that one time he asked a girl to dance and she said "sure, but I'd rather fuck." That left quite an impression on Jack, but it only happened once. Stuff like that never happened to me until Carol seduced me. Remember, I grew up in a small town and Jack grew up in a big city. This is relevant.

What we men don't realize is that we are always being manipulated, that seduction is always controlled by women. That foreplay was developed by women is probable, and that men evolved away from forceful sex like cavemen are supposed to have done. I suspect cavewomen waved their naked fannies about when seeking coitus for breeding purposes. Since there were no records about cavemen we don't really know how foreplay and flirting evolved. Women are by far superior when it comes to flirting. They can be masterfully subtle. Don't fight it guys.

As a trivial fact, horses ejaculate twenty times more semen than mankind and a man will ejaculate on average about sixteen quarts of semen in a lifetime. A man squirts over 100 million sperm each time a man fires and only about 200 little swimmers actually reach the egg's chambers. Then only one, or sometimes two get to actually mate. Two and a half teaspoons of semen into 16 quarts seems light to us, but you do the math for a lifetime sperm count. Who cares?

Chapter 17. Who Was That Masked Man?

To keep the game alive and hoping to turn on Julie and hopefully get Carol to talk more, Jack volunteered another story. This was really getting interesting.

Another time, an old girlfriend of Jack's, Glenda that had always welcomed a chance to have sex with Jack ever since their high school days, was the subject of this story. Jack explained that Glenda, at the time of this story was married and had a year old baby, and they were just good friends. Glenda was an old girlfriend that he knew intimately. They had frequent safe sex in high school.

Jack told us that Glenda had requested the strangest thing he ever imagined. Glenda explained that she had this girlfriend of hers that really wanted to have sex with Jack, but didn't want him or anybody else to ever know about it. If Jack agreed, this modest secret admirer wanted Jack to be blindfolded and the dear friend Glenda would supervise the set up, but not interfere with the special event. In fact, Glenda agreed to act as the "moderator," agreed to set up the event and disappear into the bathroom so this secret admirer could have her way with Jack with no repercussions or witnesses.

The guest partner did not want Jack to ever know who she was, nor ever call her later, or for whatever reasons, it was imperative that Jack never know who she was. Well, Jack figured he would get that information from the moderator someday, so he agreed. Jack also trusted Glenda.

Jack began anew, "when I arrived at the designated motel room my good friend, Glenda, met me at the door, she was alone. She hurriedly stripped me down and while I was standing, put a black silk blindfold over my eyes. Apparently the mystery guest was waiting in the bathroom. Glenda sat me down on the bed, which the sheets had been exposed, and then placed a black hood over my head keeping my nose and mouth free. That was two blindfolds. I wondered if that was necessary to prevent my peeking. Glenda gave my cock a gentle tug as if checking to see if I had changed. Glenda was being funny and flippant setting this stage. She was humming. She tied the hood on tightly on top of the blindfold and made me swear that I would not touch the blindfolds, no matter what would happen. I agreed."

Jack continued, "I was now lying naked on a motel room bed with my hands free and my promise not to touch the blindfold. I sure felt vulnerable. The first thought that came to my mind was that some homely virgin was going to abuse me. To my surprise when the secret admirer, Madam X, first touched me, she put one hand on my chest and one hand on my cock. She gently kissed me on the mouth. I felt her entire body as quickly as I could, and she let me. I had to confirm she was a she. She was small; I guessed about five foot two, and had shoulder length thick hair. She straddled my chest and patiently allowed me to touch her breasts and genitals. She felt really sexy. Nice breasts, nice ass, and never spoke, only a slight whisper as if that would hide her identity."

Jack stated that the mystery guest was obviously using her anonymity to be able to do things she would never do if her identity were revealed. What an unusual way to lose one's inhibitions. This fine lady, according to Jack had no flaws that he could feel. What an unusual idea for someone with no self-confidence, or maybe a chance to practice gaining some confidence. Hmmm.

"She was handling my cock as if she were exploring something she never felt before. I was pretty sure she was putting my cock in her mouth (It might have been her pussy) and she felt inexperienced, but aggressive. The oral sex was not necessary, but I have to admit that being blindfolded my senses were rising. I was totally focused on feelings. I can understand why blind men could hear and feel things better. All my senses were greatly sharpened. She tried to sit on my face without crushing me, and she didn't seem to know what to do. I tried to lick her but not knowing the angle made it difficult. So, the mystery guest assumed the bottom position and simply whispered to me to "eat her," which I did. I could then use my fingers and hands and she held my head and made some really nice sounds of pleasure, quietly but never speaking. Obviously Glenda had told her about my "licking skills."

"As she began to get noisy with pleasure; she whispered for me to lie on my back. I then felt more oral sex and then she fumbled around trying to mount me. She changed course to put a breast in my mouth. I caressed her breasts and then grabbed her ass. She did rub my cock against her clitoris, which I assume is something women wished would happen more often. I sensed that some previous lover was too hurried. She sure was tight and wet. She sat on me very gently. She didn't seem to know whether to bounce or undulate, but I'm pretty sure she had another orgasm. And it didn't take her long and she was quiet and restrained in her passion. But, she was in control, but not sure she knew what she was doing, nor could she be embarrassed. I guess that was the idea. Yet, she was too good to be using me as a practice dummy. I think she was more excited because she could do more uninhibited things, and I think that was her personal objective. She was definitely in control of my pleasure. She was taking her time and I actually had to concentrate not to come too soon. Eventually she stopped fucking me, dismounted slowly and manipulated me onto my hands and knees. She slapped my ass a few times. She maneuvered herself under me and on her back, put her hands on my waist and whispered,"

"I want you to fuck me Jack."

"And it was like I was turned loose. I was on top, but she was too short to kiss on the mouth. I grabbed her ass and lifted her off of the bed using my forehead as a fulcrum. It was like she could not move, but her reaction was very passionate. I think that original technique that only us tall guys can do was unexpected on her part. I rode her hard and fast and I swear she came again when I did. She was very vocal and being blind, I was more aware of our pleasure levels. She clung to me until her breathing calmed and she commanded me not to move. We lay motionless for about a minute with her arms and legs wrapped tight around me. And I did as I was told. She guided me off of her and crawled out from under me and jumped off the bed. I could hear the pitter patter of her bare feet running to the bathroom."

"In a moment, I heard Glenda's voice. Glenda soothed me and applied a warm washcloth to my penis. Glenda massaged my penis while the mystery guest dressed in the bathroom. Glenda kept massaging my cock; at least I was sure it was Glenda because she said so. Glenda asked me to be patient."

Jack said that Glenda whispered, "I peeked and I promised not to, and saw the whole thing in the mirror. That was such a beautiful sight, and you were magnificent."

I asked "Are you going to take these rags off my head?"

"Glenda shushed me and the two ladies whispered something. Then there was silence and I heard the mystery lady exit. Glenda had covered my mouth with her hand. I tried to listen to what they said, but alas, I know not what they said."

Glenda said, "Listen, Jack, I have a favor to ask now that we are alone. I have gained twenty pounds having a baby and I am very self-conscious about my body. Watching you was too much excitement for me. I am now so horny. Can I sit on your cock for a few moments while you are still blindfolded? I want you to remember me as I was; I'm embarrassed about how I might look to you."

"I got a second erection with her massaging me, so I said OK. When I felt her ass she was fully dressed except for her bare ass under her skirt. Glenda had a quickie at my expense, she washed me again and when Glenda untied the tight strands, I noticed she was fully dressed and no signs of having sex. I had given her a shot of cumlite and she was quick and it still felt good. Glenda kissed me sweetly and thanked me for the secret service. I am often amazed at how easily aroused we can get with a new pussy climbing on board. I accepted her apology and then asked who the little lady was. I also understood and appreciated how understandable it was for Glenda to spy on us and get horny. She was telling me how much they both enjoyed the experience and how wonderful I was. I liked hearing that so I again asked who the mystery woman was."

"She said, look Jack, please don't ask. She is a good friend and we planned this well in advance. You have met her, but would not remember her. She would be terrified if anybody ever found out what we did, so please don't ask again."

"I made the promise, but figured that someday I would find out. The fascinating thing about this event is that I have no idea who I fucked."

Jack confided in us that so far and what was to be forever, he never found out who the mystery fuck was. In a way, that is special, because Jack's senses were intensified and he felt the "Blind man" novelty was a big turn on. Jack never knew who he fucked and when you think about it, doesn't that make the experience special? Imagine how many people would like to fuck someone and no one would ever know about it including the partner. I think the major lesson when retold is how trustworthy Jack was and the fact that to his dying day he never knew who the mystery lady was.

Carol then interrupted and exclaimed,

"You know, that really is a turn on. I can think of a few guys I would have liked to fuck, but I would never give them the satisfaction of knowing I was interested. Gee, Jack, you opened up a whole new arena of possibilities. Julie and I could probably recruit a few new prospects for you."

Julie then said jokingly, "Jack, can I blindfold you?"

"What for? I already know it's you," replied Jack.

"Well, I just don't want you to see what I want to do," said Julie while grinning.

"Heck, that brings us all to acts of bondage, doesn't it?" I asked.

We all agreed that under the right circumstances bondage might be fun. The problem is one seldom hears of men tying up women. I wonder why?

This raises an interesting point. Does bondage increase one's sensitivities? Does bondage only work for the bonder and not the bondee? I think sadism is too kinky and Jack and I agree that pain should not be part of sex or foreplay, although we have experienced a few women that liked rougher sex. By that I mean a gentle slapping of the labia or maybe spanking that simulated fanny fucking. Sometimes lightly tapping a woman's genitals through clothing can be more effective than rubbing a dry finger against a clitoris. Even contact through silk or cotton panties with gentle massaging usually can lead to more contact. It is like foreplay is comprised of a series of advancing moves. The caution of a woman's acceptance is easily recognizable. The obvious lesson is that the tongue is our most sensitive organ and sensuous sex is always more desirable than hand jobs.

Women masturbating a man with her hands is not very effective. That can be painful unless a girl is really experienced. Such manual sex may work for avoiding menstrual cycle lapses, but if you really want the man to come back for more, oral sex is a great honor for a man to receive before he reaches the intercourse stage. In High School during the early battles of the Great Pube Wars, we guys would settle for rubbing against a woman and ejaculating into our underwear. If we were lucky and overly excited we might get our penises touched by a feminine hand and climaxing would not take much effort. All sex practices evolve. When you reach the right level of sophistication you will enjoy everything more. Your goal should be to never stop learning how to please another. Each person should learn to enjoy giving pleasure. I loved Cynthia's description of how much she enjoyed sucking cock even if she didn't mean it. That statement will forever stimulate me. Foreplay is an art, not a science. I can't repeat that enough.

Actually, to reiterate, many woman can better climax with hard fast strokes and there may be a fine line between rough sex and some effective pelvic slapping. Jack relates that he had occasions to fuck hard and fast for two continuous male orgasms. I think those women simply needed more foreplay. Circumstances will dictate the individual preference. Sex can be so complicated without good communication. Maybe too many lovers are left frustrated feeling a partner climax and being left behind. This is why God made so many individuals and the challenge of good sex is to live by the Golden Rule. If a woman desires hard and fast, she should say so immediately. Then she can hope that that request didn't promote premature ejaculation. Premature ejaculation is almost always a result of a man getting too excited. The best technique is to go for seconds and keep adding foreplay. Otherwise your reputation will not have to beg for a second chance. You better hope you can be so convincing. The best apology for premature ejaculation is to start licking.

Chapter18. Dance With Me Horny?

Carol said, "Well, I have done some weird things that I thought were very exciting, and I don't want you guys to think that I am some kind of "out of control" female predator. I think women ought to be able to have some secret adventures without being judged. To repeat, men get away with anything they want, but women are so restricted by social boundaries, it isn't fair. If we become aggressors, we are considered promiscuous, and how do we know that the guy isn't telling everybody about what he did with any woman and identifying her. We can't control that. I mean, if you give a guy a great fuck, he's out there bragging about how good he was and maybe dropping your name like you were so weak you could not resist him. He might have been a lousy lay while he ruins your good name. Maybe all new male conquests by women should be blindfolded until we decide what to reveal. Women should control the first experiences to decide if there should be any "repeats." At least Jack can't brag about the blind fuck because he doesn't know who it was. Now that is fair, and her reputation is protected. Women can't brag about conquests, period."

Carol continued. "We are defamed unfairly. Hell, we can't even discuss our fantasies with other women without being labeled sluts. Fortunately, I had some close girlfriends that formed our own feminist movement, but never told any guys about it. We discussed much detail about what we wished men could do to us, and not so much about what we wanted to do to men. I wish now we had discussed solutions and how to teach men what was good and what was not. You know, sex is so much more fun if you can get away with something exciting and no one has to broadcast your performance from one point of view and you are thereby judged. It takes more skill for a woman to have an adventure and get away with it. I'll give you an example."

Carol continued, "Last summer after I started on the pill, without my parent's knowledge, we had a big charity ball at our country club. I wasn't a debutant or anything like that, but I was present along with a few other good-looking girl members that were unescorted. We were supposed to just make good scenery and appear as hostesses. We stood around, made charming conversations and danced with guests when asked. It was a formal affair and I had worn a full length skirt, high heels and no stockings because of the heat."

"I was admiring an older man, he was about forty five, slightly graying, but really built. He looked like a movie star. He had broad shoulders and a nice ass. I didn't know if he came with anybody or not, but he was dancing with other older members. This guy reminded me of a Young Gary Cooper. He must have caught me admiring him. I was fantasizing about him and getting turned on by myself. I suspect he caught me staring at him and if I had a cock I'd had an erection. He approached me and asked me to dance. The first dance allowed me to look professional and show off my dance steps and moves. After all, I am a trained professional dancer. He was a great dancer and twirled me around like Fred Astaire. Then the band played a slow dance and we kept dancing. I purposely pressed against him. I gave him the full frontal pelvic bone push and a double-breasted full court press. I was in charge and I knew I was successful because I could feel his erection growing, and I did my best to tease him by using a few well planned pubic rubs. I mean to tell you this guy didn't know what hit him."

"I think I was subtle, but he knew I wanted him. No words were spoken. When the dance was over, I held his hand and led him to the balcony, down the stairs and out to the dark parking lot where I had parked my car. You guessed it, a Cadillac convertible. The convertible top covered the car; it was quite private. Neither of us spoke. He was watching me and I just smiled. I unlocked my car, stood next to the open door and boldly lifted up my full-length skirt and took off my panties while he watched. I casually threw my panties into the front seat. I climbed into the back seat and bared my tan legs from a half standing crunched up position. I was holding my skirt at my waist reflecting my bare pussy and flexed legs in the moonlit back seat. I was semi squatting, which is a real sexy move. He was like putty in my hands."

"This handsome dude pulled the door shut, unbuckled his belt and dropped his pants and with no hesitation sat down in the middle of the back seat. He had bared a magnificent flagpole. He held my hips, and kept my gown out of the physical contact path. I climbed on board, and yes I rubbed his erection against my clit first. When I sat on him we really made eye contact for the first time, but never kissed. Immediately, we were both focusing on each other's genitals. I guess I was trying to stay unruffled and not smear my lipstick. While sitting on his cock and before I began to bounce, I unbuttoned my blouse and bared my breasts unhooking my bra from the front. I buried his face in my breasts, grabbed his neck with both hands and started riding him. I was not bobbing, just sliding on his cock. His cock was nice and fat and hard. He held on to my hips tightly while I did all the work. I engineered my own rub and pumped like crazy. The angle was perfect for me, he tried to buck a little, and I moved one hand to the cloth ceiling. I came, he came, we rested for a moment and we smiled at each other. I reached into the convertible rear well where I kept some paper towels. I lifted my right leg and gave him a paper towel, and stuck one between my legs; he dried himself, which was in itself sexy and pulled up his pants, opened the car door and helped me out. I was closing up my blouse, but carried my panties in my left hand. We again held hands and casually walked back to the hall. He stopped and faced me. He spoke for the first time."

"That was the most spectacular dance of my life. I loved the finish. Thank you for dancing with me." He said, as he bowed.

I said, "You are most welcome, that was also my most spectacular dance ever, and I'm glad you enjoyed my grand finale. I gave him a deep curtsy."

"It was truly unique and spectacular," He said.

"We laughed, never exchanged names and I never saw him again, but my pussy tingled for days. I must have used that experience to fuel many fantasies and I can still close my eyes and dream about that dance and with a little help I can masturbate to an easy climax."

Carol continued, "Please understand that this was a rare event for me. I had gone months with just my vibrator. I can get so horny sometimes and when that happens it is always special because the sexy feeling lasts so much longer as I replay that dance first as foreplay. Even the music makes me horny and I'm not telling anybody what song it was. That's my secret."

"I have several good fantasies in my memory bank and that includes meeting Will for the first time. Will, I want you to know how good that new experience with you was for me. I can count my seductions on one hand. It proves I know when to act and when to pass. When to hold 'em and when to fold 'em. Seducing a man is very exciting, but to pull it off with success, you have to make the guy feel like it was his idea and he thinks me irresistible. That gives a woman terrific satisfaction and certainly a big boost in Ego and one's self confidence. I am not always that aggressive, but when the horny feeling builds up, I have to try and satisfy it. In fact, a good seduction is when the guy thinks he made it happen. I like taking charge. In Will's case I was satisfied because he was a beautiful victim and I gave us a hell of a ride, right Will?"

I actually blushed.

Carol continued, "Now I ask you, do you not think that guy is bragging to his friends about his no name fuck, when I actually was the conqueror. I never told anyone until now. And I never told him my name." Carol smiled.

"You think there is a double standard that favors men? If a man tried that back seat stunt and unbuckled his pants he could be arrested." I noted. "An attractive woman can get away with stuff like that. Perhaps her confidence is that important. Have you ever heard of a sexy woman being denied?" I asked.

Jack asked Julie, "Could you seduce a man like that?"

"I'd be terrified that I'd get hurt or someone would find out, like my Mother following me to the car or something worse. I guess I don't have the nerve or the courage," answered Julie.

"She has a good point. I have no fear, but I also think I could recognize a potential problem. If I was denied an adventure, I would assume the guy was too intimidated to act. It has to be a judgment call, and I don't take chances as often as I'd like. I do fantasize about seducing men more than actually doing it, however."

Carol added. "It makes you wonder about the inequities of sexual adventure. I'm sure there are many who have such fantasies but never act them out. Guys will usually dream on some experience and then masturbate. Do girls fantasize as much and I wonder if they masturbate as much? Are the imaginary partners faceless? There are many things to analyze. There are no accurate statistics about such things. I can tell you I wish anyone of Jack's stories had been about me, and I assure you, I will replay that blindfold story as if it happened to me. This talking is fun."

When the opportunity seemed appropriate, Jack would confess the blind adventure to a new woman dating prospect and their reaction was usually one of exceptional interest in hearing more about the unusual sensuous blind feelings and how he felt about never knowing who the woman was. The story actually served to arouse interest in Jack's vulnerability, which Jack felt might subconsciously make women more curious about him as a victim. If they were aroused by the story it was an obvious favorable introduction. I agree with Jack and I wonder how much mileage I could have gotten if I lied about that experience and pretended it was me.

Carol and I talked a lot more after that night. Carol suggested to me privately that she would like to try some adventures, different positions, different places, and even discuss our separate techniques and how we affected each other with an eye toward expanding our pleasure horizons. We agreed to be both scientific as well as passionate. The stories motivated both of us. Thus it continued, the sexual revolution was in full force. I was recruited as a private single partner.

I later asked Carol what her favorite fantasies were. She said that if at a restaurant, or the country club where the table cloths hung low, and a sexy waiter waited on her even if with someone, she would fantasize that the good looking waiter would sneak under the table and lick her pussy while she ate her favorite meal. I can think of a few waitresses that could have climbed under my table and actually I could create a few fantasies. I just needed to put a face on my fantasies.

Carol also told me that she often dreamed that while showering, a man would be sitting on the shower floor eating her while she shampooed her hair. I am not judgmental, but these fantasies turned me on so that I imagined being the sex slave. I later performed many of these fantasies on my wife as you have already read. And vice versa. Fantasies can fuel a healthy creative sex life. I hope we are providing you with some ideas. There is much more to cum.

Chapter 19. Tease For Two!

Carol and I asked Jack for occasional privacy by appointment and he agreed for the time being that is, until it interfered too much with his sex life. We always were considerate and adjusted and tried to accommodate each other for privacy, but Carol was now a close intimate teammate and it didn't bother us if Jack was on the other side of the curtain studying or having a guest as long as the guest paid us no apparent attention. It was very difficult being quiet, but we were great silent lovers; we could have been studying. And Jack was not being selfish. We were both being considerate giving a priority to who was getting laid and with whom. It turns out that even if Jack were alone and separated from us by only the curtain, he pretended not to notice.

It was only if Jack was with somebody new that our room might look like a brothel. Carol and I discussed our experiences openly with Jack and we agreed to disclose anything unusual or exciting that we might learn or accomplish. The discussions were extremely beneficial because we all were all pursuing knowledge. Obviously the discussions were motivational and arousing. We even discussed our athletic bodies. One time Carol challenged us to a pushup contest, which Jack and I won handily. The three of us talked about penises and sizes and uses and tight pussies and just about anything no matter the level of intimacy. Carol didn't even flinch one time exchanging bathroom passes with Jack when naked. Carol was simply nonchalant about being exposed and Jack tried to be the same. Carol had seen us both naked many times.

One time, Carol brought a dance costume over and danced for Jack and me rather seriously. We had requested the dance. She brought her tap dancing shoes and did a tap dance accompanied by a soft shoe shuffle. She danced in her cheerleading costume. She showed us a few bare footed ballet steps, and some really good imitations of Ginger Rogers and the ultimate sexiest dancer of all time, Tula Finklea, who later changed her name to Cyd Charisse. Actually, Carol had some real talent and she did eventually go on to Broadway after graduation. This particular evening was like three athletes showing off some skills other than shooting baskets. Carol was very professional and her training showed. Her dancing was sexier than our shooting baskets.

A major event occurred soon thereafter that private dance show when Carol insisted on coming with us as one of the guys to visit a strip bar, where Jack wanted to revisit an old girlfriend. She was appearing at this strip club in a nearby town to avoid the on-campus restrictions. We put an old letter jacket on Carol, but she couldn't hide her ponytail under the billed baseball cap, so we obviously had a female guest. With jeans and sneakers and a fat coat she might have passed for a guy except for the ponytail and make up. My letter jacket hid her breasts. But her objective was to present herself as one of the guys. She had never seen a live strip show.

We ordered a beer and observed several dancers strip down to just bikini panties. They were all bare breasted. This was an "eighteen year old" bar serving pizza, low alcoholic beer and no liquor. We were more into making fun of the dancers than lusting and I thought lusting was the general idea. Carol commented on the various breasts as if she was really interested. I think she was just playing with our interest in the dancers pretending she was interested, like one of the guys. I think she was studying our reactions to the various dancers. She did seem interested in their moves. The dancers looked like college age girls. I guess anyone can earn a few bucks however possible.

In the car driving home, Carol asked if we really enjoyed strip teases. We had not frequented such establishments, but who could knock nude beauties wiggling their asses, and yes they did suggest sex acts. Yes, we confessed to being horny as a result of the strippers.

Carol said, "Listen you guys, you haven't seen anything, I could do any of that silly stuff without rehearsing, and I can do a better job. Would you stuff a few bucks in my panties if I did a strip tease for you?"

I tested my machismo and said, "I got something to tuck in your panties."

"Hmmm," muttered Carol, "no coins please, and I suspect you would need a helping hand. I think your tucker needs to be tucked. Are, "go tuck yourself," or 'tuck you" appropriate sayings?"

"You're on," we interrupted her together. We had challenged Carol to perform a strip tease. She seemed thrilled to do so. On the drive home, Carol and I got into some heaving petting in the back seat. She had a few drinks, which seemed to make her hornier. Carol and I were so turned on that we could have had sex, except for the tight clothes and limited time. We were trying to loosen her tight jeans so I could get my hands in her panties when we stopped at our dorm. I had unlocked her jeans and with my hand under her panties was rubbing her bare pussy and she was really wet, so the stripper dances must have made her horny too. I think the whole idea of seeing strippers strip should turn women on. Either that or we raised a competitive interest in Carol. She acted like she had to prove something; perhaps that she could turn us on to a greater degree. We arrived home too soon and that left Carol and I with "foreplay interruptus." We made ourselves copasetic and the three of us went to our room.

Carol was now anxious and had risen to the challenge. She was determined to show off and tease us big time. She was not embarrassed and was about to strip from tight jeans, blouse and a fat letter jacket. She took off her sneakers before beginning. She was barefoot. The cheerleading uniform would have been more effective as a stripping garment, but alas, we could not wait for that trip to her room for a change of clothes.

We were her teammates and good buddies, except we owned complimentary parts, and our relationship was about to get more subjective. We owned "tab A, and she had a great slot, B." This was to be Jack's first total exposure to this amazing talented nude supple body. Carol was to strip to our soon to be well used record of "Night Train." Our three-way relationship had become a sports jock thing with open conversations readily exchanging the raunchiest of jokes and comments. So, Carol had no second thoughts about stripping in front of us. She felt privileged being in a threesome of jocks that all had nice bodies. However there was to be a transformation of attitudes from teammates to sex object. I'm sure that is what Carol wanted.

We had asked Carol what made men sexy and she said attitude first, eyes, smiles, then shoulders, chest and a nice ass. She admired muscle definition, which Jack and I surely had. Basketball is much like ballet except our moves are unrehearsed. You can rehearse basketball plays, but the opponent's reaction and game circumstances is unpredictable. Carol also thought penises were magnificent. Those were her words and such a comment made us more confident in someday exposing ourselves to women in private, of course. I don't think any man would gain recognition by simply taking out his penis, Bill Clinton excepted.

The dance was sensational to say the least with Jack and me cheering her on and making all the motivational exclamations that complimented her very good dance steps. Remember, we are in very close quarters. At one point Carol was dancing in the open letter jacket with only panties showing. She would hide her face and peek out from under the coat when flashing her bare breasts. I think she had seen strip teases somewhere in her past. She would flash her breasts in a very professional teasing manner until she finally took off the jacket. I loved the way her ponytail bounced with her breasts.

Carol confided in me later that she had practiced in front of a mirror when she was younger and into daily dance lessons. She was far more professional than the dance hall girls. Each time she removed an article of clothing she would toss it around and throw it at one of us, or hit us with her panties. I think what got her even more motivated was the heavy petting session we had in the back seat while Jack drove us home. I had my fingers inside her and that left her frustrated; it was not intentional, but now working in our favor. So Carol had sex on her mind and coupled with the potential excitement of having fun teasing her best friends made for a very hot sexy dance. You can assume she had been adequately "foreplayed." Carol could bump and grind like a pro!

Carol wiggled out of the tight jeans while moving her ass in bumps and grinds to the music. Carol was licking a lollipop, of all things, and she gave us the impression that she was pretending it was a lemon-flavored cock. When barefoot, she did a little soft shoe shuffle while taking off her bra, va . . . . .voom, there they were. Gorgeous heaps of well nippled flesh. Carol could flex her chest muscles and make her breasts rise up. She waved her arms over her head swaying with the fast beat. She danced with the sucker stick sticking out of her mouth, and occasionally she would suck on it like she was performing fellatio. Both the licking and sucking was sexy. Remember, Carol is only six feet away from us. It is a small room, so the closeness is an added attraction, much closer than the strip tease club. We did not touch her. I guess that was a carry forward from the dance club.

I wonder if she planned the lollipop trick, or if it was spontaneous. Where did the lollipop come from? And her breasts were too firm to spin or wave, but she sure could move them; her breasts looked even better when she raised her hands over her head and waved her arms about with the music. She even did a handstand with the splits

191

while only wearing panties. Her breasts did not fall. She was really enjoying showing off for her good buddies.

Then, Carol began doing an intermittent lap dance on me. I was sitting in my desk chair next to my bed. While she kept moving, she rose not missing a beat, pulled off my pants and lap danced on my underwear. She then slipped out of her panties, as a grand finale for the strip dance. That's when she slapped us both with her panties. Her ass was practically in Jack's face, as she never missed a beat. Finally, she laid her panties on Jack's head.

I was wrong, that was not the end of the tease. That was unexpected since the dance hall girls did not strip completely. Jack stopped clapping and the music stopped. There was a very quiet silence and Carol was the focus of everything, we were watching her and she was admiring our erections, which were now exposed. Jack had taken Long John out of his pants so he could better see what was going on. Exposing Long John was a form of applause and obviously a tact to urge Carol on to greater heights. The room was only lit by a single candle. Carol was really turned on and seeing our erections did motivate her. She was playing a very aggressive controlling role. She was covered with beads of perspiration. I loved her confidence and I really was proud that Carol was so uninhibited in our company. But then, so were we obviously uninhibited.

Carol sat on my lap facing Jack, took the lollipop out of her mouth and passed it between her labia. She sort of combed her pussy with the lollipop while licking it intermittently. Jack said he saw her lift and spread her legs and poke the sucker into her vagina a few times, while she wrapped her other arm around my neck and was kissing me thus stretching her breasts. That action really features a woman's breasts. Then she would put the sucker in my mouth for a few pulls. There was no music, and Carol was acting the sexiest of roles as if in a silent movie. She made no sounds. This was truly sexier than the previous strippers. If it was a silent porno movie, it was superior because of the mutual passion. Porno movies are so mechanical and the sounds are usually dubbed in after the fact. This dance would have made a best-selling porno movie.

While still facing Jack, Carol began sort of an Arabic sideways head movement and continued moving her arms ballet style. She reached under herself, turned around, put her moving ass toward Jack, pulled off my underwear, found my cock, and sat on my cock while facing Jack. She mounted me with the traditional labia rub and the gentle sit while we all watched our genitals greet each other. She continued the dance moves with her arms and hips while sitting on my cock and waved the lollipop at Jack. It was dark, but not that dark and Jack was only a few feet away. Carol made Jack lick the lollipop. She was bobbing up and down on my cock and had a very serious look on her face. She starting having an orgasm facing away from me and she began vigorously rubbing the lollipop against her clitoris. Jack felt his erection would burst just watching. Carol hooked my neck and kissed me on the mouth and did not let go while she reached an orgasm. When she felt me coming, she pressed and rubbed the sucker harder against her clitoris causing a mutual orgasm while Jack kept watching.

Carol could not help making short gasping sounds, which seemed to prolong her orgasm. Carol had developed the ability of making her orgasms last longer than normal. She would gasp with short panting breaths with intermittent moans. She could make her orgasm last for a full minute and that is rare. She later told me that with a vibrator her orgasms were too fast and that the foreplay made the climaxes better. Carol did not usually climax during sex when she was on the bottom, but she sure knew her way when riding a cock horse, even backwards as she just did. We had no idea what role the sucker played but it was an added stimulus. I think the lollipop representing a tongue and she was enjoying a fucking orgasm accompanied by cunnilingus. If that was spontaneous, it was spectacular!

Jack had exposed his erection and was playing with himself. Carol leaned forward and while sitting on my spent but still hard cock kept sucking on the lollipop and was eyeing Jack's exposed penis. She watched him play with himself as if she had never witnessed such an act.

Carol broke the silence and just before going down on Long John apologized, "Oh Jack, I'm so sorry to see you like this. Will and I have both had great orgasms and you know my rules. I only fuck Will, but I will give you a "best friend blow job if that will help."

Jack quickly stood up in front of Carol, who was still sitting on my cock. Carol proceeded to give Jack a nice blowjob. Jack looked a bit wobbly while standing. Strange thing, she rubbed the sticky lollipop on Jack's most sensitive nerve. She also rubbed the sucker under his testicles. When Jack was climaxing Carol bounced on my spent cock that never went soft as if she was participating in Jack's orgasm. She also rubbed the lollipop on her clitoris when Jack was coming. She swallowed Jack and hummed while doing so, making a delicious sound. When finished, she licked her lips, licked the lollipop, looked up at Jack and said.

"Do you feel better now? I know how frustrating that scene must have been for you, but Will got to me in the car and I couldn't wait to end the dance so I could fuck him. You understand what happened don't you? I am sorry to have left you frustrated, and I hope you feel relieved."

Jack pretended to stagger back to his bed and collapsed. Jack said' "I have never had such a good friend do that to me. You are a super buddy. Thank you."

After we came down from the mutual high, we had to ask, "What was with the sucker?"

"Oh that," said Carol. "Well, that trick goes back many years and this is the first time anybody saw me do that. When I first reached puberty I was exceptionally horny and I didn't know what was going on. One time I was by myself, obviously, trying to see myself in a mirror and I was sucking on this sucker. So I touched it to my clitoris, which was at that time only the best spot to touch on my body, and I wasn't sure why. But my pussy was slippery and the sucker was sticky and had a nice tongue like feel to it. The texture was very stimulating, so I began my pre-vibrator era. I have to wash myself down with clear water when done, I don't know why. The sticky sugar might have been uncomfortable, but the cool water also enhanced my fun. Sometimes I would use the sucker and water at the same time, which required some body flexing. When I was in high school, the kids made fun of me telling me to grow up and give up candy suckers. Little did they know what I could do with a lollipop. It still is an easier way to come than just using a finger. Sometimes the lemon flavor tingles more than other flavors. I later tried a mentholated cough drop and that did tingle more. Jack, what did you feel when I suckered you?"

"That felt like a tongue to me, and it might have got me off except for the desire to keep me warm and wet. I don't think I'll start using suckers, but we can keep a supply here for you hoping we can have more lollipop parties." Jack grinned.

Jack excused himself to the shower and Carol asked, "I feel you still are hard, how about you climb on me and give me a hard fast fuck. I hate to see an erection go to waste. I think I am so wound up I might even come with you. I think that dancing turned me on more than you guys."

"I don't think so, but I am ready again, lie down here."

Carol and I were going at it hard when Jack came out of the shower. He watched for a few moments admiring the show and then turned away, probably with another erection. He went to bed.

After Carol showered and left, I thought about what women did to masturbate. I wondered if my fingers being used on my high school girlfriends in the early days had any positive effects. Certainly the ladies were not going to suggest anything. I wonder how popular I might have been if I sucked on suckers in my early days and while making out tried to get a lollipop between some unsuspecting girl's legs. I think that would have been just as perverse as suggesting my tongue, or maybe suggesting both. I'm sure I would have been on post office "wanted posters," offering a reward for the capture of the lollipop pervert with my picture sucking a lollipop.

Jack and I often discussed what an amazing woman Carol was. She truly was like one of the guys, but no comparison regarding sexual maturity. She seemed sexually advanced compared to us, yet not promiscuous. Her athletic ability was certainly in our class. Every time I saw her doing her flips during time outs, I thought about how great she looked naked. Shame on me being distracted from the game even if only for a moment. Obviously the memory of that dance is firmly implanted in my mind. I found myself more aroused after a game and no matter how tired I was; I appreciated having this cheerleader in my bed.

What has stayed with us is a new curiosity about inhibitions. Do all women have such potential buried in their attitudes? I believe with compliments and a lot of licking, during that interval between cunnilingus and intercourse lovers would perform many uninhibited acts. This is another way to prolong sex. Most people think the pleasures of sex do not last long enough. I think experimenting and changing positions also enhances each sexual event. It may be difficult to interrupt extreme passion because converting from passionate sex to sport sex may be difficult once motivated and acting. Also, too many men have the uncontrollable urge to fire their weapons to feel the "big bang." They don't want to interrupt their climax, or they may lose the final punch. This type of control takes practice. Married couples should talk about games after the passion begins to slow during longer relationships. These joys of sex require energy and too many lovers are tired. This is what makes sex routine and couples should contemplate sport commingled with therapeutic sex.

Therapeutic sex requires a whole new agenda. Some tired couples lie together sixty-nine and alternate giving each other oral orgasms. The woman should always climax first. The man comes second before he dozes off. It's a gentle way to relax. Stay clean. How did I get from the sexy dance to "sixty nine?" I'm not that well organized; this is my first book.

Chapter 20. Three is company

That strip tease event opened up another new sequence of sex experiences. Jack and I moved our mattresses to the middle of the floor when preparing for, perhaps once a week threesome games. When Carol came to spend the evening, she never spent the night. When we were feeling especially scientific, Carol and I would try unusual positions and sometimes allow Jack to watch and even orchestrate some positions. It was more of a sport, or game than serious sex. Actually fooling around with Jack sometimes present was a form of foreplay often stalling real orgasms. Carol, being a contortionist was a major contributor, and humor plays a major role here. Sometimes we felt like we were posing for cartoons. We tried many impossible things. Often we would end up laughing and making fun at some of our attempts.

After Carol and I had passionate sex, Carol would sometimes give Jack a blowjob if we all got too worked up, but Jack never expected it. It amazed us that she could be so casual about giving oral sex to Jack. I watched and when her cheeks would flex when Jack was coming, I would get hornier. Carol would often comment that she could only do it to Jack because we were such trusted friends, but then, she was getting her share of licks prior to such aftermath activity. She just didn't think giving Jack a blowjob was a big deal. It didn't seem like sex to her rather just an accommodation preferable to Jack's masturbation. However, I noticed she was only receptive to any fooling around or game playing only after she was sexually satisfied. Sometimes I thought she could never be satisfied. The three of us became even closer and loved discussing these experiments.

A few times Carol and I would play what would be defined as roughhousing games. Wrestling one on one with Carol with me trying to fuck her. I even did a little tickling and Carol a little cock grabbing. It was just a naked couple fooling around. Jack served as a referee and one time he held Carol down while I fucked her. I held her legs apart so only our genitals made contact. It was simulated rape, more like bondage, but with her consent. She was trying to see if she could forcibly prevent entry and we did more laughing than fucking. She was not allowed to bite, strict rules. As to moral judgments, you decide.

We once experimented with threesome acts involving me fucking Carol from behind while she performed fellatio on Jack, but only as a final act, and, as I said, Carol was more receptive to threesomes after she had been satisfied with our private sex. One time when I was performing oral sex on Carol, she was performing oral sex on Jack. I didn't mind because Jack's involvement kept the threesome at a sexual arms length saving my conscience from hiding these exceptional experiences from Cynthia, my high school girlfriend. These games were objective and not so serious as relationship builders. We were taking advantage of experiments for later use in life.

These threesomes occurred after basketball season when Jack was dating less. Julie was still a factor, but required condoms, so Jack was considered a safer participant by Carol when not being so sexually risky. Jack no longer brought Julie to our place since she had her own private room in another dormitory. Julie was not aware of our experiments. These games were not as frequent as I will now relate, I don't want to give the impression that we were obsessed with sex. It was fun that was driven by fun when it would first start. I would estimate there were only about three big sessions altogether, but a few separate sessions that were shorter in length.

Guys need experience to benefit future relationships and these games should not be considered harmful. These scientific games were not comparable to orgies or drunken orgies. I think we more resembled wrestling matches than heated sex. It makes sense that such experience would benefit future relationships, but again, the double standard comes into play. A man might resent knowing his girlfriend had too much experience. Obviously, Ego's do come into play. Actually women participating in such games is unlikely because of a lack of trust, but Carol was right, there was a double standard and our activities had to be kept confidential. Some women think they have to present themselves as innocent and inexperienced to win a relationship with a man. I think the new trend towards women's liberation was changing all that. I don't think any woman would want a future relationship to know about how many learning experiences she had. Perhaps men should not brag on his past to a future wife.

We advanced to playing these few games initially as pragmatic or sporty, but eventually turning into passion. We tried athletic positions as if a non-existent judge challenged us. One time Carol did the naked "crab walk." She put her legs over her elbows and could walk on her hands. She could bend her head under her arms and backed onto my cock, which I held in place. She could then bob her ass on my cock pivoting on her arms without losing her balance. The position worked like a teeter-totter and we could both watch our genitals perform. It was very sexy and seemed to tighten Carol's pussy whenever we tried flexed positions. That was really something. I don't think the average married couple should try such moves. We sure talked them out in detail. Jack did not participate, but sometimes watched.

One time, when I was kissing Carol while she was naked in my bed, she spread her legs wide and was caressing her pussy while I was kissing her. She was almost masturbating, or fore playing herself. To her surprise, Jack sneaked over and began to lick her pussy. She pushed me away to see who was doing what to her and she liked it. Carol had already had an oral climax with me, but the newness of Jack's tongue brought her quick seconds. A new tongue urged her on with a new passion and the sporting games were forgotten. As a result of Jack's foreplay I was then ridden hard with Carol immediately climbing on me; she had a great ride with my holding her ass so I wouldn't lose her. This time, Jack was lying on his back watching her fuck me and petting Long John. Carol rolled off and there was Jack lying on his back, stretching his foreskin hoping for a blowjob. The erect hard cock was too tempting for Carol. Carol rolled over to Jack and surprised us both by squatting on his cock. She dropped down, put her hands on his shoulders like clutching a horse's mane, and rode him hard and he came quickly. Carol was perspiring and was beaded with jeweled like droplets. She rolled over on her back exhausted and said:

"Well, that was the first time I ever fucked two guys and I came twice while riding two magnificent cock horses. I couldn't help myself. Are you guys OK with that?"

"Sure," I blurted. I was thinking to myself that Jack's involvement would assure me that Carol would not have a change of heart and talk about a love relationship. Yet, I could not deny that I loved her. It was a different kind of love. I kept that thought to myself and never expressed it. The next several weeks, with the school year winding down, consisted of the three of us trying to take advantage of this amazing athlete with some real contortionist's moves. Perhaps, a total of four threesome sessions over a six-week period.

One time Carol also tried doing the splits and bobbed on my cock, that did not work well. Now that really seemed tight. Carol tried letting me fuck her standing up, but I was too tall. She then did some splits and exposed herself upside down while standing on her head, but I couldn't fuck her when she was in that position. But it made for some interesting cunnilingus. I had to sit in a chair to do that.

We tried the "wheelbarrow" position with Carol supporting herself on her hands while being fucked from behind. With her great body strength she could actually push off a chair and make for a "tighter" situation, but I was too tall and that test did not work well either. Carol had the ability to flex muscles most of us didn't know we had. Not everything worked and we did laugh at the failed attempts to fuck. We tried me fucking her while the Jack enjoyed receiving oral sex, but in an unusual athletic position. Carol tried to sit on my cock facing me while bending over backwards and sucking on Jack while she was upside down. We could have been porno stars. Once we both performed in succession by holding Carol's hips and fanny fucking her pussy while she bent over a chair. She could not be worn down, she was too athletic, but a fun challenge to see how long we could last with hard and fast rear-ending her vagina. We only did that once to get her feedback on fanny fucking. It was more like an athletic event. That was not so passionate, but a perspiring Carol said she loved the action. She acted like it was a natural workout at a gym.

Carol said she really enjoyed doggy style, but not for orgasms. She said the hard and fast flapping against her ass felt great. She was not aware of her "G" spot and at this time of the sexual revolution, "G" spots were not that discussed.

One time, I was even interrupted studying when she appeared next to my desk upside down, naked with her legs apart. The thought of a public drinking fountain came to mind. I leaned over and gave her a few licks. She could not reach an orgasm in that position because she said it was too strenuous. But a stand up version of cunnilingus was doable, and we could do it. She could squat anywhere with amazing resilience. Carol could squat on my desk for licks while I sat in my chair. That move always interrupted study habits. Sounds like weird stuff, but, damn it was exciting.

I don't think we did anything perverted, nor did that question arise. And, as I said, this was not a nightly series of events. The majority of the time Carol just came over to study with me and spent some bedtime alone with me. The fun and games were often spontaneous and more often not on school nights. The school year was winding down. I'm just summarizing some of them for expediency and to get on to the grand finale, our final session with Carol.

What you are hearing about is a very rare set of circumstances where a woman athlete became "one of the guys" and just happened to have the same sex drives as a man. Carol was truly one of us and as long as our relationship was confidential it was deemed unique. Jack participated more later in the year when he wasn't involved with other coeds. That was a cleanliness rule. There was one time when Jack had a date and did not have sex, which was a common experience in spite of what you might deduce from this book. Jack was raving about how he was teased and frustrated while I was driving us home from a party. While he was relating his frustration, Carol opened his fly, took out his cock and gave him a quick blowjob to release stress. It was more of an accommodation rather than a sex act and she performed kneeling on the car floor with three of us in the front seat and me driving. Carol never fucked Jack without doing me first and without her having an orgasm either with my tongue or riding me. I didn't count, but I would guess she fucked Jack about four times in my presence. They were never alone. That was an example of the kind of consideration you could get from really good friends. Carol and I had great sex later after that oral gesture. By the way, Carol often showered before and after sex and that included mouth and pussy hygiene.

I again pondered hormonal balances for both men and women. Did Carol have more testosterone than most women? She was definitely heterosexual and knowing her so well I never heard her mention any curiosity about experimenting with other women. I had read that women can sometimes experiment with each other and neither of them had to be Lesbians. This was a whole new area that I knew nothing about, but it is a universal belief that all men would like to watch beautiful women perform sexual acts with each other.

We also had informative discussions on sex including masturbation. Carol felt she had masturbated more than most women. She had many questions about our masturbation habits. She had us both demonstrate our handling ourselves, but not to an orgasm. Carol felt that stroking a penis and pulling the skin over the gans (helmet) might be a worthwhile skill for her. She tested what was too tight a grip and what action was too fast. Carol tried to masturbate Jack hard and fast and he did ejaculate, but told her she held him too hard. The climax felt good, but more of a novelty. Carol said she hoped she would not have to use her hands in the future anyway.

After our many experiments, we discussed the sensitivities of foreplay. We compared the force behind masturbation, that the force behind the masturbation was more a powerful orgasm, but short-lived. That was debatable. It was also true with her vibrator. Her orgasms were more powerful, but less sensuous than masturbating with self-foreplay. One time Carol showed us her vibrator and we watched her climax. Then she put a little vibration on our cocks, but it was too much vibration. We tried using the vibrator behind my testicles while I was working her pussy with tongue or cock. It was a distraction. Sometimes good sex cannot be rushed.

We concluded that "self foreplay" and sex toys when unaccompanied by partners should involve fantasizing. Our conclusion was that masturbation was also an acquired skill, or an art form, and was a contributing factor to a good sex life. We thought that these many adventures would someday serve as fantasies and perhaps our recounting these experiences will fill your fantasy requirements. That is one reason why I am giving the reader so much detail. Masturbation as a substitute for the real thing will eventually improve your sex life, and even better with sexy fantasies.

Carol taught us that cunnilingus was the most important skill for a man. She was a great teacher. Carol would provide us details on how to use our tongues. She would tell us how fast to lick and what direction to push her skin between her legs with our tongues. She helped us master the slight sucking technique on her clitoris so as to not be too gentle. We later learned that sensitivities were different with each pussy and only by experimenting and communicating would we be successful. Some clitorises were more sensitive and some much less. Women's orgasms were to be of different durations, but the important thing we learned was to communicate about sex with the idea of making sex more pleasurable. Reciprocity was a reward beyond description. Never, never stop licking until directed to do so.

Carol was also a good student in the art of "blow-jobs." She paid strict attention to our instructions and reactions. Fellatio and playing with cocks were fairly standard operations for most women. It was more acquiring the skill of prolonging men's orgasms. That simply means that men should not be in a rush. Fellatio is primarily a method of foreplay and women need to know when to stop to prevent a premature firing, unless that is the objective. Foreplay involves more tongue teasing than sucking.

The advantage of knowing Carol was exceptional in all ways. She truly thought like a man, but with pure feminist sex drives. I wondered how many men she would meet that accepted her attitude. She knew many men at college and her conversations were flirty, but not outrageous and she only shared sex with the two of us. I doubt she fucked another classmate besides Jack and me. I believe most of her skills were natural and were developed with her extraordinary imagination.

Later in life Jack and discussed women who were so sought after, were so attractive that they became spoiled. They were so spoiled that they felt reciprocity was not necessary on their part. They felt that "giving up" a piece of their precious ass was all they had to do. There are also some men that feel insulted if asked to perform oral sex on a woman. It was as though they were so spoiled that foreplay on a new partner was not necessary. They think their cocks have all the appeal required and just getting it inside a woman and firing was to be a big thrill for the woman. I hope no readers are in these categories. Remember the golden rule about sex . . . . do unto others . . . .

Chapter 21. Tease and Sympathy

More recent studies conducted in the 21st century begin to define the clitoris and vagina as being part of the same organ. I once read where it was referred to as the "vaginal complex." The little fibers clumped together in the clitoris may attach themselves about three and a half inches into the vagina. The question raised was to what could women feel with their vaginas? There are conflicting theories. Women often complain that they are being cheated during sexual intercourse because there wasn't enough feeling in their vaginas. They don't feel as much pleasure as men. The most frequent complaint from women is that they have trouble achieving orgasms during sexual intercourse. Since our experiences are limited compared to larger scientific studies we can only give you the benefit of our experiences.

If women couldn't feel as much as men, Jack and I often wondered why women seemed so anxious to spread their legs and try for that "filled up" feeling if they lacked any feeling at all. Surely they could feel a penis moving inside them. We feel confident that women can feel the end of a penis stroke because of the closeness of the clitoral contact at the completion of a thrust. I guess the mechanics of sexual intercourse will never be completely understood by men, or even women for that matter, otherwise, why did God put the clitoris so far from the vaginal contact? Why didn't God put the clitoris inside the vagina? I suspect women's sex drive had to be more restrained to emphasize foreplay and intimacy.

The facts are that every individual has a different hormone balance. Do hormones have anything to do with vaginal feelings? I honestly don't know. I do believe that hormone levels make up the libido. The libido is defined as the psychic drive or energy specifically as that associated with sexual desire. I'd like to believe that women with higher testosterone levels and therefore a bigger libido would have more sensitive genitals. I realize that statement supports the theory that the brain is still our major sex organ. In fact all studies conclude that our brains are our main source of pleasure. That means we can all improve our sex lives by better understanding and better communication skills. Our premise is that if the brain is our main sex organ then this book will stimulate your brain.

Why do most women claim they cannot feel enough with their vaginas? I have never seen that percentage statistic as to how many women were tested about the sensitivity of the vaginal complex, but what should the percentage be, half, or 75%, and how many women were polled in these scientific journals? We believe that vaginal sensitivity will make a difference if the clitoris were engorged. Doesn't that mean that the objective surveys should be conducted after cunnilingus?

Our experiences found that an engorged clitoris enhanced a woman's pleasure and that was most important for good sexual intercourse. We also found that an engorged clitoris can pretty much take care of itself during intercourse if it becomes overly sensitive. It will voluntarily cover itself or expand to adjust to the many degrees of physical contact, wet or too wet or the desire for more direct contact. The clitoris is far more sensitive than a penis. It is just less mobile.

Sex always feels good for women as long as there is foreplay. That doesn't mean it is not uncommon for women to desire intercourse with a "jump start" without foreplay, but orgasms get more important with continued relationships. In other words partners must deliver the goods if they want to maintain a long-term relationship. Flirting can be foreplay.

We never understood if foreplay, or fucking felt better to a woman if her vagina were stretched. In other words, was a fat cock better than a long cock? Our studies found that the fatter the penis the more pleasurable the sex for a woman. I suspect a pussy feels tighter with a fat cock, but only women can determine which is more important. It appeared that a fat cock stretched a vagina more and that might increase vaginal sensitivity. Also a fat cock would tend to pull the clitoris closer to the vagina for better contact with a pumping cock. According to women we talked to, it was impossible to tell the length of a man inside them. The first contact between cock and pussy is also important because most women can feel that first thrust that opens her up and initially pulls the clitoris toward the stroking. No woman we talked to said length was better, or made a difference. Clitoral contact was always the most important factor. Most women don't care about penis size; it is the overall performance that counts!

Jack had a female friend (Glenda) previously discussed, that when gossiping with her girlfriends about this foreign guy who bragged he could wear a wrist watch around his cock, the girls requested Jack's help in a little experiment. Jack's old friend, Glenda, planned to ask to see the fat cock and wanted Jack to approach the car at the right moment so she could escape the event without any repercussions. She wanted to report back to her drinking girlfriends and Jack's role and physical presence would make the inquiry safe. She approached the guy at the bar and simply asked if she could see his cock and the wrist watch trick. He took Glenda to his car in the parking lot and Jack watched to see where they went. He went looking for Glenda at just the right time interrupting the moment; the guy did a quick cover up before Jack got closer. The guy did put his watch around his hard cock. That was the end of that story, but continued to raise the issue as to how important fat is to how long. Length makes no difference, only foreplay does. Penis size has nothing to do with good foreplay. Foreplay makes a man a good lay, not his cock! Foreplay trumps fat cocks.

It should be noted that during cunnilingus, if a man pushed his fingers into a vagina it would stretch the skin bringing the clitoris closer to the vagina. Strangely enough, the three-fingered poke did not affect female orgasms in our experiences; it was all in the tongue action. I don't think we can make any generalized conclusions because again the excitement of the moment may change or enhance the feelings emanating from the brain. I wonder if when a woman masturbates, does she have a desire to stretch her vaginal opening? I don't think so, but again, our sample groups are limited even though very subjective. The women with good sex lives who confided in us masturbated often, but did not play with their vaginas when masturbating. Many women enjoy cunnilingus more by stretching their own labia while her man performs. It makes the clitoris stick out more.

It may be a different set of conclusions when vibrators are used, I have only seen in porno movies where women will use two vibrators, one vibrating the clitoris and the other simulating fucking. We never met a woman that admitted to using two vibrators, but remember, our sample is small, but subjective.

Carol Mason discussed this with me and claimed that when she masturbated she didn't bother touching her vagina. She did admit that a man's caressing fingers in and around the vagina during cunnilingus was more sensuous. She also admitted that "stretch" pressure on the vagina felt good during intercourse. Carol felt that it was easier to climax during intercourse if she had an orgasm with cunnilingus first. I think that is a general foregone conclusion.

Carol described her best vibrator as having a "head" on it that resembled a golf tee. The cup at the end of the tube attached to her vibrator had a deeper head that could surround her clitoris. The vibrator offered speed choices. The theory being that vibration surrounding her clitoris was more effective and avoided direct contact with the head of the clitoris. Direct clitoral contact brought her to an orgasm too quickly and made her clitoris too sensitive. She obviously controlled the vibrating tool and could make it perform any way she wanted. She said she preferred the slow "surround sound feeling."

Carol claimed her best orgasms during oral sex when performed on her occurred when I pinched her clitoris ever so gently between my tongue and my front teeth. The gentle pinching was like a gentle flicking but with the clitoris caught between tongue and teeth. With this technique, there was little contact with the head of the clitoris. I learned to do that when she was finally reaching a climax because that technique made her climax last longer. As long as I kept flicking Carol would continue her orgasm, but within limits. This technique extended and accentuated her pleasure, and in my experience was an individual thing that only worked for Carol. What I did resulted in a flipping action that was constant, and I thought was too intense. Carol said that once she began her orgasm the harder pressure felt good, especially since the action prolonged her orgasm. I have since learned that some clitorises get too sensitive to touch during a woman's orgasm. We learned to blow gently on a sensitive clitoris as it came down from the high.

This tongue and teeth technique worked very well for Carol Mason after only the first few trials. I could sustain her orgasm for more than a minute and that is a long time for an orgasm. I noticed that other women could not withstand such hard tongue action. I believe every woman has a different level of sensitivity and that feeling has to be worked out between partners. It requires a type of trial and error to find the right moves for each woman. Jack once performed cunnilingus on a woman whose clitoris was as big and hard as the end of his thumb. This woman only reacted to hard pressure, almost a bite before reaching an orgasm. Again, I don't believe our sample is large enough to draw any conclusions other than no two pussies are exactly alike.

Orgasms are measured in seconds. Everybody either imagines or hopes for orgasms to last for minutes. Carol often had uncontrolled hip movement during cunnilingus, which can do serious damage to a guy's nose. I had to keep a hand on her pelvic bone to protect my nose. When her clitoris became too sensitive, I would blow on her clitoris for a few moments, and she could eventually start over and go for multiple orgasms if patient. The usual reaction was a strong desire to be fucked. The interesting thing about Carol was that she could go for multiple orgasms after a brief respite even after fucking. The good news was that second orgasms only made her want to fuck more. It could become an endurance contest, which men cannot win. Nothing wrong with that, huh?

Once again, I believe Carol's testosterone level was abnormally high. It was an enigma that she was so feminine, yet horny like a guy. I wonder how many women would admit to such urges. I wondered if there was any way to treat women with hormones, or take a pill before sex like Viagra. I read where Viagra can enlarge a clitoris. Viagra didn't exist during the sexual revolution.

Obviously you hear about some women just not being in the mood. Think about it; what does it take to get a man in the mood? Men are so easy. But there are some women who will never say no and some who seldom say yes. This will always be a man's challenge. It is difficult for a man to accept rejection from one he loves. Yet women can reject sex from someone they love. This raises an interesting question, which we felt was related to a woman's hormone levels and her time of the month. Is having a partner readily available reduce the desire or cause routine. Routine is a nasty sex policy, it comes off as inconsiderate. Couples should routinely kiss each other "goodnight." The adage is, "never go to sleep angry or stressed. Sex can be therapeutic and even "make up sex" can be passionate.

Some people believe women climax better during a full moon. Hmmm. Women have more water in their bodies than men. Men supposedly have more muscle. These opposites should be compatible. Is there such a thing as a "tidal fuck?" Perhaps that lunar "pull" promotes romance. Such is the sustenance of romantic novels. Maybe there is such a thing as a "lunar orgasm." Why not give it a try.

In conclusion, recent findings concluded that the clitoris retracts itself during intercourse in order to protect itself from possible damage from men's pelvic bones or penis hilts. In my humble opinion, women have better sex regardless if it is oral or intercourse when the clitoris is engorged. So, we disagree with some of the professional sex scientists.

I would like to interject a most important rule about cunnilingus. Never, I say never, never stop licking until you get a signal to stop. There is nothing worse during sex or foreplay to stop an act when your partner might be about to climax. If you guys can imagine that while getting oral sex your partner stops when you are about to climax, how would you feel? Cunnilingus is often performed as foreplay, not intended for finality, and only may be an intermediate step moving towards intercourse. Unless your partner has easy vaginal orgasms, you may be robbing her of her chance for an orgasm. Remember, sex is an art, much more so than a science. Biofeedback is imperative.

Another point for the ladies about cunnilingus, you cigarette smokers should be aware that tobacco tastes are transferred to the vagina. Often times the excitement of any partner's reaction or passion may overcome tastes and odors, but if to be performed regularly, I would make cleanliness a priority. I mean, would you garlic up prior to possible sexual encounters? Many spicy foods can also be detected in any person's body, mostly emanating from skin. In my opinion, sex is much better on an empty stomach. Sex is by far better when sober or not drugged. We believe that the notion that sex when drunk or high on drugs is a myth. If both partners are drunk how would they know if sex is better? The chemicals may make them more uninhibited or enhance the mood. I also read later in life that Viagra works better on an empty stomach for older guys.

I personally like the clean natural taste of a passionate woman. Is it an insult when propositioning a woman to ask if you can taste her? You may get your face slapped, but I guarantee she is thinking that over. That is not a likely offer for a first date, but should be a good test of attitude after positive preliminaries. A woman's natural taste should be a motivator for men. I even prefer a hot pussy taste to any hint of soap. Women should only clean their pussies with clear water, but I have no scientific evidence for that conclusion. I have also read that under unusual conditions, whatever that may be, a woman can clean herself with a dab of toothpaste. Toothpaste kills bacteria and the mouth and vagina have similar characteristics. Minty flavors might be too much of a tingle and I'll discuss "minty" sex later. We have a minty sex experience to relate.

Jack and I have enjoyed eating a lot of pussy and I personally feel that when a woman climaxes with my tongue, I can feel the sensation through my entire body, even to the point of possibly ejaculating. There is the same theory that many women, when more passionate, will experience a "mini" orgasm when bringing her partner to orgasm. I have had women tell me that they feel a different type of orgasm when a man comes in her mouth.

There will always be the controversy over the taste of sex. Semen is salty and resembles lump free caviar. Pussy is also slightly salty or sometimes fishy, but taste is related to diet. When people are passionate their taste buds become neutralized. Bathing prior to sex is not always convenient, but a quick rub of rubbing alcohol around the genitals is helpful. Remember the use of hair treatments on pubic hair lasts a good 24 hours. It is also possible for a woman to swallow semen without tasting it. Swallow quickly and swallow saliva afterwards. And men can always apply their own saliva to pussy, the fluids are compatible. Mother nature has provided us with glands that secrete stimulating odors. Men supposedly release body odors that attract women; clean men perhaps more so. Perhaps an attitude adjustment is needed. You have to think sexy.

On the other hand, is there anything that is more disappointing than when your partner performs oral sex with hesitation? How can sex be fun if your partner looks like they are going to get sick with the idea that salty semen will cross their lips? Semen and vaginal fluids are clean stuff unless utilized under dirty, unhealthy conditions, or by force. Sex under duress is not considered sex. There is little logic or satisfaction in performing sex on someone who is doing so under duress, or simply not in the mood. How bad can it be for your self-esteem when someone performs oral sex on you and you know they are uncomfortable, or wish they were somewhere else?

I know how to train a woman to enjoy fellatio and that is by performing cunnilingus first. I can remember Carol Mason telling me that she had a personal rule that if asked to perform fellatio at the right time and under the right circumstances, she would suggest that the guy go down on her first to earn the pleasure. She was referring to her older high school boyfriend who wanted too many blowjobs. Carol actually only had less than five partners up to the time she met us. Carol said that any woman who gives a blowjob first when promised reciprocity second is foolish. She says men lose most of their urges after an orgasm, whereas a woman has a big advantage; she is just getting warmed up. This is another case that can be made for a man to always begin sex with the best mutual results by starting with his tongue. The enhancement of a man's orgasm is very significant if he pleases his woman first. I believe I have repeated that point several times, and that may not be enough.

Many of our (Jack and Will's) conclusions may not be as scientific as they should be for the purposes of this book, however we think our experiences are more conclusive than scientific interviews because we have been more subjective. All totaled, we probably have experienced over 100 women, and yes, that may be a small sample, but all of our combined experiences were good. There were no complaints. You have to admit that meeting unusual women was a rare experience for the two of us, because we could get their input based on the pleasurable experience. What we don't know is the size of our "sample" for specific questions and answers. It is impossible to count because we didn't record experiences when they occurred. Our tests were not official or scientific, yet we feel they are more meaningful. We really wanted to take advantage of our unusual experiences to be constructive and learn to communicate with women without offending them. Our results are from good sexy memories.

Actually the communication between men and women can be and should be an essential part of foreplay. Perhaps that can be said as a major contributor to the art of seduction. If a man wants to talk about sex hoping to turn on a woman, he best lace his comments with frequent compliments. Sounds of pleasure emanating from your partner is important. You should always tell your partner how good something feels. Most women really want to show off their assets, they just need to be motivated to do so. Remember, trust is a main factor. Sex cannot be rushed, and both partners need to be considerate of that factor. Especially since men are more often in a hurry. We are well on our way at this point. This next event proved to be another breakthrough that will probably never be applicable to most couples.

None of these technical sex studies were available to Jack and I back in the 50s and 60s. Women, generally, were even more confused about how their bodies worked. If you add to this confusion the moral codes, or the many restrictions that were just considered improper to discuss, then you can handicap the communications between the sexes again. Jack and I were forever trying to evaluate each of our experiences to what was happening to us as a result of our concerted effort to perform with excellence.

To have a relationship with Carol Mason that was so intimate, yet did not involve a love relationship with repercussions was very exceptional. I think Carol loved us and we loved her, but not in the same way that couples loved each other preparing for marriage. Separating love and sex has usually been exclusive to men, yet here we were, two young college men having this very unusual relationship with a best friend that just happened to be a sexy woman. I promise you again that trust plays the more important role in our experiences. That and our obvious respect for women, especially women who opened up to us (no pun intended) and came out of their "shells" for us.

Chapter 22. Putt Butt Golf

With just a few weeks to go during our junior year, and Carol's senior year, Carol invited Jack and me to spend a weekend at her parent's country club. Her parents were traveling elsewhere and the condo at their club was for our exclusive use. The weekend was to feature a golf tournament between the three of us. No strokes were given and none taken. I'm talking about golf here! Carol insisted the match be played on the men's course. As it turned out "strokes" were to highlight the weekend, and I am not referring to golf.

Jack and I drove the 100 miles in Jack's old clunker and Carol drove ahead the day before. The condo was pure luxury. It had a big master king size bed, which we three were to share, and this condo sported his and her bathrooms. We arrived Saturday about ten in the morning and after unpacking our minimum travel items, we went right to our tee time. It was a beautiful spring day, about 70 degrees and sunshine. Ladies teed off first from the men's tees and after 18 holes Carol was two strokes ahead of us. We could drive better, but with no control and Carol was an excellent putter. I came in last' Jack won. We headed back to the condo in a private electric cart and showered in separate bathrooms. This lady was quite a golfer. Perhaps her ability to stroke was improved by golf? We kidded a lot about giving each other strokes.

Carol had given us an envelope that we were to open after showering at the condo after the golf game. The envelope contained written instructions about the special bedding event that was the purpose of this special weekend. We were to shower and apply the same after shave lotion, wrap towels around us and meet her in the bedroom. Why before dinner? It turns out that being hungry during and having dinner after this event was important.

We were puzzled at the written instructions, but they were a script telling us exactly what we had to do. Apparently we were to participate in a special sexual event. I won't tell you what the script said; I'll just relate to you what happened. This "ménage a trios" was well thought out and probably is something that can never happen as a part of any normal sex life. You might say this experiment should not be tried by casual lovers. Perhaps in a porno movie, but our results turned out to be passionate beyond description while most fascinating.

Carol came into the master bedroom naked, but freshly showered and made up wearing only a gold chain necklace. She was pony tailed and tanned and looked formidable as an athlete. It was so neat that she was so relaxed being nude with her good buddies. We dropped our towels while Carol closed the drapes giving the room a "night time glow." She asked us if we had any questions before we proceeded and we nodded having discussed the script in the bathroom.

We both lay on our back and allowed Carol to play and suck us erect. She would lean over us and we caressed her breasts while she proceeded to see if she could mount us separately moving from cock to cock. We did not penetrate her but a teasing single inch; she was teasing us by rubbing our cocks between her labia. It was more of a test thing than actual sex. Our conversation was rather casual and we talked about the sex as if were normal conversational material. She handled our cocks like she was testing our equipment. These were lighthearted fun moments as we relieved some tension from our soon to be experiment, or whatever. We joked about the golf game and how important strokes were. (A double meaning game)

This was not really an experiment as it was to be the most unusual thing we would ever do.

During these relaxing preliminaries, we played around in a sporting manner and smothered Carol with licks and caressing. We made yummy sounds and raved about her skills. While she was moving about us we would occasionally hold her down, sort of bondage like, to give her a few forced licks. One of us would hold her legs apart and the other would dive in her pussy. Even though she was in control, we tried to give her the feeling that we were so anxious to taste her that we made her pause and enjoy while we performed. She began to get serious and rolled us over and set a few personal records by moving from erection to erection with her mouth, and yes there were the lollipops. Carol sucked on our cocks a little at a time, but stopped before it felt too good. Jack and I held her down and while one of us kissed her face and caressed her breasts, the other would rub the wet lollipop against her pussy. We would alternate sucking the suckers and rubbing them alternately on her pussy. We licked the sugar off of her pussy after each lollipop. I even tried applying two lollipops; I gently stroked her clitoris with one sucker and gently moved the second sucker in and out of her vagina while Jack held her down. The two lollipops really turned Carol on. We did everything she requested and followed the proposed schedule. We were candle light lovers. She claimed that no woman could ever experience two 6'5" well built lovers with such a meaningful relationship. She said she loved us both and wanted us to never forget her. We never did forget this teammate.

Carol then lay down between us and we began the explicit outlined routine of us alternately licking her pussy each time to create an orgasm for Carol. Her focus got serious and we lost count of her orgasms. We purposely stalled the main event building up her passion.

We were given written instructions as to what techniques we were to use. The non-performing teammate was kept busy with caressing her breasts and kissing her. We were required not to be in a hurry and I think Carol was going for some special multiple orgasm record. She alternated orgasms between our turns with our faces between her legs, and each climax seemed higher and more powerful. No woman could possibly have this good of foreplay. She was concentrating on every touch and lick knowing this was an opportunity of a lifetime, something most likely never to be repeated. We circled her counter clockwise so while one of us had our face between her legs, the other's cock was in her mouth upside down. The "in mouth cock time" was irregular as she began to focus on what was being done to her. But even a cursory suck from a passionate woman was exciting because we could feel her rising passion. We both rotated to lick and suck on her breasts when passing, while the other was licking her pussy. She was in pure ecstasy. We were required, according to the script to keep four hands and two tongues going all the time. There was no talking, just heavy breathing now, and Carol's noises of pleasure. We were following the written script.

When she was ready for her final act, I was pushed flat on my back. She mounted me with the usual clitoris rubbing, bent forward, and rested her chin on my chest, which intentionally raised her ass up higher. She was too low on my chest to kiss me, so she watched my eyes and I watched hers. Her eyes were twice their normal size and she was as high as you can imagine. She had prepared herself for this moment even though she was so high. Carol smiled at me, her chin resting on my chest, and waited as if she was waiting for an injection before surgery.

Jack took the squeeze bottle of gel and began to lubricate her anus. Per her instructions, he injected a few drops into her anus. Jack applied the lotion to Long John Silver. Jack began to very gently enter her anus, which according to the script was a first time for her. Yes, her eyes widened, and Long John was a bit too large for a first time anal "hot beef" injection, so she did grimace. She was feeling a new sensation for the first time, two big cocks in her bottom at the same time. She later confirmed that two big cocks was a slight discomfort, but it felt fantastic according to her subsequent comments while recapping the event.

When Jack was completely inside her, Carol began to rock in rhythm with Jack's strokes while sliding up and down on my cock. Carol tried to ride my shaft to the same rhythm started by Jack. Jack was kneeling behind Carol and holding her hips trying not to bang against her too hard. I remained motionless, but I could also feel what was happening better than they could. I felt that I was wedged tighter than normal and in my pinned down position I could feel Jack's cock moving inside her. At the end of each stroke, I thought I felt Jack's cock touch my nerve. This was really weird and I wondered what to concentrate on, Carol's rising passion, my pleasure, or what the hell was going on, or in.

Carol's goal was to have two cocks fucking her with the idea of all us having a triple orgasm at the same time. Carol was very vocal and grunting with each stroke, but reassuring us it all felt good. Her grunts seemed louder and she was digging her chin into my chest with each stroke. Her hands were cupped on my shoulders. Her eyes were bulging and I think not really watching me, but deep in a trance. I even heard some of Carol's prayers telling God how good she felt. Her loud panting had become a hard grunting.

" Oh God, I'm so close to coming, please come with me. Don't stop, Jack harder, harder," she moaned.

Jack picked up his pace and Carol was sliding on my cock at the same pace. Now here is the strangest feeling. There is apparently only a single layer of skin between Jack and me. Our penises are facing each other with our nerves touching each other through a single layer of skin lubricated on both sides. Jack's cock ran the full length of mine and reversed as he withdrew. It seemed like I was being fucked and fucking at the same time. All three of our sensitive nerves were touching at the same time. Carol's skin at her vaginal opening was stretched so that her clitoris was taught and really enlarged. Her clitoris was rubbing the base of my cock, which was not in motion since Carol was sliding on my cock with each of Jack's strokes. The rhythm was unusual because we were all in sync. We were all moving at the same rate with this single silky layer of skin between me and Jack and Carol feeling everything, but more intensely.

Here is a strange lesson; the rectal side of a woman apparently had more feeling than the vaginal side. Carol was experiencing more internal feelings. She swears she could feel our cocks touching inside her and the feeling doubled her pleasure. Her entire body was poised to burst by being so full of cock. Everything was rocking and her brain was ready to explode trying to assimilate so much pleasure. It was a first for everybody. Jack and I fired simultaneously and we both felt the other man climaxing. Our pulsations were exactly the same and Carol was exclaiming loudly that she could feel us both coming and there was no doubt she was enjoying an orgasm. Her orgasm began before we fired and continued after we came because we did not get soft. The excitement was almost too high. Our minds had shut out reality and we were in a dazed world of heightened pleasure.

The three of us froze while we finished pulsating. Carol was looking at my face and she was drooling a bit. Saliva was running down her chin and onto my chest forming a small puddle, I don't know why. She had dropped excess saliva onto my chest and was not aware of it. I was watching her eyes and she was as wide eyed as I had ever seen her. She claimed she was concentrating on feeling both of us ejaculating and it was a sensational pleasure.

We lay motionless and silently, breathing heavily with Carol sandwiched between us. Jack had never put any weight on us. He was more like kneeling behind Carol and he had been holding tight to her hips. Jack was straddling my knees, as they were flat on the bed. Our breathing was slowing. No one spoke. Carol was smiling at me waiting for Jack to withdraw. The original plan was for Jack to remain until he softened, but we sensed Carol's discomfort at being bent so tightly. Jack withdrew slowly; Carol sat up, straightened her legs forward parallel to my body and held me inside her. Her feet were aside my head. She was stretching her breasts and reached behind her neck to give Jack a kiss. She was sort of catching her breath and stretching from being sandwiched. Jack moved to lie down beside us, with Carol now looking at both of us, but still sitting on my erection.

Both of us still had erections, which was no surprise, except I was still inside her and she felt extremely tight. I was wondering about the correlation. Carol raised her knees and sat still on my erection. I was not softening. I think I had a case of "shock jock cock."

Carol smiled and looked at me, while sitting on my cock and asked what I had felt. The first thing I told her was that I could feel Jack coming as if we were touching each other. Her interest exploded when I said that. Her green eyes flashed with new sparkle.

"I could feel the same thing in every detail, something I have never felt before. It was like my vagina had big feelings. What felt so good to me was that my anus and my vagina were stretched to the limit making the fucking more sensitive. I mean, I could feel more than I ever imagined. There was tremendous pressure, like I would burst if you guys were any bigger, but the slight pain felt so good, beyond belief. When you both came, I felt every squirt each of you made and my whole body was reacting as if I was climaxing during a train wreck. I could feel you guys coming. I mean to tell you guys that my clitoris was pulsating right along with you both and it was a strange sensation, but wonderful. I actually felt like I was ejaculating something. That was really weird. I felt so full of cock and they were both mine and I made them fire. Wow, that was unbelievable. That will be the greatest orgasm of my life. I can't begin to describe the power of that wonderful sensation."

"If you think it was strange for you, I could never imagine feeling Jack's cock against mine, really, that certainly was not a homosexual thing, but surprising and confusing. I felt like there were little tongues inside you that were licking me while I was being fucked. I was distracted, yet enhanced by your orgasm Carol, and feeling Jack was actually a shock. It certainly did not distract from my orgasm or the power of the three of us coming together. The energy was like a bomb exploding, or rather a series of bombs exploding. I sure loved your reaction, Carol, your orgasm went through my entire body," I said.

"Wasn't that the purpose of the script?" Jack asked.

"Well, I am still stunned at the extreme pleasure, but I had no idea that you guys were in such close contact. How could I know that? Now that you mention it, that makes the whole thing even sexier. And why should you guys be concerned about that male thing when guys can't even touch each other during a threesome, other men might think your feelings a bit homosexual." Carol added.

"Frankly," Jack said, I didn't notice the contact as much as Will because I was stroking and holding your hips and that was sexy. But, I was also distracted by your pleasure level, Carol. I might add my view was very sexy because your ass is so beautiful. I never even saw Will. I guess my animal instincts overcame my feminine side. I did feel an awful lot of pussy activity that was different. And, Will was motionless while I was stroking, but I did feel Will come with me, and that sensation was inexplicable and totally unexpected. I was so high."

"OK, "I said, "I'll tell you both what happened. Imagine a cock being inside a nice pussy and the pussy has a partner inside there that starts rubbing against your cock. Come on, that is a big difference from any other orgasm isn't it? Jack, could you really not notice inner movement as if there were little "pussy elves" running around inside there trying to add to the pleasure. Remember how men joke about a pussy being able to suck or pull a cock around? Well there you have it. I suggest that because of the unusual circumstances, we are not embarrassed about the penis contact, and overlooking the fact that the thrill involved another guy. I was motionless and you were rubbing your cock against mine with only a thin membrane between us. That is probably why you will only see this trick in a porno movie because no two normal guys have an incentive to feel another cock. If that were the sole purpose of the act it would probably repulse us. Carol's passion is what made the situation so sexual. I suggest we deal with this as an unusual situation and we will keep the pleasure secret. The pleasure was indescribable. I wish women could develop vaginal muscles that could stroke us like that."

"Men! You are always trying to be so macho. Maybe you need a little more estrogen to make you enjoy sex more. What the fuck difference should it make to you if your penises rubbed against each other? This was about filling me up with quality big cocks. I will never find two guys that I can trust to do me again and I will miss you guys. This double-pronged fuck felt great and will probably be the highest moment of my sex life. And you guys will never find another pussy that can duplicate that, my pussy is about as athletic as any woman can get. I doubt you guys will ever do this again, look at both of you, you're still semi-hard. I mean, I can feel Will inside me and he is still hard. Maybe this will give you guy's permanent erections and man will I be proud. In fact, I may brag about this to all the girls. Do you think the other girls will think you guys are gay, or will they envy my accomplishment? And what are the odds that any woman will trust two guys as much as we trust each other. Trust is the most important thing and second is the ability to communicate with each other. I do love you guys and I really appreciate your bringing me such fascinating fucking ecstasy." Carol just lectured us.

I think that experience leaves much room for discussion. Was it not really only important that Carol had this once in a lifetime experience? It was her request. The vast majority of men will never trust each other to not admit to homosexual contact, even if that was not the intent. Jack and I had done a few doubles with Carol after basketball season and never once did we ever touch each other, or even accidentally bump into the other. That was not intentional; it was a natural thing because we were concentrating on pleasing Carol. Male contact wasn't purposely avoided; it was just a guy thing because we were concentrating on Carol's reaction, which increased the passion. The primary goal of threesomes should be to please the woman first, not the male partners anyway. I think that makes us unselfish heterosexual lovers. Two or more men fucking a woman in tandem without the "Queen bee" foreplay defeats the purpose of threesomes unless the goal was to please the men. The type of threesome should be agreed upon first. It is, again, a communication problem.

I began to wonder if a woman would consider putting a false cock, with ripples, of the right comfortable size, stick it in her anus and fuck her lover to see if he could feel the fake cock rubbing against him. The woman would have to be on the bottom on her back and the stroking male could not avoid the ripples in the false cock stuffed in her anus. I don't think it would be necessary for the plastic anal cock to vibrate, but that also provides new sensuous ideas. This idea opens up a few new ideas for marital sex. It depends on how a woman feels about anal sex. Secondly, this may be a communications test for a married couple. They could feel if the female's vaginal sensitivity might increase with her lover's penis rubbing against the plastic toy through inner layers of silky skin; that could be sexy. The two female channels are parallel. I have never read anything concerning the layer of skin between the vagina and the lower intestines. Maybe I just haven't read enough sex manuals. I was unprepared for the new feelings.

I had read where some men like to have fingers inserted in their rectums during intercourse, but that thought never crossed my mind. Probably because I am too tall for women's reaches. Jack and I talked about anal penetration as a variety with women and we are in the group that prefers pussy. Anal sex during menstrual periods may be something to try. I never did. In history, anal sex was often a form of birth control, but I wonder about women's enthusiasm for anal sex during medieval times, cleanliness not being what it is today. We cannot judge others who prefer anal sex. Yes, the anus is surely tighter, but unnaturally lubed. It is a personal taste thing. Jack and I have been so obsessed with pussy that we never discussed anal sex with our partners. We never thought of "analingus" either. That was not a sexual revolution priority.

Carol dismounted and I still was erect, but softening. She excused herself to her private shower. We took turns in the men's shower and talked some more about how hot Carol was. We all got dressed and had a wonderful fancy country club dinner. We toasted our great relationship and our exceptional basketball season. We toasted Carol's future on Broadway. We toasted the most interesting and sensual sex act we ever even imagined. It was quite an event.

Sex is definitely better on an empty stomach.

Once again it boils down to sexual attitudes. Is love necessary to have good sex? Does good sex distract from love? The vast majority of married couples would never share sport sex with others. I think most men would be concerned about being "outperformed." Women might find two men more exciting because they might be too involved to make judgments. And, it has been firmly engrained into our moral codes that sex is bad if not with a loved one. Ego problems could abound.

The dictionary defines the "id" as the inherited instinctive impulses of the individual as part of the unconscious. The "Ego" is the part of the human mind that reacts to reality and develops a sense of individuality. Social standards and rules are developed to restrain or control these feelings of self importance or gratification. We are constantly fighting with our basic instincts trying to rationalize or justify certain unapproved actions or feelings.

God has given mankind some basic enjoyments to be derived from our life's adventures. I classify them as accomplishments, sexual pleasures, and the enjoyment of food. The latter two are appetites that we learn to control as being civilized. We list vices and sins, but all vices are related to abuses. Sexual abuses are harder to define. Drunken orgies are rare today compared to the Old Testament and ancient empires like Rome. They had different Gods for eating and sex and conquering enemies. I never read about a mythical fucking God. (Phallus?)

Today, accomplishments and degrees of success are necessary for developing anybody's self esteem. And that includes things not sexual, but we are talking about sex here so let's concentrate on sex.

Imagine how it builds your self-esteem when someone flirts with you, or tries to seduce you. Imagine the good the seducer feels if you reciprocate with compliments, or acceptance. However, no compliment can mean more to self-esteem than success. Is any compliment or any accomplishment as good for your self-esteem than when another desires you sexually? In our opinion, someone finding you sexually attractive is a bigger measure of success than making a lot of money. These are difficult comparisons because everybody's ego is different. There are some people who could care less about sex and a funny thing; they often excel at non-sexual accomplishments. One need not pursue every compliment, but the impact on your self-esteem is wonderful.

There is an adage that whoever isn't getting enough sex gets to make the rules.

We are of the opinion that a sexy attitude makes a person sexy whether they have sufficient self-esteem or not. You may have to fake it using your attitude. Your attitude should be like the "Golden Rule."

Sex works that way. We all want to be appealing and attract the opposite sex. That may be our greatest self-esteem lift. Our "id" demands that our instincts be normal. That makes for a strong sex drive. Our ego demands that we show self-control, yet our egos have conflicts with our id. There is a song, "I like to have women I've never had." Yeah right, but what about the women's rights? Do women want to have every man they never had? I don't think so.

Are these things really related to sexual desires? All women must fantasize about lovers and what lovers do to them. Men are more basic than that. They just have a strong desire to fire their sexual weapons. We cannot imagine the hurt people must feel if no one ever shows any desire for them. That is a subject we will leave for the psychiatrists. We want to examine the ways to achieve desirability using common sense.

So, in concluding the tale of this fantastic threesome, did I learn anything about sex? Do I have more respect for women? Yes, more than ever. I am amazed at what women can do for a man. I learned that valuable lesson from Carol Mason, as did Jack. I am just as confused about my natural desires sunk in my "id." I don't feel my ego needs any strokes because I am an accomplished person and I am successful. I am exceptionally well read on most non-fiction subjects. I enjoy acquiring knowledge. I will always have a difficult time rationalizing or justifying my sexual experiences because I think about sex often. I enjoyed everything I did and I figured as long as the information was not made public or would not hurt someone else's feelings I could justify my actions. I never felt immoral. I'm sure there are many who would judge me as immoral, but then would they feel the same way if they had as great a sex life as I have had? The bottom line is that I ask you and myself if my experiences made me a better husband.

Jack and I were exhausted after that very athletic threesome event. The three of us cuddled and tried to talk, but sleep soon overcame us. We slept in the same big bed with Carol between us. The next morning I was awakened by the gentle rocking of the bed. That was the ideal alarm clock for me because I awoke with one of those early morning hard-ons that prevent men from losing bladder control in their sleep. The bed covers were off the other side of the bed and there was the most beautiful sight; Jack was on top of Carol and was gently fucking her to the most pleasant rhythm. Carol had wrapped her arms and legs around Jack and was sweetly awaking him. An interesting observation about Carol; when sleeping naked, if I brushed up against her, her legs spread as a reflex. (?)

The two of them were not vocal. It was quiet sex. Carol's legs were rocking with Jack to give him depth with each stroke. Jack's orgasm was quiet; he sort of held his breath, exhaled a big sigh and kissed Carol. He looked so peaceful. He lay there resting on his elbows enjoying the tenderness of the moment. Carol was rubbing his back and occasionally stroking his head as he came down from the morning wake up call. Jack would begin his day with what I call therapeutic sex. When Jack had his wakeup fuck and was coming down from that pleasant release, Carol held him with her arms wrapped tightly around his mid section during his climax. When she was satisfied that Jack was fully awake and satisfied, she released him and Jack pulled out and staggered to the men's bathroom although he looked only half awake. I arose and followed Carol into her bathroom and peed. Carol watched me pee.

"If you splatter on my toilet and don't put that seat back down, I will slap your wienie silly. You guys all need bathroom training and men are something else when it comes to bathroom etiquette."

I asked Carol if early morning sex without foreplay was good for her.

"Carol," I said, "does sex always feel that good to you that you gave Jack that nice early morning ride without foreplay?"

"Honey, it always feels good and my intention was to show you guys how much I appreciated last night. I feel so close to both of you although I'm in love with you; Jack is about sex because I trust him. I want you to come back to bed as soon as we both pee, and please ride me for your early morning wakeup call. I want to start out this fabulous day with my pussy tingling. Now what do you say to that?"

Carol knelt in her bathtub and splashed cool water on her pussy. I watched; that was sexy.(Both bathrooms had shower stalls with benches and this room had a gigantic tub.) "I sure do love this stuff," she said referring to Jack's semen.

I think she was draining her pussy and didn't mean that she liked keeping all that juice inside her. I think she was rinsing herself to better accommodate me. I did not ask.

"You said you loved me, but you also said I was going to be a fuck buddy. Has something changed?" I asked.

"Now wait a minute, that's true and our fabulous sex life was the center of our relationship, but I couldn't help but fall in love with you even though we both know nothing can come of us after this week when I graduate. I can't help but feel love for you Will. It is impossible for you to give me so much pleasure and me not feel the female thing about love, but with no commitment. My need to not commit to a long relationship is hard to maintain, but I can handle it. I have my personal goals; I just didn't expect us to be so good together, so compatible. Damn, I will miss you."

Carol reached for my cock and gently ran some cool water over my cock using her hands.

"Well, I can't help but feel the same way about you. You are such an exceptional woman, you are every man's ideal and I have had the extreme pleasure of spending so much quality time with you and inside your fantastic pussy. You will have the distinction of having spoiled me for life. I have to tell you how much our close intimate relationship means to me. You are truly my best friend."

"Well, I feel I have truly raised your standards higher for good sex. And believe you me you have made me feel extra sexy. I guess I needed that reassurance, although that was secondary to the excitement and fun we had. I think every woman needs to feel sexy and you and Jack have set some high standards for me too. It will be years before I settle down with a husband, but I will have some fun first. Now, please come to bed and fuck me and let me try and kiss your face. I think I will get more face kissing in the future with some shorter men."

Jack was still shaving and showering. Carol sat on the edge of the bed and took my cock into her mouth making it nice and hard as I stood and watched. Then she rolled over on her back and spread her legs so wide while she scooted up the bed. Her knees were raised and her legs were at a right angle to the body. That was some stretched out spread. Carol was very limber. I mention this because I realized again how sexy a woman is with her legs spread and knees raised. She held her arms out as if she was going to embrace me. What a sight, all those open arms and legs open and beckoning me. When she saw me looking at her pussy, she did something unusual and uninhibited; she spread her labia exposing her pink parts. She began to rub her clitoris as I mounted her. She jerked her hand away when I entered her. I arched my back and scrunched up so I could kiss her face and mouth while we started fucking.

The early morning warmth of her pussy was something else to be remembered. She was wet, warm and tight. I enjoyed the pleasant stroking while we gazed into each other's eyes. The eye gazing was something we developed that was personal. The eye contact is far more intimate than eyes closed or cheek-to-cheek fucking. When I came, I pumped faster and I pulled back so we could look into each other's eyes when I was coming. I stopped stroking so I could concentrate on my ejaculation. Carol loved watching my eyes when I came and I noticed her eye reflex when she opened her eyes wider as she felt my orgasm. She had the most considerate moves; she would try and move her hips as if reaching for my cock. She tried to rise up against my weight. I thought she was angling for clitoral contact.

We had done that often; we watched each other's eyes during orgasms. I stayed inside her until I softened naturally. She finally released me after purring like a kitten. Carol took me into her bathroom and we showered together. I sat on the floor of the shower stall making my face ideal to lick her pussy. Carol was in a semi squat and I had my head against the shower stall bench. I licked her pussy while water cascaded over my face. The water poured over her stomach and cascaded so much that I had to breathe like a swimmer. I felt I owed her that treat, and she was very appreciative. Carol squatted over my face in the full pouring water. I could easily recognize the sounds she made while climaxing. She would actually pant with quick short bursts of air. I knew when to stop. She bent over me to kiss me on the mouth with water dousing our faces. She said she could taste herself on my lips and I once asked about that. She said it just tasted like good sex. That sexy shower orgasm got her hair wet, which delayed breakfast. Carol sat on the bench while I shampooed her hair. She put my cock in her mouth while I shampooed her head. We were giving each other head. I did have another minor orgasm which made me realize how light headed we can get during sex. Especially while standing. You are reading about how sexual gratification can build momentum. Once up and passionate it is sometimes hard to stop because one never has time to cool down.

We were drying off and after she kissed me she said,

"It's moments like this that proves you a sweet exceptional considerate man. If you act like this the rest of your life, you will bring some lucky woman so much pleasure and I guarantee there will be reciprocity beyond your sexiest dreams. Will, you really are a great considerate lover and you have exceptional tongue skills. And you really get into eating pussy, which makes you great. Don't forget that."

What made that experience important was that we felt that this morning Carol was so unselfish about satisfying us with no concern for her own orgasm. When confronted, her point was that it is not always necessary for her to climax. We concluded that most women will fuck just to give her partner the pleasure as a priority because basic sexual intercourse always feels good to women. I suspect many couples just fuck because men are not made to be unselfish sex partners. Women are far more unselfish. I can't imagine a man satisfying a woman while sacrificing his own orgasm.

Carol said fucking always feels good whether she had foreplay or advance orgasms or not. The morning wake up sex we had was not about quickies because we were still fired up about our "two pronged" sex.

Carol told me something I will never forget. She said that early morning sex without foreplay was in itself foreplay. She said that to awake with a man between your legs was such a pleasure. Imagine waking to a man caressing your pussy with a hard cock and you are hugging him with both your arms, legs and vagina. There are no thoughts of stress because we are coming from pleasant sleep and sweet dreams, especially after our previous night. And when a man reaches an early morning orgasm a woman can feel his body swell and recede, she can feel his muscles tense and relax and his entire body releases a giant sigh, a release of tension accompanied by such pleasure, which she is providing. It is like rocking a baby in a cradle of love. Perhaps a little too many maternal feelings, but the same satisfaction as nursing a baby. I admit I crave that feeling.

Carol expounded, "Morning sex feels so good to me. I feel such satisfaction and I feel my entire body tingles with a gentle sweet pleasure, because I am so relaxed from sleep. I am so lucky to wake up under a man and feeling so much pleasure to start my day. I love the feeling of taking you inside me and making you appreciate me and my starting my day by sharing these wonderful feelings. I am the source of your awakening; the source of mutual pleasure, and knowing and sharing an orgasm is indescribable. It makes me feel so alive and so important. My reward is feeling that special orgasm that I feel while I am so relaxed. The passion is replaced by the comfort and warmth of holding you. I gasp and sigh right along with you. I learned this from you Will."

Carol continued, "I do have this awful feeling that I will regret my many experiences because, by comparison, I may never meet the right man. I want a man like you, Will, and I hope there is another like you out there. The warmth and tenderness of our relationship is really my important lesson. We have learned sex together, but more important we have learned to communicate and yes, how to make and feel love. Separation of sex and love will always be mankind's problem, and now mine."

Speaking about tall male sex partners, Carol made another interesting observation, which we had not thought as unusual. Both Jack and I had a technique that sometimes during sexual intercourse with us on top, either of us could use our foreheads as a fulcrum, brace ourselves with our foreheads over Carol's shoulder, arch our backs and lift her ass off of the bed while still on top and fucking. The reason I occasionally did this was by holding Carol's ass and hips I could change the angle and do some fun strokes while her hips were held motionless. I could fuck faster because I controlled the speed of the strokes, whereas a woman might not react fast enough to rapid fucking with a man on top of her restricting some movement. Carol said my holding her ass off of the bed felt good and she confirmed she couldn't move that fast being underneath all that weight. She said she had better clitoral contact when we tipped her ass and held it off the bed. Obviously the man has to be considerably taller than the women to perform this feat. She once challenged us to a fast fucking contest, and if she could be on top, she was faster. It is too difficult for fucking couples to work and coordinate fast strokes unless the female doesn't move. She also concluded that shorter guys could not do that "grab ass" trick. Try lifting the woman underneath you while arching your body and putting weight on your neck. Not an easy feat; try that, folks! We outweighed Carol by over a hundred pounds.

After a country club breakfast and more sex talk, Jack and I headed back to school. I had one more final exam. Carol's parents drove to school for her graduation later in the week. I took my last final exam with ease and took Carol to dinner and a campus movie. (She used her credit card). When we got back to my room, Jack was out for the night with Julie. Carol climbed in bed with me and spent the night. I gave her a special long gentle effort orgasm with my tongue. I teased her into a frenzy. When satisfied, she mounted me and undid her ponytail and swept her locks down over my face forming a tent. She then took her right breast and put it in my mouth. She watched me like she was nursing me. I sucked for a few minutes. This is so strange. After all the final exam pressure, here I was relaxing with a breast in my mouth. Why does it feel so good for a grown man to suck on a nice breast? Another point for discussion? How much better my test scores might be if I could take the tests with a breast in my mouth. Nah, the school would probably not allow that.

Carol slid down on my cock and slid her breasts along my chest while exiting my face. I had to put a pillow under my head to prop myself up for those few wonderful kisses; remember Carol is only five feet four inches tall. There is more than a foot difference in our heights. Our height differential certainly made no difference when she was on top. In fact, I think she had an advantage especially being so acrobatic. She could mount me in a flash and once on me, she rode me hard. She could make the bed shake rattle and roll. We were a great sex team by now and she was great at making us reach for our climaxes together. As soon as I knew she was firing, the reaction brought me up to the same moment. We achieved an almost violent climax. Then she fell forward and lay motionless with her head against my chest. She began to weep. I cried too, and I was not embarrassed. Carol whispered she loved me and she would never forget me. I dittoed that sweet comment. She stayed on top of me for a long time as we began to doze off. Carol spent the night with me and, of course, I had my wake up pleasure ride. We dressed for breakfast and her graduation ceremony.

We promised to write and we did correspond the next year, but sadly our paths never crossed again. I always hoped if we played in the New York area, she would come to our basketball game. We never played there.

After Carol's graduation ceremony, Jack and I met Carol and her parents for dinner. Her Dad was thrilled; apparently he was an active alumnus and had season tickets for our home games. He knew who we were, but he never knew how well we knew his daughter. Carol was proud to be able to have two big star basketball players as her dates. The Masons drove home after dinner in two Cadillac's and Jack and I walked back to our dorm for one final night. Well, Jack was in a hotel room with the graduating Julie, so I was awake most of the night stunned, rethinking what was to be a most spectacular sensational year of my sex life.

The next year, Carol sent me a program where she had the lead in an off Broadway version of South Pacific. She then moved to Hollywood and we lost track of her career. We heard she was on several TV shows as a dancer. She must have been involved with someone because she said little about herself in her letters.

Can you believe we were at the beginning of the sexual revolution and something this amazing happened to me? This was incredible. For the next thirty years the battle of the sexes was more about women's liberation rather than a battle for dominance. However, dominance did play a role, but very difficult to define the motives. There were the new battles in the work place where women wanted equal pay for equal work. There was also an increase in divorces as women became more independent. So there are other problems that did not involve sex that played roles here. Jack and I decided not to study these trends; we wanted to focus on sexual pleasures and how the revolution might impact people's sex lives.

Chapter 23. Then Cum Summer

Jack and I returned to our hometowns and talked by phone every two weeks or so. We were trying to meet to play some "one on one" basketball. We were determined not to lose our edge. Jack came to visit me for a few days and we played some of the local talent two on two. No one could play at our level, not in my town.

I had a summer job as a law clerk.

I began dating Cynthia more frequently for the summer before entering law school. I would never have divulged the Carol Mason experience to anybody and I never did. But the experience stayed in my head. I felt pretty seasoned and qualified to make love to any woman, particularly Cynthia. But she proved to be a difficult conversion. Cynthia was much more beautiful than any of the girls I met or saw in college and her body was far superior to any woman I had ever seen.

My sex life was now a struggle. I was back in the past with Cynthia. I wanted more than she was willing to give up and condoms were a big turn off. Discussing condoms, preparation time and the idea of putting them on was time lost from the mood. Cynthia and I spent little time talking about sex. She was always embarrassed.

Her approach to our relationship was an innocent flirtation with a lot of touching, and not realizing how frustrated I was. I became more aggressive, but gentle and tactful. After many attempts to get Cynthia to disrobe, I finally got her to bare her breasts. They were small, but firm. I got to play with them whenever we could get privacy. I gradually advanced to kissing and caressing her breasts and she became a very willing subject, or rather her breasts did.

It was late summer before I got to put my penis in her gentle hands. I was advancing very slowly. She was easily embarrassed, but willing to cooperate because she loved me. She hesitated to put my penis in her mouth and I decided not to press the issue. We did simulate sexual intercourse by rubbing my cock against her bare stomach. We were getting used to each other and her comfort level was rising with her passion and curiosity. Remember, this is near the beginning of the sexual revolution.

Finally, before we departed for college, Cynthia and I tried fucking with a condom. It was not very passionate. It was more like a physical exam to see if our parts matched. I did try to get my head between her legs, but she pushed me away, mostly because she was embarrassed. It would be some time before she would be interested in such possibilities.

The condom felt like a thick rubber inner tube and much feeling was lost for me. It was a fumbling experience that I guess everybody goes through with varying degrees of success. Cynthia was only reacting to the idea that she had lost her virginity. She did not respond like it was fantastic, rather that it was a deed that eventually had to be done to keep my interest. Sex at this time in her life was almost a fearful thing and the challenge was mine to convert her. I loved her and was anxious to lead her down the path of pleasure. I really appreciated my previous lessons in love making provided by one Carol Mason. Regressing was really frustrating.

Jack and I entered our senior year with a new focus on basketball. We had to surpass our past records and the competition was out to defeat us even more so after we beat them all the previous year.

Our sex life was to be disappointing without the sexy icon, Carol Mason. Well, that was my case. Jack always had a good exceptional sex life, but he just had a slow start. I had double pressure starting my first year of law school during my senior year. Last year I finished in the top one percent of my class in spite of the rigorous basketball schedule. But I had the dreadful fear of falling behind there also, so I tried not to think about sex. I was also writing Cynthia often.

Jack had a few partners in our room, some noisy, some quiet and a few gigglers. He told me nothing was exceptional, nor did he meet any really interesting coeds. Jack and I always discussed cunnilingus and women's reactions hoping to build some credentials knowing how different each lovely woman was. It was just the usual group that had crushes on Jack and he was very gracious. He made them all understand that sex would be fun, but he had to deal with basketball and made no promises or commitments. It seemed like some really beautiful college girls just wanted to experience Jack. Many of these girls didn't want to be exposed as just plain horny, so Jack was very discreet. There probably weren't more than six lovelies the entire year and they all had repeat sessions not knowing about the others. I didn't get any offers. I wondered if the word was out that Jack liked cunnilingus. We will never know. These new coeds were certainly open for repeat business. They felt privileged to experience Jack. I sensed this because I did get to talk to them, but not about sex. That would have been nice, but I was interested in what Jack told me about the one's I met. That made me horny.

Therefore, I will summarize this year and move on to our careers. We won the conference championship again and went to the national NCAA tourney. I completed the first year of law school with my usual great grades.

Jack graduated from business school and had an offer to train on Wall Street. He moved to New York right after graduation. And no, Carol Mason had moved to Hollywood.

Perhaps the most interesting thing that happened our senior year was when two nubile graduate students in nursing school challenged

Jack and me to a secret game of serious strip poker. Jack had been having a fun sex relationship with one of the girls and apparently the challenge was made during one night of light drinking, to which I was not present.

The big game was set for a Saturday night a week in advance and with no basketball conflicts. I have little interest in card games, so Jack had to teach me the fundamentals of poker for dummies. This was a form of liar's poker whereby a single hand is dealt to the lead player chosen by a high card draw.

The game was to consist of four players, boy-girl and boy-girl, a foursome sitting on a king sized mattress. The first player could draw up to four cards of a five-card hand. That player would then tell the group what he was holding and then laid the cards face down on the bed. If the player to the first player's left picked up the hand they had to draw to beat what the first player said, whether the first player lied or not. If the second player refused to play the hand and when exposed, the first player told the truth, then the second player lost the hand, or in this case was to remove one article of clothing. The object of the game was to lie or beat what was claimed trying to pass the challenge on to the next two players. Eventually the hand would get too good to beat and the hand had to be challenged. The excitement was not knowing which players were telling the truth.

Jack and I went to the girl's apartment ready for action. Here were the rules. Each player was allowed six removable items. The girls had blouses, bras, pants and panties, shoes and socks making six items. We had jackets, shirts, pants and underwear, and shoes or sox counted as one item each. Losing your shoes and sox was like a warm up to get to the serious part of the game, which was eventual nakedness.

What confused me was the little thirty-second sand clock that was prominently displayed. The game was to be played with four candles on each corner of the playing bed. The bed was a mattress on the floor. I guess the game had some complicated features that I was to learn as I progressed. The first person to get naked when incurring further losses had to perform whatever the hand winner wanted for thirty seconds. Hmm, I wonder what that meant. Perhaps the most exciting part of the game was the two uninvolved winners got to watch. That put added pressure on the loser. I soon learned that when the biggest loser was down to one item, the other players tried to lose their underwear before their shirts. Go figure; you will.

Let the games begin. Keep in mind I am not a poker player and I was winging it. The girl to my left won the deal and she played it safe telling the truth on a hand that Jack felt he could beat. Jack drew three cards implying he had a legitimate pair. I don't know whether Jack beat the hand or lied. My problem was by the time I got the hand I had to decide if the player to my right was lying or I might beat the hand.

I naively picked up the hand, drew two cards, and everybody was laughing knowing I had to lie to pass the hand. I lost and took off my shoes. And so it began. I seemed to be always at the worst position even though the loser was subsequently dealt the next first hand, which was never challenged. The losses were unfair, in my opinion, because I was always at the hard end of a cycle making it impossible to beat or lie. I was the obvious loser. I was down to my underwear and Jack still had shirt and underwear on. The girls wore blouses with bras off under blouses and panties when I was totally naked. What do you think would happen if I lost again to either girl on either side? All I could do in self defense was to try and get any girl to take off her panties and that required two winning hands on my part. What were those odds after my obvious lack of poker skills? The game was exciting even when I was the big loser. Think about admiring two beautiful playful women about to get naked.

I eventually lost to the girl on my right; I called her a liar and she was telling the truth. I was told I had to lick her pussy for thirty seconds. She had removed her panties in anticipation of winning a hand, so she had kept her blouse on. Her bra had also been discarded in hands she had lost to Jack. Her partner turned the thirty-second clock and monitored the time. OK, I enjoyed it and so did the winner, but the good news was that if the girls could reach an orgasm in thirty seconds, more power to them. But the guys could not climax or they were out of the game except for tongues. I felt otherwise; I thought I sensed I was in demand because the girls seemed to want to specifically beat me so I had to perform. The girls were freshly showered and sweet smelling. Obviously the odd couple was going to get turned on by watching the loser perform. Fortunately for them I was good at performing thanks to my advanced lessons from Carol Mason.

The next half hour consisted of Jack getting his cock licked and sucked while I spent all my time eating pussy, that is, for thirty-second intervals. The girls were really turned on, thanks to me, and Jack loved the game, thanks to my stupidity at poker.

Finally I lost to a naked woman who demanded thirty seconds of fucking as her prize; hard and fast she demanded. The rule was the man could not reach a climax or he was out of the game. Prior to the thirty seconds, I had to use a condom from a dish of handy condoms to be used only one time each.

After everybody was naked the hand was played to see who got fucked and who watched. Jack did get to lick a few pussies on demand, but when he won, he called for the loser girl to sit on his cock for thirty seconds, and wiggle or bounce. Long John was a big star and the girl's goals were to get fucked as much as possible by either of us. The cunnilingus was limited once the game progressed.

The game ended when I finally lost to the girl on my right and I told her I could hold off no longer. I put on a fresh condom, she laid back and said, "go for it, I'm ready too." So, screw the sand clock, I had a good old-fashioned jump fuck while being watched. When we were finished I stayed inside her and we looked over and the other couple was hard at it. Jack had also given up on the enforced foreplay. It was a great game; I tasted two nice clean pussies and got to fuck two girls at intervals, there was plenty of laughter, and it was fun, fun, fun. I had fucked Jack's old partner and we both got to fuck the new partner. We never had a rematch. I don't know why, but such events should be recorded. I did accidentally meet my "coitus" partner on campus and she was delightful as if nothing had happened, but an obvious good attitude about sport sex. She did wink and I think winking is sexy. She asked if I had improved my poker skills. I think she was hoping I would ask her out, but I was too involved with Cynthia and school and basketball to find time. I must have been crazy.

Jack had his nurse friend that Jack had done a few times after the poker game, but the best I could do was watch, which I did. I did get to talk to Barbara about sex a few times, but she was not so sophisticated. She just wanted to fuck Jack and liked it when I watched. Of course I had to masturbate while watching, but they could not see me or did they care. Oh well, that was better than nothing and I believe a normal reaction. There are not enough words to describe two beautiful people fucking when you can smell the smells and hear the delicious sounds. Sex is such a beautiful act. I think that when we get older and can't see ourselves, we can imagine that we look beautiful and that will work in our old age. Old people just don't look good naked any more, but someday, these memory images will play an important role in maintaining good sexual attitudes. Remember, your brain is your main sex organ.

Jack graduated in business finance and I received the same undergraduate degree, but as a step towards completing law school in six years, three years of undergraduate business school and three years of law. My four-year degree was a business degree with a law major.

I spent another summer working for a local law firm and Jack and I talked by phone frequently. We were really close friends and I think Jack needed my support when it came to his new job confidence. You might say I was his lawyer and confidant.

My final year of law school was my sixth year of college. I graduated at the top of my class. Cynthia and I got married the summer before my sixth year and of course Jack was my best man. Cynthia started on the birth control pill and we rented a small apartment off campus. Cynthia taught grade school nearby and supported us. I had a six-year scholarship and our expenses were low. Our life was routine and so was our sex life. We made love about three times a week and I did perform cunnilingus each time. I was learning Cynthia's desires and we finally began to talk about sex.

After Jack returned to New York, I began to tell Cynthia about Jack's sex life with the understanding that we might learn something. I didn't tell her everything, just stories that I felt would enhance her knowledge and abilities. I did not want her to ever hear about my yearlong affair with Carol Mason. Cynthia could have never accepted my experience as simply learning some valuable lessons. So, this pattern began early in our married life, but Jack's stories were not as frequent until we both ended up in Denver a few years later.

I believe my relationship with Cynthia was along a normal trend. Religion and moral codes play a more important role when any partner is older and has no experience. What people miss today is the gradual growth of pleasure and sexual experience. When you move slower, you savor each step. Perhaps going slower promotes better communication. Communication is a maturity factor and my adopting Cynthia's sexual growth having my undisclosed sensational experience was a contributor to my better developing her sexual maturity.

Men should learn at an early age how communicating and being tactful can enhance your sex life. Being forced into such a situation works great. However, there are many stories of boys who are too aggressive and they tend to handicap those of us that are more considerate. And there are some women who obviously enjoy having a man pursue their bodies aggressively. A man losing control, or too anxious over a woman might be a compliment to the woman.

I remember a high school buddy of mine confiding in me that his girlfriend thought he might be gay and was concerned about their pending marriage that he may not have enough experience. A week prior to his wedding at his bachelor party I advised him to get involved with his fiancée and pretend to lose control of himself, begin to caress her breasts, which he had never touched and when she reprimanded him for the deed, apologize and claim that he was so anxious to have sex with her that he lost control and would she forgive his enthusiasm.

The next day I inquired what happened. He explained it worked perfectly except she never made him stop. That really impressed him and they did withhold intercourse, but thought they had confirmed what would be a good wedding night. The reason he said they did so little during their engagement was because of their strong Christian principles. I can't say whether that example is typical or not, but it does illustrate religious influence on learning about sexual techniques.

Chapter 24. Infurred Sex

To give you an example about Jack's first year in New York, Jack was seduced by an older wealthy woman on Wall Street. His first affair was a co-worker, about forty years old and had the body of a movie star. We often described women as to what movie star they resembled. This new lady was a slightly older Catherine Zeta Jones type, Jack said. Her body dimensions were about the same.

What at first appeared normal, she invited Jack to have dinner at her apartment in Manhattan. Jack said it was obvious that she was to seduce him. Jack was to her, the new stud on the scene and yet she was discreet as far as the rest of the office's knowledge. It was a gossipy scene and Jack appreciated her attitude. They had only flirted in private and occasionally at lunch.

This sophisticated lady had a luxury apartment in Manhattan. She had invited Jack to a private candle lit dinner. The initial shock was that she opened the door to greet him dressed in a full-length mink coat. And during the catered meal she would flash her bare legs since the coat only came down to her mid calf. She wore high heels and no stockings, and her legs were nicely tanned, a tanning booth type. They played games using sexual innuendoes.

Her coat remained buttoned until dessert when she unbuttoned her two top buttons and pulled her mink coat off her shoulders revealing a very low neckline that turned out to be braless. She was beginning the seduction by flirting in the mink coat and flashing skin wherever possible. They began kissing and she sat on Jack's lap. Jack reached inside her coat to feel her breasts and she was completely naked under the coat.

Jack asked, "What is with the mink coat?"

She replied, "I want to have sex with you while keeping this coat on. I paid for it myself and it is my most prized possession. Next time we can get naked, but I have this urge to get fucked wearing this coat."

Jack expressed real interest in the game and asked, "Whatever floats your coat, but I have to tell you, you feel much better than the coat, you have fabulous skin."

"Thank you sweetie, but please, just for me, feel the mink and pretend it's me. This is something I have fantasized about and you fit my dreams perfectly. You are one hunk of a man."

She led Jack into her bedroom and undressed him raving about his beautiful body. She never removed the mink coat, ever. She went down on Jack and Jack thought he was being eaten by a bear, or a very large mink. She pulled the coat over her head while giving Jack head. That was unusual and a first for Jack. Jack had that subconscious counterproductive vision of the closeness of an animal's teeth against Long John. Jack said he held her head by holding the coat around her head. You might say they went "head to head" with infurred pleasure. It was only foreplay. There was some continued apprehension on Jack's part, but admittedly exciting.

So Jack pulled her away from his cock and went to kissing her bare breasts. When Jack kissed her breasts, the mink was pushed against his face; she cuddled his face in mink while he kissed her breasts. When he moved his tongue down her nicely tanned body, she closed the mink cover with him so he felt like he was making love to a furry animal, a furry passionate animal. The mink fur was always in Jack's face. She was lying on most of the coat, yet there was sufficient mink to close the unbuttoned part as Jack moved his face between her legs.

Then, she almost suffocated him in mink; it was like he had buried his face into a live animal. Her enthusiasm carried the moment, she was moving her hips wildly and Jack had to put a hand on her pelvic bone to protect his nose. She was rubbing Jack's head while covering it with mink. Jack ignored the weird feelings knowing he was eating a wild pussy that was making lots of noise and, thank goodness, not growling. She was having one hell of an orgasm pretending she was a mink, or perhaps, some wild animal. (Of course the term, "fucking like minks" comes to our minds.)

At the moment of "coitus beginnus," Jack felt like his cock was searching for a pussy hiding inside a very furry animal. He had to move Long John around under cover of mink searching for the wet spot. Once inside and he could not see her pussy, Jack said he felt like he was fucking a bear. Maybe, there was more to this game than he thought. Then she asked to be fucked from behind and again, Jack could only see the mink coat, not her ass. Jack was holding her ass covered up with mink, a weird situation to say the least.

Then she really got more weird, if that was possible, she took the coat off and insisted Jack wear the mink coat and fuck her some more in two positions, with her riding Jack with a closed coat, and with Jack on top so she could caress her coat on Jack's back. She always caressed the coat while Jack fucked her. She clutched Jack's ass outside of the coat, never touching his bare ass. Then she got on top of Jack and buttoned the coat shut so Jack looked like a bear. She lowered herself flat over Jack so she could rub her breasts on the mink. I can imagine that felt different to her, but good. I have seen gloves used to caress lovers and I suppose a mink feel would be a real luxury.

These two nuts played sex games by cross-dressing with the mink coat. They ended up with Jack on top, wearing the coat, so she could have her orgasm hugging Jack with her arms clinging to the coat. Jack said she caressed the coat madly when she was coming. Every time she had an orgasm, she yelled it out. Jack said she was obsessed with feeling the mink during sex. However, she never once suggested that Jack growl. When resting after sex, she did exclaim how sexy the game was and Jack agreed. I think he agreed just to appease her. Jack confided in me and said he thought the sex really did feel exceptional.

Shall we analyze that situation? Hmmm. Does that mean hairy backs are a turn on? Most women Jack and I talked to did not prefer hairy men. Jack and I are always clean-shaven and have no hair on our backs. We even have very little chest hair. Our basketball bodies were shiny and we were told by Carol Mason that we glowed in the dark with muscles that rippled. We both have great muscle definition. We lifted weights as part of our basketball routines, but not heavy stuff. Our muscles were well defined, but not like weight lifters. Should Jack be labeled a "bare fucker," or a "bear fucker?" You make the call. I hear a massage with mink gloves is a good thing. I will surmise that feeling mink during sex or having mink rubbed against you probably feels pretty good. I would hate to be the guy who got cum stuck in that expensive coat. Jack had several more encounters with this sexy "fur freak." Her enthusiasm for fucking like minks never waned. She was a bit too possessive so Jack moved on and occasionally went back for infurred sex.

So is this a hairy thing or an obsession with the feeling of fur? Is there a hint of bestiality here? Or, did she really love her coat that much? Every explanation seems too weird, yet Jack said the sex was fantastic without analyzing the weirdness. Jack never had a chance to interview the coated lady. He dated her only a few times and then copped out even though she was always available. However, Jack said the next few times they screwed only he got to wear the mink and she was always appreciative and equally passionate. He said performing cunnilingus with his face in the mink coat was the weirdest thing of the entire experience.

Who decides what is kinky and what is not. I suspect relating the experience to others would make it kinky, but privately it can be labeled as unusual at best. The term often used is "fetishes." Now there is a subject for discussion. I think it is beyond our pay grade because we can only evaluate what we experienced and cannot draw conclusions about Lord knows how many fetishes are out there. I would hope that these unusual tastes and practices do not involve pain.

We heard of a guy that had a leather strapped swing bolted in the ceiling over his bed. The woman sits in the swing naked and the swing straps raise her knees so her pussy is featured on the bottom of the swing. The swing is then twisted so when released the guy puts one inch into her pussy and the leather swing slowly turns and literally screws the vagina down on the penis. There are also games that swing the pussy into the cock. It also serves for some unusual rear entry options.

Jack and I have never tried drugs in spite of passing through those culture modes. My total alcohol consumption might total ten ounces during my lifetime and Jack, while enjoying an occasional cold beer was never into much social drinking and has never been drunk. I use the least acceptable social excuse; "I don't like the taste of alcoholic drinks." I was forever labeled a "nerd." However Jack once had sex with a woman who was high on "grass." He thought she might have enjoyed it more. I believe people who are both under some mental influence cannot get any higher than with just good sex, but we now must disclaim any conclusions about drugs never having any experience. Jack and I always felt that complete control over ones faculties is a must. I saw too many people make fools out of themselves or get their asses kicked while drunk. I swore that would never happen to me. Drinking and drugging simply made no sense to me.

I guess the mink coat may not be so weird after all. That was fair and balanced reporting; you make the call, weird or sensual?

Chapter 25. A Lousy Lay

Here's one more Quickie we will let you evaluate. I will now relate to you what Jack described to me as the worst sex partner ever. This babe, named Cassy should be in the record books.

Cassy, short for Cassandra was a New York celebrity. She did local TV weather reports, some modeling, and some TV acting from New York City. Jack met Cassy at a "due diligence" meeting. Cassy was a model hired to promote a new product to be released by a cosmetic company. It was lip gloss of some new type.

Jack said she appeared unapproachable; at least that was what one of his co-worker's said. No one apparently approached this lady because she was so beautiful. So Jack said he asked her,

"I heard and I believe it that because you are so beautiful that you are unapproachable. Do I dare tell you that I am attracted to you?" Jack asked.

"Why thank you, aren't you sweet, and so handsome. I thought men avoided me because I am so tall, but you make me feel a lot shorter. Can I invite you home with me for a drink? I'd like to read your horoscope." (That was quick.)

"I am honored and privileged. And I want to prove those guys wrong that told me you were out of my class." Jack responded.

"Who told you that?

"Never mind that, I am proud to be in your company; let them eat cake."

Well, Jack said when they got to her place she excused herself and Jack proceeded to stand at her bookcase and read some titles. His long arms spread from one end of the bookcase to the other. Her books were about horoscopes, health, and paranormal behavior. Suddenly Cassy appeared under his extended arms wearing a sexy negligee and asked if she could read his horoscope. She began to undress Jack by first removing his tie, while she asked about his birth date. Did he have to be naked to get read? The alignment of the stars seemed quite important to Cassy

"I apologize for this, but I haven't been with a man in so long I think I'm growing shut. Are you OK with this?"

Jack replied, "I am so flattered that I can be here for you. Perhaps we can open up your . . . . . . .potential?"

Cassy never heard anything Jack said. She only had a "sender" and no receiver. Cassy undressed Jack down to his underwear and led him into her bed. She had plenty to say about how great Jack's body was and what great shape he was in. She asked about his vitamin intake. A pesky cat followed them and she shooed the cat back into her living room. There was no door and the small apartment was like one room with the bed at one end. Jack said he removed her negligee and she seemed to pose while he did so. She was six feet tall and had a coke bottle figure with nice medium sized breasts, and great legs. She even had makeup on her legs. She sort of looked like the lady that played "Wonder Woman" and I can't recall her non-screen name. But, Cassy talked too much. She talked incessantly about health and the star alignment and how this intercourse with Jack was meant to happen. It was written in the stars.

Jack laid her gently on her bed. He took off his own underwear and he swears she never noticed that he was erect; she never looked at their genitals. She was still asking Jack questions about his horoscope while Jack was caressing and kissing her breasts. As she watched Jack kiss her breasts and not seemingly getting in the mood she began to explain that her Chinese herbalist was the same as some famous Chinamen. Her herbalist had advised her that sex gave her renewed energy and that her focal source of energy was about four inches below her navel. She was anxious to recharge, she said.

Jack could have cared less about her herbalist even though she promised to make him a carrot juice drink after sex. She talked about sex like it was a distant subject. So, Jack went down on her while she kept talking. Jack flattened his tongue on her clitoris and waited for a response. There was none. Her pussy tasted like vitamins. Jack said he gave it his best "lickity split" shot and felt liked he failed to deliver. She paused occasionally, went quiet for a moment and then began quoting her herbalist. Jack raised his head and asked her if she was OK and she responded by explaining that she had been rubbing vitamin "E" between her labia as instructed by her herbalist. She began to explain the theory behind that Doctor's prescription when Jack gave up and mounted her. He said he tried a slow fuck while trying to kiss her, but she was still explaining why she put the vitamin "E" in her pussy, so Jack decided to fuck fast and hard. She shut up and seemed to feel the thrusting, but showed no emotion. Jack had to lift her legs for a better entry, she seemed not to notice. When Jack was about to fire, she yelled, "Oh Jack, Jack."

Jack let the juice fly and continued pumping thinking he finally got some passion from her.

Cassy yelled, "Did you see that? My God, my cat just jumped from the book case to the mantle, an unbelievable leap."

When Jack withdrew, she began to explain that he had just enhanced her energy center, like charging her battery. Jack wondered if her cat got charged.

"What energy?" Jack said, "You never moved a muscle, I even had to lift your legs into the air and hold them there so we could fuck. Couldn't you have at least wiggled a little or reacted to what was happening to us?"

"Now just you wait a minute, you mean that did not feel good, you obviously were satisfied and you did finish."

"I must not have noticed your passion, did I fail somewhere?"

"Jack, you were wonderful, why do you seem upset?"

"Well, I was worried about your cat and all."

"Oh, did you see that incredible leap?"

Jack said, "No, I was busy fucking and I wasn't watching the damn cat."

Cassy seemed insulted and said, "So you did not enjoy having sex with me?"

"I'm sorry, I enjoyed having sex with myself and I did enjoy using your equipment, but frankly, that was the worst sex I have ever had."

"Will you please get dressed and leave, and excuse me," She pouted.

"Ok, I'm sorry, are you going to replace the vitamin "E" in there, and do you want me to pay for it?" Jack was shouting through the bathroom door.

Cassy had run to the bathroom and slammed the door shut. Jack got dressed and left.

A few months later Jack and friends went to a Chinese restaurant and there was Cassy hosting the seating. She gave Jack a dirty look. Later when things were less busy, Jack went over to Cassy to apologize.

"So, Jack," she said, "have you managed to find another woman to have sex with you?"

"Yes," Jack replied, "and I think I am gaining some good experience. I think I'm improving, How's your pussy . . . cat."

"I see you are still a smart ass."

Jack did the gentleman thing and simply said he was sorry for all the trouble he caused her.

Jack heard later at his office that Cassy was having an affair with the rich owner of the Chinese restaurant and he was a foot shorter than her. Apparently her Chinese herbalist fixed them up. Jack never did get the carrot juice and never saw Cassy again. Jack's thought was that it is possible to meet a woman that is a lousy lay. I wonder if we can learn anything from this event. Did Cassy have a low libido? Did she only need the reassurance that she was appealing? Was she only satisfied about being appealing and that was the end of the urge? Was she that inhibited or that inexperienced? Should Cassy only have sex during a full moon? She had been married to a US Naval pilot, who was gone a lot overseas and she divorced him, so she must have been somewhat experienced.

That was the only bad experience either of us ever even heard about. I don't know what to make of Cassy, but I think there is a lesson here. Bad sex is when one partner shows no emotion or reaction. One should contribute something other than just being present. It is most unusual that any woman about to get fucked would not raise and spread her legs. It is not natural to offer one's body for sex and not want to contribute. It is possible for someone really inexperienced to reflect innocence, but even under those circumstances there would be a display of passion or at worst enthusiasm. This goes back to the beginning of this story, that reactions to a partner's foreplay are absolutely necessary for good sex.

I'm sure you have heard the stories of women faking orgasms. Why would a woman fake an orgasm? To make her partner feel he has succeeded, or to end the session? In either case adult communications would have solved the problem. The faker should know how to tell her partner what to do to improve the feelings, or find a new love. We cannot emphasize enough about good foreplay and adult communications.

Talking about sex should be considered foreplay. Unfortunately when people get old they get physically tired and even routine sex takes too much energy. The energy level is a trade off for pleasure. We believe foreplay works on the tired and weary partners, but one partner has to have the energy to perform foreplay or lose the moment. How many tired women will perform oral sex to get fucked and how many men will go down on a tired woman taking the time to warm her up. It may be easier to just climb aboard and be quick. Consideration becomes the most important factor and this is where many marriages go wrong. People need to take care of each other's needs and when older the consideration will make for a better marriage. Perhaps a new attitude is the prescription for a renewed sex life. Energy levels and old age determine the frequency of desired sexual pleasure. I think that problem is bigger than this story since all participants in this story are more energetic.

I think the biggest complaint among married women is that their husbands grow into therapeutic sex and become routine. Many married women complain that they become holes in the mattress and their husbands are no longer romantic; they feel taken for granted, or as some say taken for "granite." Isn't this an attitude adjustment? The only advice I have for those circumstances is for wives to initiate foreplay and hope for reciprocity. Try straddling his leg first and undulate showing some hunger, after all you're about to get laid anyway, maybe you can offer yourself for foreplay. ("Honey, I want you so much, will you eat me first") If you don't get a reaction mention it and beg for foreplay. There is something very sexy about a wife who asks for foreplay, or shows the desire for it. Secondly, once he enters you express some excitement and ask for more strokes. You can also initiate foreplay before bedtime.

I apologize for all men that sexual gratification comes so easily that consideration for others is a fault. It is the fault of the guy's little head and we have little control over those things.

I wonder how many women will listen to that theory? Hey guys, I tried.

256

Chapter 26, Josie Wails

There was this amazing woman named Josie that Jack met while he was working in New York. Josie worked as a secretary at the same securities firm with Jack. Josie was only five feet tall and was a cute red head that resembled Sissy Spacek. Jack and I, whenever possible described women by whatever movie star best resembled them. It was a game we played and I had mentioned this before in this story.

Josie was a very curvy girl for a small person. Her red hair was cut short like a man's cut and was wavy and curly. The shade of red was almost blond and it was natural. It is unfair to describe her as cute when she was very beautiful. She was always smiling and was green eyed. She had a small mouth, but full lips. She resembled a child's doll, very delicate and that image was very deceptive.

A strange event happened to Jack, that sounds unlikely to me, but I have no reason to doubt Jack. Jack met three women that lived together including Josie; they were her roommates. After sharing drinks at a local pub, Jack found himself at a hot tub party with these three women in a basement recreational room that was available by signing up for its exclusive use by tenants.

The women had been drinking and not drunk, but teased Jack into their private hot tub club. The tub was reserved for tenants and was a red wood tub. There was a bar across the room stocked with beer and hard liquor, a BYOB bar. (Furnish your own) The small room was furnished with five big black beanbag chairs. The room was carpeted red and had nice wood paneled walls and locked from the inside to assure privacy. There was a great sound system playing Elvis music. Elvis was at his peak in popularity. The girls were taking turns dancing with Jack, and each other. The girl's dances were very suggestive and their pleasure was outnumbering Jack and trying to embarrass him. Jack was both confident and game knowing he could hold his own.

During a musical break, the girls huddled and Jack overheard them say,

"I will if you will. Ok, let's all do it at once."

The girls began to undress hurriedly with little warning. They all got naked and climbed into the hot tub and started the jets. Jack focused on Josie, who had this tight body with a cute ass. Only one percent of the population are redheads (She was a real redhead) and this delightful little lady had the amazing quality of always smiling, even when she talked. Her small patch of pubic hair was a perfect red match. She smiled at Jack while she undressed knowing she was being watched. She was not the least bit embarrassed. She was always looking at Jack, took her time and when she caught his eye, she would wink. Jack was undressing slowly because he was enjoying the strip show. Josie's smile was exceptional because some people's smiles are more contagious than others. The girls chanted to Jack, that since he was the slowest, he had to do a strip tease before he could join them in the tub.

That reminded me of a game we played as teenagers. All the guys would have to pee in front of a car in the dark and the first one done could turn on the headlights. It was a dumb game and caused a lot of wet pant legs for no good reason. Fortunately no girls were allowed to play, although their participation would have certainly upped the ante. I think I already mentioned that.

So, Jack proceeded to take off his clothes slowly to the music. The girls applauded gleefully and Jack pretended not to be embarrassed. Fortunately, Jack was blessed with the kind of software that dangles nicely before being aroused. Some men grow more when aroused and some shrink more than others. It really doesn't matter, but being exposed in a small crowd of admirers, it helps to be well hung. My "thing" seems to hide from public exposure, but always ready for immediate action. The ladies were admiring Long John Silver.

Jack climbed into the tub and the ladies were concentrated on one side leaving Jack half the tub to himself. Once in the tub, while the ladies were bunched up opposite Jack, Josie was closest to Jack's right. The setting was imbalanced and the girl's breasts were barely submerged. The boobs seemed to be floating. Jack was slowly growing an underwater erection, which is not an easy task under hot water. He thought the circulation and the power jets contributed to arousing everybody. Also, adding to Jack's arousal was each girl standing up and doing a little dance to the music hoping Jack would take a turn. The girls being shorter were exposing only their breasts when dancing. The tub was just deep enough that the girls knew that Jack being six feet five inches tall would have to eventually expose Long John Silver.

The girls seemed to enjoy performing the big tease, while urging Jack to stand up. Jack stood only briefly revealing his half erection. His minor problem was being outnumbered, but not wanting to show embarrassment. Jack was trying to figure out how to isolate Josie. The girls were loose and giddy and just drunk enough to praise and admire Jack's half erection, but they did not reach for it. Long John's exposure time was limited to seconds, just enough for the girls to want to see more. Their eyes were fixated on the magnificent Long John Silver. Jack introduced them by explaining John's name, which gave them a second look. It was a sexy move and Jack did touch himself a few times to accentuate Long John, and the ladies were getting very horny. This was a big role reversal here with a Man tempting women rather than the reverse. This was a new role for Jack and an interesting study into wondering about how many women would enjoy such a show, or would admit to the game. The girls were really turned on, but gaining courage making more suggestive moves towards Jack, looking but not touching. Josie was running her tongue over her lips while watching Long John. Obviously, Jack had no fear of the situation, but was focused on Josie, who was less drunk and reflecting more serious arousal.

Josie, on the other hand, seemed more in control; and since she had not really been drinking a lot, her teasing was more sober and calculated. She just smiled and when she stood up and danced she made eye contact with Jack and winked with each of Jack's admiring looks. All he could see was her breasts, but her hip movement even underwater was stimulating. Her timely winking and constant smile was really sexy. Josie had cute perky breasts. Dancing women that are bare breasted almost always raise their arms over their heads to better pull the breasts higher. It is a great pose for breast admirers. Josie looked very professional.

Any breast more than a mouthful is supposed to be a waste anyway, but Josie had the smoothest skin. She was almost pink in that dimly lit room. Perhaps such skin would be a disaster in the bright sun; definitely not the tanning type. Her breasts had a clean appealing desirable "put in mouth" look. Josie had a confident strut to her dance and taunted Jack by pretending to move her breasts into grabbing range. Josie would raise her arms over her head and gently shake her breasts with the music. The other two girls sensed Josie's more serious attention to Jack and were more intent on watching for Jack's reaction.

When Josie was about to sit down, Jack grabbed her by her waist and said,

"Why don't you move to this side of the tub so someone is sitting next to me?"

As Jack pulled Josie over to his left side, Josie stumbled and fell onto Jack's chest. Neither person's move was intentional and Jack deftly caught Josie so she wouldn't get her head wet. He grabbed her by her waist and lifted her up and righted her position as she fell on to Jack's lap. Guess what happened, and what are the odds; Josie accidentally fell onto Jack's now firm erection. Jack's penis helmet sort of ran the crease between Josie's labia like it was plowing a single furrow, and settled with a full plunged seven inches into little "five foot" Josie. She reacted and turned her head in shock and looked at Jack, not smiling, just surprised at being suddenly impaled. Jack said, "oops." Josie twisted herself and buried her head into Jack's neck and was obviously embarrassed. She had her back against Jack's chest. One of the other girls, exclaimed, "What happened, did you sit on his cock?"

"No," Said Josie, "I just fell against it, did I hurt you Jack," Josie lied.

"I'm fine," said Jack, who was also in a state of shock, but pleasantly surprised. What were the odds of that happening considering water pressure and all? The physics didn't seem possible since human orifices close under water. Only in movies have we seen people fuck in water. I believe it is possible, but since it requires such effort, you'd think the players would move to dry land.

Jack looked at Josie, who was now grinning from ear to ear, and said,

"I'm Ok if you just don't move."

Rising up would have disclosed the unusual sitting coital position, so neither one of them moved.

"Can I move a little bit, I'd like to face my friends, but I'm not getting up. This is the most comfortable I have been in this tub." Josie winked at her two friends.

With that, Josie moved and rose up a few inches and settled back on Jack's cock smiling at him first knowing she was having a good time keeping the girls more curious and going on with some humor about having touched Jack's cock. She was facing her roommates with a big smile. The ladies were obviously envious thinking Josie was only sitting on his lap, but against his cock. Also, it was then settled that Jack was enjoying and focused on Josie, so the other girls soon excused themselves giggling and whispering all the way while getting dressed and leaving Jack and Josie alone. However, the door was unlocked and Jack and Josie couldn't move for fear of losing the "water tight" insert.

When they were alone, Jack lifted Josie up and sat on the tub side out of the water. Josie lifted her right leg across Jack's chest and now faced him without losing his cock. Her legs were now wrapped around Jack; almost, since she was so small. She looked him in the eye and asked,

"How did you do that so smoothly? I have never been entered under water. I still don't know how that happened."

Jack assured her, "I promise you that it was an accident, but how sweet of you to keep it quiet. I am surprised I entered you so easily because you are so small and I didn't want to hurt you. And you are really very tight. Are you OK?"

"No way did that hurt, you feel great, I'm just surprised, but happy to sit on you. That was the first time I ever got so familiar on such short notice."

Josie continued, "If you are really worried about hurting me because I am so little, let me give you some advice; big girls have big pussies, but us little girls, we are all pussy."

We like it when women acknowledge the term "pussy." It is the sexiest reference. Jack and I often asked the question of women to determine which terms regarding sex were offensive or acceptable, or maybe even were more arousing.

Some terms are offensive, like cunt for females or "prick" for males. The most acceptable term for a woman's vagina is "pussy." The term pussy goes back to 1530 in English pertaining to a cat. In the 17th century, there is a famous quote, actually a toast;

"Aeneas, here is health to thee, to pussy and good company."

According to Playboy magazine, in the 18th century there was a sexy banter that went something like this:

"Give her pussy a taste of cream."

That was supposed to be complimentary during Shakespearean times. Other old slang terms for pussy that never caught on were, quim, teasle, and motte.

That reminds me of the story of two Priests working the same crossword puzzle. One Priest says, "What's a three letter word describing a woman that ends in "unt?"

Why "Aunt, of course," says the second Priest.

"Oops, can I borrow your eraser?"

Sexual language and genital terms went into two different directions, one that was seductive or complimentary, and another that was to be purposely disrespectful. I don't think the latter was necessarily related to sex. The word "fuck" has many uses. "Fuck you" is a taunt or can be used to end a conversation with an insult. The words "fuck me" may not be a tender seductive invitation, but certainly can reflect passion.

The word "fuck" supposedly is derived from colonial times when wrongdoer's heads were placed in stockades with a sign over their heads naming their sin. The word "fuck" is an acronym for "For Unlawful Carnal Knowledge," but I also read somewhere that the term was used by Roman soldiers during Caesar's conquests. I read for a fact that Roman soldiers used the middle finger gesture as an insult, but I don't know what verbiage accompanied the gesture.

Women never say "what a nice prick you have." The most frequent word used by women is "cock." The same can be said for most sex jokes. Penis is a little clinical, but probably the second most used term. The term "cocksucker" has gone away as a compliment. Fellatio is always acceptable, as is just saying, "I love giving or receiving oral sex." Another term is "giving or receiving head." That refers to arousing an organ to make a little engorged head. I apologize if any terms in this book are offensive, but after polling these exceptional women, we settled on "pussy, cock, penis, and an occasional positive vaginal reference.

Acceptable sexual slang has always been a problem for too many people. To be offended, or offend somebody because you chose the wrong word is a problem. A man would never say, "You have a beautiful cunt." Or would a man proposition a woman and say, "how about a little intercourse?" It's not romantic. You would not compliment a woman by telling her she has great mammary glands. There is a major difference when using the various terms.

Here is a list of names used to describe a penis. Cock, summer sausage, sausage, Johnson, wang, willie, dick, peter, schlong, dong, wiener, pecker, prick, baloney, baloney pony, tool, the one eyed trouser worm, one eyed monster, joy stick, snake, rumple foreskin, woody, third leg, dip stick, dobber, member, pile driver, shaft, rod, Mr. happy, pole, knob, lizard, ding dong, tube steak, tallywacker, dingaling, wand, magic wand, family jewels, schwantz, a hot meat injection, pussy plunger, and any number of personal pet names such as Long John Silver and Winston. (Winston tastes good like a hard penis should).

I'll do some research on feminine pussy names, but complimentary ones are easy. Derogatory names should be forgotten. Pussy is by far the most acceptable term. Vagina is second, but lacks some complimentary image. But, I am digressing, back to Josie.

Josie wailed, "Well, that sudden wonderful impaling was better than shaking hands or even kissing, and I promise this never happened to me before. I am so pleased to meet you and hello and welcome to long John Silver. I would have liked to have met the good fellow first when he was standing at attention, but sight unseen was extra exciting. I didn't think such a move was possible under water."

Josie reached up and shook Jack's hand while sitting on his cock and officially introduced herself.

"My name is Josie Stratton and we met at the office, but not so officially as this more familiar introduction. Don't you think we should kiss next? I think I'm pretty tight from the water pressure, Ok with you?" said Josie, "so this meeting must be special, certainly different, and maybe was meant to be. I like what happened, I am excited, so, can I do anything more to please you? Do you want to fuck me some more? I mean you aren't done, are you?"

"I think we are fucking, but let's get better acquainted, please let me stay inside you; you feel so warm and fantastic."

Jack and Josie began to kiss passionately and when Jack came up for air he replied, "I think I'm turning into a prune, so let's stay attached until we move over to that bean bag." Jack's legs were still soaking.

Having said that Jack easily rose up with Josie's legs wrapped around him, and with one hand cupped her ass. He stepped out of the tub (His legs had been immersed) and easily carried her to a bean bag without slipping out of her. Jack passed by the door and Josie bent over backwards and reached the door and relocked it. She seemed to be gripping him with an unnatural tightness even out of the water. Jack wondered if her smallness had anything to do with her tight pussy. He laid her onto a big beanbag and resumed kissing her on the lips. Jack had to curl up considerably to kiss such a small woman. He finally withdrew and, yes her pussy did tug at him as he withdrew.

Jack than went down on her and Josie made so many delicious noises, that Jack had to be asked to stop. What was unusual was that when Jack looked at Josie while performing oral sex, she had her eyes closed, but she was still smiling, always smiling. She was lying on the beanbag stool and Jack was kneeling on the floor.

Jack moved to the bottom position thinking Josie could control the cock depth better, but Josie mounted Jack and bounced as if she were "all pussy." Jack was now lying on the beanbag, which formed his body shape. Josie mounted Jack and had to spread her legs further because of Jack's wide body. She sat on Jack's cock, was in control and was really passionate. She almost seemed professional, and yes, she never stopped smiling, always keeping eye contact with Jack, which she seemed to prefer. Jack allowed Josie to stroke and do all the work reaching joint orgasms. She even smiled while coming to a climax and still made those sweet noises of pleasure.

I don't think anyone's sex life would be complete without being "bean bagged." The big beanbag forms the perfect body shape for any sex act. When Jack was licking Josie, he was on his knees and the bag supported her at just the right angle. I too, have been bean bagged and I was on top. The angle was very conducive to good sex.

Jack said he was so intrigued with Josie that he invited her home with him to spend the rest of the night. He promised her breakfast and wanted the time to get to know her better. She accepted. She was delightful company, so upbeat, so happy, and it was catching. Jack was feeling very good. Her conversation was delightful and sexy. She never stopped flirting or complimenting Jack's love making abilities. Who wouldn't enjoy that?

When Jack awoke Saturday morning, Josie appeared to be sleeping with his penis in her mouth and looked like a baby with a nipple, or sucking a pacifier. Josie looked "flushed" or even perhaps "pink." He was admiring her cute well-shaped body. He woke her gently and she began sucking and smiling with her eyes closed. She was like a "Shmoo," the Al Capp creation that was totally dedicated to giving pleasure as they sacrificed their very existence. Josie was pathologically made up with this urge to please. When Jack woke her up, he praised her generous sleepy attention. She did the most surprising thing he ever imagined. As soon as Jack was hard and at full staff, she surprised him and "deep throated" his entire penis. She withdrew, smiled at him and asked if he'd like to cum that way.

Jack was stunned at the deep throat feeling, the view, and her attitude. "Where did you learn to do that?" Jack asked.

I will tell you something very private if you promise you won't judge me."

But first, they had great sex with Jack on top and Josie hanging on like a pouched animal. When completed, Jack asked Josie to tell him what made her attitude so great.

Josie nodded and Jack was now paying close attention. (I'll paraphrase and summarize the story.)

Josie said that she was raised on an Oklahoma farm and that when she was fifteen she was gang raped by four prisoners that had escaped from a local prison. The men were brutal and had burned her with cigarette butts, which was a form of torture. They slapped her and made her perform fellatio while being raped. It was painful and a horrible experience. The police became involved and soon caught the prisoners, but they were already serving in prison and years were added to their sentences. Josie was put under psychiatric care for about a year. She resented the clinic and was paranoid as if everybody in the small community knew what happened to her and was monitoring her recovery. She was most uncomfortable in these circumstances.

Then, she ran away from home at age seventeen, having first finished high school amid the small town society; she also ran away from the clinic. No one knew where she was and she did not contact home for years. She did call her Mother and told her not to worry about her.

"I made up my own mind that I was not going to let that experience ruin my life and the clinic was a nothing but a reminder of what I wanted to forget. I got angry and promised myself that without any professional help I would change my attitude about men to the opposite of that horrible experience. I programmed myself not to resent men, but to adore them realizing what had happened to me was so rare. I think people are good."

"I read everything I could about good sex. I even secretly rented porno movies, and read sexy romantic novels. I went to typing school and got a job in Dallas at a big company. I got my own apartment and lived by myself, never going out until I felt I was ready. I practiced everything that I could, but not with men. I got all the sex toys and practiced so I could deep throat and played with a vibrator until I mastered orgasms. I saw the deep throat trick in a porno movie. I learned a lot from porno movies."

"My first Beau was shocked and thought I must have been a hooker, but he liked what I did. I dumped him because I didn't like his attitude, he was immature. I seduced a married man, practiced on him and then dumped him, too. But I did learn how to give pleasure and frankly I grew into a very willing, easily satisfied woman. I won the battle of my life. I so much enjoy sex and men; I just have developed the ability to know when I will be appreciated. I know a good man when I meet one, and you Jack are sensational. You are a great lover and you make me want to pleasure you until I prove my point; that I am good and I enjoy myself, and I love men, I love cocks, I love to suck on them, and most of all I love getting fucked in style. I haven't been with a lot of men, but I know what I am doing. I'm not looking for a husband, or anything permanent. I just want to feel you and live for the moment. OK?"

Jack was impressed, and stunned. Jack said he wanted to hold her, which he did and she was like a small child. They became great friends and over the following year Josie definitely was not wailing about life, Josie was always available even if Jack dated others. At work, she would send him notes and tell him she'd like to suck on his cock and all he had to do was ask. She even wished she could do him at work, but privacy was out of the question. She never stopped smiling and did everything in her power to please all other co-workers, not with sex, but just doing little things for her co-workers, men and women alike. Jack and Josie were steady dates and she often slept over with Jack. There are many good rumors about redheads and their sexual prowess just like there are regarding blonds and brunettes, different races and even different religions. I read in Playboy magazine that when redheads undergo surgery, they require 20% more anesthesia. That seems inexplicable to me.

The amazing lesson about Josie was her attitude. I can't imagine any woman enduring what she did and to get angry and challenge and singly handedly over came her tragic past. She managed life very well and did accomplish a complete makeover on her life. Her countenance literally sparkled and she radiated joy everywhere she went. Jack said he admired her more than any woman he'd ever met. Josie wails? Absolutely not!

Chapter 27. Euro Lag Knees

This event is weird, but not necessarily crude. It begins with one of those New York City blackouts and Jack's hyper-mammiferous neighbor. Her name was Helen and she had the biggest breasts, and, in her mind that probably was the sum total of her being. She thought big tits entitled her to special privileges in life. Unfortunately there are women who use their sex appeal as leverage. A man better behave or they will withhold sex. Or, "if you are good to me I may let you touch my tits." This is a really bad attitude and usually will drive a man away. Anyway, during the blackout Helen knocked on Jack's door with a candle and said she was alone and afraid. So Jack let her in. Unfortunately she was dressed in a robe that frequently parted too much at the top.

Jacks fear was if those "things" were to escape, what would he do. Being an ex basketball player he'd probably try to catch them to prevent her boobs from hitting the floor.

Josie was Jack's main squeeze and Jack was expecting Josie anytime and was worried about her arriving under the blackout circumstances with Helen invading his privacy. The taxis were running, and Josie was late. Helen kept apologizing for her being robed. The problem was that Jack was not interested in Helen and having an affair with a neighbor would have drastically affected his privacy. Jack's NY apartment was very small. But he did have a shower stall that was big enough for Jack's Six foot five inch frame. Helen asked if she could just wash her hair. Jack argued he may run out of hot water with the electricity shut down. She reminded Jack that he had a gas hot water heater.

Helen sort of bullied her way in and Jack felt she was hoping to get a reaction out of him regarding her huge endowment. Actually, without being cruel, Jack and I were not impressed by large soft floppy boobs. They had to be restrained with special equipment and when exposed dropped and spread in all directions. I apologize to such women, but please know that an attitude adjustment is all you need to be competitive. I repeat, in my opinion, real hefty boobs are OK, but don't use them as the main attraction to promote yourself. Large breasted women usually need an attitude adjustment not a breast adjustment.

Sure enough, Helen came out of the shower holding only a towel with shoulders back and her boobs hanging out. Helen could have used a belt for a bra.

Oh oh, Josie was coming in the door and there were Helen's boobs on display. Josie immediately went to Helen, stuck out her hand and introduced herself. Helen was embarrassed and explained that she just wanted a shower. No problem, Josie was most ingratiating. Helen left and Josie was her usual bubbly appreciative self. She asked no questions. She was unbelievably trusting and cheerful. Jack told Josie how he was offended by Helen and talked about her type. Josie and Jack had a candle light dinner and warm cuddly sex that lasted for hours counting the talking and the foreplay.

During the evening Josie informed Jack that she hated New York and that her Mother had cancer and she had to move back to Dallas soon. Jack was truly disappointed. If Josie could have hung in there, I suspect she could have been a permanent relationship for Jack, but the real sad news was that Josie could not have children. Perhaps her sterility had something to do with her being attacked. At first she told Jack she was on the pill. I think Jack fell in love with Josie. Everything worked against them and a long distance love affair with a non-potential wife was not to be. I think Josie loved Jack, too.

Josie moved to Dallas a few weeks later. Jack was saddened. He knew Josie was irreplaceable and he would miss her sweet personality. The lesson for us men is Josie's rare personality and her pathological love to please her man. She was definitely a "giver." Whenever you meet a woman who is such a giving person reciprocity becomes natural. It grows on you and most men find themselves so appreciative that they become more of the giving type. Jack said he had a strong desire to perform oral sex on Josie as his reciprocity, but he so enjoyed her reaction that her reciprocity was even greater. Isn't that the case for all foreplay? There was so much more to learn from Josie's attitude.

Jack began to go to the "Village" with another bachelor friend from the office, Eddie Fannon, to listen to this really sexy German girl singer. Lena Vostadd was tall, about five nine, and had this sexy raspy low singing voice. At about their third attendance Jack told Eddie he was going to try and date Lena. After her 11:00 pm performance Jack approached Lena and said,

"I love your voice and I'll tell you why. It is so nice to hear a mellow sound compared to all the other female singers that screech. And I must say you are so beautiful that the combination of your good looks and sexy voice has captivated me."

"Vat a vonderful thing to say, vhat may I play mit you?" That comment set Jack back. He didn't know if she was playing a language flirting game or not. But Jack held his composure and blushed a bit and said,

"Can you play and sing any Irish songs? My name is Jack Callahan, and I have become a big fan of yours."

"Yes, and you are so beeg. How beeg are you, undt you say you are mine?"

"I'm about two meters tall and I used to play basketball."

"Vhen can I play mit you?

Jack said, "Well, there's this rare Irish ditty that is sort of a novelty yet funny song, it is called, "Seven Drunken Nights."

"Can you zing somezing?"

Jack sings, "As I came home one Monday night as drunk as I could be, I saw a horse outside my door where my old horse should be, well I called my wife and I said to her will you kindly tell to me, who owns that horse outside my door where my old horse should be? (Chorus next, wife sings). Ah, you're drunk you're drunk you silly old drunk, and still you canna see, that's a lovely sow me mother sent to me. (Male sings) Well, it's many a day I've traveled a hundred miles or more, but a saddle on a sow, I never saw before."

Jack explained, "The song has many verses, one for each day of the week, Tuesday, there's a coat on a hook where his coat used to be, on Wednesday he sees a pipe on his chair where his pipe should be. The wife sings "that's a whistle my mother sent to me" and he responds, "tobacco in a whistle he's never seen before." We should rehearse and you can sing the female part. Here's the final verse, you sing the female part for me, and I'll lead."

"When I came home one Sunday night as drunk as drunk could be, I saw a cock between her legs where my cock used to be. Well, I called my wife and I said to her will you kindly tell to me, who owns that cock between your legs where my old cock should be?"

Chorus: "Ah you're drunk you're drunk you silly old fool, and still you canna see, That's just another whistle me mother sent to me.

(Male) Well, it's many a day I've traveled a hundred miles or more, but hairy balls on a whistle I never saw before."

Lena sang the chorus a second time with Jack, laughed heartily and begged Jack,

"Ach de leibre, Dot ezze goot, can you teach me zat song unt ve vill play together?"

Jack had a fair singing voice, but he was not talented enough to give up his day job.

"Will you have lunch with me tomorrow?"

"Yah, dot eez very goot. You are very handsome man, I should like to play mit you."

Jack blushed again and they agreed to meet right across the street at a small Village restaurant. Lena asked Jack if he could stay until she got off work, but that was about three in the morning and Jack explained he was not a night owl. Jack and Eddie stayed for another show. When they left, Lena blew Jack a kiss. That all seemed promising.

When Jack met Lena the next day, it was one o'clock in the afternoon and it was to be her breakfast. That was fine with Jack. Lena had only arrived in New York about a month ago and was hoping to launch her career as a folk singer and guitar player. She really was good and her raspy, but perfectly pitched voice had a future for the folk music of the day. Lena resembled Mary, from the then popular Peter, Paul and Mary, except she was long legged and well built. It was hard to replay any details because she wore loose fitting hippie clothes. She appeared to be a natural blond, there were no dark roots on her head. Jack and I always had a better view of head tops.

"I grew up during zee war undt my Motter undt me spend much time in bunkers. I have guitar and practice much. I go to school in Germany undt study music. I like America. Now you tell me about you und vee play together this Irish song, yes?"

"I'm from Michigan and I studied finance and I work on Wall Street as a stock broker. My grandparents came to America from Ireland and I am a third generation Irishman. My Father and his friends used to drink and sing a lot and some of their songs were cute and as I said a novelty."

Jack had written the words for Lena and all she had to do was put it to music. After breakfast, Lena asked Jack back to her apartment, which was grungy in a sense, but what one would expect in the Greenwich Village area. Lena's apartment was even smaller than Jack's. It was all one room with a bathtub and with a very old shower and one of those toilets with a big tank hanging overhead. They sat at the little eating table, which only had two chairs. Jack sang along with Lena until she caught on to the Irish lilt, which never really worked. An Irish ditty with a German accent was hard to understand, but her accent made the ditty more charming. It was a fun day of music and laughter.

So Jack began to attend some of Lena's performances. He always got a front table and Eddie joined him sometimes. Jack simply could not stay until the wee hours, so they began to date a few times during the early evenings, or on weekends. And Lena performed Jack's song many a night. Jack did not push Lena for any sex, but they kissed one evening when Lena could not stand it any longer. She finally blurted out,

"Do you vant to fock me? I vant you and I am very vet."

"Oh yeah, I want to fuck you, but I was hoping not to rush you. Fucking you has always been on my mind, but I am so fascinated by your talent and beautiful body that I did not want to lose the moment by being too aggressive. You German's are sure outspoken and I love it."

"Very goot. Now I must tell you zat I must see you first naked undt vorking undt I vill show you mine, understand?"

"I'm not sure what you mean."

"You come Saturday at noon undt you must show me your cock undt how it vorks. I show you my pussy undt you see how it vorks before vee make love, yes?"

Jack was excited, but not really knowing what to expect, so they kissed some and Jack felt her breasts, which must have been permissible all along. She did not bare her breasts, just allowed Jack to explore.

When Jack arrived Saturday noon, Lena was wearing a long terry cloth robe and was freshly showered. Her hair was blond and was wet and she smelled great. Lena led Jack over to the bathtub and she sat down on the toilet seat. Jack had no idea what to expect.

"You vill take off your clothes please."

Jack stripped and Lena watched him closely. She was only a few feet away and her sitting view was right at Jack's "cock level." When Jack was naked, he was not hard. Lena had Jack turn around so she could see his ass muscles. Lena made no move to touch him. She stood up and motioned for Jack to sit.

"You are a beautiful man. You have nice strong body."

Lena disrobed next and stood with her legs apart. She flexed her breasts. Raised her arms over her head and turned around.

"You like, Yes?

"I like very much, yes. Did I pass the test?

"Soon, yes."

They were both naked and posing. Lena traded places with Jack, she sat down on the toilet seat and spread her legs with her labia exposed and rubbed herself a few times.

"You see pussy, yes? Now you make cock hard, yes, undt you show me how it vorks. You watch how I vork pussy and I watch how you play cock."

Apparently what Lena wanted was for the two of them to masturbate for each other. She was to demonstrate what felt good to her and she wanted to see Jack ejaculate. She had him straddle the tub so his cum would land in the tub and she would watch while she gave herself an orgasm. Obviously it was to be mutually stimulating. This was a hell of an introduction. There was no light on and the daylight shown through the open bathroom door.

Lena started out slowly, but picked up the pace by rubbing herself sideways. Jack tried to stroke Long John and keep up with her pace and watch her carefully. Her hand movements on herself were fascinating. Lena became very vocal and told Jack what a beautiful cock he had and to try and come with her. She began to yell, "Yes, yes, yes" and raised her legs up in the air, putting one leg on the tub. Jack moved his hands faster and kept quiet because he was fascinated by her action and reaction. Jack shot his semen into the bathtub and Lena was all eyes. They starred at each other exhausted. Jack waited for Lena to speak.

"Yes, I vant to fock you even more now. Next time you vill lick my pussy, and I suck your cock yes? And ve vill fuck plenty, yes?"

"Yes!"

They showered together in very small quarters and Lena washed Jack's cock. When they were toweling, Lena sucked on Jack's cock, but did not try for a climax. She said she liked Jack's cock and was anxious to meet again. Of course, the next day was not soon enough for Jack; a Sunday afternoon in bed for the initial sexual encounter was to be perfect.

They did everything for each other and what impressed Jack was that Lena was very demanding. Jack liked that. They explored each other's body with their tongues. They began with Lena on top, and they tried all positions. When Jack was fucking her, she seemed to be posing and flexing her body. She watched her own ass, which was perfectly shaped. She would feel Jack's arm muscles when she was on the bottom and when she was on top; she seemed to admire her own breasts and frequently watched her own midsection as she moved. She grabbed Jack's ass whenever she could. Jack noticed she had set the bathroom door full-length mirror so she could watch herself perform. Well, that was well and good, but she spent more time watching herself than normal. Jack thought that strange and tried to report every detail to me on the phone Monday morning.

Another lesson learned from Lena was that when sex was hot and passionate and Lena wanted faster action, she would poke her fingernail into Jack's anus thus forcing him to jerk or thrust inwards. She could force Jack to fuck faster by controlling the pokes against a sensitive organ. Jack said it was a poke that felt like a pinch and his reflex was to jump thus causing his thrusts to be coordinated with her finger. If he slowed down Lena would give his anus another pinch. Jack said that such motivation always caused him to not stop pumping until she stopped poking his anus. After he climaxed, all was quiet on the anus front.

Another strange thing happened that Jack noted; Lena had rubbed just a touch of toothpaste on her labia and clitoris. After, Lena explained that she used toothpaste before sex for several reasons. First it was clean and might enhance the taste of her pussy. Secondly, mint and spearmint contain menthol, which naturally teases the cooling nerves on our skin. A little dab of toothpaste on a penis causes a cooling reaction on each "out" stroke. Then the penis is again warmed and the temperature changes enhance sex. Lena said the temperature change helped cool down her "hot pussy." Toothpaste also absorbs moisture otherwise your mouth would overflow with soap like a washing machine. If a woman gets too wet, then the toothpaste will dry the action just enough to add to the friction feeling. Toothpaste does not work for a man wearing a condom. Finally, toothpaste kills bacteria and may contribute to safe sex when she may not have confidence in a new partner's cleanliness. Toothpaste is not a form of birth control.

(Surely you readers have heard of a "Crème de Menthe blow job?)

The real shocker was just about to happen. After sex, Lena made an unusual demand.

"Zhat eeze goot, now ve pee together, yes?"

"I don't know what you mean." Jack again was confused.

"You come, I show you how to pee mit me."

Lena led Jack to her toilet and made a small rug for Jack's knees with a towel. She sat down on the toilet and had Jack kneel in front of her. She took his penis in her hand and pulled Jack close so that his penis was almost touching her clitoris.

"You must pee und I vill join you, vee make one pee together. I hold you so you pee on my spot, yes?"

As soon as Jack started to pee, Lena joined him. She held his penis so that Jack's warm urine and his water pressure reflected off of her clitoris, which became naturally engorged revealing the "nostrils" that formed two channels. Their urine was of the same chemical base, and there was no splattering. Their urine formed a single stream and it was a very clean process. What was happening was the pressure from Jack's hot stream was hitting her clitoris, which was performing the pee function, but was also causing a pulsating pressure against her clitoris. Lena had a special kind of orgasm and she held Jack's cock so he couldn't move. She held Jack's cock against her clitoris while she came down from the high. Her left arm clung to Jack's neck and she exclaimed while having an orgasm, "Yes. Yes, yes. Eat iss vonderful."

When they were finished Lena stepped into the tub and splashed some cool water on her genitals. She pulled Jack to the tub and rubbed his penis with cool water. They dried with a towel and Lena told Jack that peeing together after sex was another orgasm for her.

She said it was clean and certainly made peeing together fun. Jack said he got more pleasure out of her reaction than anything else. Now was that weird or what?

The correct term is "urolagnia" and that is defined as deriving sexual pleasure from urination. Most forms of urolagnia involve peeing on each other, which is too kinky, maybe even perverted. However, urine is clean and Lena's obsession with urolagnia can be understood. The same nerve controls the bladder and clitoris, and that tissue is so close to each other, that the sensation is normal.

The hoards led by Genghis Khan when conquering Europe and the Middle East would bath in each other's urine so as to preserve drinking water. This was described in the book "Poland" by the woman kidnapped by the Mongolian cavalry. She described their body odors when being raped as the most offensive body odor known to mankind. Remember, in the book she appeared complicit to protect her teenage daughter. They were kidnapped as a pair when her husband was executed by the Mongolians. They even used urine to sterilize wounds. Nasty history, right?

It is just that most women don't think about urolagnia as something to do for sex. Peeing is the primary focus and sharing that would be a serious breach of modesty. I guess I should say, don't knock it until you have tried it. I tried dual peeing with Cynthia and she was not turned on at all. Jack said he tried it later with women who were not experienced in the practice and most of them could take it or leave it. Jack guessed that his big love Josie would have loved it, but that was because she had this uncontrollable urge to please her man. She might not have been honest about her reaction. I think you have to be into fun and games with a partner with whom you have established good communications to try stuff like that.

Jack dated Lena steady for several months until he was transferred to Denver. Lena was so sexy and she was always a willing partner, but insisted on peeing together as often as possible. Jack was her exclusive lover. One time when she was performing at the theater and during her break she insisted Jack accompany her to her toilet and pee with her. That practice without sexual intercourse first was not that sexy to Jack, but he accommodated her because she liked it so much. One time when Jack could not find the urge to pee with Lena, she peed anyway and while peeing she masturbated with her hand while she kept peeing. Now that was unusual, but seemed normal to Lena. It was like a quickie orgasm for her. It got to the point that in restaurants, Jack would never excuse himself to use the men's room for fear Lena would follow him there and test the privacy of a men's room stall. Imagine how her orgasmic yelling "yes" with a waterfall background would go over in a men's room with multiple stalls and an audience.

Here is a really weird thing. Lena asked Jack if she could sit on his cock and during her orgasm could she release her bladder while she was coming. What? How did that work? Well, Jack sat naked on her toilet and while she stood with her legs apart and a slight squat, Jack licked her pussy to get it hard. She then sat on Long John and fucked until she had an orgasm and she released her bladder at the moment of orgasm. Actually, her bladder burst. Her hot urine flooded Jack's penis. It was hot, but Jack later told me it was really a good orgasm for him. It was a mixture of so many feelings.

I don't know if women can control that dual orgasm. I have heard of women who pee uncontrollably when reaching an orgasm, but a very rare thing. But controlled? Lena was a rare woman. Lena told Jack that she could do that at will. She claims she has peed during orgasm in every position. Jack agreed to try each trick. Lena had to drink a lot of tea at the beginning, but Jack said she had a peeing orgasm once when he was on top and she wet the bed. It heated his stomach. When he fucked her doggy style she was leaning over the bathtub, but missed the tub and wet the floor. Jack said that she rubbed her clitoris vigorously while he fucked her from behind. Interesting? He said she peed almost the whole time he fucked her from behind and wondered when she came. Weird? Yes! Did it feel good to Jack? Yes!

I tried to get Cynthia to try that, but she simply could not pee during sex. I believe that is normal. It is a fact that men cannot

281

pee and stay hard and I have never heard of men peeing during orgasms.

When Jack spent time at Lena's place, she would sometimes ride his cock while playing the guitar. Jack would lie down and Lena would bounce on Jack's cock with the rhythm of the music and often sang while fucking and playing at the same time. One time Jack kneeled before her and licked her pussy while she spread her legs and played and sang a love song. When she had an orgasm, she strummed the guitar harder until she finished her orgasm. These things may seem more interesting for those with musical abilities. It sounded like fun to Cynthia and I, but all we could do is dance. Dancing and enjoying sex is doable, right? And some women hum the national anthem while giving a blowjob.

It never ceased to amaze me how one man could have so many unusual sex experiences. When I first realized how special our sex lives were, I couldn't wait to write this book. Both Jack and I were amazed at the unusual things women would do. Keep in mind; these experiences were not every day things. For the purposes of this book, I have condensed most relationships. Would it surprise you to know that there isn't room in this book to retell all of our experiences? I am only telling you about sexual experiences that might teach you readers something; perhaps even stimulate you to try some fun sex. Lena was definitely a learning experience.

Lena was a hot sexual animal. She controlled her own appetites. She demanded performance. Is that a European thing? It seemed to us that European women were less inhibited about sex. It made us wonder how sex with different cultures would feel. There simply was not enough time in any lifetime to do such subjective research. It is only a coincidence that Jack and I had little experience with inter racial sex. Remember, our experiences began in the late fifties and there was not that much interracial contact, even at our major university. We were certainly not prejudiced, but most of Jack's partner's pursued him as much as he pursued them. We had cheerleaders of other races, but they dated others of their own race. That was a sign of those times.

There is another theory that Catholic women are the worst sex partners because their religious background resulted in more sexual guilt. European women may be more uninhibited and more passionate because they grew up with fewer inhibitions. Many think Black women are more emotional during sex and Asians are more cooperative. Again, our samples are limited to women of our own race and only Lena as a European sample. Our women friends, or subjects, were more a result of women who pursued Jack Callahan than women we selected. Still, I think our reporting of these personal examples is interesting.

By way of interest in European attitudes, Jack's older brother was stationed in Germany while in the military. He told Jack about a barbershop in Germany that allowed you a shower and shampoo and then clothed you in a loose robe similar to a hospital gown. They washed and dried your underwear; dry cleaned your uniform and polished your shoes. After getting your hair cut by a woman, the barber would massage your back and shoulders while a pretty young girl after massaging your feet crawled up your body under the loose robe and gave you a nice blowjob. The total cost was five dollars, but tips were expected. Such service would be a crime in this country. I don't know how that barbershop advertised, if they had to, but that sure sounds like a complete service. How interesting are different cultures when it comes to sex.

Perhaps the basic difference in cultures is how they communicated. Oriental women, perhaps do not communicate much except with body language and being subservient. That bowing and excessive courtesy may directly affect their foreplay. We might not find it so exciting. Yet Lena was so outspoken that her sex appeal was enhanced. Did she intimidate most men? Probably.

Black people are more expressive in their body language. They use that racial coordination to better express themselves in dancing. One cannot deny that there are racial as well as cultural differences between races and countries. Would you honestly deny that German people might be more militaristic? Or, that Jewish people because of their strong family ties might focus more on educating their children.

It is an interesting fact that Jewish people are a small minority yet they have won more Pulitzer and Nobel prizes than any race or religion. And why do oriental children do so well in school? How come so many Armenians are such successful businessmen? Are French people better lovers or better cooks? Why do Brits have more cases of gout? There are many cultural differences and obviously they will affect their sex lives. We are once again, moving into an area, which we are not qualified to pursue. We have to stick to the sexual revolution as we experienced in America and in our small controlled test group.

Chapter 28. Magna Cum Loudly

Finally, Jack and I were reunited in Denver. I had accumulated my own clients and practiced law, although with a big firm practicing general law. Jack was working for a major national securities firm and our offices were but a few blocks apart. We began to have lunch regularly. I was trying to refer clients to Jack and vice versa.

We began working out together, which consisted of pick-up basketball games, usually three on three and with other more experienced players. We would add a player to our threesome and often play for who would buy the beer after the workout. We also did some weight lifting and had my brother teach us tennis. My younger brother was a tennis pro at a local country club. Cynthia and I now had three kids in rapid succession and I had a vasectomy. Jack was still a bachelor and open for dating. We renewed our sexual talks with my contributing how I was "training" my conservative wife, and Jack always had good advice. Later, we would begin to include Cynthia in some of our more exciting discussions. This experience really raised my wife's curiosity, not that she would participate, but the type of orgasm really turned her on. That was good fodder for later sex. I will begin this chapter with the most unusual experience Jack had on his thirtieth birthday.

Jack was dating stewardesses, local business women and women he met at our several health clubs. Jack was extremely popular and kept his sense of humor at the fore of meeting girls. Most men were envious of Jack. His blue eyes were light blue and with his black hair and superb build he was always being chased by women. What made him even more appealing was the way he treated women. He reflected so much respect, was never crude, always complimentary and polite, and then add his sense of humor, which was always evident with everybody he met, and you have an ideal guy. Jack had a way of teasing women with humor that began all new friendships with smiles and laughter.

Jack had met a younger girl named Amy that had an enormous crush on Jack. She was too young by about ten years, but was so upbeat and charming that Jack enjoyed frequenting her time and bed. Amy reminded Jack of Josie regarding her willingness to try sexual adventures such as outdoor sex. The mountains provided much privacy for sunning and sexing naked. A picnic blanket and lunch made for great weekend adventures. Cynthia and I were not included and Jack was always only a twosome. Jack bought a Harley Davidson motorcycle for exploring the mountain parks and highways. Jack was not an avid rider, like no gangs or clubs, just solo riding or with a date hugging him from behind. Jack was not into fancy cars and always drove an old "beater."

There is something you need to know about motorcycles, especially Harley's and women. The motor vibration can be very stimulating. Jack once noticed that Amy would sit on her knuckled fist when riding behind Jack. So, Jack decided to have sex with Amy in a secluded mountain spot, but not leaving the bike unattended. They were making out on the idling Harley while parked. The bike was leaning on its anchor peg and Jack was sitting on the bike when he stripped Amy naked. Jack then stripped, "gunned" the bike while he had Amy sit on his cock. He gave Amy control of the throttle. That was either a mistake or an advantage depending on how much vibration a motionless cycle could take. Jack had straddled the bike and Amy straddled Jack and they vibrated in unison.

Amy was fucking Jack with her hand on the throttle and as she got closer to an orgasm she would gun the motor causing their asses to vibrate more. Jack felt like his ass was getting numb while Amy was only working the vibrations with her own orgasm. Amy was very vocal, so much that often Jack had to cover her mouth with his hand. Yes, she was a screamer, but Amy also had the unusual skill of coming to a climax easily. She had orgasms when Jack was on top, or behind her. It made no difference if it was fucking or oral sex, Amy was extremely orgasmic, and Jack was convinced she was never faking. The problem with Amy was two-fold; she was too loud for most situations and was in the category of nymphomaniacs. Not really, but what all men wanted, a screaming never satisfied nymphomaniac.

Amy was five foot nine and relatively flat chested, and didn't care. Amy's body was the spitting image of Julia Roberts only her smile was about half size. She had full lips, brown eyes, and a beautiful infectious smile. (Very white teeth.) Her breasts were very sensitive and would fit nicely into an average mouth. She liked to spread her legs extra wide, could bring her knees to her ears, and rocked more than necessary in bed. Amy could not ride in a car without playing music and bouncing on the seat to the music. Her long legs were thin but shapely. Her hair was cut short and was jet black. Her ass was not as firm or athletic, but she sure could move it.

Strange thing about Amy was that she didn't care about having oral sex performed on her. She didn't refuse the pleasure, but she was always more anxious to get on with fucking. She seldom had the patience even for her own oral orgasm. She claimed she was more turned on by sucking cock than being eaten, although she always masturbated when giving head. Amy also told Jack that she masturbated every morning upon awakening, every morning since she was six years old. Amy would lie on her knuckled fist and move her hips as if she was fucking a man while on top. She claimed she could climax in a few minutes and she would have a nice release, sort of a wake-up call to get her day "jump started." Whatever happened to coffee? Amy was unusual; or was she, you decide.

I had read a research report from India that found that tested athletes performed better after sex. That did not mean sex immediately prior to any big game. The study concluded that the more men had sex the better they performed in everything else. Morning sex caused the body to more rapidly rebuild testosterone levels. Testosterone is what makes people competitive. A few hours after sex, men became more competitive, had more energy and had clear minds, concentrated more on the competitive task at hand. The study did not mention women. Why not? Women also use up testosterone during sex. They obviously have different ratios of hormones, but passion and sex drive is usually credited to testosterone.

There are also many studies that show that men who fire their prostate glands are less apt to get cancer. The old theory was if you don't use it, you lose it. Does that mean that people should "start out each day with a song" No! It means, start out each day with an orgasm.

Sex before bedtime is a major stress release and people do sleep better after sex. The problem for many women is that they don't often have orgasms during therapeutic sex. And many people are too tired at bedtime to perform foreplay. Sex becomes routine, but still more important for men. Sex is always a great stress release. Remember, Jack and I concluded that there were three kinds of sex, to show love and make love, affectionate sex, which should always include lots of foreplay. The second kind of sex is for stress release and we call that therapeutic sex. Finally, sex for pure fun! Sport sex also requires more foreplay, but foreplay comes in a variety of ways. Our conclusion always boils down to communication. Couples should define their sexual needs by using these three categories. Too many marriages go sour because of the lack of communication. Unfortunately, the blame for less communication between sexes usually falls on men.

This girl Amy was a pure fun fuck. She was not very well educated, didn't read books preferring TV shows. She was more interested in gossip, celebrities, movie stars and who was rumored to be doing whom. Amy was immature in too many ways. She proudly claimed she was promiscuous in high school. She told Jack that she once over heard her older sisters whispering about a local guy who worked as a mechanic in a local gas station. His Father owned the gas station and a small convenience store attached. Her sister was whispering to another sister that this guy's cock was so big that screwing him was painful. After overhearing that, Amy then walked to the station one evening and simply asked the guy if she could see and touch his big cock. They went into a storeroom and this guy dropped Amy's jeans and panties and the guy fucked her on a case of oilcans. Jack thinks she said she was only fourteen. He was standing and had arranged the cases to the right height. She said his cock was huge, but felt good. This guy ratted on her to her sisters, who then beat her up for interfering and for being so bold.

This small town environment left little to do for recreation. There was TV, in its early stages, and movies that were prudish. Give me a break! Remember when John Wayne crossed the pacific during a world war two movie, drove his jeep through enemy bombs and pouring rain, found Patricia Neal in a secluded small hospital, they ran and greeted each other with a passionate kiss in the pouring rain? Then John Wayne said," I'll be back, wait for me, we have a war to win." He climbed back into his jeep and fought his way back to his unit. Why on God's green earth couldn't John have gotten laid? Movie censors, yuk!

So Amy spent time sneaking around and spying on her older sisters and on occasion got to enjoy some voyeurism. She would watch and masturbate and thought nothing concerning sex was unusual or immoral. She was extremely uninhibited. Amy could squat and pee anywhere with limited privacy. Can you imagine a New York runway model doing that? Amy's loss of virginity came at age thirteen. Her sisters were having an outdoor summer party at a local lakeshore park. An older high school guy simply approached her and asked her if she fucked. It was as casual as asking her to dance. Amy said no, but she'd like to try. So she lay down behind a bush, dropped her jeans and the guy mounted her for a quickie. There was no kissing. She said she loved it. Amy told Jack that her

Father caught her in the back seat of a car in her own driveway having 69 sex with a man who had hired her as a babysitter. No rape charges were brought. Her parents sent her to counseling and she was punished many times over. Amy simply grew up never saying no. Did she ever use condoms? No, and it seemed unbelievable she never got pregnant or caught any diseases. She thought having sex was just fun and acceptable to society.

Perhaps another weird thing was when Amy gave Jack blowjobs during her menstrual periods. The first time, Amy was sitting on Jack's bed and Jack was standing. When Jack began to ejaculate, Amy got very excited as if she was coming too; she sort of bounced on the bed and made loud "Ummm" sounds while slapping Jack on his buttocks while he was coming. It was like she was spanking him for coming. She later explained it was because she was so excited. She said she liked sucking cocks as much as fucking. She obviously did not mean that when you consider how excited she got during intercourse. Amy was a most interesting character study. She loved semen like it was candy.

Now comes Deedee Yolanda, a cheerleader from our college days. Deedee was visiting her parents in Denver hoping to get in some skiing on a long weekend. Deedee called Jack and asked him to dinner on a Wednesday night. They met at a restaurant had a great time and even talked about the amazing athletic abilities of Carol Mason; Jack never mentioned her real abilities. They had a great time, had a few drinks and Deedee was most anxious to bed Jack. She even admitted to it, hoping to make her Denver trip something to remember. She actually asked Jack if he would fuck her. How often does that happen to the rest of us guys? They had a great night of first time sex.

Amy had previously suggested a special birthday party for Jack on the following Friday. Amy was trying to recruit a friend of hers that was open to a threesome treat for Jack's birthday the coming Friday. She was trying to recruit a girlfriend with similar interests to just perform foreplay on Jack with her, but she was planning on doing all the fucking. That turned out to be a difficult offer and Amy could find no takers in her social circle. She even tried to recruit a sister, who was equally into sex. So Jack asked Deedee if she was open to participating in a birthday threesome. Deedee said, sure, she would love to try something new as long as it included only Jack. Deedee said she had never been in a threesome, but was willing to learn. Amy also said she had never done a threesome of any kind. Jack asked Deedee and Amy to dinner the following night and when he told Amy about Deedee's offer, Amy said that sounded great and she should meet Deedee. Jack did not mention that he had just had sex with Deedee. Amy thought Deedee was an old college girlfriend of Jack's.

The threesome dinner meeting was wonderful. The girls hit it off and agreed to do for Jack whatever he wanted. You know, back in the late 1960's sex trios were fantasies and virtually unheard of. I never knew of a girl with that open-minded attitude. Even Carol Mason was unaware of the frequency of such things even though she readily joined us with such an adventure. But in her case it seemed to happen naturally rather than by a calloused invitation as if it were a common party. I must be an old fuddy-duddy. I wonder what part of the sexual revolution most promoted such casual celebrations. Humor seemed to lead because the girls kidded Jack about how he was going to handle so much sex, and was he capable of such performance. It was lighthearted kidding as if it was a usual event. Jack redirected the conversation to what Jack wanted. The subject of dual cock sucking came up and the girls were discussing in front of Jack how they could do that particular foreplay. Two female tongues and mouths in such close quarters was the issue. How could this be so casual?

Deedee said, "Have you ever kissed another woman?"

"No, and I have never had the urge either." Amy showed her very white teeth. She had a beautiful mouth.

"Well, I have never kissed another girl either, but if I had to, I could kiss you if our lips met at the top of Jack's cock. I never thought about this, but you have the most beautiful mouth, and I assure you I am totally into men." Deedee confirmed.

Amy blushed and then said. "I am all about men too, but to be truthful I sometimes wonder what another woman's breast feels like. I mean, we all were babies at one time and I think that is a natural curiosity. I am embarrassed that my breasts are so small."

Hey, don't forget about me ladies, this is to be men's night. Actually, I'd be happy to orchestrate some female interaction here." Jack spoke.

"Forget it," said Deedee. "I don't mind if our bodies touch, but Jack has some duties to perform on us, right, Amy? Are you sure you can handle the two of us?"

"Look, I'll take care of both of you, but the foreplay is the objective here. If I'm going down on one of you, why can't the other one massage some breasts, or rub some skin if you can't reach me?"

The ladies looked at each other and agreed that Jack could orchestrate whatever he wanted as long as they didn't have to pretend to be lesbians. Some kissing and touching was agreed upon. The bad news was that Jack was fighting a head cold and was not up to full strength.

Deedee borrowed her parent's car and showed up at Jack's condo and Jack had picked up Amy. Both girls were in jeans, blouses, and no high heels and to everybody's surprise; they were exactly the same height. Jack started by asking all to disrobe while he watched. Jack was undressing and the girls were watching Jack with frequent glances at each other. To Jack's surprise, Long John was still the center of attention even half cocked. But Jack was admiring how much the two girls were alike.

The three of them stood at the foot of the bed and Jack had them stand toe to toe and behold, a phenomenon; their nipples were exactly the same height and when Jack pushed them together so only their nipples touched and he commented on how sensuous that was.

"Are you ladies feeling anything here? Aren't your nipples supposed to be extra sensitive?"

Both girls were staring at their nipple contact and exclaimed how unusual that was, and how good it felt. Deedee's breasts were much larger and fuller.

Jack took one breast from each and rubbed their nipples together. The two girls reacted, as they should have. They watched Jack "flip" their nipples. When they looked into each other's eyes they were a bit shocked to see how close they were. Their mouths were inches apart, so the girls kissed. It was a very tender kiss and each reacted with eyes open and immediately began to feel each other's breasts. After they hugged during an exchange of tongues, Jack interrupted them and moved the trio to his bed and alternately began kissing the girls on their mouths. They were each lying on a side of his chest. The ladies were caressing Jack and their hands met at his cock. They dropped down and then went to work on Jack's cock. They licked long John up and down in unison and kissed at the top on each stroke. They tried to get Jack's cock in both mouths, and they were giggling, not so passionately. Jack said it was unusual and sexy when they both had parts of Long John in two mouths and even more fun when they licked him at the same time including exploring some testicle skin. A man's skin right under the testicles is extra sensitive. This was already a hell of a birthday celebration and much better than cake. Let others eat cake!

The mood was changing and passions were rising, so Jack moved Deedee to her back, spread her legs and began to eat her. Everybody was freshly clean and Deedee was hot, ready and vocal. Jack sneaked a glance and Amy was kissing Deedee on her mouth rather passionately and was massaging her breasts. Deedee then surprised everybody by sticking her finger between Amy's legs while Jack was eating Deedee. Amy's pussy was close to Jack's face and Jack was fascinated by these two heterosexual ladies exploring each other's bodies. Deedee was masturbating Amy, however clumsy it was, while Jack performed cunnilingus on Deedee. And Amy was reacting to the female finger rubbing her clitoris, she was vocalizing with her mouth on Deedee. Jack switched pussies and replaced Deedee's finger with his tongue. Amy came in less than a minute while Deedee tried to kiss Amy's open noisy mouth.

Jack suggested they try something he had read about and they agreed. Jack positioned the two girls so that they were lying like two pair of scissors. They could not reach each other to kiss. He had them spread their labia so that when fully locked, their clitorises would touch during any movement. That required a little squirming that must have felt good. The girls were watching their bodies, not eyes. Jack then gave each girl a clean piece of white paper and placed a sheet on each girl's right breast. He then began to rub the two opposite bent knees against the paper, which was wedged between each girl's knee and breast. That rocking motion however gentle created heat on each nipple, which stimulated the girls, and as a result of the "paper polishing," their clitorises would rub in conjunction with the ever heating paper. The paper raised their nipples, but they soon lost track of the knee movement because their clitorises were making random contact. They weren't ready to climax, in fact, both wanted to be fucked as a result of the limited clitoral contact. Now that was creative. Jack had seen that paper trick in a porno movie and suddenly Long John Silver was going to get into the act.

Jack pulled their legs apart and Deedee's hands immediately found their way to Amy's clitoris. Amy and Deedee were doing a lot of tongue work while kissing and they began to feel and rub each other's genitalia. Jack again felt he was losing control, so he broke them up. Jack knew how much Amy loved "doggie style" sex, so Jack moved Amy to a kneeling position and mounted Amy from behind while Amy continued to kiss Deedee and kiss her breasts. Deedee couldn't control her passion any longer, so she boldly shuffled up the bed so Amy's face was between her legs. She spread her labia with both hands. Amy may have been startled but she did not hesitate to lick Deedee's pussy while she was being fucked from behind. The licking seemed to come naturally to Amy even though she insisted she had never been down on another woman. Jack believed her; her first attempt was cautious, but the newness of another woman's tongue between her legs was all Deedee needed. She quickly climaxed. Her hips went wild while Amy was being fucked harder. After many strokes Jack pulled out because he was bouncing Amy too much while she was trying to perform oral sex on Deedee. When Jack pulled out, Amy turned her body around and went sixty-nine with Deedee lying on their sides. Jack tried to find an angle where he could enter either girl, or at least find some activity. It wasn't working.

Jack watched for a few moments and he swears Amy was having multiple orgasms and yet her sounds were muffled as she began to lick faster with her face buried in Deedee's pussy. Jack also noticed Amy was trying to spank Deedee, but not violently. Jack broke the licking party up and orchestrated a new position. The girls were totally into the mutual sex between women and were more focused on each other than Jack. That was totally unexpected.

Jack moved Deedee, "doggy style" to her hands and knees and positioned Amy underneath Deedee so that Amy's face was level with Jack's penis stroking Deedee. Jack had to straddle both Amy and Deedee. He was big enough to do so. Amy, now lying on her back with her legs straight ahead, was lying under both Jack and Deedee. Amy wrapped her arms around Deedee's waist to pull her face closer to the action. Amy was now face to face with the two opposing genitals. Amy kept one arm around Deedee and started by licking Jack's cock and then with one hand guided his cock into Deedee while she simultaneously licked Deedee's clitoris. Amy had to keep one arm around Deedee's waist while her other hand was free to work Jack's cock and stroke his balls. She had to raise her head up to meet Deedee's pussy. Deedee began to react, almost too passionately to being fucked from behind while simultaneously having her clitoris licked. Amy let go of Jack's cock, which was now moving too fast for her to participate in the fucking action. Amy wrapped both of her arms around Deedee's waist with her face actually in the fucking action, but with her tongue flicking Deedee's clitoris. When Deedee started to have an orgasm, Amy began slapping Deedee's bare ass. Jack took his hands off Deedee's hips and lay back slightly to watch this most unusual performance. It was too much pleasure for Deedee. She began pleading not to stop and finally she pleaded to stop. Jack pulled out and Deedee demanded she and Amy change places.

"You cannot believe how good this feels, let me get under you." Exclaimed Deedee.

Amy moved to the doggy style Fucking position, which might have been her favorite anyway, and Deedee gave Jack his preliminary entry licks. She did guide Jack's cock into Amy since Jack was hands free above the action. Jack was holding Amy's hips. This time Jack put a pillow under Deedee's head to bring her face closer to the fucking without straining. Amy now sort of squatted lowering her pelvis closer to Deedee's face. Jack was now between Amy's legs not straddling them and Deedee's legs were straight and close together. Jack was straddling Deedee's legs, but between Amy's legs. This squatting position allowed Amy to lower her body closer to Deedee's face. This was a very sexy threesome.

The comfort level improved and so did the action. Jack began a gentler fucking so Deedee could find Amy's clitoris with her tongue, which she flicked sideways. She even tried to suck on Amy's clitoris, which seemed like a natural thing, but hard to do with the difficult angle and Jack's cock rubbing on her chin. Deedee's tongue never seemed to tire and Amy was her usual too noisy self. Deedee wrapped her arms around Amy's waist while Jack held Amy's hips. Then Deedee began to slap Amy's ass, which made Amy yell even louder. Amy was yelling instructions to both Jack and Deedee. Amy liked being fucked from behind because she liked the spanking effect of a cock and balls slamming into her ass. The harder the better. Wow! This was a major new sensation.

"Fuck me harder Jack, don't stop licking, yes, yes, give it all to me, harder, and please don't stop. I'm coming, I'm coming, Damn, am I being fucked." Yelled Amy.

Jack fired; he couldn't take the passion level any more. Deedee, with her face next to Jack's balls felt Jack ejaculate; she was holding his testicles with one hand. After Jack stopped trembling, Amy pushed Jack way and moved down and literally dove between Deedee's spread legs and began to lick Deedee.

Soon, Deedee was eating Amy with a similar vengeance while they were side by side. They seemed to be having continuous mutual climaxes. Finally, both girls rolled over in complete exhaustion. The term sexual frenzy again comes to mind. A feverish non-stop fit of pleasure.

Jack, still kneeling at their side, spoke first and said, "Wow, I have never witnessed such extreme passion. You are both so beautiful and both so unbelievably sexy. You both lost complete control of yourselves and I think that proves that women are so much more sensuous. The barriers disappeared, as they should. By the way, aren't you going to at least sing "Happy Birthday" to me?"

The girls, now very close and chummy knelt over Jack's soon to be new hard on and while one sucked and hummed, the other sang Happy Birthday. They alternated singing and humming after each line. After creating Jack's second erection, the girls decided to have a contest by riding Jack's new erection, ten strokes each and have a contest to see which one would get to make him come. Jack's head cold was now working in his favor weakening him and giving him more staying power. The threesome now resembled Russian roulette as to which pussy chamber would take the cumlite bullet.

Amy went first mounting Jack while Deedee sat on Jack's stomach facing Amy so they could kiss and play with each other's breasts. Amy, facing Deedee, was massaging Deedee's pussy while Amy was riding Jack's cock. After Amy gave her best ten strokes, Amy backed off to straddle Jack's knees while Deedee advanced forward mounting Long John still facing away from Jack. Deedee was now riding Jack with her back to him. Amy did something unusual; she tried to lick Deedee's pussy while Deedee was undulating on Jack. Amy squatted as low as she could with her ass high in the air. Amy was lapping

Deedee's pussy with doggy licks and clasping Deedee's ass with both hands. Deedee leaned back as best she could exposing her clitoris, but the angle did not work well, so Deedee clutched Amy's head with one hand as if she were more trying to feel Amy's tongue licking her pussy than cockriding Jack. Her other hand was supporting her backbend. The frenzied act excited Jack too much. Jack rose up on his elbows to view the action. Jack was just a pawn in their action. It is confusing isn't it? Jack bobbed as best he could and ejaculated in Deedee's pussy because he could see Long John Silver being ridden better from behind Deedee and Amy's muffled moaning and pulling on Deedee's ass contributed to Jack's excitement. Deedee's body curves, her flexed ass and body action were a sight to behold. The view was exceptionally stimulating. Deedee felt Jack ejaculating and announced her victory while Amy spanked Deedee. The girls shouted in unison, "And many more!" That was one spectacular threesome!

The girl's showered together, and were both confessing how good everything felt and that they reaffirmed to each other that they were not converted to lesbianism. Jack sat on his toilet waiting his turn and was interested in what they were saying. When the girls stepped out to dry, Jack suggested he buy some sex toys. He suggested a strap on plastic penis and that they should meet the next night and fool around. Both girls agreed that more advanced sexual experiences were in order.

The next day, Jack bought a two-headed plastic cock, a vibrator shaped like a penis and a strap on plastic dildo. Both girls were on the pill, which was the popular thing for this period of the sexual revolution. Jack spent the non-shopping part of the day in a steam bath hoping to recover some new energy and less nose blowing. He had kept Kleenex next to his bed and its use went unnoticed. The girls arrived early about seven o'clock and they had snacked at a fast food chain together discussing their new found relationship. They said they could not understand why or how they managed to have so much fun and not be embarrassed.

Back at Jack's condo, everybody showered and got naked and Jack explained how the sex toys worked. They sat on the bed, cross-legged in a circle waiting instructions from Jack as to how to use the toys. Jack suggested he perform cunnilingus on both of them to get them flowing with that good pussy juice. When Jack went down on Deedee, Amy tried to get her tongue into the action by licking "cheek to cheek" with Jack; she said she wanted to try and learn what Jack was doing. They couldn't both lick Deedee, but Deedee said she appreciated the dual effort. She watched at close range. Both girls admitted that Jack's tongue technique was superior and they both demanded lessons. However, Jack later learned, neither girl ever did another girl. They later wrote each other as best friends and looked forward to the day when Deedee returned to Denver. Amy only discussed the relationship a few times and never brought it up again. She did admit she was confused and hoped Jack would not share what happened with anybody.

Jack positioned the girls with their legs spread and split like two scissors locking together. It was the same position as the paper trick. Instead, the dual headed cock was evenly distributed between them. He had carefully placed the two-headed plastic cock and inserted it into each partner, half in each. The girls couldn't reach each other to kiss, but they used their hands between their legs to rock alternately on the toy. They couldn't climax, but Jack thought their fingers on each other's clitorises contributed more to the action than the double-headed dildo. It was not as good as the other games.

They then kept the dual head inserted and used the vibrator so both of their pussies vibrated together. Amy always came first and loudest, which seemed to get Deedee off soon after. The girls agreed the vibrator was fun, but too quick. They wanted the fun to last longer, so the vibrator was set aside.

Jack separated them and strapped the fake penis dildo on Amy. He advised her to perform as if she were Jack. So, Amy performed oral sex until Deedee had another orgasm. Then she mounted Deedee and began to fuck her in the missionary position as if she were a man. What made the act exceptional was that the base of the toy dildo rubbed against Amy's clitoris causing her to feel each stroke and forced her own orgasms. I think the sex toys were designed to do that. It worked very well; Deedee said when finished,

"No offense Jack, but that felt better than you because of her reaction."

"None taken, but are you suggesting if I yell like Amy, you will come faster?"

"Maybe, that is something men should think about. After all, you get turned on when we are vocal; it works both ways, and men, unfortunately are rather passive lovers when it comes to complimentary sounds."

The girls changed places and Deedee strapped on the dildo and with Jack's instructions, had Deedee go down on Amy before entering her. Jack felt the cunnilingus was more necessary when using a plastic toy. So Deedee did the full routine and when they kissed after Deedee entered Amy with the toy, Jack noticed how easy sex must be for those of the same height. Deedee had the same reaction, the base of the toy was rubbing on her clitoris, so she stroked to adjust and as usual Amy started to climax too soon, so Deedee kept pumping going for her own orgasm. It made no difference to Amy; she was too orgasmic to notice how Deedee was coming. When Deedee exclaimed she was coming, Amy raised her pitch and passion and began to spank Deedee. The harder they each came, the harder Amy spanked.

Jack then held Amy fast and entered her from behind while the strap-on dildo was still inside Deedee. Amy then fucked Deedee with the strap-on cock while Jack fucked Amy from behind. Both Amy and Jack were in sync as if Jack just went along for the ride. Jack forced a faster harder pace, which the girls seemed to prefer. Jack was actually fucking two women at the same time. Amy apparently had an active "G" spot and the strap on penis rubbed both clitorises. This was very sexy!

This whole spanking thing we always thought was kinky. Yet Amy seemed to think it was normal. There was no deep psychological reason for the urge other than just plain enthusiasm. However, getting violently spanked as foreplay did not appeal to either of them. Although sometimes Amy liked a soft patting on her labia as foreplay.

For their next act the girls wanted to ride the strapped on cock horse. Amy went first, didn't bother to lick Deedee, and just climbed on the strap on toy while it was strapped to Deedee. Amy rode for her own pleasure and because she was so enthusiastic, Deedee watched with fascination as Amy was straddling her. The strap on had a small tab that stuck out from the base that lightly rubbed the fuckee's clitoris. During the straddling position Deedee, on the bottom, was doing her best to rub Amy's bouncing breasts, and when Amy came, Deedee spanked her bottom. Jack wasn't sure Deedee came, but she was very anxious to get her turn on top. Once Deedee found her riding groove, she reached her orgasm herself, but Amy, unbelievably turned on, never seemed to stop coming. Apparently her clitoris was always in contact with the toy. Jack thought he might be getting envious and he raised the issue after they were finished. Jack was also concerned that neighbors might think he was killing women in his spare time. He kept expecting to find the police at his door complaining about the screaming.

Jack explained that watching two women was a common male fantasy, but he was frustrated and asked if he could get into the action. The girls immediately apologized and agreed to fuck Jack in appreciation for his teaching experience. The girls requested that instead of the missionary position, could they have him perform the same trick he taught them yesterday. It turns out that the doggy style fuck with the other girl underneath licking the clitoris was most unusual and would be hard to duplicate for the rest of their lives. Jack passed on the missionary stuff. The girls seemed very anxious to perform the fuck/lick ride. They didn't think they could ever duplicate that fantastic feeling of being fucked and licked at the same time, so Jack agreed. These girls concluded that this position was the most pleasurable thing that could happen to any woman.

Deedee quickly rolled over and squatted with her ass up in the air, ready for action. Amy assumed her position under both of them with her face in the action. This time the pillow became a necessary prop because it raised the "under girl's" head for easier access to the face to face view of coitus. The top girl had to squat slightly and Jack had to kneel inside the top girls spread. This time Amy stroked Jack's testicles as he stroked in and out of Deedee. A man's testicles usually tighten up against the base of his shaft when fucking. The ball positions did not interfere with her licking. Deedee's build up was gradual, and they both appeared to be making it happen slowly to extend the pleasure. The girls were enjoying the longer moment. But Deedee eventually could not help herself; she could not hold back her orgasm. We had previously discussed how teasing or changing techniques prolonged orgasms and made them stronger. The girls were learning that technique on their own.

They anxiously changed positions so Deedee was underneath doing the licking. It was very difficult for Jack to restrain from coming. It was a more difficult task for Jack because Amy wanted harder strokes and Deedee hung on to save her teeth, so to speak. Jack's testicles occasionally banged into Deedee's chin, and that was OK, she later said. Also, Amy was forever getting wetter with each orgasm and Deedee seemed to not mind the wetness. All wetness was running down Amy's face and she loved it. Deedee said later that she could feel Jack's penis pulsate when he reached his orgasm. She was also stroking the underside of his balls this time instead of wrapping her arms around Amy's waist.

When Jack tried to withdraw, Amy held his cock so he had to stay kneeling behind Deedee. Amy continued to lick and suck. Deedee reached down and held Amy's head fast between her legs until Deedee was completely satisfied. Jack thought that act was weird. It was as if the passion had gotten out of control and the girls didn't want to lose any of the fluids. Amy kissed Deedee and they seemed to exchange leftover fluids. Their cheeks were covered with the juices of sex. It seemed strange to Jack that while the taste of sex was a big turn on for guys, it was interesting that they seemed to enjoy the blended tastes. The good smells of sex also permeated the room and Jack said he thought the odor lasted forever. It made him sleep better thereafter. There was very little spanking that day. The girls hugged each other in exhaustion.

Jack excused himself to the shower first. When he came back to towel off, the girls were trying something different. Amy was on top and they were eating each other. What was different was the angle. They had to look at each other's anuses. Jack bent over the bed and suggested they finger each other's anuses, and so they did. Jack felt he had created two monsters that couldn't get enough of the new thing they were experiencing. That was their last same sex contact, so they said. They showered bragging about how good they were. Everybody was so happy. Their faces were flushed and full of color as if they applied make-up.

Jack was anxious to talk to me, Will, to try and unravel this situation of uncontrolled passion. Was it normal? It seemed extreme to us. Men have a safety valve; once they ejaculate they become less passionate and have to be re-stimulated. Women seem to get more motivated with each orgasm. We wondered if because they had no loss of fluids they seemed never to be satisfied. Women get wetter with each orgasm, which may protect them from soreness. If a woman gets fucked and did not climax first, she might get sore. We must leave that theory to the scientists since Jack had not experienced any women who didn't always want more sex after an orgasm. Most couples rest after sex and know that they can enjoy each other later if wanted. These two girls might have been trapped knowing they could not repeat the experience.

The social codes and sexuality issues faced them whether they liked it or not. Was guilt to be an issue? Jack said it was never evident with Amy. She took it all in stride and if it made her hornier, Jack could not tell. Amy's sexual appetite was perhaps not normal and Jack felt that was consistent under any conducive circumstances. Amy would be an easy sex partner as long as the guy was sexy and attractive, and preferably a celebrity. I suspect there are many women who feel that way, but more self-controlled. I wonder how many women would react to same sex experiences in such a passionate uncontrolled manner. I wonder how many women would perform this way and retain exclusive heterosexual interests. We never asked.

Deedee left Sunday to return to Michigan, and never lost contact with Jack. Amy later told Jack that she was unbelievably surprised about what had happened. She tried to assure Jack that she was all for him and was not ever looking for female encounters. She was embarrassed. Jack reassured her the experience was normal and that most women confuse having sex with a lesbian, or a masculine woman, when two beautiful heterosexual women might be broad minded enough to get into that mode. We wondered if Jack's presence enhanced the sex. It is highly unlikely that two women would request such an arrangement without a very close trusting heterosexual relationship with a man present.

Jack told Amy that he knew a girl in high school that was so beautiful, but had a thalidomide arm, an arm that stopped growing. This girl was so self-conscious about her arm that she wouldn't date. So her best friend, then Jack's lover, during a twosome sleepover had confided that she had just been laid by Jack and her crippled friend began to cry. She complained that she would probably never feel what sex was all about. Jack's girlfriend then confided to the handicapped girl every detail about having sex with Jack, which turned them both on. So this dear friend used her two fingers to try to simulate sexual intercourse for her crippled friend. They hugged and kissed so they could share kissing while finger fucking. The handicapped girl was so turned on that she went down on her friend and they both ended up having orgasms. Jack's friend allowed that to happen and she confided in Jack hoping he would understand. Jack did understand. She did not mention whether she performed cunnilingus on her handicapped friend. That idea was not prevalent at the time. Jack caught on when his friend tried to explain it without actually disclosing who licked whom and Jack suspected the licking was mutual.

The two girls did do each other whenever the occasion rose, but only on sleepovers, not on dates and never to be divulged to anyone. Their sessions consisted on a lot of caressing and touching until driven to more sexual contact. Jack's prowess was used as the main stimulant. They hugged a lot. When Jack's friend went on to college, her friend went to another college and eventually found a man who loved her in spite of her handicap. She later thanked her friend for showing her some tender love making techniques. Jack and I thought that was very touching and not a lesbian relationship. I don't know how many women experiment with good friends. I do think men would never experiment with each other unless they were gay or bisexual.

As for Deedee, she and Jack remained infrequent lovers for the next 25 years, perhaps meeting as little as once a year during skiing season. What was most interesting about Deedee was that Jack later introduced me to Deedee and she was most cooperative discussing her experience with Amy and Jack. Deedee became a member of our inner circle for intimate discussions and she made significant contributions. We had so many questions about how that same sex experience happened and about the many exceptional reactions. Deedee and Jack even met after they were both married and would meet occasionally when the opportunity arose for a sweet afternoon of reminiscent sex. I don't know if that is the right term, but their sexual chemistry never faded nor did their friendship. No one ever knew about their relationship except Cynthia and me, and this woman offered a rare opportunity to learn about female reactions to all things sexual.

I was often invited to lunch with Deedee and Jack. Using our movie star I.D. recognition system, Deedee reminded us of Catherine Zeta Jones. I realize how unusual this seems that Jack seemed to meet only exceptionally good-looking women, but equally as extraordinary was their willingness to discuss many deep emotional and intimate feelings. My descriptions of some of Jack's feelings were supported by Deedee and perhaps more insightful than Jack's feelings. It was extremely helpful to have Deedee's mature insight.

Deedee claimed she never had sex with another woman after the experience with Amy, but she did admit she would gladly do it again if the circumstances were right. She was comfortable that she was heterosexual under any circumstances. I hinted at such a treat with Cynthia and Deedee and Cynthia declined. Cynthia simply would not share me with any other woman and it was not that she lacked confidence, it was a moral thing. Oh well, I can always fantasize.

Deedee said that beautiful women were subliminally attracted to each other. Men can admire another man's build and athletic skills, but seldom do they think about sex. We do not care how another man does in bed. On the other hand, women are physically created as sensuous sex organs and one woman admiring another seems normal for desires to touch. Especially when heterosexual women are clean smelling and admired by men. Men fantasize about heterosexual women fore-playing each other, but probably not involving another masculine lesbian. Two women exploring each other's body's makes men feel like they are the missing link and men can fantasize their required involvement. Women's bodies are themselves sex organs and why would they not welcome admirable touches from other women. Women, fortunately can share emotions by hugging and crying together. Men seldom do.

There is a big difference between two heterosexual women giving each other pleasure and lesbian sex. It has to do with hormone balances. A percentage of men and women alike are born or develop hormone imbalances and I don't believe that balance can be changed. Supposedly about 10% of men and 5% of women are born with hormone imbalances.

I should mention how trustworthy I was when on one occasion there was no time for hotel rooms and after a nice lunch meeting, I drove the freeway while Jack and Deedee had sex low in my back seat. What was most memorable was after I finally adjusted my rear view mirror so I could catch some glimpses, Deedee caught me looking and winked and smiled and waved at me while Jack was stroking away. All I could see were her bare legs rocking because this wintry "nooner" was not conducive to taking off clothes. Damn that was sexy and again reminds me how sexy women can be when in a trusted situation. Never underestimate the potential for sport sex.

Many people would do it if the circumstances were right and they were sure they would never get caught.

Deedee kissed me on the cheek and thanked me after the short thirty-minute drive. It seemed longer, but then doesn't good sex seem to stand still for time, even if for the moment of climax. Jack and I did reveal that experience to Cynthia, but much later after it happened. That was after Cynthia's transformation and resulted in Jack again requesting reciprocal viewing rights. Jack offered to let Cynthia and I have sex in the back seat while he drove. Such an occasion never arose.

Subsequent to that threesome experience, Jack was always wary about Amy. She was not his type for a serious relationship and she seemed to only want sex anyway, which was not a bad deal for Jack. Amy eventually started fucking a TV celebrity that promised her a Hollywood career. Amy followed this guy to California. Jack thought she would enjoy being a call girl if she could only do good-looking guys. So, Jack stopped seeing Amy as she moved on to some variety, probably never finding anyone she could trust as much as Jack.

Women are more sensitive than men and they liked to be touched more than men. Men are basically in a rush to fire their weapons. The lesson for men is to learn to take more time with foreplay. It's too bad we can't withstand a nice massage without getting an erection. I am referring to men that are horny, which can include some women, like Amy. She was a most unusual experience. We hope you learned something about the possible favorable results about women who masturbate frequently. A lifetime of better orgasms? Go figure!

I have heard about professional massage therapists who will message women and tactfully ask if they can massage breasts. The next step is to tell the client to say when to stop and the next service performed is cunnilingus. I knew of some wealthy women married to older men who had weekly sessions with such massage specialists. For men, the perfect ending to a massage is a blowjob or a hand job. I think most men will be aroused when getting a massage by a woman. I suspect such services are more prevalent that we realize. Obviously they are confidential.

Deedee told us that she and a girlfriend sometimes went to a male massage therapist in Detroit who used a large "thumping" type vibrator and that during the inner thigh massage the therapist would hold the big thumper against their labia for a moments and if the women didn't say stop the therapist would hold steady until the therapy included an orgasm. Deedee said it was very professionally done and a great stress reliever. The thumper vibrator was about six inches across and the signal she gave was that she spread her legs while lying on her back and relaxed for the several minutes required. The slow thumping made for an unusual but pleasant climax. She was covered by a towel so the privacy angle was preserved. She said the problem was trying not to be obvious and controlled when she wanted to yell out her pleasure, but kept quiet. Her signal to the therapist to move on was a hand signal. I'll bet there are many unusual ways to perform sexual gratification acts that would not be considered masturbating.

When Cynthia heard this story, she had me buy a "big thumper," and I became an occasional therapist. Actually when applied to me, it was a great lower back massage, but did nothing for me sexually. But Cynthia liked to finish her massage with brief labia thumping pressure. It seemed dignified and she pretended it was just a great massage, but it was fruitful because it always made her horny. This proves that the fast or slower vibrations have their place. I think every woman should own a vibrator with speed variations.

Chapter 29. Fat Chance

What do people who feel overweight do about sex? Do they have a harder time overcoming inhibitions? I think so! Jack and I have some definite opinions on sex for overweight people. As we get older, we lose our shapes; we don't look as good naked any more. In our opinion, weight should not make a difference, especially if you are in love. However, no matter what the relationship, the individual attitudes are both the problem and the solution. Overweight people are entitled to good sex, they just have to plan more. They need to develop sexy attitudes.

Overweight people lose confidence and understandably don't want to be seen naked. I want to address this issue using a rather "sweet" experience Jack had with a co-worker. Dorothy was big boned and at five feet six inches tall weighed about 155 lbs. The positive things were, she was beautiful and with a beautiful round face, a most pleasing disposition, and a wonderful smile. Using our "movie star" ID factor, Dorothy resembled an overweight younger Elizabeth Taylor, sort of. She had that kind of coloring with dark eyebrows, and big brown eyes. Her skin was flawless. She was just overweight. Weight can be loose or firm and in Dorothy's case she was firm.

Loose weight is easier to lose.

Jack was playing the field and Jack's reputation around the office was that women chased him to where it might be considered an inconvenience. Well, inconvenient for Jack because he didn't believe in affairs at the office where he works. Jack probably passed on more sex than most guys get.

All the women in the office seemed to have a crush on Jack, and if for no other reason, he was so attentive to all of them regardless of their age or how they looked. They all flirted with Jack and he charmed them all. Jack always had cute tasteful jokes to tell.

Dorothy spent more time starring at Jack than working. She did not work for Jack directly, but had a clerical job nearby. Dorothy owned her own small house, paid for by her parents. Her Father subsidized her. She was overweight, but had a flat stomach. Her legs were very shapely and she was always neat and well dressed. She wore great perfume and was a smiley person. She was big breasted, and they appeared to be firm. It appeared her excess weight was on her thighs and ass.

The biggest problem with overweight people is when both sex partners have big a big belly. They better be younger and more supple. Also, we think fatter people should always be more freshly cleaned. Perspiration does not become them. Their biggest problem is when they are obsessed with their weight and complain about it incessantly. If you exercise regularly and eat less, and perhaps do a few sit-ups daily, anyone could stay sexually competitive. Dorothy obviously had a problem with her self-confidence, so Jack purposely tried to be friendly and flirtatious with her. She blushed regularly and loved having Jack's attention. Jack never acted like he wanted to date her, but Jack treated all women with respect. He had a readily compliment for each of them. Or he shared some humor. He was fun to be around and humor is always sexy. Dorothy had a great sense of humor and after overcoming initial shyness, she had a very charming mature personality. Dorothy had a major crush on Jack.

Dorothy asked Jack if she could talk with him privately. Jack invited her into his office, which was encased in glass so all could see, but not hear. Dorothy was very nervous. She stood rather formally opposite Jack's desk. Jack asked her if she had a problem. She responded,

"Please forgive me, but I want to share a problem I have and your advice will be kept confidential. You have such a nice sweet manner about you and I believe every woman I know has a crush on you. I have a strange request for you, but you must promise me that if I ask you about my weight, you will keep an open mind and help me not to be so embarrassed."

Jack said, "Look, you are very kind with your comments and please know that I find you very attractive. I just never asked you out because I don't believe in office romances."

"No, no, that isn't what I'm suggesting, I need some advice on weight loss and you seem to be in perfect physical condition. I need to talk to a man that I can trust and knows about women. I admit I have a crush on you like everybody else, but I just get to dream about you and I don't have to share that with anybody. But can I ask you something?"

"Dorothy, you can ask me anything. We can be friends and who knows, I may need some advice from a beautiful woman someday. Gee, will you tell me about your dreams in detail?"

Dorothy blushed and ignored Jack's comment.

"Jack, I weigh 155 pounds and I'm five feet six inches tall. I haven't had a date in years and I want to be in that scene. I think I am a loser because I'm fat."

"Hey, wait a minute, you look pretty solid to me and I don't think you are fat. Maybe you just need to join a gym and workout regularly. Maybe you just need to firm up a bit. I'll bet you'd meet a guy in no time."

"Please forgive me, but hear me out. I'm always dieting and I never have success. I hear about diet programs that if you wager a friend and stand to lose money, you will take the diet more seriously. I have tried everything and I know I need to get on a regular workout schedule. I need advice and I need an incentive. If I can't lose fifteen pounds using your advice, I'll pay you $500.00."

"Dorothy, you don't have to go to that extreme. I'll tell you what I would do to lose weight and we can do it as good friends; Think of me as your personal trainer."

"But will you advise me how to get a date, and will you discuss my body candidly?"

Jack commented, "I don't feel that qualified, but I'd be happy to try. I can tell you a few things that men look for and like, especially if we agree to be candid and private. Can you talk about sex freely?"

Dorothy began to tremble a bit and blurted out,

"If I lose 15 lbs, will you bed me as my reward? No long term expectations; I'm not asking for a relationship and I am so embarrassed for what I just said." She looked at the floor and was quite embarrassed.

Dorothy looked like she was about to cry. Jack grabbed her arm and said, "Sit down and let's talk about this. Please don't be embarrassed. I am complimented that you would choose me, so let's talk. I'm certainly not offended."

"Please know that I will understand if I asked too much. Please don't think me foolish, I have not had any experience with men to speak about and I think it's because I'm too fat. If you will just help me lose weight, I'd be just as happy."

"Hey, wait a minute, I just heard you make me an offer no man would refuse, are you backing out already? I thought that was a really great offer, especially with no strings attached. I can be your friend and personal trainer. I can show you a few things about men while I'm at it. You just have to promise me that this is just between the two of us?"

"Ok, if you are sure you are OK with this. I consider these terms the most worthwhile challenge of my life. Do you have any exercise ideas?

"Well, jog for about a half an hour each day. If you jog more than that you are doing more than just trying to lose weight. Use very lightweights for bedtime exercises and concentrate the most on sit-ups. You can do a sort of curling exercise by lying on your back and raise your head and knees and raise your knees to your chest. I will tell you that sometimes exercising will cause a weight gain, but ignore that gain. As long as you are firm, weight may not be a problem. What makes a woman sexy is a curvy body. Measure your bust, waist, and hips and watch for losing inches. Also posture plays an important role. Do not slump and do not hide boobs. Your hips should not be wider than your shoulders, but that is not critical. Sex appeal is in your head. You work out to gain confidence and self esteem. If your attitude is about loving sex then you will reflect sex appeal no matter how you are built. Women often make that mistake when it comes to self-analysis. Remember, if you act interested in sex, then you will be sexy. All partners are sexier when they take good care of their bodies, stay clean and always smell good. You have underestimated yourself and I guess that is OK for now. Keep me informed on your progress."

Dorothy was taking notes as fast as she could. Jack then complimented her wardrobe, and said, "Good luck gorgeous, I'm hoping for your success and especially since I am now your teammate. Don't make a scene here, write me notes or call my extension, and I'll do the same. I'll use you to request stock reports as often as possible to keep wagging tongues silent."

Jack told me about Dorothy so I could advise him on the psychological aspects of her contract. She had given Jack a tape from a weighing machine to record her start point. We agreed that we would do everything possible to build up Dorothy's confidence and esteem. I made a special trip to Jack's office so he could request a stock report and introduced me to Dorothy. I agreed she had a nice quality about her innocence. She did not know that I knew about the contract.

Jack tried to call Dorothy on the inter-office phone weekly and each time he referred to her as "gorgeous." Dorothy always blushed when Jack called her gorgeous, especially on the phone. Jack could see her answer the phone. She was reporting to Jack the weights she worked with and that she had joined a health club. Jack told her to try swimming or working out in chest high water. After about two months Dorothy reported she was losing weight and inches. She said her bust line declined a few inches, her waist about an inch and as much as three inches off her hips. Jack also noticed Dorothy was buying newer clothes, which were very stylish. Once when they were alone in the elevator, Jack reached over and felt Dorothy's breasts. She jumped, blushed and Jack commented on their firmness. Jack urged her to keep up the good work. All she could do was blush. Jack would occasionally pat her on the ass when no one was looking.

"Nice, very nice," Jack would say.

One time Jack decided to tell Dorothy an old weight loss joke to sort of test her sense of humor and her ability to deal with some sexy talk.

There was this big newspaper advertisement about a health clinic guaranteed to lose five pounds on the first visit if you passed a simple physical exam. The test was an endurance test that tested heart rates, a stress test actually, but the initial cost and each test was $50 with a money back guarantee and was for men only. This skeptic and slightly overweight man insisted on taking the test even though he had to sign a release exempting the gym from any liability. After he signed up he dressed in shorts and sneakers and was placed on the ground level of 50 flights of stairs. At the next half level was a beautiful sexy young girl in perfect physical condition that was stark naked, but wearing sneakers. Around her neck was a sign that said,

"If you can catch me, you can fuck me." A bell rang and the naked lady had a ten-stair head start and took off. Each time the man rounded a corner he caught a glimpse of that sexy ass. After thirty flights he began to tire and she disappeared. By the time he reached fifty flights, he was weighed and did lose five pounds.

So the man asked for further tests thinking if he practiced he could easily catch the bait, but when he returned with the second $50, the trainer discouraged him telling him the second test was always more difficult and dangerous. The man insisted and bragged that he was ready for anything and really didn't care whether he lost another five pounds or not. The trainer assured him he would lose weight. This time the man was put on the first flight level and gasped as he saw a 600 pound male gorilla in a cage with a sign on the cage that said, " When I catch you I will fuck you." The bell rang and the man ran for his life. (Well, I think it's funny!) Dorothy loved the joke and passed it on to her co-workers.

Jack was dating a woman lawyer and Dorothy was aware of that. Jack thought that information would keep the contract on the "trainer" relationship out of the rumor mill.

Then came the big day, Dorothy first asked Jack if he still was her reward. She hoped so. They had become friends and were discussing her body parts freely, especially her breasts. Dorothy handed Jack the weight scale tape reflecting her weight at 140 lbs, down from 155. Jack said "Ok, well am I ever proud of you. Let's have dinner tonight to celebrate and we can talk about how to work this wonderful upcoming event."

By way of comparison, Carol Mason at 5'4" weighed 130 pounds, but was all muscle, and you could see her ribs under her breasts. I don't think weight is much of a factor if a woman has a flat stomach and nice breasts. And asses are always appealing if shaped right.

Dorothy and Jack went to dinner and Jack began by asking Dorothy how much experience she had with men. They had developed the advanced ability to communicate as intimate friends.

"When I was in high school, I allowed my boyfriend to touch my breasts. He did get his hand inside my panties, but we never had intercourse. He put my hand on his penis once when he made me feel inside his pants and he wet on my hands."

"You mean you are still a virgin?"

"Oh please don't say no to me, I want to learn about men and I trust you. I'll do whatever you want. I have exercised myself with my fingers a bit so I just know I'm ready. Please don't let my lack of experience change your mind. I am a virgin, but I sure wish I wasn't. Please help me."

"Well, I will have to change my strategy quite a bit, but, yes I can handle it. I hope you keep this as an objective experience. You know what they say about virgins; they tend not to move on. They get stuck on the guy who deflowered them. Don't do that to me, I don't qualify. You would make some lucky guy a good wife and you need to take dating seriously. I will advise you how I think you should handle dating, but please know I'm just your confidant, and soon to be best friend because I will know intimate things about you that no other will ever experience. I will see parts of you that you will never see. A first time is always only once. You must keep what I do with you, to you and for you as just a learning experience. I will show you how to be a great sex partner. Do you agree?"

"Yes."

They drove to Dorothy's house in separate cars. And Jack asked for candles, which she had. Jack kept reassuring Dorothy to calm down and not be nervous. He said he would explain everything as they progressed and would stop at any point if she wanted to reschedule the next step.

Jack took Dorothy directly to her bedroom. She again was almost trembling because she was so nervous. She had a nice queen size bed and a well-decorated room. The candlelight is always a perfect setting for sex. Jack had Dorothy stand with the bed to her back and told her to undress him and ask any questions that came up. Dorothy was very excited and she took off Jack's shirt and T-shirt. She ran her hands over his muscles and exclaimed how beautiful he was. Then Jack had her sit on the bed to take off his pants. Jack had removed his shoes and socks. Now Dorothy was more nervous than excited. She dropped his pants, got up and folded them neatly on a chair next to the bed. She sat down again on the bed and hesitated to drop his boxer shorts, so Jack said,

"Go ahead, be gentle, it won't bite."

Dorothy surprised Jack and said, "What if I bite?"

Jack helped her and stepped out of his shorts and he was soft. Jack explained,

"Let me introduce you to Long John Silver, and he is a non-circumcised penis. Take a good look, because he won't be lying down for long. When a man gets aroused, he gets an erection."

"I read about that, but now that I am this close, I think Long John is magnificent. Do all penises look like this?"

"Well, close, all different sizes, I'd say the average length is between four and six inches, I'm a bit longer, but women once engaged would not feel the length. You can handle any length, but being a virgin may make you tighter than usual, and I'll have to be extra careful because I have a wider tread than most. I may be bigger around and I'll have to be extra careful. By that I mean no sudden thrusts. Go ahead and touch me until I get erect. Use your finger tips and be gentle."

Dorothy nervously touched Long John and used her fingertips to massage Jack. She kept asking if she was doing it right and Jack urged her on.

Once Jack was hard he changed places with Dorothy and began to undress her. He unveiled her breasts and they were beautiful, full and firm. Jack said, "grapefruit size." He had her raise her hands over her head and raved about her shape. He took off her skirt and left her panties in place and laid her gently on the bed. They began to kiss and Jack whispered as many compliments as he could and caressed her breasts. He licked them and sucked on them telling her how sexy she was. Jack was caressing her inner thighs and he sensed she was really ready to advance. Jack then put a firm pillow under her hips and told her to put a pillow under head and watch him as best she could. Dorothy had no idea what Jack was about to do. He took off her panties and spread her legs. She was preparing herself for intercourse when Jack began to lick her labia. Dorothy gasped and pulled back as a reflex. One cannot describe the level of passion Dorothy had achieved.

Jack said, "I have to taste you first, and you tell me what you feel. If you want to, hold my head and concentrate on my tongue."

Dorothy's thighs were both big and beautiful. They were perfectly shaped. Together they could cover Jack's head, but her skin was unmarked and her thighs were firm and a perfect invitation to paradise. Dorothy had no wrinkles. Her size was shapely and was not unappealing. Strong looking legs are a big turn on for most guys. Dorothy was very limber. Her spread was delicious looking and her legs flexed as an invitation to sex. Her calves also flexed and were very sexy. Big women when well shaped were just as attractive regardless of size. And most important, her willingness to fuck was more important.

Dorothy held his head and watched intently as Jack continued. He massaged her clitoris with the flat of his tongue and alternated between licking, flicking and blowing. Dorothy did not know what to expect and didn't really know what a climax would feel like. She was purring and trying to move her hips. No matter how objective this lesson was Dorothy could not control her emotions. She trembled and twitched and moaned like it came naturally, which of course it did. Jack pushed his thumb into her vagina and it was wet and tight. Since she didn't know how to climax, Jack thought she was ready for long John. So, he rose up on his knees under her legs and told her he was only going to enter her by one inch and she should tell him what she felt.

"I'm OK, everything feels so good, and you are definitely not hurting me."

Dorothy was breathing hard and her eyes looked she was going to burst. Jack assumed she had never been so "high."

Jack pushed in an inch at a time and then withdrew. He started over again several times and each time Dorothy's pussy seemed to be begging for the whole penis. He watched her face for any sign of discomfort. When he looked at her, she appeared to be nodding approval and was focusing on what she could feel. Once Jack was in up to his pelvic bone he placed both of his arms clamping her head between his arms and kissed her. He told her not to close her eyes and said,

"I am inside you all the way, are you OK?"

"It feels soo good, go ahead and keep doing it."

Jack pulled out completely and took out a condom. She watched closely as Jack unrolled the condom. Jack reentered her slowly. He began to fuck her slowly, but gradually picking up the pace. When he reached an orgasm, he looked her in the eye and said,

"I'm coming, hold me, hold me," and she hugged him with all her strength. Jack pulled back and said,

"I wish I could stay inside you and cuddle and talk, but condoms are dangerous when I get soft, so watch me take it off. Look, we could have done it longer, but I don't want you to get sore. Take this into the bathroom, see how much semen you could have had, flush it down the toilet. Always try to pee soon after sex. Come back here and let's talk, OK?"

Dorothy jumped out of bed and delicately carried the condom into her bathroom. Dorothy was really sexy and had a great ass. Jack heard the toilet flush and she was back in a flash. Jack pulled her to him and hugged her and told her she felt and looked fantastic.

"Are you ready to talk?" "Yes, yes, I am." She answered.

Jack explained cunnilingus and fellatio and explained how important these skills are to better sexual relationships. He explained in detail what he did to her with his tongue. Dorothy then asked Jack to teach her fellatio. Jack had Dorothy kneel between his legs and explained the focal point, the all important nerve on the underside of his penis. He told her that his penis nerve was similar to her pussy nerve, they had the same function. While she was kneeling in front of Jack, he reached between her legs and touched her clitoris and she jerked and gasped.

"You are touching my pleasure nerve and I am touching yours. The objective to get them in harmony; that is what sex is all about."

Jack continued, "Look, your tongue is your most versatile organ. It has not only has taste buds, but it is so coordinated that it allows you to chew food and not bite your tongue. Your tongue can be gentler than your fingers and has many more nerves than your pussy. You can create more pleasure with your tongue, but be careful not to cause it to ejaculate a man during foreplay. A correct blow job to bring an orgasm involves being on the down side of a penis, but if you can't get to that angle then allow the sides of your cheeks to rub the man's nerve. Remember that I tell you this, never, never allow your teeth to make contact with a penis. Try to cover your teeth with your lips. You can blow on a penis to cool it down, and you can lick them like a Popsicle, or mouth them like a cob of corn. Actually "cobbing" a penis with your teeth is OK, but never bite or scratch a penis with teeth. There is unlimited room for creativity. Pretend that you are doing to a penis what you'd like to have done to your clitoris with a tongue. It's kind of like the golden rule of oral sex. Put your lips together and pretend your mouth is your pussy. Kiss my little head and gently suck my penis into your mouth as if I were entering your pussy."

Dorothy did exactly that. She pursed her lips and took Jack's soft penis into her mouth and as it grew, she did what was normal. She bobbed and licked and Jack had to stop her. It was feeling too good. Jack handed her another condom and asked her to put it on Long John. She did so and then looked at Jack for further instructions. Jack straightened his legs and asked her to climb on. Dorothy looked confused, so Jack continued,

"Put your left knee down and lean to the left. Then put your right foot flat on the bed and tip to the left. Rub my penis up and down your labia and after a few strokes find your vagina and sit slowly while leaning back to the right. That's good, now settle down slowly. Perfect. Fall forward and put your breasts on my chest and slide gently on my cock. She moved slowly and said it felt great. That is one technique. Now, sit up straight, lean back and put your hands on my knees. That shows off your breasts and will further stimulate your partner, which you are. Ohhh that feels good. Put your hands where you can feel both of us and see if you can feel yourself move on my cock."

Strange reaction, Dorothy was sticking out her tongue and curling it as she adjusted her hips. That's what Mother's do when spoon feeding a baby. That's what Michael Jordan did when shooting a basketball. It's funny how tongues can aid concentration. Jack told her to find a good move that made contact with her clitoris. She tried, but her lack of experience was showing. Jack began to bob, and he sat up and hugged her. Jack began to bounce Dorothy on his lap and his cock and when he was close to climaxing he kissed her and kept eye contact. Then he maneuvered her under him without withdrawing and laid her on her back and began a more powerful stroke until he came for a second orgasm. Jack then cradled her head again and said,

"My dear Dorothy, you have just gone from an innocent virgin to a terrific fuck in one session."

"Dorothy smiled and said, "Better than I ever imagined."

Jack continued, "I'll tell you what will be your problem. You may come off as too experienced, more experienced than your new lover. You have to be very careful. For example, don't offer to suck his cock. Wait for him to ask, and then ask him to tell you how to do it. You also don't want to be the aggressive un-dresser. You have to let the man lead off or, undress him and you. Don't be embarrassed and always show confidence in how you look. You have to be subtle. You can innocently show off your breasts by finding a reason to raise your arms. When you first lie down, put your arms over your head. Stay with language that is not crude. Ask your new man what you want him to call your genitals. Always be open to ask innocent questions and when you react, exaggerate your reactions, be vocal, compliment him often. Establishing communications is your most important policy. Believe me, no man will react badly to questions or compliments."

"You will be there for me when I have questions? Can I relate what is happening to me and ask advice confidentially?"

"Well, don't call when you are doing it, otherwise, absolutely. Any questions are fine. Could we be more intimate? I have been deep inside you and you delivered unbelievable pleasure for both of us. You might get a good vibrator and take care of needs that build up, and after what we did, you will become hornier. You'll have to deal with the urges now that you know you are good and it feels good. You might practice having orgasms with a vibrator since I wasn't sure you recognized the different categories of pleasure. I will get you a vibrator."

Jack and Dorothy showered together and that increased her comfort zone. Dorothy had matured greatly in just a few hours with Jack. It was a job well done, but did it raise more issues? Experience and innocence play important roles in seduction. That is another separate marketing skill. I think much of that will come naturally. Would it have been better for a woman or two lovers to struggle through inexperience together?

Can you imagine the religious promise made by Mohammad that a martyred Muslim warrior that killed some innocent women and children as an act of valor would earn 72 virgins in heaven? What the heck would any guy want to do with training 72 virgins as opposed to having 72 courtesans or some hot women that were experts trained at providing men pleasure? It is a strange world. I'll address Women's human rights in our final chapter.

I don't know where to draw the line on size. Jack felt that size made no difference as long as she was firm, clean and had a sexy attitude. Overweight people involved in a long time serious relationship faced a new set of problems that we are not qualified to analyze. There are some men that crave big breasts and some men crave big women. They just have to find each other.

Chapter 30. Aiding and A Bedding

Several weeks had passed, Jack was still dating the woman lawyer, but she offered no lessons for this book. She was a good sex partner, but nothing worth reporting. She was well educated and somewhat inhibited, but classy. They went to more stage shows than movies and doubled dated with Will and Cynthia on occasion.

Dorothy had met a nice guy at her health club. He seemed interested and Dorothy was hoping he would ask her out, which he eventually did. Meanwhile he hung around with her sharing exercise machines and discussing fitness rather than fitting.

Jack had a free weekend and was planning a motorcycle ride exploring the mountains. It was expected to be a nice warm weekend, but the mountains were always cooler. So, Jack called Dorothy and wanted to know if she wanted to go for a ride with him, have a mountain picnic, and get caught up on his advice.

Dorothy seized the opportunity and was anxious to try her first motorcycle ride. Jack showed up to pick up Dorothy at her house and she was asking what would be appropriate to wear since she had never ridden a Harley.

"OK, the mountain climbing shoes are fine, the jeans are good, I have a helmet for you and the jacket will do. I don't have an extra leather coat. But, take off your jeans for me, please?"

"I beg your pardon? Surely you don't want me to ride naked?"

"Trust me for a moment and you'll learn something," said Jack.

Dorothy must have been well trained and even though it had been a few weeks since she lost her virginity to Jack, she didn't hesitate to drop her pants, but she had to take off her boots first. Funny she didn't ask Jack why she was undressing inside at her front door. She may have thought there was something special about how she was to wear her jeans.

Jack then handed her and instructed her to wear a tight fitting jock strap.

"What is this and what is it for?"

"This is what male athletes wear to protect their balls."

"Really, and what are you suggesting I do with this thing?"

"Trust me. Just put it on. Here let me help you."

Jack fitted the jock strap so the stretched cup was hanging loosely over her pussy outside of her panties. He then took a small soft red ball, about half the size of a tennis ball and fixed it at the base of the jock strap so the ball was pressed gently against her "pantied pussy." He then helped her into her jeans and she had to re-lace her mountain climbing shoes.

"Trust me. You will soon understand. And consider this a valuable lesson, OK?"

"I can hardly wait," replied Dorothy dryly.

They mounted the motorcycle and Jack fired the engine. He looked back at Dorothy who obviously now understood the purpose of the little red ball. The ball was wedged between her clitoris and the slight hump in the passenger seat. Her legs were wrapped around Jack as were her arms and her pussy was vibrating with the motor. They were simulating a sex act. She smiled at Jack as Jack gunned the engine for a quick rumble. He then took off and headed for the highway. Dorothy was treated to a scenic ride with her clitoris being gently vibrated. Jack asked her to keep track of her feelings and if she had an orgasm to nudge him. Dorothy began to nudge him every few seconds, and she was grinning from ear to ear. She kissed Jack on the back of his neck. What a great pleasant surprise this outing was, she thought. Was Jack considerate or weird?

They rode for about an hour. The scenery was picture perfect. Jack turned onto a narrow dirt road that went uphill into some beautifully wooded pastures. They dismounted and Jack covered the bike with a tailored plastic cover and carried a backpack with wine coolers, towels, and a picnic blanket. Dorothy did not ask where they were going; she just followed Jack up a steep climb.

They came to a very secluded spot surrounded by some boulders; it was a small bed of grass. Jack spread the blanket, opened the wine coolers and patted the ground next to him. They drank and talked and Dorothy admitted that the cycle ride was orgasmic, but she really couldn't tell the difference when one orgasm ended and the next began. Dorothy seemed to have expanded her sexual attitude and appetite as well as her sexual sense of humor. She said she took his advice and was practicing masturbating with the quality vibrator he had given her. Their conversation involved a lot of kidding and sexual overtures. They were teasing each other and that was a reflection on Jack's success about training her to have a less inhibited attitude about sex and being naked.

Jack took off his boots and as he began to undress, he asked Dorothy to do the same. She did not hesitate. When naked, Jack put his boots back on and Dorothy did the same. They were both standing in the sun surrounded by trees and boulders. Jack handed

Dorothy a towel to carry. If by chance they should meet anybody, which was most unlikely, she was to wrap the towel around herself for cover. They hiked over to another cluster of boulders, which were about three feet high that covered the view of a small creek that was bubbling downhill.

Jack climbed over the smaller boulders, straddled the stream, dipped his hands in the cold water and playfully rubbed Dorothy's breasts with cold water. Her nipples rose on both breasts. Jack crouched and licked the cool water off her breasts, kissed her mouth and caressed her breasts while standing naked in the warm sun. Dorothy bent over to catch a handful of cold water to rub on Jack's erection. She was getting into the sporting fun and the naked game. Outdoor sex always means nice breezes and smells and new heights of excitement.

When Dorothy bent over the stream, she was standing on a smaller boulder and she was leaning over the boulder on the bank of the stream. Her ass was the perfect height for the next lesson. Jack grabbed and held her from behind and held her hips tight, not allowing her to move. He reached under her and stroked her labia with his penis from behind her. The old expression is "plowing a furrow." Dorothy froze her position and gasped. Jack found her vagina and slowly pushed in. Dorothy balanced herself against a smaller rock in front of her and braced herself with her arms against the boulder in front of her. She pushed off the rock and grunted with each stroke as Jack's body slapped into her firm ass. Rear entry sex is like spanking and the contact noise and the banging against her ass is what makes the act exciting. A woman feels the banging more than any clitoral action. Supposedly the "G" spot should come into play amid the controversy whether it exists or not. I think it exists. Dorothy was speechless and had braced herself against the last rock next to the stream so she could look back over her shoulder. Her breasts swung hard and that too felt good. Dorothy was stunned as to how good this felt. She raised her head, tried to look back at Jack's face as well as the thrusting action and she purred how good she felt.

Jack told her that was her lesson for rear entry sex and pulled out. They stood and faced each other. Jack was dangling a nice erection and Dorothy was breathing hard being frustrated at "coitus interruptus." Jack wanted to know if she thought she had a "G" spot, which was always tested with rear entry sex. Dorothy said, she wasn't aware of her "G" spot, but raved about how sexy everything was and how good the hard rear strokes felt. Jack was pulling a condom out of his boot and Dorothy quickly told Jack he didn't need a condom. Dorothy said she had started on the birth control pill hoping to meet a new man. She didn't expect Jack to introduce her to outdoor sex or she would have mentioned the pill. That was good news for Jack; he hated condoms. They reduced sensitivity for all.

Jack led Dorothy back to the blanket and told her she was about to get fucked outdoors with her boots on. And she would never forget it.

"Are you kidding? This is already unforgettable. But have at me, what can I do here? Can I start saying "fuck" now, because I really like fucking. I've had to fantasize about you with the vibrator you gave me. This unexpected opportunity is always an unexpected pleasure. I am so happy to be here, it is so beautiful. I promise you if you want to fuck until it gets dark, I am ready and I am already too wet to get sore.

"Wow. Have you ever matured? You should hear yourself talk. You have grown into such a sexy partner and your firm body is ever more fantastic. I admit that I haven't been able to get you out of my mind, but I think we have to hold to our original understanding. Put that towel under your hips and let me get downhill from you. I want you to concentrate and see if you can identify and feel an orgasm. Tell me when you get close, talk to me; tell me how it feels and if I should keep a particular tongue move. Take your time. Feel the sun and the wind and watch the sky. Concentrate on my tongue. Pull your labia apart and stretch it without hurting yourself. I want to see your clitoris rise and get a little hard, OK?"

The scene was now Jack eating Dorothy in a secluded sunlit mountain meadow. Her booted legs were high in the air and she was holding her labia apart stretching her skin in order to tighten her clitoris. It was a very sexy scene and don't forget "Mother nature" provided the perfect setting with smells, breezes and a warm sun. Jack took his time teasing her erect clitoris. He was lying on a towel, Dorothy was on the blanket and Jack had the warm sun on his back. He used more flicking and less massaging with his tongue. They were not in a rush, just concentrating on the pleasure. Dorothy had built up a tremendous frustration and was reaching the point where she was going to burst with an orgasm. When she began to move her hips and exclaimed she was coming, Jack began his tongue action just below her clitoris and flicked faster. That technique is sometimes referred to the "butterfly flick," or the "hummingbird lick." Finally Dorothy yelled,

"Yes I'm coming, Oh God, thank you, don't stop, Oh God, thank you."

Jack blew on her clitoris and moved up and mounted Dorothy while she was still high. He rested on his extended arms and looked down at her as he began her first outdoor fuck. The scene is sometimes referred to the "Adam and Eve" setting. They took their time fucking, again enjoying the special circumstances. Finally, Jack had reached a peak and he began to increase the speed of his strokes. Dorothy exclaimed,

"My God, I think I'm coming again."

They came together, if she really came, and, after a brief rest, Jack rolled her over without exiting her and put her on top. They lay together and enjoyed the moment that they couldn't do the first time with the condom. They held fast and just kept quiet with Dorothy's face at Jack's chin level. Dorothy was whispering how wonderful this scene was. Jack whispered how wonderful she was and held her tight until he softened naturally. When he fell out Dorothy was resting on his chest and said she could feel him leave her. She still did not move. Mother Nature was beautiful and Dorothy was asking Jack how she could ever expect outdoor sex from another man. Jack suggested she be the hostess.

They arose and took a short naked walk back to the stream. Jack washed off his penis with cold water, which felt good. Dorothy squatted and splashed cold water on her pussy. She then asked how and where she was going to pee because she had a strong urge to do so. So, Jack showed her the "woodsman techniques." She squatted, he held her hands and she blushed as she leaned back without touching her ass to the ground. She peed; no splashing. Jack was balancing her as a counterweight. She grinned with delight and was not embarrassed. Jack felt like he was molding her into having fewer inhibitions because they were giggling about it while it was happening. It was natural.

"You better hope I don't let go, you'd be in deep pee," laughed Jack.

"Don't you dare let me go and please don't watch me." She said.

"Nonsense, it's too late to become inhibited with me. Hey watch this."

Jack turned sideways and peed while she watched. They acted like two little kids laughing about their casualness.

"You are right; I have never seen a man pee before. I don't know if I needed that information, but that was interesting."

"Ever hear the story about the two third graders when on a picnic sneaked off to pee? When the little boy took out his little penis to piss the little girl exclaimed, "What a neat thing to bring on a picnic."

Jack washed his penis; she squatted over the little brook and again splashed cold water on her genitals and once again and they sat on the boulder. The breeze increased and it was getting cooler. It looked like it might rain. Dorothy was not about to let the weather interfere with this unexpected opportunity to play with the man of her dreams. Dorothy soon kneeled in front of Jack and took his penis in her mouth and began an "outdoor" suck. Jack was out of semen so he leaned back, put his hands behind himself and looked at the sky and enjoyed the feel free sensation. Man, life is good! Jack soon became erect and shifted himself higher on the boulder, so Dorothy could straddle him while he sat upright. Dorothy sat on his cock like a pro. The deep knee bends pushing off the ground were easy for her with the rock and cock at that height. It was custom made for fucking.

Dorothy was enjoying a slow smooth ride, sort of a cuddling mode with her arms around Jack's neck. It began to sprinkle, then, it rained harder. They faced upwards so the rain fell on their faces and they did not stop fucking. Dorothy was bouncing rhythmically on Jack as he held her hips. He could suck on her breasts, which he did frequently, and the rain was cascading on his face, which was also sexy.

Dorothy's hair was now soaking wet, but she was going to ride this bucking bronco as long as she could. Jack was actually bucking because he was reaching a climax. Men's orgasms in close sequence don't carry much semen. There is still pleasure, but the term for frequent ejaculations is, "blue balls." That is a pleasant feeling, but causes a slight ache deep within the testicles. Regardless that again was such a sexy scene that a small orgasm was always welcome. It was like a big sigh. Jack made a big vocal scene when he came; he made a giant sigh, a gasp. Dorothy was having her finest hour. The sexy scene, the rain combined with the mountain scenery was too much beauty. She was getting so much satisfaction from the entire day so far that she could care less what the weather was going to be.

They walked naked in the rain carrying their towels and stuff and started the descent down to the bike. Dorothy was sipping the last of the wine coolers. They were only wearing their mountain boots. Jack walked behind Dorothy and watched and raved about her muscled body. He never even thought of the "fat" word. By the time they got to the bike, they were soaked and it was getting cold. They climbed down to the bike and got under the cycle cover, which became a convenient tent, as they were half sitting on the bike. They dried with the towels and Jack started the motor for the extra heat. Jack and Dorothy dried off and got dressed under the cycle cover. Jack put the jock strap back on Dorothy for the "red ball" express ride home. Their clothes were somewhat dry from being in the backpack. They would get wet again. Dressing involved some giggling and some slapping and some sexy touching,

"The ball goes outside your panties." Jack reminded her.

Dorothy grabbed Jack's cock through his jeans and wanted to know if his balls vibrated too. So the fun went on. The ride was difficult at first. The dirt path had become muddy and Jack kept the bike at ten MPH. Dorothy chugged the last of the wine and threw the bottle into the brush. Jack stopped and retrieved the bottle and chastised Dorothy for littering. They started downhill slowly.

Dorothy began to sing to the tune from "Sound of Music."

"Climb every Mountain, bend over every stream, catch a cock with my big ass, get fucked until I scream." Jack laughed, but concentrated on steering.

"Climb every penis, suck every cock, lick my little pussy, and fuck me round the clock." I could have been a decomposer, Jack. If I could play a guitar I'd be a star."

"Dorothy, I think you've had too much to drink. Listen to me, when you find the right guy, don't drink on the first date."

"One for the money, two for the show, better get ready cause I wanna fuck around the clock tonight, gonna fuck fuck fuck til the broad gets it right."

"Dorothy stop it, I'm trying to drive here."

Dorothy paused and then sang back to the Sound of Music, "Straddle that big hummer, ride the little red ball, Strum my little clit, until I feel it all."

Dorothy continues to sing using the "Sound Of Music" tune.

"No, I got a better one; Ride every Harley, vibrate my little clit, when I'm wet and ready, fuck me in my slit."

" No, no wait; this is better, ride pussy ride, ride the little red ball, when my pussy tingles, come and fuck it all." With that Dorothy began to undulate against Jack and pressing the red ball against his back.

"Come on Chief, give me a little rumble." Jack gunned the engine and Dorothy yelled, "Ride em cowgirl, yahoo, I'm coming again."

Jack finally reached some pavement.

"That's enough Dorothy, you're driving me nuts."

"Can I drive with your nuts?" Dorothy was rubbing Jack's crotch and he moved her hand away.

However Jack could not stop laughing, and his threat lost credibility.

"Jack, I have an original idea. Why don't we fuck on the motorcycle while the engine is running?"

"Here in broad daylight? Are you crazy? We would go to jail for indecent exposure. And, it's raining even harder, I'm going to stop at the next underpass and wait it out, OK?"

"Maybe we could do it in my garage on the bike."

"And how about carbon monoxide poisoning? That would be your last fuck, and I know you don't want that."

"Hey, it ain't over til the fat lady sings."

"Damn it Dorothy, you are not fat! Haven't you learned anything, now shut up."

Dorothy was pretending to pout and was silent for a while. Then she began to sing softly into Jack's ear,

"Make him lick your pussy, before he fucks your ass, keep your mouth shut until the overpass, then (Louder) climb every penis, suck every cock, rock him in your pussy, until you get his cream."

"Climb every mountain, forge all the peaks, fuck him in the sunlight, until your pussy squeaks. (Change melodies to "You are My Sunshine")

"Fuck me in the sunshine, fuck me in the rain, and fuck me till it's over, until he comes in mine. You are my sunshine, my only one shine, you fuck me happy, when sky's are gray, you'll never know dear, how much I fuck you, please don't turn off my . . . . engine, awe shit, that didn't rhyme."

Dorothy sighs and then goes silent the rest of the ride. When turning in her driveway, she apologizes profusely.

"Jack, I'm so sorry, I don't know what came over me. Please don't give up on me. That's the first time I ever reacted that way to wine, it must have been the altitude. Please forgive me?"

"Dorothy, you were hilarious. I see a side of your personality that I didn't know you had. You are very witty. I love your sense of humor, I'm glad you had a good time."

Dorothy said her sex life was ruined because she would never find another Jack. They went back to Dorothy's and fell asleep from all the wind and fresh air. They were dressed. Jack woke up a few hours later, undressed and headed for the shower. Dorothy joined him and they laughed about her drunken fit.

Dorothy began to sing again, in the shower.

"Climb every penis, feel it on my clit, fuck him till he comes, and have another fit."

They laughed and went to bed and had an old-fashioned missionary bed fuck, hard and fast. Dorothy said she was hooked and probably would never be satisfied again. Jack was sore.

Jack reminded Dorothy about the joke about the God "Thor" paying a visit to mortals so he could get laid. He and this beautiful woman fucked for hours. When done he beat his chest and said, I am Thor.

"You think you're thor, said the fair maiden, I'm so thor I can't touch mine with a powder puff." It was an old joke, but Dorothy had not heard it.

"I wish I could tell somebody I am now a successful mountain climber except I climbed a big cock when I got to the top. No one would believe me anyway, but I should have shouted it from the mountain top, I've been fucked and I am good at cock climbing."

"Oh my God, what have I created," mused Jack.

Ladies and Gentlemen, it is a fact; liquor makes both men and women less inhibited. Liquor makes seduction more efficient. Too much liquor can also spoil the act, and too much continued drinking can lead to sexual disaster. Liquor does not enhance orgasms. Sobriety and good foreplay and a sober attitude and willingness creates better sex. I'm sure you have understood from this book that we are emphasizing cunnilingus as the most productive act for better sex and a better sex life.

Another two weeks passed and Dorothy confided by phone that her new boy friend finally fucked her. She confided in Jack that she hoped her anxiety to begin fucking was not too obvious. She told Bill, her boyfriend, she just started taking the pill hoping he would get the message. A condom may have made Bill too insensitive on his first try. She said he did not do cunnilingus and the first time while they did fuck like beginners, he came in about two minutes. The newness and Bill's passion carried the day. Jack explained that fast ejaculation meant he was too excited and to stay with him. Don't say anything about his performance, just stay interested and keep telling him how much you enjoyed yourself regardless of your disappointment, be patient.

Dorothy asked Jack about how to advise the guy to try new things without hurting his feelings. She said that each time after he left she had to satisfy herself with her vibrator. A few days later they were walking to the parking lot together and Dorothy complained how much she missed being eaten and that if her new boyfriend didn't offer to do her she was going to threaten him, "eat me or leave me." ("I'll never be lonely." Isn't that an old Doris Day song, "love Me Or leave Me?")

"My, my, I have created a monster haven't I?" said Jack. But we are still best friends aren't we?"

"Yes and all I can do is fantasize about you. Can you tell me something or suggest something I can do with my vibrator in case this guy never goes down on me? Shall I show him my vibrator and hope he catches on?"

"Buy an instruction book and show it to him." Jack advised. Let him read it and let him suggest cunnilingus, or maybe ask you about oral sex."

Jack changed the subject. "OK, I'll tell you what, how about a simple new contract between us? I have an experiment for you. Let's try some mutual oral sex as a release. I'll eat you first and then you give me your first complete blowjob. I'll show you some more moves and you can learn cock sucking. If you suck on his cock maybe he'll catch on to oral sex."

"Yeah, when, and where do we do this, and will that get me all of my Girl Scout badges?"

"Right now; in my front seat. I'll show you how to practice. You keep watch while I do you first and I'll keep watch while you do me. What do you say?"

"That is an offer I can't refuse."

Jack had Dorothy remove her panties. He watched her struggle in the front seat and he had to comment how sexy it always is when a woman lift's her dress and anxiously takes off her panties, and or panty hose. Jack told her to practice that move in front of a guy and the more she could struggle and appear anxious, the better the stimulation. Jack reclined the passenger seat so she could see out the window. The underground parking lot was almost empty and they were out of anybody's sight. Dorothy lifted her legs up and rested her feet on the seat on either side of her per Jack's instruction. Her beautiful legs were spread with her knees at her chin, and her pussy was presented like candy on a serving tray. Jack took his time licking her clitoris, this time when he stroked her little head with his tongue licking upwards, she had an orgasm. She kept orgasmic sounds to a muffled groaning and whispered a sweet "thank you" continuously. She later recognized when she came because she had practiced with the vibrator Jack gave her. Dorothy admitted Jack's tongue was far better than her toy penis. She was learning.

Jack reclined his seat and undid his pants and took out Long John. Dorothy said,

"Well, hello Long John Silver, I finally get to give you a good licking."

Dorothy went down on Jack and she was wonderful because she seemed anxious to be good. Her inexperience did not show. Jack had to be careful he didn't bang her head against the steering-wheel as he had to lift his hips off the seat as he came. He told her when to expect each squirt and she reacted by sucking and swallowing. She did cough a bit, but assured Jack it was just lack of experience. Jack explained that the oral sex contract was supposed to be a safety thing for releasing tension when fucking was inconvenient. They both agreed their first try at therapeutic oral sex was successful.

There are new statistics that reflect an increase in "Fuck buddies," a term for people who are just good friends but have reached a comfort level and a mutual understanding about sex just for immediate needs. The reason more such sex takes place is because of the understanding to keep it secret. Such sex requires an attitude adjustment and involves mutual trust. Many married people stray and have such relationships to satisfy sexual desires that are not satisfied at the home front. Some people rationalize that variety motivates them on the home front. The older the partners the more justified the outside activity. Sex friends do not involve love, just an understanding about helping to meet private needs. Oral sex is probably more often used, but probably not involving cunnilingus. It surprises me that so many women will give gratuitous blowjobs.

Jack once attended a noisy outdoor concert and was joined by two ladies. One was beautiful and tall, but Jack later found out she was an expensive mistress for a rich German guy. Jack danced with her and was striking out. She left by herself leaving Jack stranded with the not so attractive lady. It turns out the stranded lady was bisexual and was hitting on the same beauty. Both had struck out. Jack was complaining that he had been turned down by the sexy beauty and his new friend offered to give him a blowjob just to relieve his frustration. A consolation prize? Jack had an excuse and declined, but wondered what was to be gained by this lady and her offer. A lonely woman willing to suck cock? Men offering to perform cunnilingus as a final act is unheard of. I'm sure this woman was offering a blowjob hoping it would motivate Jack to fuck her. Many times less attractive women will use this technique. There are so many mysteries concerning sex that we wondered if we would ever learn it all. Back to Dorothy.

"How about some more practice time, "Coach?" She grinned as Jack tucked Long John into his warm "barn."

Jack ignored her and said, "So, do you still think you are too fat to fuck?"

"I think I'm still overweight, but thanks to you and my exercise routine I am staying firm, but I still think I'm too big. Maybe I'll have to find a big man who by comparison makes me look smaller."

For the next few months Dorothy was training her boyfriend as subtly as she could. He was an accountant at a big firm and was conservative and inexperienced sexually. She said her sex life was nothing compared to Jack, but she thought this guy was getting serious and their sex was lasting longer and improving. She felt she was still short-changed on climaxes.

Dorothy requested an oral re-engagement of their new contract, and as a result, she and Jack did the front seat oral exchange thing a few more times as winter grew close. Dorothy said she wanted to improve her blowjob skills, but Jack realized the cunnilingus was something Dorothy was enjoying most. It was very pleasurable as well as a mutual release of tension. If either felt the need, they agreed they would try to meet and pull it off, so to speak. Dorothy said she always felt she deserved a good licking. The oral sex contract kept Dorothy and Jack close as friends and confidants. They would have fucked, but Jack's car was too small and there were time constraints. And as Bill and Dorothy got serious, Jack backed off, which was the right thing to do. Dorothy told Jack that she was teaching Bill cunnilingus from an instruction book she kept at bedside, per Jack's advice. Bill was getting into it and obviously was not aware of where Dorothy was learning her techniques.

Dorothy finally had a marriage proposal from Bill, the accountant, and Dorothy was anxious to start a family. Jack and I attended her wedding and Dorothy continued her contact with Jack just for the advice, which went on for a few years. Dorothy became the sexual aggressor much to Bill's enjoyment. Jack had taught her well. Dorothy had a great marriage and said when she eventually taught her husband how to perform oral sex and he thought it was his doing even though she had purchased the book. Women always seem to have the upper hand when it comes to sex and love. Dorothy never again questioned her bigness. She had enjoyed an effective lesson in self-esteem and self-confidence. She accepted it for what it was. The lesson here is for all lovers to overcome bigness fears. It is all about attitude. If you think you are or will be sexy, you will become what you eat. Oops, that was the wrong expression.

Chapter 31. The Story. Blowing In The Wind

It gets to the point where Jack's experiences are too many to report. I have tried to keep the adventures on subjects that are exceptional because of the characters, attitudes, or new sexual techniques. This may seem like a strange way to get experience, but I assure you it worked for my marriage to Cynthia. Some of these stories were eventually told to Cynthia and brings us back to the beginning of this story. The unusual sexual events in this chapter actually happened and really stimulated my wife Cynthia many years later.

I want to relate another story because I felt this particular woman had an exceptionally sophisticated personality. More important, Jack and Ann had the most unique sexual experience, perhaps one of the most creative sex acts we have ever even heard of. Her Name is Ann Collins. She was a divorced single mom about ten years older than Jack. Ann had a dry sense of humor and was an outspoken up-front woman that withheld no punches. She could match Jack telling sexy jokes and had mastered the accents and body language of storytelling. She was a Texan through and through. She was Five feet eight inches tall, red hair and greenish eyes. She reminded Jack of Josie because of her coloring, but Ann's red hair was darker, sort of an auburn color, a dark reddish brown. Jack met her at the Houston airport while on a business trip. Ann was an airline reservations supervisor. It is only a coincidence that many of these adventures are with redheads or green-eyed women. Remember, only 1% of the population are redheads and I don't have any statistics for green eyes, especially green eyed redheads.

Jack had a client named Ron Carlson. Ron owned a business that manufactured forty-foot sailboats. They were custom made and because of some patented boat building techniques, Ron was successful. Jack was acting as an investment banker for Ron. They became fast friends. Ron was ten years Jack's senior.

Ron had trucked a completed boat to Miami and asked Jack to spend three days with him rigging and testing the boat. Ron was married, but invited his pretty young travel agent to join him for the delivery. He agreed to pay her way and included her older sister as well. The travel agent's name was Gloria and her older half sister was Eve. They had different Father's and Gloria was not very Italian. Eve was Eve Garoldini. Ron told Eve about Jack being single and showed her a photo of Jack, and Eve, a single divorcee, was embarrassed about her younger half sister maybe accompanying a married man, but readily agreed to accept the short paid for vacation, especially if she could meet Jack, a handsome single man.

Jack called Eve and assured he was not an aggressor and she had no obligation toward him and they would just see what happens. Eve agreed. But on the Wednesday prior to the planned trip, Eve's only child got sick and she apologized that she had to cancel on short notice. Jack was at the Houston airport that Wednesday night, it was ten o'clock PM and he had to wait for a midnight redeye flight. The ticket counter was closing and Jack was inquiring about the possibility of an earlier flight. The supervisor was Ann Collins. There were no other flights. Jack hung his head in disappointment and gave Ann his classical puppy dog look and said,

"Damn, I wish somebody would sympathize with me and at least buy me a cup of coffee."

"Honey, I'll sit with y'all all night of I can just look into those big but sad blue eyes. And if it's sympathy you want, you just met the right woman. Damn, you are a handsome dude."

Jack blushed and they strode to the coffee shop two doors down. Ann had closed her counter.

Jack said, "Listen gorgeous, what are the odds of me meeting a sympathetic person with any airline at this hour. Do you always work this late?"

"Darlin, I got me two fine boys to raise and I need all the work I can get. I like my job and my oldest boy is fifteen, so I can leave them alone some work shifts. Y'all got any kids?"

"I'm not married, still looking."

"Don't bullshit a bullshiter honey, a big stud like you must be corralling a herd of fillies with their tails raised."

Jack tried to blush. "Yes I date some women. How come you are not married again? I'll bet you have a few stallions chasing you."

"Darlin, this old mare don't have time to go wagging her tail. I just swish it to keep the flies away." She laughed, Jack laughed.

They sat down and ordered coffee. Jack asked if he could tell her a sad story and ask her advice. So Jack told her how he had this airline ticket and how he got stood up at the last moment by a blind date. He told her about Ron and the boat and then popped the question.

"Listen to what I have to say, gorgeous, you just won a free three day vacation in Florida, all expenses paid and I will be your escort."

Ann abruptly got up and left the table. "Don't yew dare move, I'll be right back."

"Jeeze, you are not going to have me arrested are you?"

Ann waved him off and entered a phone booth. She talked for a few minutes and returned to the table.

"Ok, you big stallion, this old mare got her tail up and out of the way and if y'all are serious, I'll accept the prize. I just called my mom and told her I just won a trip and she agreed to watch my kids. Let me ask you first, do y'all like my tits?"

"Well, yes, why ask?"

"Cause they ain't mine and I'd rather y'all not touch em. I can take em off and y'all can take em home with yew, but what little I got will sure be thankful for any attention. I'd hope y'all wouldn't think big tits are important."

Jack said, "The only thing that matters with tits is if the "feelee" enjoys the touching and sucking, anything bigger than a mouthful is wasted anyway. Are your nipples sensitive, now that you brought the subject, and by the way, I love your candor."

"Honey, y'all better stop talking that way or I'll get stuck to this seat like a rubber tipped arrow. I got a stored up urge and I haven't seen such a sexy stud as y'all in all my life. I got a special place for your sympathy, I just hope y'all didn't bite off more than you can chew."

"You don't scare me. But I have to admit you do excite me. I love your outspoken manner. Can you reopen your counter and change this ticket to you. Here's my credit card."

Ann put her arm around Jack and led him to her ticket counter, opened up her computer and had Jack sign the ticket over to her. Jack insisted on up-grading her to first class and she patted him on the ass in gratitude. Ann had major discounts working for the airline and didn't need the upgrade.

"Honey, I promise y'all the time of your life. I can't thank y'all enough for the vacation. I need a trip badly." Thank yew so much. Damn your arms are hard."

"That's because you are feeling them. They weren't that hard before you touched me."

"I love the way you talk, you big bullshitter, I'll walk y'all to your gate, y'all better get moving."

When they got to the gate, Jack pulled Ann aside and kissed her. She clung to him like she was having an orgasm. Jack said he would meet her plane in Miami.

Ron and Gloria showed up in Miami first, and then Jack, and they were waiting for Ann's arrival. Ann surprised Jack when she walked up to him. He didn't recognize her at first. She had a "fall" attached to her hair giving her a long full red ponytail. Her auburn hair sparkled in the daylight. She was dressed in an all white suit, tight skirt, white high heels making her a few inches taller. Her ass was tight in her skirt and curved out better than Jack remembered. In fact he would not have recognized Ann if she hadn't come straight to him. Her Texas cowgirl image was advanced to a very classy model. She had make up on and dangling earrings, all enhancing her image. She gave Jack a big hug and he kissed her. Introductions were made and they caught a shuttle to their hotel on the beach. All were happy and excited about the sailing trip. When they got to the adjoining rooms, both rooms had king sized beds. Gloria immediately and nervously piped up that the girls would get this room and you guys sleep over there.

"Hey, hey, wait just a fucking minute here, I didn't come all this way to sleep with you honey, If I can't sleep with Jack, I'm going back home." Ann seemed upset.

Everybody looked surprised. Ron winked at Jack and Jack pulled Ann into the other adjoining room and shut the door. The couples met later in the restaurant, and had tons of laughs. Ann could sure tell great sexy jokes. Her language was a little crude as she seemed to get excited about closing in on bedtime. She kept her hand on Jack's leg and told some jokes that would make a vulture blush.

When in their room Ann went right for undressing Jack. Jack tried to reciprocate as he tried to undress her, but she ignored his efforts. When Jack was naked, she sighed and had him stand still while she undressed. She would not take off her "falsies." She kept reaching for Jack, stroking his muscles. She even licked his chest while taking off her tight skirt. Jack took charge and laid her on the bed. When he began to lick her pussy, she kept saying,

"Yew sweet man yew, y'all are so good, how sweet to be treated this way. This I am not used to, oh fuck, I'm coming already. Please don't stop, oh my Goooood."

Ann began to undulate her hips and moaned sweetly to herself.

Ann continued, "What am I going to do, I want to fuck and I want to suck on your cock, y'all are one sexy fucker, God am I living right, or what?"

Jack said, "Relax. Remember we can do more tomorrow. We have to get up early. If you like being eaten so much, then I'll give you all you want. Let me get inside you, I'm also ready to fire and I can't wait either." They fucked for what seemed like a long time and after, quickly fell asleep. There was no morning wakeup sex because they had to get to the sailboat early.

The next day they all helped rig the new boat with Ron's supervision. They got under sail about noon and the wind was ideal. Once out of sight of land, Ron had Jack take the controls, a big spiked wheel. Ron and Gloria went to the bow, out of sight, took off their bathing suits and sunned themselves naked using globs of lotion.

They must have had sex the previous night to be that familiar. Jack could not see them once they lay down.

Jack was standing in front of the steering wheel in his shorts. Ann was fully covered in white cotton and wearing a big brimmed hat to protect her from the sun. There was a giant awning over the center cockpit. Ann couldn't wait to get the festivities started so she kneeled in front of Jack and pulled his shorts down. She began an enthusiastic blowjob, "blowing in the wind," as it were. Jack lifted his head high and was breathing in the sea breeze. There was Jack, standing at the helm, the wind in his face and his cock buried in a beautiful mouth. Could life get any better?

Jack did not plan on ending the moment with a blowjob. He sat on the bench behind the wheel and Ann took off her slacks and white panties and climbed on his cock. The boat was heeling to port and the breeze was providing some extra stimulation. Ann's big hat made it difficult to kiss her, but Ann was taking a prolonged sweet gentle ride on Jack's cock also hoping not to end it too soon. Jack kept the boat on course while being serviced like no helmsman in history, he imagined.

Ron and Gloria reappeared and caught them in the sitting on a lap sex act.

Ann said, "Hey, how about some warning? Damn why aren't y'all fucking and taking advantage of this time?" She stopped riding Jack, but didn't get up. "OK, why don't you guys steer and let us move to the front?"

Ann climbed off of Jack's cock and got up naked from the waist down, and Long John was exposed. There was no place for Long John to hide. Also exposed was Ann's beautiful ass and shapely legs and an auburn pussy that sparkled in the sunlight.

Gloria stared at Long John in complete disbelief and tried to pretend she wouldn't be noticed. Jack pulled up his shorts and his penis was bulging out of the top of his partially pulled shorts. Ann stayed naked from the waist down and the two of them crawled to a space just ahead of the first mast. Ann rolled her white cotton slacks in her hand and pushed them forward.

The boat was a twin masted ketch. Just ahead of the bow mast was a small windshield exposing a front inside cockpit. This is hard to describe, so "bare" with me. There was a small white nylon awning attached to the bottom of a short boom facing forward. That small sail was an extra "jib" attached to the bow mast. Jack rigged the small tent attached to the underside of the boom to keep the sun off of Ann's red headed more sensitive skin. She was wearing her fall fixed in a ponytail, which was blowing wildly in the wind. A stainless steel railing was set on the deck about four feet apart and was only about six inches high. There was a small mattress that Ron had left fastened between the low deck railings. There was another two foot railing that ran the length of the boat to prevent people from falling overboard.

When Jack and Ann positioned themselves under the six-foot awning, the tent was too low and they could not have sexual intercourse. Ann couldn't sit on Jack and Jack could not mount Ann. Jack's ass didn't fit under the small tent, so Jack tried to get downwind of Ann to eat her pussy, but the rail was too short and Jack's ass was dangerously exposed to the elements, wind, sun and the heeling of the boat. There wasn't sufficient room for a tandem of bodies. The wind was extremely forceful. Jack had to stay under the awning with Ann because she could not expose herself to the sun for any extended time. The boat was heeling sharply, and the wind was hitting them so hard, they could hardly talk without shouting. Jack came up beside Ann, but she had spread her legs and was holding her labia open allowing the high wind to blow on her clitoris. Actually the wind was so strong that it blew her labia apart. Now that was truly uninhibited. So, Jack turned around, sixty-nine and tried to get his head positioned to help with some licking, but his head blocked the wind and was interrupting the wind flow. More adjustments were necessary.

Try to imagine what is happening. Ann pulled Jack on top of her so his chin was on her pelvic bone, but kneeling while holding his weight on his elbows. That put Jack's ass above Ann's head. Ann had one hand holding her pussy open and with the other hand she pulled Jack's cock so it was positioned over her face. With the heavy wind separating her labia she let go and moved both of her hands to try and hold Long John. Jack's testicles were sort of sitting on the top of her head. They were trying to adjust to their height difference. Jack was straining to get his tongue on her clitoris, except he was licking her upside down. He would push his tongue as if he were pushing her clitoris toward her vagina, while keeping his head out of the wind flow beating against Ann's clitoris. The wind was blowing so hard that if Jack would have opened her vagina with his finger, she might have filled up with air. Jack had the same problem with his mouth being open.

Ann also made the same adjustments, and they could not hear each other, they were just reacting instinctively. She was licking Jack's penis stroking her tongue toward his little head and as long as his main nerve was on her lips, she imitated Jack's tongue action, at the other end, so to speak. If Jack flicked sideways, she followed suit.

There was no way she could get his cock in her mouth and keep Long John's helmet warm, because she was upside down. After she released her hand holding that was holding her labia open, Jack used one of his hands to spread her labia apart while he strained to flick his tongue sideways in a most awkward position. But as the wind pummeled her clitoris, Jack's tongue complimented the wind current. Ann did the same tongue flicking to Long John as if they were coordinating their tongue actions. They finally got in rhythm and it gave Ann the biggest thrill she had ever imagined. She would occasionally stamp her feet when climaxing. Her legs were under the small tent and the flats of her feet were on the mat. Her knees were pushing against the small tent.

Jack could not thrust because Ann held his cock firm, but never seemed to tire licking. She licked faster when she was having an orgasm, which appeared to be constant. She didn't want to stop. The wind was pounding her clitoris during Jack's licks. Ann could move Jack's cock sideways, but in order not to lose her concentration, she kept licking Jack's nerve sideways. She was hanging on to the small railing with her other hand.

The tease was more than Jack could handle. He could not move his body. His knees were embracing Ann's head and he also had one hand on the railing to hold them steady as the boat heeled. His right hand was spreading Ann's labia and his licking in the wind was more effective than he realized. Ann continued to stamp her feet, when coming again and he could feel her mouth humming.

The wind was whistling around Long John, but with less velocity. It was swirling across Ann's mouth and Ann could hear herself whistle while she worked. As Jack's frustration rose, Ann went crazy with pleasure causing Jack to ejaculate. She was stamping her feet even harder. Jack burst and his semen shot down Ann's body so Jack actually felt some moisture on the underside of his own chest. Ann began to pull his foreskin as best she could as his cum streamed down her chest. She also filled the cleavage of her false bra with cum. She never took her bra off.

Jack rolled off Ann, turned around and squirmed up against her. Ann, again did not have to hold her labia apart, the wind did all the work; she wasn't going to miss the wind pressure whether Jack was there or not. She was enjoying the high wind and the occasional salty splash. Jack had withheld his orgasm from when they were fucking before at the center cockpit, so his orgasm was a bigger than a normal build up. Ann's belly was soaked with cum all the way to her pubic hair. Jack began removing her bra and false breasts and she allowed the move. She then spread some cum over her flat chest and Jack did the same. Jack yelled that he never felt anything so good in his life. He wasn't sure what she was doing to him, but it was a major tease. They were both "teased off."

Imagine these circumstances. A penis has the foreskin tightly stretched; the exposed male central nerve is technically called the "frenulum." What we call the little helmet is technically called the "Glans," and the ridge at the bottom of a man's helmet is called the "coronal ridge." During intercourse, the frenulum is rubbed against the vaginal walls. A man pumps and strokes creating his pleasure. The woman gets pleasured when the penis is fully inserted and the clitoris gets "touched" and is pleasured more with the frequency of shaft contact. The act is enhanced by the passion of the partners. To have the penis motionless, no thrusting, and have the butterfly flicking as the only driving force makes for a more violent orgasm. The prostate gland is forced to fire without the thrusting, thus requiring more energy. The flow of semen somewhat resembles capillary action. Very seldom are orgasms reached this way, especially mutually. The male usually needs the warmth of the vagina to complete the act. This mutual orgasm was very unusual and the energy release was far superior to sexual intercourse.

In this case Jack's penis was held tight and it could not move, so the fucking sensation was in his mind. Ann had the big advantage of the wind blowing against her erect clitoris. The tongue contact was not directly on her clitoris. Her frustration level was having a vagina begging for a penis when in reality, the wind was doing a better job, especially when the male tongue was contributing to the pleasure, albeit it secondary to the wind pleasure. The mutual orgasms were major eruptions driven by frustration. Perhaps a form of bondage? You decide. These circumstances would be difficult to recreate.

They clung to each other for about five minutes and when they tried to kiss, the wind created a slight whistle. They could not describe what happened to each other. They had teased each other to orgasm without direct organ contact. It took a lot of energy to climax that way and they felt exhausted. Jack had never felt such powerful urges to fire without being inserted somewhere. The sensation was something new. He would never forget the feeling, and he would always be alert to fucking in the wind, if the circumstances were right. Ann put her bra back on and the two of them crawled naked back to the center cockpit having just performed the most original sex act ever imagined. Ann had replaced her hat, which was strapped on and covered her shoulders with a white blouse. She was holding her long white slacks.

Back at the center cockpit, Gloria was naked and while lying on her stomach was leafing through a magazine in the heavy wind. Ron was naked and fighting the wheel. Gloria said to Ann,

"You still have your bra on?"

Gloria sat up exposing her much younger firm body and perfect tits. She was waiting for a response.

Ann spoke, "Listen to me honey, I don't have any tits. The good lord decided to handicap me with a flat chest. These tits aren't real and I am too embarrassed to stick these fried eggs out in the open? But looky here, see this ass, I got a great ass, a tight pussy and nice hard little button between my legs that fires whenever I pull the trigger. Honey I can come like an automatic weapon. I see your tits and they are beautiful and y'all got a nice body, but how in God's good creation can you sit around and not be sucking cock or fucking. If I could start over, I'd never let a good cock pass me by once I got naked with a good hard man. Darlin, y'all are wasting some valuable time reading that magazine."

Ann was posing with her ass pointed to everyone. She turned and grabbed her pussy like a football player adjusting his jock, and shook it once while she finished speaking. Gloria didn't know what to say, and Ron and Jack laughed.

When evening fell, Ron mounted a charcoal stove that hung from a bracket out over the water. They were now anchored in a small cove on Biscayne Bay. Each couple had a cabin, one for'd and one aft. They all met for the boat dinner naked, except for Ann's bra and Gloria's bathing suit bottom. Jack and Ron were naked and soft. Ann demanded Gloria take off her bathing suit bottom and she did. All three applauded Gloria and she gave a cute bow. She apologized if she offended Ann with her comments and Ann gave Gloria a little hug, which meant her bra made contact with Gloria's bare breasts.

Ann then took off her bra and said,

"Y'all take a good look and don't say anything. Y'all my friends now and Honey you look at my tits and let me tell you how lucky you are. I expect these guys to be admiring your tit's and not looking at me anyway."

Ann and Jack amused all with jokes and short funny sexy stories. Jack told them about the world's worst lay. He also talked about the use of toothpaste during cunnilingus, which held everybody's attention.

Gloria seemed to be watching Long John and when Ann caught her staring at Jack's well endowed "softee," she winked at Gloria and licked her lips. Gloria blushed. Ann later whispered in Gloria's ear,

"Honey, y'all don't have to put a whole cock in your mouth. Just take what you can and pretend your mouth is your pussy. I expect to hear Ron screaming all night about your tight pussy. Take it from an old broad, you got what every man wants. I have to work harder at it. You want a cock sucking lesson, I'll demonstrate if you want."

Gloria nodded and blushed.

After dinner, they were enjoying the moonlight and Gloria had a few drinks. She blurted out to Ron, "Ann said she would teach me how to suck your cock Ron, can I try?"

Ron jumped up and asked, "Where did he sign up." Ann had Gloria sit next to her with Jack on her other side. She kneeled in front of Jack and began to play with Long John with her tongue and described what she was doing. Gloria's face was but a few inches away and she was truly fascinated. Jack got hard quickly and Ann demonstrated how to suck cock. The lesson lasted about one minute and Gloria tried the technique on Ron. Ron was already erect as Gloria went down on him. Ron said, "I can take it from here." Ron and Gloria excused themselves to the aft cabin. Both guys were laughing and praising Gloria. Jack and Ann went to the front "V" shaped quarters.

What was unusual about the small "V" bunk is that Ann pushed her feet against the boat ceiling and used her feet to move her ass better. They had to rest awhile after the windblown scene. Jack and Ann were a bit sore from blowing in the wind, so they had an amusing sporting good time with creative foreplay. Ann tried to sit on Jack's face and Jack was pretending to spank Ann's labia. Ann sat on Jack's cock facing his feet and during intercourse she stuck her finger in Jack's anus. I hear that is more of a common practice than we thought, but perhaps Jack's relationships did not get to that stage.

Is anal stimulation fundamental or not. I have never seen any such surveys. Ann's mature attitude was what this chapter was about until I described the wind "tunnel" orgasms. Jack and Ann talked about their windy experience as a once in a lifetime experience. By the way, Ann was not a promiscuous person. She just had this stored up sex drive held at bay by her busy work schedule and raising her two boys. She had many good Texas girlfriends that all talked like her and loved group "cock-talk."

On Sunday, they sailed into port and had to be properly dressed. No one got sunburned, but Gloria sported a new tan. It was a sporting event for her because she knew Ron was married, but she confided in Ann that she needed the lessons and the experience. Gloria confessed Ron was only her second experience, and she probably would not have an affair with him. She confessed she was only nineteen years old. Ann felt very motherly. They kept in contact by mail and Ann helped Gloria mature.

Jack did see Ann a few times when he could direct his travels through Houston. One time Jack had only a few hours layover and Ann took a break, sneaked Jack into her back office, dropped her slacks and panties and bent over a desk and had Jack fuck her from behind for a quickie. Jack felt that was extraordinary airline service.

The lesson here was the tongue stimulated orgasm and the exciting personality of Ann Collins, a single Mother that knew what to do, was uninhibited, but her urges were creative rather than gained from experience. She said she did not date much, but was always looking for a good man. She said her problem was she was being hit on by less attractive men. If she ever found a good looking pilot that married or not, she would fuck him in a heartbeat, she was forced by her job to remain "sweet and innocent." Ann brought up the subject once discussed with Carol Mason, that women simply could not be aggressors without ruining their reputations. Ann was forever careful, and that is why she unloaded on Jack. She knew he was too good to be true. What a pleasant surprise she had meeting Jack.

Chapter 32. Tourette's Sin Groan

Tourette's syndrome is a rare disease whereby some people have a speech problem causing them to emit obscenities. Technically it is a neurological disorder; an obsessive compulsive disorder that involves a "tic" or motor nerve, vocal, involuntary action resulting in uncontrolled emissions of obscenities. Some think the disease is a reaction to excessive stress. One version of this disease has to do with sex where a person during sex will shout sexual obscenities because of insecurities or nervous tension, if there is such a sexual disorder thing. I say that because if you yell obscenities during sex it may not be Tourette's and maybe not a sin, but still a form of groaning or moaning, perhaps uncontrolled. I don't think yelling obscenities during sex could be a disease and why are we debating this anyway. It's just that passion during sex may cause you to exclaim something, but if you call sex by unsexy names, it might cause a problem, especially if someone overhears you. Obscenities, or "dirty talk" may or may not be a turn on.

I know of a true experience where this large religious family invited an Uncle from the local nursing home, and they only knew vaguely of this elderly man's dementia, to join the family for Thanksgiving dinner. During the Thanksgiving festivities and during the prayer the elderly man shouted that he would fuck the turkey and to hurry the prayer. The hostess paused in shock and he then blurted, "and I'll fuck you to." The man had Tourette's syndrome and kept mumbling obscenities during the meal, so the host escorted him back to the nursing home before desert.

One of our objectives here is to showcase as many different types of women that might teach us how to respond. There are more types than we could possibly talk about, but if there is a lesson to be learned, then we should report it. That is the purpose of this subjective survey. I'm not sure whether this unusual type has any meaning, but we will let you decide. Sometimes you meet women that are always victims of men no matter who is to blame. I actually witnessed this next adventure.

On this occasion Jack invited me to come to Miami with him and view and sail a new boat before it was sold. The boat manufacturer was Jack's client. The Ketch" was docked at a private yacht club for showing to clients. We were having a quiet dinner in the club's dining room and Jack noticed a beautiful woman sitting at the bar by herself. What could he lose, so he approached her and said:

"Look, my buddy and I are enjoying dinner and admiring how lovely you are and if you are alone or not meeting anybody, why don't you join us for dinner and we can have some pleasant dinner conversation."

She agreed and followed Jack to our table. We introduced ourselves and her name was Melanie Lampman. She resembled Charlize Theron, the movie star, but was heavier and about five feet ten inches tall. Melanie had a perfectly formed bust line and as part of her introduction she mentioned she was a former Miss Texas and just recently retired as a Las Vegas show girl. Melanie paraded on stage topless using her breasts as a backdrop for some more talented dancers. Those were my thoughts. Melanie had long blond hair and a models body and probably weighed 140 pounds, which suited her just right.

It turns out the mistake we made and there was no way to know, was that Melanie could not stop talking. She bloviated about all the famous people she knew from working in Las Vegas and was determined to impress us with celebrity. She was a smoker and lit one cigarette after another, which ruined our meal.

Jack and I had adjoining rooms with a door between us. I excused myself early after dinner and left Jack to deal with Melanie. After dinner and drinks, Jack decided to show her the boat. Maybe she knew of a buyer and Jack would get a commission. As they strolled down the dock Melanie talked incessantly about all the famous yachts she had been on. Ron's 50-foot Ketch was a sailing vessel and Jack showed her this well furnished boat. When he got to the bow cabin, which is a "V" berth bedroom, Melanie became defensive. Jack put his hands on her waist to help her pass by him so she could lead them back to the upper deck. As she passed by Jack her breasts brushed against Jack. The passage was narrow and Jack was being a gentleman. Melanie slapped Jack in his face and began to tell him off.

"How dare you touch me, I'm a married woman and these people living her all know me. They see me come down in this boat and they will suspect we are fucking if I don't appear back on the dock. Who the fuck do you think you are grabbing me like that?"

"I'm so sorry, I did not grab you. I assure you I have no intentions of hitting on you, I just wanted you to see this boat, which I have for sale. I grabbed your waist to help you pass by. I assure you I am a gentleman."

As they walked back Melanie resumed her tirade about being seen with Jack. She kept motioning to all the windows and patios as if there was a crowd watching them. Nonsense!

Jack calmed her down by saying,

"Ok, OK, calm down, I'm not hitting on you. Please forgive me, I admit I am attracted to you and you are a very beautiful woman, but I would not have grabbed you, I was just easing you past me."

"Well did you enjoy feeling my tits? I think you were trying to get me in that bed and fuck me weren't you?"

"Let me ask you a question. Help me out here. You are the sexiest woman I have ever been close to next to that bed, but I assure you I am a gentleman and I would never offend you. If the circumstances were different and we were alone, would you have found me attractive?"

"Well, yes I am attracted to you, but I have a reputation to protect and you being so handsome makes me look even more guilty. Yes I would love to fuck you, but I won't. And you can't come to my room because I expect my husband to phone me anytime. My husband is elderly and easily upset."

"Ok, I feel better knowing I had a chance and I appreciate your telling me. So, my apology is accepted?"

"Yes, I am flattered and I'm sorry I accused you of trying anything. But you have to understand about my husband and there's no reason for me to be seen going to your room either."

Jack never asked her to his room.

"Well, there is a cigarette machine outside of my room, which is 1440 by the way in case you change your mind after your husband calls."

"I beg your pardon; I am not going to risk exposure by coming to your room. You certainly are sure of yourself."

Jack is trying to exit by not letting her think she is not attractive. Why confront her weird insecurity were Jack's thoughts.

"I was hoping for the best, can you blame me for wanting you? I just want to leave you knowing how much I will miss you, and again, I'm sorry for the problems I have caused you. Do you care if I at least fantasize about you?"

Melanie ignored that comment.

"Well, I don't have any reason to go wondering around the halls late at night. Don't you understand that? You are one cocky fucker aren't you?"

"Yes, I apologize, I understand. I just think we could have had a good time and worth the risk, but, again, I don't want to get in the way of your good life here. Do I have your permission to jack off? Can I pretend I'm fucking you?"

Melanie turned abruptly and walked away from Jack.

They parted and Jack came back to the room and told me the details of this weird situation. We talked about how much difficulty Melanie was having with her conflicts of interest. We thought Melanie rather funny and wondered why she couldn't shut up. Perhaps guilt, nervousness and desire were her problems. She sure appeared tense. Suddenly there was a knock on Jack's door and I hurriedly stepped into my room and left the inter room door ajar so I could see and hear what was going on.

It was Melanie holding a new package of cigarettes and impatiently tapping her foot.

"Well, dammit, are you going to leave me standing out here? I mean somebody might see me, oh, what the hell am I doing here, I should not have come here, I needed the cigarettes, damn you anyway."

Jack pulled her inside and closed the door. Melanie kept on talking.

"This trip better be worth it. You better be good. I am a nervous wreck. What do you want me to do? You want to fuck me, right?"

Jack calmly said, "This is a pleasant surprise, but first you have to stop talking. Listen to me carefully; I am about to take a quick shower. I don't want to hear you talk anymore. When I come out of the shower you can either leave quietly, or you can be naked in my bed and not talking."

With that said Jack quickly closed the bathroom door. He showered quickly and when he shut off the bathroom light, the room was dark and he could see Melanie's clothes neatly stacked on a chair and she was lying in his bed naked. Her breasts were magnificent. Jack dropped his towel and crawled over to her and before he could kiss her she pushed his face between her legs and began talking.

"Eat my cunt you bastard. I came here at great risk and you better lick my cunt real good."

I peeked around the door and watched Jack. Melanie was literally pounding his head and yelling instructions at Jack using the foulest language I had ever heard. Jack tried to cover her mouth with his hand and he told me later he was terrified at her getting that nasty mouth anywhere near Long John. Melanie yelled her Tourette's vocabulary in so many words I could not write fast enough.

"Come on, fuck my cunt you son of a bitch and fuck it hard, she yelled."

Jack knew he was in over his head, but he did become very competitive and drove her hard, but with her wiggling and, slapping his back and shouting how good it felt while insulting Jack, Jack fired prematurely. Melanie sensed Jack's ejaculation and said,

"Did you come? You bastard, big fucking athlete, came in two minutes, what a waste of time you are. I risked my reputation to get fucked by a quickie wimp?"

Jack gritted his teeth and kept stroking begging Long John not to get soft. Jack became really competitive and decided he would fuck this bitch right through the mattress. It was now a contest and Jack was determined. So Melanie began again telling him to keep going and fuck faster.

"You better keep fucking, you son of a bitch. Do you like my cunt? Well fuck it harder and faster, you bastard, you soft piece of meat. Is that all you got?"

I think she soon realized she met her match. I didn't time Jack, but he kept stroking fast and hard for what seemed like too long for normal satisfying intercourse and Melanie began to yell she was coming. She pounded his back and kept calling him names, names I never heard come from a woman before. Jack was persistent and ignored her and concentrated on longevity. It worked. Finally Melanie shut up and said she had enough. Jack rolled off and headed for the bathroom. Melanie followed Jack into the bathroom and began to fill the tub. She urinated in front of Jack and looked away from him. She and Jack soaked quietly together. Melanie was quiet. She actually looked like she was pouting as Jack massaged her shoulders. Jack soaked sitting behind her. Silence!

According to Playboy magazine the average time for sexual intercourse is seven and one half minutes. I think Jack and I have bettered that average, but we obviously did not time ourselves. If you count foreplay I suspect lovemaking lasts an average of 20 minutes. But foreplay may commence and last for hours as in the case the VW chapter. Foreplay with Carol Mason was always longer because she demanded oral orgasms prior to performing intercourse. Actually, as a result of this book and these adventures, my wife almost begged for oral sex performed on her as she began to grow into a hornier woman. I think that is one of the keys to this book.

Melanie doesn't sound like she cares about foreplay although her demands worked for her. I suspect her language was part of her self-stimulation. Jack's endurance test with Melanie was record breaking, but I don't think his pleasure level was a positive factor. It was more like an endurance test, but for Melanie, I suspect she enjoyed every lasting stroke. It was as though her sex life had been in a void. That is a lot of clitoris banging and she seemed to concentrate on that feeling as she became less vocal. This was really a strange situation especially with me as an objective observer. She had called herself a cunt as if she were a third person operating her genitals. Jack told me he was glad she wanted hard fast fucking and less pussy eating because her pussy tasted like an unwashed ashtray. Remember tobacco stays dominant in body fluids.

Without speaking she kneeled outside the tub and tried to go down on Jack and when Jack was hard she tried to mount him on the edge of the tub, and that would not work. Now Melanie was focused on Jack's cock as if she was obsessed with fucking him, but no longer vocal. They moved back to the bed half wet and began a much slower pace of intercourse with Jack on his back and Melanie riding him, but more gently and as if she were in a trance. Now Jack could kiss her and I think they set a record for multiple climaxes. I tried to sleep, fell asleep and when I awoke, they were still fucking. I peeked and Jack was riding her doggy style, but quiet. Melanie was pushing against Jack hard with each stroke and was pushing against the headboard while grunting. It appeared as if they had reached a truce, but were still trying to prove who could last the longest. Melanie appeared to have ended a long dry spell, which she later confirmed.

Melanie left about five in the morning claiming she had to catch an early morning flight to New York for a dental appointment. The last thing she said to Jack was that he made her sore.

"You son of a bitch, my cunt feels like I've been fucked by an army. I hope you had a good time, you bastard."

What an unusual attitude. Why avoid guilt by being a victim when she actually advanced the event. Does that leave room for discussion? Unfortunately Jack had given Melanie his business card when she had calmed down during what was a great sexual encounter. Her appetite was one for the record books, but her personality was food for a psychiatrist.

Melanie's husband went bankrupt a few months later and abandoned her. She had married Mr. Lampman to escape Las Vegas and the environment that hardened her so much. She was too often asked to perform sexual acts on rare occasions and only for real "high rollers," as they say in Vegas. So after her divorce and Lampman having abandoned her, she moved to New York City and went to work as a receptionist for three elderly real estate owners, who knew Lampman. Jack felt sorry for Melanie as he got to know her better and she confessed she had no skills and with a chronic heart problem she was trapped with no future. She reluctantly became the mistress for these three wealthy elderly real estate landlords who kept her as a receptionist and paid for her apartment, which was quite nice. Each old man would visit her, or basically owned her for a week at a time and only came to visit her for sex.

Melanie confided in Jack that these old men were not good sex partners; for these old guys could barely get it up, or had to fuck lying on their sides or with Melanie on top. And being on top was delicate. Melanie was very sexy even being in her early forties. They never took her out to dinner, just wanted to see her naked as much as possible and after a few drinks have her perform oral sex and intercourse however limited because of their age. They never performed foreplay and sometimes played with her pussy with sex toys. These old men were too obsessed with sticking objects into her vagina. It was like a slave/master power play for rich old men whose sexual abilities were fading fast. She was a slave that was too often physically abused. Fortunately these old men were not much of a physical threat. Melanie hated her existence and often wished she had gone to college when she had the chance, but Las Vegas offered a naïve young girl a show business career. Her Las Vegas stage experience was parading around bare breasted and that did little for one's future job applications. Her new employers knew of her background and knew her ex husband. They were smelly rich old men taking advantage of her sad circumstances.

Remember the story of the guy who while sitting a bar smelled so bad the patrons and bartender demanded an explanation. The guy explained he worked for a circus and was an elephant trainer. He bathed elephants and cleaned up after them. An elephant had gotten sick and threw up on him and he was having trouble getting rid of the smell.

"My God man, why don't you find another job?" said the bartender.

"What, and give up show business?"

Back to Melanie, who was also smitten with show business. But, Melanie had this small cute poodle named Apollo, which seemed to be her only companion. She cared for this dog like it was her child. Melanie was lonely and miserable, so Jack became her close long distant friend and her personality changed drastically. It makes us think that the sexual Tourette's was a reflex caused by stress, or rather extreme stress. Jack could not stay with her at her New York residence, but he did sleep with her a few times while she was in Miami in his room until the boat sold. Jack saw her in New York only twice after she moved to New York City and secretly in Jack's hotel room. The sex was passionate with Melanie almost begging for good sex. Once she ceased the Tourette's she was a spectacular sex partner. She claimed Jack was all she ever enjoyed. Sometimes she cried after sex because she was so sad.

Jack felt more compassion for Melanie as he got to know her better and she became more relaxed. Jack's contact with Melanie was mostly by phone and letter. I wonder how many women fall into this trap. Melanie's parents had died when she was young and her career as a dancer was a fluke by Las Vegas standards. She was never a prostitute, but was threatened by her employer if she didn't accommodate certain favored clients with some kinky sex acts. Her employer did pay her bonuses when client's complimented her. She claimed she had to perform privately about once a month for tips, usually just a strip tease or a lap dance in a private room. Her worst experience was when an old couple made her perform oral sex on an old woman while that women's husband watched. These stories bothered Jack and he asked why she didn't leave. Melanie said she needed the money and had nowhere to go until Lampman took her as his trophy wife. Lampman was a sweet stately gray haired man that treated her right and was a seldom lover and poor sex partner because of his age. He was not a good businessman.

Melanie confessed that she went to a hotel room with a five-man rock band after a Las Vegas concert. There was drinking and drugs and when everybody was high, she noticed she was the last woman at the party. The group told her she would have to fuck everybody in the band. She said she was too drugged to know what she was doing do they disrobed her and bent her over a footstool and took turns fucking her in the ass. Melanie said she really didn't feel anything until the next day when she awoke at home and her anus was sore. Jack told her how stupid she was and that would only bring her serious trouble. Melanie assured Jack she was not into drugs because her "captors" would not allow such behavior. The point to be made here is why people do stupid things when drunk or drugged. I think in Melanie's case she had such low self esteem that she was always unhappy and felt trapped or doomed. Escape becomes a major force in her life and she did not care what price she had to pay.

One time when Melanie was flying to New York back when she was married to Lampman, she sat next to a famous man in first class. It was night and dark and no one across the aisle from them. They were whispering and bragging about important people they had in common when suddenly the man exposed his erection to Melanie. She was surprised and had a problem, should she yell and make a scene? She tried to ignore the man, who she refuses to identify, when he grabbed her head and pushed her face down on his cock. Jack asked her what she did and she said, "What was I supposed to do?" She claimed that raising a fuss would get her in more trouble, so she gave him a silent blowjob. The man zipped up, said nothing and dozed off. He acted like nothing happened. This story was a direct conflict with the aggressive personality of this poor woman. Did she really handle the situation correctly? A loud challenge and a denial by the celebrity might have gotten her into more trouble than just complying. After all, she said, it was only a blowjob.

Women are so vulnerable and that is truly unfair. There are many women who have sexual circumstances forced on them and keeping quiet about what happened may be the safer course of action. One wonders how many date rapes are not reported for the reason of not wanting to be exposed to the repercussions. Jack and I were flabbergasted at hearing about these things. We could not fathom ever being so intimidated. We were never confronted with bullies, which today is a major problem among teens at school. You can understand why women felt safe with us. Our respect for other people was something we were proud of and such attitudes are fading with our evolving society.

One time Melanie called Jack at his office and told him that she was being invited to go to Spain with one of her sponsors for a two-week vacation. So what is the problem Jack inquired? Apparently her predecessor went to Spain with one of the sponsors and never returned. Melanie thought that they might have her murdered and find a younger replacement. These old men feared reprisals from their old wives and the entire mistress operation was clandestine. Jack said such a drastic threat was unlikely, but Melanie argued that if she was of no use to these guys, she was out on the street. Jack said he would try and help her get a job in New York, but she'd have to downgrade to a smaller apartment and possibly find a roommate. Jack had a few old friends living there that might help. Jack felt badly for Melanie, but wished he had not gotten involved. Melanie also had a worsening weak heart problem including high blood pressure and complained she could not afford her medication if she got fired.

Jack had not heard from Melanie for several months and when in New York would never call Melanie, but walked to her apartment building and she was not registered there anymore. Jack found the superintendent and inquired about Melanie. The Superintendent said it was strange, but Melanie had gone to Spain for a vacation and never returned.

We don't know what happened to Melanie nor will we ever know, but we like to think fondly of Melanie although as a sad case. Getting into such difficult situations can happen to men or women, but when it happens to beautiful women it is far sadder. Beautiful women are more likely to be victims of crime and unfortunately rape. As the US population grows and now with the internet, too many tragic cases are being revealed. Any person would feel compassion for Melanie and we wonder how often such sad situations occur. This lesson was a downer, but made Jack and I understand how vulnerable some women can be, especially sexy women. How disgusting some men can be taking advantage of such tragic circumstances. I wonder how many women take advantage of innocent men. Actually, we don't want to go there. We are more interested in relationships that can teach us how to be more aware of people's sex lives. But amateur delving into personalities is always interesting.

I think television, Hollywood, and the Internet creates more social problems because parents have to adjust. You can't keep watch on your children 24/7 and social temptations are literally forced on immature young people. Peer group pressure unfortunately grows worse during the sexual revolution and too much exposure through the growing competitive media worsens the problem and proportionately does not grow solutions. Parenting is much more difficult today and fortunately Jack and I raised our children with more supervision and parental involvement. I actually believe that our sexual adventures made us better parents. By learning to communicate with women during the "Great Pube Wars," we were better trained to deal with changing mores.

Therefore, a better sex life with good adult communications makes for better parenting. Go Figure!

Chapter 33. Splitting Hairs

Jack's female lawyer friend played the "exclusive or else card," and Jack quit the relationship. He was not ready to make any commitments and she was a little too controlling for him. Jack thereafter suffered a dry spell, so to speak. Dorothy was now unapproachable and Jack often thought he let another good deal slip away with Dorothy. He really enjoyed Dorothy's personality once she became uninhibited. He was thinking about what a good time he could still be having, but perhaps not ready to become a family man. Sometimes good men get spoiled with so many good relationships too soon in life.

Jack was subsequently sent to New York for a day for a company meeting and once there had no evening plans so he decided to go to a movie his only night in town. Melanie was gone and he had no prospects. He was sitting at the counter in the coffee shop of the Waldorf. This young girl sat next to him and was looking over his shoulder at the movie schedules. Jack asked her if she wanted to see the schedule and she apologized for looking over his shoulder. Her name was Joan Davidson and she worked at Macy's as a sales clerk. She said she was waiting to catch a train to the Bronx. They began to talk about movies. Joan was somewhat shy, but obviously attracted to Jack. She asked all the right questions. She politely asked Jack if she could go to the movie with him and she would buy her own ticket. Jack agreed and they walked to the theater, which was midtown and fairly close. They walked and talked about their favorite movies. Joan sort of resembled a younger heavier Debbie Reynolds. Joan was about five foot three and not skinny, but still sexy in a juvenile "Tom boyish" sort of way. She was too young for Jack and he was not interested in anything more than a movie companion. He bought her ticket.

After the movie, they were walking back toward the hotel when Jack asked if he could give her a taxi ride to Grand Central Station. Joan said she had missed the last train and was going to go down to the village to spend the night in a free flop-house. Jack asked how that worked and she explained people sleep on floor mats. She said she would sleep in her clothes. Jack asked,

"Aren't you afraid of being molested by some old drunk, or something?"

"I don't have to worry about that. I have slept there before; although I better call my three roommates and tell them I missed my train. We can only afford the cheap rent in the Bronx. Anyway, nobody messes with me because some did try, but you see, I don't have a vagina. They make fun of me, but most are too drunk to attack me, and I'm pretty tough."

Jack stopped walking and took her arm and said, "that's not possible, what do you mean no vagina? Don't you menstruate?"

"Yeah, but I don't know where the stuff comes from. I was born this way."

"Have you seen a Doctor?"

"No, I can't afford one."

Jack asked," You have to menstruate, I mean, you look healthy, something's wrong here. I'll tell you what, I have two beds in my room, you can stay with me and I guarantee your safety. Maybe we can talk about that."

Joan was so pleased to be in such pleasant surroundings. Jack had not seen anybody rave about the hotel luxury before. Jack told Joan to take a nice bubble bath and he was going to watch some news on TV. Joan came out of the bathroom about a half hour later wrapped in a towel. Jack said, "Look, I'm no Doctor, but I have seen quite a few pussies. Can I examine you?

"Sure," Joan dropped the towel and was not the least bit embarrassed being naked. Jack threw back the covers and patted his bed. Joan climbed into Jack's bed and said, "What do you want me to do?"

Jack put a pillow under her hips. Joan, looked at a soft Long John and exclaimed, "Jesus, you are really hung."

Jack ignored her comment and turned Joan toward the bed light. He spread her labia and felt where her vagina should be. She was right, she had no big opening. There was a very small opening that would have allowed for her periods and Jack gently tried to poke his little finger in her orifice. It was too tight.

"Does this hurt?"

"No." Jack then kissed her very clean clitoris.

Joan jumped and said, "What did you do?"

Jack explained what the clitoris did and how it was not related to her problem.

"Have you not played with yourself?"

"Well yah." Joan grinned.

SPLITTING HAIRS

"Show me with your finger what you do." Joan rubbed herself. Jack then told her to concentrate on his tongue. Jack performed some basic cunnilingus on Joan. Joan became very passionate and Jack thought she had an orgasm. She was definitely a novice and a virgin.

"Wow, that was powerful, man, how do you do that? Should I be doing anything to you now? I have made a few guys come with my hands."

Jack interrupted her and said, "Hands won't do, can you use your mouth?"

"I guess so, but I'm not very good at blow-jobs. A guy once held my head on his cock and sort of fucked my mouth. It was not pleasant."

With that said, Joan began a rapid bounce with her mouth on Jack's cock, a stroke twice every second. Jack stopped her and suggested slower. He took Joan's two fingers and demonstrated by sucking on her fingers. She tried first by sucking on Jack's fingers. Jack was losing interest. Joan seemed anxious to try again. She started out fairly smooth and Jack decided to try and end the lesson. He allowed himself a half-assed hurried climax. Joan kept a steady pace and as soon as Jack started to come she removed her mouth and used her hand catching Jack's semen. Nothing ruins a blowjob more than the sudden loss of pressure and heat. Jack just shrugged it off as a lost cause. Joan ran into the bathroom and washed her hands. Jack decided she needed plenty of work, and he was not going to take any more time with her.

The next morning, Jack called a college alumnus gynecologist friend, who knew Jack from his basketball career. Jack said he would pay for her examination. Joan agreed and went to see the Doctor the next day after work. Apparently her hymen had grown over her vagina. It was like a piece of gristle and with local anesthetic the Doctor performed the simple surgery in his office. The Doctor told Joan to exercise with a candle as soon as the soreness went away.

Joan called Jack in Denver and expressed her gratitude. She asked if Jack would teach her how to fuck if she waited for his next NY trip. Jack agreed, although he never expected to hear from her again. He wasn't going to call her; in fact he had lost her phone number.

Six weeks passed and Jack was still looking for a new partner. He was horny, but stayed with his non-aggressor policy. When he returned to the Waldorf six weeks later he met with Ed Fannon, his old bachelor buddy from when Jack worked in NY. Ed met Jack at the cocktail lounge in the Waldorf lobby on this Thursday night during the cocktail hour. The big surprise, unbeknownst to Jack and Ed was the convention of female models at the Waldorf. The bar was literally stacked with tens of beautiful women. There was a shortage of seats in the barroom, but decorated with a flood of pulchritude. Jack saw this gorgeous woman that looked like Audrey Hepburn, and approached her as she searched for a table. Jack invited her and her friend to join them. The girls looked at each other and nodded and followed Jack back to their table. Jack ordered drinks and they began to get acquainted. Most women will sit with Jack when invited, especially being a single man.

Her name was Heather, what else would a model be named? Her specialty was eye makeup. Heather had posed for several eye makeup commercials and showed Jack a copy from a prominent magazine. Her green eyes were exceptionally beautiful and she had the long neck like Audrey Hepburn. (Green eyes again!) She looked delicate, but slim and shapely. The girls acted like they were pleased to be sitting with two handsome younger guys, since the bar was stacked with older men hoping to get lucky. "Money talks and bullshit walks," was the expression of the day. Jack told a few tasteful jokes and had Heather eating out of his hand. The guys asked all the right questions and the ladies seemed to enjoy the conversation. Heather commented on Jack's build and said he should be a male model. Heather watched Jack closely, but she was young and shy.

Then, Jack heard himself being paged. He excused himself, which allowed Ed time to tell the girls about Jack's basketball career. Jack was being paged by Joan Davidson, who had called the Waldorf every day for the past few weeks asking for Jack. Joan pleaded with Jack to do what he promised, a promise he never made. She purred that she had been practicing with her candle and was hoping to be christened by Jack because she trusted him to be gentle. Jack was in a hurry and told her he would leave a key in an envelope at the front desk with her name on it. He could deal with her later. He told her he was busy, but to wait in his room. He suggested she watch TV and treat herself to a bubble bath.

Jack got to thinking, since he had a sure thing back-up, he could proposition Heather and if she accepted, great, but if she was offended, he would spend some time apologizing before excusing himself. The night was young, and so was Heather. He had nothing to lose. He was not sure Heather would accept his proposition and he decided to ignore tact. If Heather refused to take Jack to her room, he was prepared to rent a second room.

Jack sat close to Heather in the crowded noisy room and whispered in her ear.

"I can't take this anymore. You are so adorable, and so beautiful; your eyes have hypnotized me. Take me to your room and if you let me feast on you, I'll eat your pussy and fuck you to paradise."

Heather pulled away and looked at Jack in shock. She did not smile.

She whispered in Jack's ear, "You are really something. You men have it made, you can say something like that and what do you care about me; you don't even know me. What about pregnancies and diseases? You expect me to jump into bed with you just like that?"

"I'm so sorry, I couldn't help myself. Forgive me. I see you and talk to you and I can't get making love to you out of my mind. I will dream about making love to you anyway, I'll just be alone. I'm sorry, but I want you to take my proposition as a compliment. I confess I am smitten by you; look, I have a condom and I also want to taste you. Please forgive my boldness, but life can be so short and you are so sexy, and I can't help myself. I hate to let our meeting pass us by. I beg you to not let this moment pass, I feel strongly about my desire for you and I'm not ashamed. I promise you I will make you feel so good that we will have to get together again soon."

Heather made eye contact, smiled at Jack, blushed, and said nothing. She looked in shock because she obviously could not hold back her desires and that was a damn smooth proposition. Jack got up and presumptuously reached for her hand. Heather hesitated, rose and took his hand and walked with Jack to the elevator. She spoke not a word. Ed Fannon and Heather's friend just kept talking. They did not excuse themselves and Ed pretended not to notice where they were going. They walked into the elevator and Heather pushed the correct floor. She was very nervous and Jack put his arm around her and squeezed a hug.

"I can't believe I'm doing this, I'm not the easy type, but you are irresistible, and you make me feel weak and that is scary. Please be careful, I have not done this before."

"I guarantee you I will give you complete control. You don't have to do anything you don't want to do. I'll do whatever you want as long as I can see your eyes."

Heather blushed, but she was smiling, as she was nervous. She had given in to her desires and was obviously curious. She seemed to trust Jack, but was obviously inexperienced. When they got into her room, she explained her roommate was at a Broadway show and Jack could not spend the night.

Jack said, "I have a special favor to ask. Can you keep your eyes open and watch me. I am under your spell and I want to stay there."

Jack kissed Heather and the kiss seemed to release plenty of frustration in Heather. Still, she remained stiff and still seemed in a trance. She was not smiling and was very nervous. Jack calmed her down and said he understood why she was uneasy, but reassured he would be very gentle. She kept her eyes open as Jack requested. Jack kept his lips on hers and licked her lips. She responded by exploring Jack's lips with her tongue. While they were lip locked and with eyes wide open, Jack began to undress Heather. He removed her blouse and bra. He stepped back and took off his shirt and commented she should be modeling her breasts. Heather blushed and began to caress Jack's muscles. He pulled her to him and pressed their breasts together. That created another spell and they kissed wide-eyed some more. Jack sat on the bed and unzipped her skirt and it fell to the floor. He kissed her navel and midsection while she held his head. Jack laid her gently onto the bed and stood up and took off his clothes while she watched. Her eyes opened wider when she saw how Jack was hung. She said nothing. She realized Jack was a well-built beautiful man, more than she expected.

Eye contact is a major indication of sexual arousal. Eye contact during sex is very erotic. Partners should always try making love watching each other's eyes when delivering pleasure. Eye contact definitely increases intimacy. The idea that closing eyes to better feel, or focus on pleasure is different with some people, but I believe once you use your eyes more, you will enhance your pleasure as well as your partner's. Eyes sparkle and the pupils enlarge with jolts of pleasure. People should try keeping their eyes open during sex because what they see being done to themselves is pleasurable. Sex is beautiful. It is like a smooth ballet dance when properly done. Two people actually do become one. Watching someone's eyes while they are having an orgasm is really special.

Jack put a pillow under her hips. I guess you recognize Jack's style by now. That is to raise her pussy off the sheet and allows Jack to get his knees under her legs so she can watch being entered. It was a very effective technique. It featured the woman's hips and sort of put her "unit" on a pedestal. Jack took off her panties and raved about her body, but they still had eye contact. Eye contact is very sexy. I guess I am repeating myself regarding eye contact, but I'm not sure about making such generalizations. This theory begins with Jack and me, and we know not what the accuracy of our conclusions.

Jack kissed her thighs and rubbed his cheek against each thigh. He finally reached her pussy and to his surprise, she was completely shaved. The only things protruding from her thin but shapely body were her breasts and her pelvic bone. Her pelvic bone looked polished. She smelled so good and her labia were easy to lick. Heather had large "labia majora," the term for the outer layer of protective skin. Labia resemble a protective envelope, or folds of skin forming a furrow. Women also have "labia minora," an inner layer. Women have both labia, but sometimes hard to distinguish one from the other. Like fingerprints, no two labia are alike.

Once your tongue is there labia size really makes no difference to a woman. And there is so much unrecognized beauty in labia. Remember, foreplay is an art form. When a man runs his finger or tongue along the crease of labia, it is arousing for both partners. In my opinion, labia that are suspended about a half-inch better identifies the area and spreading the labia is the ultimate sexual invitation. Any man in a rush to fuck misses so many wonderful parts of a woman. They are truly works of art and perfectly designed to give a man pleasure even while he spends time admiring those delicious parts. A woman's skin is a wonderful sex organ for both partners to appreciate. Thighs are a specialty. Lick them, kiss them and rub your cheeks against them. Wow! This woman was spectacular once undressed. Her gorgeous eyes were only the initial "hook."

Labia also add to the feeling that a penis is being caressed even though having gained full entry. The effect of plowing the labia as if the penis were a plow rubs the two critical nerves together. Some couples have sexual intercourse by laying the penis between the labia and ejaculating into her pubic hair. Young folks have tried this for centuries as a form of birth control. It can sure feel good, but difficult for a man to fight the natural urge to penetrate.

Heather was again falling into a trance, but her eyes were on Jack. Her mouth was open and she was even drooling slightly. Her breathing was hard. The nice thing about focusing on eye contact is that it is hard to break contact once the enhanced pleasure kicks in. People become hypnotized with sex, especially first time sex.

Jack flattened his tongue on Heather's clitoris and she twitched. She did not seem experienced at being treated this way. A pillow was under her head and she tried to see what Jack was doing. Jack's opening proposition about eating her pussy must have rung a bell. Surely this was not her first time being licked. Perhaps she had been licked as foreplay, but maybe not to orgasm. Jack began his exploratory technique measuring each tongue movement with her reaction. He sucked gently, and that raised some vocal pleasure sounds. Jack took his time. Heather seemed not to know how to climax, so Jack changed tongue movements as she became more vocal. She began to move her hips. Her hips and mouth sounds became almost uncontrollable at the same time. Her words were incoherent. Jack went for broke and flicked his tongue on the raised top of her clitoris. Heather had an enormous orgasm, perhaps her first with a man's face between her legs. Jack blew gently on her clitoris and rose up to kiss her mouth. To Jack's surprise, her beautiful eyes were filled with tears. She was sobbing.

"Oh my God, I'm so sorry, did I hurt you? Are you all right?"

"I'm not hurt, are you serious? I have never felt such pleasure and it felt so good I began to cry. I can't help myself. That is the first time anybody has done that to me. I did not know what to expect. You are so good at that, wow, please keep going."

Jack rose up on his haunches and pulled on a condom. He entered her and asked again for eye contact. They stared at each other while Jack began a slow fucking. Heather opened her mouth with each in stroke and closed her mouth as Jack withdrew. She was still sobbing, but not as much and her sobs sounded more like gasps and grunts, very feminine grunts, of course. She still did not smile, but her pleasure was emanating from her body language. She was so passionate having been eaten for the first time and having it performed by a real expert. Heather really got into the fucking. Her slender body showed amazing strength as she moved enough to move Jack. Jack finally looked into her eyes and told her he was coming and to hold him. She wrapped her arms and legs tightly around Jack and her mouth was wide open and her eyes bulged as she watched his facial expressions as he came. Jack rested on his elbows and began kissing her. She was sobbing again. Jack withdrew and told her not to move because the condom had to be disposed of. He explained it was so full he had to be careful. While Jack was flushing the condom down the toilet, he confessed from the bathroom he had not been with a woman for months and that she drove him to such pleasure because of her beautiful eyes.

When Jack came out of the bathroom, Heather attacked him naked with a big hug. She began to thank him for the wonderful pleasure, and exclaimed, for having enjoyed sex so much with him. She could not recall having so many orgasms. She asked him how long he would be in the hotel and if she could see him again. Jack told her was going to Boston early the next morning, but wanted to exchange contact information. Heather worked in New York City. Jack promised to call next time he came near New York. Jack pursued his only long distance relationship. Heather even came to Denver at her own expense. She was delightful to be with, but oh so young. Jack thinks he awakened her libido. Jack's dry spell had ended with a big bang, no pun intended.

He covered Heather with the bed blanket and kissed her goodnight. She was off in a contented sleep before he dressed. Heather never said anything about her relationships with men and Jack assumed she had a relationship with someone else. Perhaps someone in her industry. Jack was probably an unexpected pleasure that made her rethink her other relationship.

Jack was not so enthusiastic about Joan waiting in his room. He was fucked out and tired and had an early morning flight. Heather was unexpected and incomparable and she was all that he could think of. When he opened his door, Joan was in a bed and drowsy. Jack showered and while he was showering he wondered if he could get another hard on. There is a proverb that no man can avoid seconds with a new sexy partner. He would probably be short a load of semen. His body could not recover manufacturing new semen so quickly and his shots with Heather were full load deliveries.

That was not to be the end of a relationship for Jack and Heather. The next summer Heather visited Jack for one of his famous "red ball" express rides. I'll add something about that later.

Joan greeted Jack with a big kiss when he came out of the shower. She aggressively led him to his bed and sat down and began to suck on Long John. She claimed she had been practicing fellatio on her penis shaped vibrator, which replaced her candle. To Jack's surprise her enthusiasm was quite stimulating. She climbed into Jack's bed and spread her legs. Hmm, now that looked pretty inviting. Jack made a cursory move with his tongue and her enthusiasm made him harder, but he was still thinking about the deep impending soreness when you are about to fire from an empty tank. Jack was not used to rapid firing with new partners, but he was very capable and seldom refused a good thing.

There is an old story about the world's greatest sexual athlete, "Superstud." He was performing on stage by fucking ten naked women in succession. After a standing ovation, Superstud mounted lady number one and when he climaxed he waved the condom about and dumped its contents in a measuring beaker. Then on to number two, and three, each time a big round of applause. And then on to number four and five, each time a big round of applause. As the stud approached number seven, he staggered and fainted. The crowd booed. Stagehands rushed out and carried him away. The announcer took the mike and apologized to the unruly crowd, who were demanding refunds. The announcer said, "I don't understand what happened, he was fine during rehearsal today." Guinness book of records? Nah, it was just a crude joke. Back to Joan.

Jack had done the pillow prop and with a small lamp aglow, he performed on Joan as he had on Dorothy. One inch slowly, then two and his final plunge was wonderful. He pulled out and put on another condom, his supply was waning. Jack started over and by comparison, his performance was a quickie. Joan never knew the difference. Jack felt an orgasm and there was that empty feeling, he was all huff and no puff. It was like a climax using hot air for his rush. He put on a good show because he wanted Joan to feel accomplished.

And she did. She asked Jack if he could do it again. Jack was truly tired and fucked out. He explained his early morning departure and invited her to stay in the room until she had to get to Macy's in the morning. Jack told her that he most likely would not get back to New York for some time and wished her well. She hugged Jack and thanked him for saving her life and doing his thing for her. Jack had paid the medical bill and never heard from Joan again. He thought it his good deed. Regarding his "dry spell," it had ended with a bang. He just wished he could have had Heather return to his room with him and spend the night. It would have been worth postponing the Boston trip to meet Ron for a few hours. Can you imagine explaining how too much pussy interfered with his scheduling?

Ron met Jack at the airport and drove to his factory, which were a few miles outside of Boston. They discussed his profits and whether Jack could help Ron with an underwriting. It did not look promising. After lunch, Jack fell asleep on the couch in Ron's outer office. He was surprised when he was awakened mid afternoon by Eve, the girl he had missed for the sailing experience. Eve explained that Ron gave her a job because she lived close by, and he knew her sister Gloria so well. Jack inquired about her son, who was fine. Eve looked very Italian, a bit like a big version of Sophia Loren. Eve had those big Italian brown eyes, almost fawn looking. She sat on the foot of the couch, had brought Jack a cool bottle of Coca cola. Don't coke and Dr. Pepper taste better in chilled glass bottles, ummm. Eve apologized for missing the trip and said her sister said Jack had found a hot replacement. She said she was glad it worked out for him. It made Jack wonder just how much Gloria had told her about the boat trip. Jack asked her of she'd like to have dinner that night; lobster with Ron and his wife. Eve said that was up to Ron to approve. She said she hadn't been on a dinner date in years, but wanted to go. Ron approved and Eve met them at this famous lobster house tavern.

They had a delightful time. Jack was his usual entertaining self and Eve was obviously charmed. After dinner Eve was to give Jack a ride to his motel. Upon arrival, Jack asked Eve if she'd like to come in for some desert. Eve seemed naïve and said, "Sure." Once inside, Jack quickly took off his dress shirt and tie and excused himself. Jack assumed Gloria might have set him up with an enthusiastic sister that just might like to get laid.

"I have to brush my teeth."

When he came out of the bathroom, Eve was standing by the door and said, "This is not a good idea, I have no idea what I'm doing."

Jack apologized and said he was sorry if rushing to the bathroom seemed inconsiderate, but nature had called.

"Look. I understand how you feel and I didn't mean to appear so aggressive. You do whatever you want. I was hoping a good-looking woman like you would share some bedtime with me, but I am really sorry if I have offended you. I am not an aggressor. I just misread the situation. At least let me pay for your baby sitter."

Eve said nothing and took off her coat and asked if she could use Jack's toothbrush. Jack provided her with a new one he kept in his traveling "dop" kit. Eve brushed her teeth and when she came out of the bathroom, she apologized to Jack for leading him on.

"This is my fault. Yes I thought about coming here, but now that I'm here, I have no idea what I'm supposed to do. I have not been with a man for years. I'd like to experience you if you're OK with that."

Jack went to her and kissed her. He began to take off her clothes and Eve did not fight it or help him. She wanted to keep kissing. Jack took off his shirt and unhooked her bra and before she could react, or he could look, he pressed their bodies together. Eve had been hiding some nice big breasts. Eve hummed a good sound as their bodies touched. They undressed, but Eve seemed ashamed and embarrassed about her body.

Eve was overweight and said her husband had abused her and she has since been hesitant even thinking about sex for lack of confidence. But she admitted she found Jack irresistible. She admitted she had no confidence and would never have tried to seduce Jack. She was running her hands over his shoulders and arms. Jack turned off the bedside lamps and turned a small light behind the louvered shutters in the closet. The setting was more romantic, and the shadows loosened Eve up a bit. Jack lay Eve back onto the bed and kissed her breasts. He could not help but notice that Eve had hair around her nipples, not a lot, but noticeable on his tongue. Eve had hairy arms and her head of hair was black, long and very thick. She even showed a slight hairline on her upper lip, which she obviously had been processing. Jack sensed she was embarrassed because of her hairy body.

This raises an issue about sex. How do partners react to excess hair? Jack's chest was almost a polished finish with nary a trace of hair. Yet he had a full head of wavy black hair to offset his bright light blue eyes. It is unusual and wonderful that God made so many varieties of humans. Hair, eye coloring and sizes are necessary to make for enough variety to support a race of humans. Billions of people and no two look alike, except for identical twins.

Jack thought that if he reacted negatively to her excess hair he would ruin Eve's confidence forever. He sensed she was anxious to get laid, but she was nervous about revealing her excess hair. Jack began to kiss her stomach while caressing thighs. Her thighs were smooth and big, but shapely and sexy. When Jack pulled down her panties, she resisted for a moment by pulling her panties up, but her urges won the battle; she pulled them down herself when Jack looked like he was going to back off. To Jack's surprise she had the biggest plot of pubic hair he had ever seen. Her hairline was almost to her navel. Her pubic hair was longer than normal.

Jack felt sorry for Eve, but he was determined not to hurt her feelings. He pretended not to notice and before she could react, Jack found a part in her nest and flattened his tongue on her clitoris. Eve held her breath and Jack began to make a circle on her clitoris with the flat of his tongue. The secret to invading a fresh pussy that you don't know what to expect is to use plenty of saliva. Jack drenched her pussy with his saliva and put his thumb in her vagina and stretched it hoping to increase her sensitivity. Jack was determined to make her enjoy his action so she would forget about her hairline. After all, does hair have anything to do with a warm pussy? Eve's desire played a major part here; that contributed to her sex appeal. Eve acted like and exclaimed she had never felt such pleasure. She obviously had not been eaten often, if ever. Funny thing about cunnilingus, if a man finds a good lay that some other man has denied oral sex, she will always be a willing partner, and may never go back to a non-aficionado of pussy if given the choice. Jack stopped licking, perhaps prematurely, he couldn't tell. He rose up on his haunches to apply his last condom.

"You don't need that thing, I can't get pregnant. I have to tell you, you are such a considerate man; you are way beyond my wildest dreams and thank you so much for not saying anything about my out of shape body. I want to get fucked so badly and I can't believe I am so lucky to be here with you. You are beyond my wildest fantasies."

Jack set aside the condom and entered her fast as if he couldn't wait. She was very warm, extremely wet, and surprisingly tight. Jack decided to fuck hard and fast, because she was almost too wet. And after all the sex he had during the last day, he knew he could last a long time. She was very vocal and grunted each time Jack hit her pelvic bone with his shaft. It was easy to keep going because Jack was not really out of practice after his recent increase in serendipitous activity. They had a good old fashioned full frontal fuck, which lasted longer than normal. Eve's knees and legs were around Jack during the act and her legs bounced off of his back during the action. Eve had created a perfect angle with her legs and knees raised and did her best to move under Jack's weight. She was a great lay because she was trying to participate, which raises that issue again. A good lay is enthusiastic, passionate and tries to contribute to the moves. When Jack was spent, he stayed in her for almost five minutes while he softened and she talked about how good he felt and how much she appreciated him. It was unusual for Jack to stay on top of a woman because of his weight, but Eve seemed to like holding him with her legs tightly wrapped around Jack for the afterglow. Eve was beautiful in spite of her lack of experience or confidence. Those big brown "Sophia Loren" eyes were very lovely even in the dark. Lovers lying together in the afterglow of great sex can be most rewarding and more time should be devoted to such moments. Too many people are in a rush to separate after sex.

We think the art forms of the afterglow are important. Staying inside a woman after sex for a brief period is a very intimate moment. The "after sex" conversations are bonding in nature. Most men will, or should roll a woman over and allow her to lie on top of you until softness occurs naturally. Very little is written about "afterglow." If mutually comfortable, we believe the moment should be more enjoyed. A man seldom needs to put his weight on a smaller woman and propping some weight on his elbows is common. Afterglow significantly adds to the joy of sex. It may be as meaningful as the seduction and will always add feelings to any relationship. That sort of demeans "quickies," or one night stands does it not? The worst reaction I have ever heard about is either partner rushing to a shower immediately after sex to wash away the smells and juices. That is seriously dysfunctional. Oops, Eve is waiting.

"My ex husband told me I was a hairy bitch and I know I am, but I can't seem to remove hair. I feel so ugly, and you are so considerate. Why are you so good to me?"

"I guess whatever hair problem you have it does not distract from your sex appeal. Not every man will agree with me, but I have learned that what you consider a negative about yourself it makes you fuck better in case you don't get another chance. If I come to Boston, I hope to see you, but I am not good at long distance relationships. I won't have time to communicate, but I have to tell you, your pussy was hot wet and tight and I feel sorry for the guy that passes you by because of your hairline. I don't know what to tell you, this is not my area of expertise, but I'd check with a dermatologist. I'd hate to see a great fuck like you go to waste. If you get a hot proposition, tell the next guy that you feel you have too much hair and if that turn's him off, too bad. You can also say that you are a good lay and you hope that excessive hair is not a turn off. In my experience, communication and straight talk is all you need. Keep a sexy attitude and learn to talk about sex freely."

"Were you sent by God? You are amazing."

"Can you say the word "fuck" freely? You can say that God blessed you with a tight pussy and cursed you with too much hair and if a guy can't handle that, end it right there and keep your confidence level. Do you know how to suck cock?"

"Probably not, I have never tried, but, I have read about it and it appeals to me."

"Does it matter that my cock, named Long John Silver by the way, has just been dipped in your great pussy juice. Can you taste yourself on me and not be offended?"

"Just show me what to do?"

Eve was gaining self-esteem and Jack was saying all the things she wanted to hear. The lesson here is how people should handle these circumstances from both sides of the problem. Jack had the previous experience with the mink coat, but never asked any women what she felt about men's hair. I have read studies where baldness can be sexy. Not for bald women, in my opinion, but men with long hair, or hairy backs, or really hairy chests may all be rated separately. Jack and I are not prepared to conduct any surveys on hairy men or women, nor did this issue ever come up over our time during the sexual revolution, or the "Great Pube Wars". In our opinion, hair should not be a factor as long as the hair is clean. Remember, the use of hair conditioner on pubic hair. Clean smelling hair can be a turn on regardless of quantity.

Jack enjoyed her fellatio for a few minutes and then stopped her claiming he had "shot his wad" and as good as her mouth felt, he was completely satisfied. Eve was happy as a lark, dressed, kissed Jack and drove herself home smiling all the way. She just got laid after her long dry spell and had gained some new confidence. Jack had on a few occasions seen Eve when he visited Ron in Boston, and she remained a very appreciative friend and always a willing sex partner. Jack never asked about her sex life and she never said anything other than how much she enjoyed seeing Jack. She apparently told her sister that she went to bed with Jack because she later told Jack that her sister thought Jack was really hung.

I guess a regular question is about whether men who hang soft more than four inches are sexier, or does it make a difference once erect as to whether an erection is sexy compared to a long "softee." Some men shrink down to two inches from six; does that matter? We have spent many hours in a locker room and no man ever paid any attention to another, so we wouldn't know. I wonder if a woman could watch men shower if such a comparison was of interest.

I remember once staying in a hotel in NY with my window adjacent to a women's locker room at a dance studio. I watched about fifteen women undress, shower and get dressed and all I could do was check out tits and asses and body curves. I didn't have time to analyze in a scientific manner.

Actually these are dumb considerations, but as a matter of interest I wish we had asked more questions as to how women felt about these comparisons. Our best source of opinions are Carol Mason and Cynthia Mc Masters. Neither mentioned thoughts about comparative softies, but both thought erections were magnificent. Whether they said that at the time or that was their profundity is not known. Wouldn't it be interesting to see some anonymous polls regarding sex and opinions on different body parts? I mean what turns women on about men physically and how important is that? Carol Mason said; eyes, broad shoulders, not too much muscle, but good definition, and a nice ass made men sexy. From what we did learn, weight lifters were not as sexy as slim muscles. Most women consider personalities and cleanliness as most important. Of course, those men who were concerned about foreplay were always favored. I repeat; in this day and age, most people on average experience eleven sex partners if a lifetime.

The worst thing I ever heard was about a guy who as soon as he finished sex he would hurry to wash off his penis like he thought a pussy left some unwanted sticky substance on him. How stupid is that?

During this single business trip Jack had experienced a shaven pussy, which was a real turn on, and an extremely hairy one, which could have been a turn off were it not for Jack's ability to not judge at first contact. The third experience in rapid succession was a virgin that had an overgrown hymen. It also must be noted that men like Jack are just so damn respectful of women that he always inherently tries to build their self-esteem. By doing so, he was always rewarded by grateful extra reciprocal efforts. Women like sensitive considerate men. Eve was fortunate to have her "comeback" experience with Jack. Her decision to not resist the temptation is of course attributable to Jack's charm and his ability to be frank in communicating with women. It takes a certain skill to know when you can say something shocking, when to advance and when to back off.

We believe that shaven pussies are sexy, but extra amounts of pubic hair is not a problem. A shaved pussy may appear cleaner, but it seems like a lot of trouble to keep it shaved. Stubble might be a problem. Heather was smooth as if she had removed her pubic hair. This raises the question as to what was God's purpose in issuing pubic hair. Nose hair screens bacteria and small insects, and head hair may be a warming factor. Then why do Semitic men have more face hair than Eskimos? Beards get in the way of eating and present a cleaning issue, but I don't know how women feel about facial hair. Are long beards a sign of wisdom? I think that is bullshit! Do long bearded men think they are sexier? I guess you ladies will have to opine on that. That may be another useful poll for the general population. It seems to me that the male models on TV today seem to need hairstyle, a bath, a shave and a clean freshly pressed wardrobe change. Go figure! I can remember when "crew cuts" were in, then came long hair on men and now, today, shaved heads seem popular.

As a minor fact, earwax is a repellent to bacteria and small insects and it may smell bad, but in an emergency, earwax can serve as an antibacterial cleaner. I have heard of men who will rub earwax on their penises after sex with a questionable unclean partner. I don't know how the wax was extracted, but I have heard jokes about it. Today there are commercial hand cleaner lotions that kill bacteria. I believe that would really help clean a used penis if needed.

It is too bad Heather lived in New York, although Jack slept with her on the next successive trips, which were not frequent enough to suit him. Heather lived to hear from or meet Jack, although we suspected she had a boyfriend. Heather was simply too young, but so beautiful and "big eyed" innocent looking. It raises the question about how sexy are innocent women. Is there exceptional satisfaction for a man or woman in "breaking in" a novice? That is another common fantasy for both men and women. Jack lost his virginity to a brother's date when he was five years her junior and considered a minor. I think many women fantasize about breaking in a young male virgin.

When Heather visited Jack, he took her on a motorcycle ride into the mountains for an amateur photo shoot. Heather, being a professional, posed nude in many mountain settings. The pictures were very tasteful and Jack has them to this day. There were colored photos of Heather standing ankle deep in a mountain stream with her hands on her hips surrounded by golden Aspen and colorful mountain flowers. She was slender, but perfectly shaped. Most of Jack's photos included her eyes, mostly eyes and bare breasts together. They enjoyed great outdoor sex, but no pornographic photos. Jack claimed he fantasized more about Heather than any other woman in his lifetime. I believe Heather was one of Jack's regrets for having not pursued her as a wife.

In my opinion, Heather became one of Jack's favorites along with Dorothy and Josie. I also think Jack wished he had married Dorothy. She looked like a healthy child bearer, and her personality was blooming like uncovering the tip of an iceberg. Jack never propositioned Dorothy once she was married, but he sure thought about it. It's funny how it takes retrospect to realize what you have missed. Maybe there is a disadvantage for having too many relationships.

Chapter 34. A Cock Shocker

I feel it is necessary to report another unusual experience from Jack's past. I would have to call this a "phenomenon" and we have no idea of the scientific repercussions, but again very unusual and deserves some investigation. I also think Jack fell in love with this widow and never recovered.

Jack Callahan had a married couple as clients at his securities firm. Mickey O'Leary and his wife Madelyn, nicknamed Maddie, were active stock traders, which was unusual for a young couple. Mickey was a successful and serious investor. Mickey was five foot ten, 155 pounds and a super wannabe athlete and fanatical sports fan. Mickey tried out for football and basketball, but never made any team or had exhibited any athletic skills. He followed most sports as an obsession. He watched college and professional football and basketball and loved betting on the games. But, his favorite sport was auto racing and Mickey owned a Corvette. Mickey did business with Jack because he admired Jack's athletic past and his awesome athletic build. Mickey had followed our college careers. Mickey and Maddie would join Jack for lunch on occasion.

Mickey's downfall was his Corvette. He kept it pristine, polished and in racing form. It was loud to get attention. Mickey's Corvette eventually killed him when he attempted a mountain curve at high speeds and crashed into a rock wall and then drove off a cliff. His death was quick.

Fortunately Mickey was well insured and Jack fueled their stock account with the added insurance benefits and invested for Maddie's future. A year had passed since Mickey died and yes Mickey's widow, Maddie, was subsequently enamored with Jack. Maddie was the spitting image of the movie star Meg Ryan; even her personality resembled the "cutie" parts often played by Meg Ryan. Maddie was an artist, both sculpting and painting. Mickey had been a successful young Pharmacist and well insured.

Jack had established an income Trust for Maddie and I did the legal work, so I was familiar with this exciting woman. Maddie trusted Jack and asked if he would pose for a portrait. Maddie also had posed nude for an art class and although slim, had a model's figure. Obviously she was not easily embarrassed, or she had some great confidence. She reminded Jack of Heather, the New York model of recent affairs past. Jack being a single male was concerned about approaching his client's widow, but Maddie was so charming and was obviously interested in Jack that something was bound to happen.

Jack was in Maddie's studio above her garage and Jack was to pose bare chested so Maddie could paint a picture of Jack from the waist up. Since Jack knew of Maddie's famous body, he was always teasing Maddie about him trying to paint her nude with some lessons. Maddie teased Jack that she would want to sculpt him nude first, so the games began. Maddie was a big tease and had this wonderful sense of humor. She was also a playful "prankster." Maddie was 5'7" tall and about 125 lbs.

At Jack's third sitting and with the portrait well on its way to completion, Jack kissed Maddie while she was measuring his face for a close up. Her response was very passionate, so Jack soon had Maddie naked, which was from some very tight fitting jeans and "T" shirt. Maddie had brown hair, brown eyes and a "tom boyish" figure, but with perky breasts, a firm well rounded fanny, and nice long legs.

When Jack kneeled in front of her couch and put his face between her legs, Maddie was surprised. Apparently ole Mickey was not into cunnilingus and this was to be Maddie's first licking. Her reaction was wild and during Jack's slow moving tease, Maddie expressed extreme anxiety at getting on with the fucking. Jack felt it was her first time with a cunnilingus climax, so there was no rush and Jack's teasing drove her into a wild fit of passion. Are artistic types more passionate? I don't think so, but Jack thought so at the time.

When Jack entered Maddie for the first time he experienced this unusual surprise. Once he was completely inside her vagina there was this tighter grip on the end of Jack's penis. As best Jack could describe this to me it was as though she had a grove for about four and a half inches and then her vagina stopped and a new path was formed, a new groove that tugged or grabbed the end of Long John Silver. With each new stroke the end of Jack's penis he would enter a tighter passageway that caused just enough resistance to feel like there was a sucking sensation at the end of each stroke. Jack was fascinated, but it was so sensitive that Jack stroked faster when he was coming and ejaculated into that tight pocket deep inside Maddie. Now that was a sensation Jack had never felt before. It was inexplicable, but Jack was determined to find out what he had discovered because this deeper probe added a great sensation to fucking.

Jack and Maddie had a great relationship and they could not resist having sex frequently and when moving to her bedroom and with new positions and more foreplay, this was a "hot" relationship. The same sensation occurred when Maddie was on top, sitting in his lap, or with rear entry sex. Maddie did not seem to notice anything unusual about her pussy and that drove Jack to finally ask if she knew how good she felt.

"Listen to me, please, I've got to tell you something that is so special about you and I can't figure it out. When I am deep inside you a part of your vagina grabs me and holds on like an extra tight passage deep inside you? Can you explain this phenomenon?"

"Gee, I have no idea what you're talking about. You are only the second man I have been with and Mickey was never a talker."

"If I'm not getting to personal, what kind of lover was Mickey? I mean, how could he not notice that sensation? Was he experienced with other women before he married you?" Jack inquired.

"I don't know, I assume he had other women, Mickey was a few years older than me and I was a virgin on our wedding night. Mickey was, well, a lot smaller than you, but we had a great sex life. We had sex almost every day. Mickey was very different from you. He never licked me; actually he didn't find time for foreplay. I guess I didn't know the difference, but Mickey went very fast and kept it up for a long time, I guess."

"You mean he just sort of jumped you, or climbed on and was too fast?"

"No, no, I didn't mean too fast, I really liked sex, I guess I never knew the difference because sex with you is really much better and I love the foreplay. You make love to me more gently at first and I get to savor the feeling more, and the feelings last longer with you. I don't know if I had orgasms with Mickey or not, I remember his fast hard strokes felt good and when he came he was quiet and I guess he didn't stop until he was finished coming. You sometimes stop before you are finished and I really enjoy holding you. I never held Mickey, when he was done he was gone and off to sleep. He was affectionate in his own way; he just never talked about sex. He just did it and he liked doing it and I guess I was always available and I thought that was what it was supposed to be like. Mickey never missed watching sports on TV and at halftime during football games he would pull down my pants and do me from behind, hard and fast and then thank me for the halftime service. You might say he was always sort of playful rather than passionate. He never reacted like you do."

"It sounds like he needed to be macho. I am surprised to hear this. You said he was small, did you mean his penis was small?"

"Well, compared to you he was very small, and I never saw or felt another man, but I have to admit you feel better inside me. I guess I didn't know what I was missing, but Mickey was a good man in his own way. I think he was disappointed that he was not a bigger man or didn't excel at football. He often said he wished he was a good jock, but maybe that's why he drove that damn Corvette so fast. Sometimes I think he loved that car more than me." Maddie kept talking.

"What did he do during your periods? Did he ever put his penis in your mouth?"

"No, he only wanted sexual intercourse, but sometimes during my period he would stick it in my rear, you know what I mean? I would kneel in the bed and he would do it that way."

"Did that hurt?"

"No, he would rub butter on himself and started out gentle, but I guess it didn't hurt because he was not that big around. Did you want to do that to me?'

"Baby, let me tell you something, you have a special feeling deep inside your pussy that I have never felt before, and I simply could never pass on that sensation. That doesn't mean I wouldn't enjoy any contact with you, but I'm still trying to figure out that extra tug you give me that feels so good. I wonder if Mickey plowed a grove that fit his penis and with rapid strokes made you feel good because he was hitting your clitoris fast enough for you to get off."

"What do you mean, "getting off?""

"Maddie, getting off means that at the end of his hard fast strokes your clitoris was being hit enough to give you an orgasm."

"I guess I don't know. I don't think I had orgasms, but doing it felt good, even without foreplay. It always feels good to be made love to no matter how you or Mickey reacted. Your groove theory sounds logical. Does that mean that all future lovers have to keep getting bigger? . . . . Just kidding."

"Maddie, all of your pussy feels tighter to me, it is just an added pleasure and I love your reactions, you are a passionate sweet considerate lover. Did you ever give him a blow job?"

"I guess Mickey never did it in my mouth because he was so fast and that may be why he didn't do it that way. How is that supposed to work because I'd like to learn that for when I get my next period."

"Are you on the pill?"

"No."

"You never mentioned that, why didn't you tell me? Shouldn't I be using condoms?"

"Jack, Mickey and I could not have children and after we were tested, it was me. I hope that's OK with you. I have never felt a condom. What about me putting my mouth on you? Will you show me what to do?"

So Jack taught Maddie how to suck cock and their relationship continued for years, even after Jack met Angela. Jack and Maddie always had a great time. They were having great sex and great conversations. Maddie was a prankster, which Jack loved.

Jack and I discussed this groovy thing at length and eventually told Cynthia. Cynthia agreed that it seemed logical that Maddie's vagina was grooved and that groove was never changed until Jack came along. Cynthia wanted to meet Maddie, and we did double date many times, but the subject of sex never came up. We had delightful conversations and Maddie even aroused Cynthia's interest in trying arts and crafts.

Jack initiated Maddie on to the "Red Ball Express" and they enjoyed many outdoor adventures. Jack even tried some of the techniques he learned from Cynthia and me and tried some of the discussed adventures. Jack and Maddie explored "tree sex" and urolagnia, and Maddie tried nude dancing for Jack, strip teasing, and even lollipops for an added lick. Jack would relate these adventures to us and we many times enjoyed sharing adventures and comparing reactions. It was always a learning experience, but the discussions were also motivational and contributed to many a good session of foreplay. It was unfortunate we never included Maddie in the discussions, but Jack was adamant about keeping her not knowing any more than necessary. He wanted that relationship to remain private.

Maddie as a joke once sculpted Long John Silver, which was the result of Maddie having mastered blowjobs. She would sculpt and then suck alternating between the two tasks. I mention this because I have not said much about Maddie's playful personality. She eventually molded a vase over Long John's statue with a sliding circular opening. Maddie then would put flowers in the vase and when alone she would open up the sliding window and see Long John enshrined under flowers. Then as a practical joke she had a duplicate vase loaded with flowers delivered to Jack's office. Jack felt the anxiety of hoping no one would find the sliding window, but when he finally opened it up, there was no Long John statue, Maddie had made a duplicate vase without Long John as a reminder that the empty vase bottom needed to be filled. It was subtle yet indicative of Maddie's charm.

Maddie O'Leary became a famous artist. She had her own art shows and would do portrait sculptures for a fee. She started a new business doing pet portraits, which caught on big time. Maddie was madly in love with Jack and kept that fire burning the rest of her life. Maddie remained Jack's best account and soon began to contribute her earnings to her account. Maddie became very wealthy. She understood Jack's desire to have children and when Jack met Angela, Maddie stayed in Jack's life for the rest of his life and was his secret mistress. Maddie readily accepted that role and became so involved with her career that she was content with the relationship. Maddie was very discreet. Jack truly had the best of all worlds.

Jack told Cynthia and I about an unusually sexy thing he and Maddie had done. I will tell you about this thing because Cynthia and I couldn't wait to try this.

Jack had Maddie kneel in a doggy style pose and spread her knees as far apart as she could. He then took a wad of toothpaste and dabbed a dot behind each of her ears. He then painted her neck with a stripe of toothpaste, applied wet, but soon dried as it tingled. Jack drew a line of wet toothpaste down her chest and looped around each nipple with a little head of toothpaste on each nipple. He next drew a line down her stomach around her pubic hair and left a dab on her clitoris, then continued from behind her pose and drew a line over her anus and up her back, down the middle and back to her ears. Jack proceeded to wet and lightly lick away the toothpaste starting with her ears and neck. He lay under Maddie and licked the line away until he got to her clitoris, which by this time was aroused and engorged. Jack wrapped his arms around Maddie's waist and she dropped her arms, which were getting tired and clutched two big pillows. She had her head comfortably rested on her pillows with her ass high in the air with Jack under her performing cunnilingus. Maddie's knees were aside Jack's head. She moaned in ecstasy and when she was satisfied she rolled over onto her back and slide down Jack so he could clear the toothpaste off of her back. Then she rolled over and took his cock in her mouth and began a gentle sucking.

Jack moved her back into the first position, wet and blew the paste off of her anus and then with her head low on the pillow and her ass raised high, Jack entered her pussy and rocked her face against the pillows with gentle strokes admiring her lovely ass. Maddie reached down and enjoyed feeling Jack's cock moving into her vagina and felt Jack's strokes as she stroked her own clitoris. After Jack came, she sat in his lap facing him without losing him, a brief gymnastic feat, and they both sat upright there kissing until Jack went soft. Why don't you readers try that act? That is good sex.

One of Jack's co-workers was marrying his live in girl friend and as a honeymoon special asked a few of his close male friends to write a script for each night of the honeymoon. The groom picked the folded instructions at random and tried to act out the written instructions. Jack had submitted the "Around the World with toothpaste" and won the favorite award of the bride. You see, people can do some creative things if they just learn to share ideas. Cynthia and I performed that act both ways traveling around my body getting equal travel time. I have heard of couples using body paint as foreplay; now you can add toothpaste, which kills bacteria, is clean, and has that special cooling tingle effect that may be more arousing. Imagine adult couples trading such ideas with each other. Perhaps they should form clubs like book clubs and relate new ideas for making love. Maybe Jack and I are on to something.

This relationship between Jack and Maddie opens up many possibilities for moral judgments. How can a man love two women and how can a woman love a married man and keep such a relationship forever? Is it normal to restrict love to selected people? People love different things about each other. Is it possible to love someone for a second intimate relationship? Who decides whether sexual pleasures are to be regulated? Our growth through the sexual revolution has left us with many unanswered questions, but our interest in finding answers never waned. If the sexual relationship is immoral, who gets hurt in this situation? Does it make you wonder how much of this goes on in life? Is it a cultural thing? It always boils down to whose feelings are damaged and how many lives are damaged. In Jack's case the answer is none.

I have never heard of the grooved pussy before. I would think that all human sexual organs would reshape themselves or at least hold some form. We know that breasts sag with age and that pussies lose their shape after childbirth because some women have themselves surgically tightened. We know that older men have more erectile dysfunctions. I think sexual desires will always exist. Remember, you are only as old as you think you are.

Remember the story about the old man sitting at the curb crying? The policeman asked what his problem was and the old man replied, "I have a beautiful sexy wife, I live in a mansion, I have a personal chef and . . ." The policeman interrupted him and said, "My God that is fantastic, then why are you crying?" "I can't remember where I live," Answered the old man.

Rising divorce rates are a whole different ballgame. Jack, Cynthia and I are not psychologists and are not qualified to talk about bad relationships because we experienced so few bad ones, and that is unusual. Couples get divorced because she wants an older more mature man that offers more security while she dreams of happiness. He wants a younger woman that is less mature than he is so he appears more mature and if he gets lucky he finds a younger new body to play with. Men are so stupid when it comes to trying bachelorhood at middle ages. The hunt goes on and we wonder how many later realize they should have tried to make that first marriage work. This brings us to our same conclusions, learn foreplay and learn to communicate. Isn't that just common sense?

Chapter 35. The Breeders Cup

It was God's plan that Jack Callahan gets married and has children. Perhaps he had been avoiding that issue too long. The problem with men like Jack is once they get the urge to find a wife they tend to be in too much of a hurry. That is but my opinion and Jack would argue the case back when it happened.

Jack met Angela at a tennis tournament. Jack and I were playing in the men's doubles as guests at an exclusive country club. We were formidable because we were natural athletes, but not sufficiently experienced to win. We were spreading our golf and tennis skills too thin. We seldom practiced, certainly not like basketball. We played basketball with the best and many considered us the best, but for minor sports, we were just good competition that enjoyed the game.

Angela won the women's tennis title easily. She was graceful, tanned and as it turns out, was also a tournament golf player. Jack challenged Angela to a tennis match and got his butt whipped. He could beat her in golf, but only because he could drive the ball further and was a fairly accurate putter. Putting resembles some basketball skills. But Angela could always outlast Jack in tennis. Her shots were accurate. You'd think the tennis would require more endurance and strength. Jack liked Angela's competitive spirit. In my opinion, she was not sexy, but Jack thought her a challenge. Angela seemed more interested in competing with Jack in sports than dating him. She was not dating anybody else.

Angela had an exceptional sense of humor. That dry, half smiling witty digging kind of humor. She was quick with any comeback as long as it involved sports and not romance. Jack and Angela teased each other more about sports techniques than flirting. But Jack was persistent. Angela was built like and resembled Winona Ryder. She was not well built, but her muscle tone made up for being flat-chested. I mean, she had the bumps where her breasts were to be; sometimes a result of more testosterone giving her a slight masculine look. She had the hips of an athlete and her legs were shapely and muscled even though she was slender. Women who are avid sports players tend to lose the waistline making them sort of straight up and down from waist to hips. Angela stood about five feet seven inches and weighed about 120 pounds. She had a similar build to Maddie. Her athletic form while serving at tennis or swinging a golf club was perfect.

Jack asked her out only after they became mixed doubles partners. Angela didn't seem interested in Jack sexually and her kisses were not very passionate. That urged Jack on even more trying to break the ice. Jack complained to Cynthia and me that Angela didn't seem to get passionate when necking. When Jack touched her breasts she did not stop him, but seemed not to feel aroused. It was like whatever he would do was for his pleasure. After months of no advanced sexual contact, Jack had to simply proposition her. He asked her if she would like to sleep over and her reply was, "what for?"

Jack was very patient and began to kid her about not being interested in him.

"You have this very talented body and you deserve to put it to use with some good sex. Do you always have to compete with me?"

"What did you have in mind that would make sex competitive?"

"I bet I can make you have an orgasm. What can you bet? I'll tell you what; I'll give you five strokes in golf. If I win, I get a blow job, if you win, I'll perform oral sex on you."

"Don't be ridiculous Jack, those aren't prizes."

"Angela, do I appeal to you at all? If not, stop leading me on. I want to make love to you and if you don't ever plan on bedding me, let's end this relationship now."

"My goodness, if it's that important to you let's do it. Maybe sex will improve your tennis game." Angela chided.

Jack had Angela over to his condo for the big night. Jack did not know whether Angela was a virgin or not. He asked.

"No, I'm not a virgin. But I have had enough sex that I did not find it to be a big deal. I think men want sex all the time and I just don't feel it so necessary."

That's all the challenge Jack needed. Angela cooperated with Jack when undressing and if she was hiding her real desire, she did a good job. Jack said she enjoyed cunnilingus, but very reserved, no sounds, and he could not tell whether she climaxed or not. She was a tight fuck and moved or reacted little. Jack said using a condom was also a distraction. Angela's reaction was she hoped he felt better after they were finished. Angela's semi-uncooperative reaction only made her a bigger challenge. Jack was determined to melt her coolness. However, Angela did tease Jack more about sex and made witty remarks about if he did well, he could come and get it anytime. Isn't that a control position? A woman shouldn't offer sex as some sort of reward for conforming to her demands that are not sexual.

That attitude is the worst coming from any woman. I can remember when in college Jack and I overheard a conversation at a restaurant between this very chubby woman and her mismatched good looking well built boyfriend. She was telling him he better behave or he wouldn't get "any" that night. What the hell was that all about? Pussy being used as a reward for good behavior? I guess men could play that game too, but why bother? Sex is a mutual thing, not a fungible thing to barter. Angela was close to having that attitude, but Jack was determined to change her attitude. He next tried humorous sex. You know, laugh and giggle, wrestle and slap and chase each other around. The guy tries to insert and the woman tries to resist. Instead of pinning her to a mat, the male wins when he gets penetration. Well, maybe once in a long time, but not the best game for orgasms. A sexy mental attitude is essential for orgasms. Another problem was that Angela simply did not like the idea of putting Jack's cock in her mouth.

The unexpected happened. Jack and Angela got married. Jack may have felt it was the only way to dump the condoms because Angela got pregnant quickly and two times in succession. They had a boy first, then a girl. Those kids grew up with wonderful dual parental attention. After the daughter was born, Jack was back on condoms as Angela lost interest in sex fearing further pregnancies. Even after Jack's vasectomy, Angela seemed to focus on her babies and not sex.

To make a long story short, both of their children were good looking and talented tennis players, both winning college scholarships. Jack coached his son, Ryan in every sport. Jack was a devoted father.

About five years went by and Jack had a vasectomy. We were both sterile and Jack was still hoping to convert Angela to a great sex partner. It never happened. Is that not a strange turn of events?

Jack's first extramarital affair came soon after his vasectomy. That is except for an ongoing relationship with Maddie, his mistress. Jack was not "on the hunt," women simply chased him and as I have mentioned, Jack turned away as much pussy as some men get. Jack also met with Maddie weekly, so his appetite was always satisfied. Maddie was a safe haven from the trials and stress of marriage and raising kids. Maddie also desired Jack and Angela was indifferent; actually showed no interest in sex. But it is only natural that men when confronted with temptation of something new, a new adventure, the decision to avoid excitement is hard to do. I think that as we age, both men and women develop a curiosity about the other gender. We want to have our sex appeal reconfirmed. Many women only need the attention and are satisfied with the flirting, but men are not so advanced. Anytime a man meets a woman and she shows interest in him, any man would like that reassurance that he is appealing. Who follows that temptation and how far they go depends on whether they think they won't get caught. That is truly the reality of temptation.

For women, my goodness, if their husband becomes routine or takes them for granted, how many married women fantasize about attracting men. Compliments mean a lot and most women simply enjoy the good feelings without pursuing a sexual relationship. Women are too emotional to have simple sex affairs, and their risk is always greater. Men can get away with more because their requirements are simpler, but a man screening women and knowing when to back off takes real skill.

I think oral sex may be more prevalent for older people, although I think most older women would be uncomfortable letting a man put his face between her legs. I think a man that pursues that kind of sex might be more successful. Older women performing oral sex on a man may be easier to do than cunnilingus is for older men. Oral sex is sometimes considered not sex, thanks to President Clinton. All flirting requires new communication skills, as we get older. That makes sense because most people's attitudes have matured. The idea that a woman being offended by sexy compliments is losing ground. A guy ought to be able to sense what he can get away with. Older people actually need flirting.

I know of a man, a Doctor, who would frequently ask women if he could "eat their pussy," and yes he did get his face slapped a few times and his reputation preceded him, but he received a surprising number of acceptances. He didn't proposition his patients, but was known as a horny dude among the hospital staff. He always promised secrecy and actually had many good sex partners. It kind of makes you wonder what goes on in secrecy in the sexual revolution.

One of his clients, ten years Jack's senior, a wealthy woman who had Jack manage her investments wrote him a note asking if she could take him to lunch. After a few cocktails, she asked Jack if he ever fooled around. Jack said, no, but was interested in what she had to offer. This client belonged to a woman's investment club with mucho bucks and all middle-aged housewives, desperate housewives. Jack was invited to a hotel room after work and had a ball fucking this very horny older woman. This client's husband was a rich oilman and traveled too much and was apparently not servicing his wife. She needed monthly "lube jobs" when her husband traveled. The affair seemed harmless to Jack since she was equally concerned about not getting caught. So, Jack began meeting her demands. She paid cash for the motel room. This lady was an avid skier and had a hard body and simply loved to fuck. What could be the problem? She also had grown children and was not a threat to Jacks marriage.

When Jack was coaching little league football, one of his little players was part oriental. The boy's oriental mother always attended practice with her son and Jack could not help but admire this lovely shy woman. Jack would flirt with her, which thrilled her even though she would turn her eyes away and blush. Jack soon learned her husband was in the military and was stationed overseas for two years. Her name was Suzy and she was definitely a shy blusher. She stared at Jack constantly but turned her eyes away from Jack when blushing.

She asked Jack to follow her home one time promising him a cup of coffee so she could discuss her son's football progress. When home, her son ran off to play with some kids and it was two hours until dinnertime. Suzy was showing Jack her neatly kept house, one room at a time and when Jack was commenting about her recreation room, Suzy had moved into her bedroom. When Jack rounded the corner, Suzy had opened her blouse and was flashing some very lovely bare perky breasts. She said nothing and was not smiling and could not look at Jack. Jack pulled off his shirt and when doing so Suzy hurriedly took off her jeans and panties and lay back on her bed. As Jack took off his pants, she held her legs apart and watched Jack undress. She spoke not a word. Jack went down on her, which was unexpected on her part and she began to make oriental type noises, her sound was a constant, almost like a chant. She was very passionate and a very enthusiastic fuck. She wiggled a lot. Jack was hooked. Suzy bowed and thanked him and when Jack told her he was sterile; she said nothing, smiled and bowed. As Jack departed, she bowed again and thanked him for so much pleasure and would he please find time to see her again. Jack acquiesced. Thus began Jack's newfound luck. Angela would never know, even when they reached old age together. Jack knew how to qualify partners. No deep love affairs and meeting only qualifying women who were equally discreet. Any sign of trouble and Jack was gone. I would guess Jack saw Suzy twice a month until that relationship was replaced by another. It ended after football season and then her husband returned. His "dance card" was filling up.

I don't know if Suzy's reaction was an oriental thing or not. We had nothing to compare her to. She seemed needy and with her husband gone, I guess she felt sex with a lover was acceptable. Doesn't everyone have sexual needs? There are women like that, but again, we were not qualified to judge or generalize. Also, those tactics only happen to guys like Jack. Many women fantasize about him and I suppose eventually try something bold. If baring one's breasts causes a man to run away, then women must adjust to unexpected rejection. I suspect a "good looking" woman would not be rejected and who succeeds and who fails with that open seduction depends on that particular women's status and attitude. Women have an advantage with exposure seductions. Men can be arrested for exposing themselves, unless you are President of the United States.

I suspect such blatant sexual exposure as a means of seduction might vary by country and foreign customs. For example, flashing your goodies might be more acceptable in France than say, Saudi Arabia. Those are two extremes.

Morals and acceptable behavior make for interesting studies. I remember reading that Eskimos would offer their wives to male visitors as a courtesy to keep the guest warm in an igloo environment. I had a friend that I met later in life that would allow his wife to sleep with "good friend" traveling male visiting guests as part of her request for variety in foreplay. The male host would get aroused and have better sex after she returned to his bed. The sex was an agreed upon policy and subject to the wife's discretion, although this wife and husband liked talking with each other about detailed descriptions of what happened with the male guest. Condoms were required. The qualified male partners were limited to the same few who knew what was going on in that marriage. That husband sleeping with female guests was not part of the deal. I suspect there is no end to strange bedding practices.

When this husband relocated to another town and they didn't want to move their children to different schools, the wife stayed behind and as part of an agreement, either spouse could have affairs as long as they disclosed the deal to each other. This guy called my brother and asked him if he would service his wife for a month and my brother declined. I was curious as to what happened and heard that she had several lovers and was readily available for giving blowjobs. The last I heard was this couple reunited and never had a marital problem. This seems strange to me. But is that not a separation of sex from love?

Strange conversations happened between Cynthia and Angela as we frequented taking our wives to dinner. Angela once said to Cynthia, "I see all these women flirting with my husband and it makes me wonder what they see in him. He is not easy to live with. Thank God he is such a great father."

Cynthia was shocked to hear Angela say that. Was she that naïve? Angela didn't seem to care and was more into demeaning Jack with humor. Like he was getting old and had a hard time rising to occasions. She would tease him about spending too much time watching sports on TV. Jack would reciprocate with his humor, which we thought crude. When Angela was recuperating in the hospital from giving birth to their daughter, Jack brought her a get well gift wrapped like roses, but when opened revealed a set of toilet cleaning brushes. I thought that was funny, but I suffered reprisals at home from my wife who did not think it funny. I'm not sure what Angela's real reaction was after the fact.

Angela never approached Jack for sex and would not even consider sucking on his cock. She was "out of the sex business" and was only concerned about her children and her sporting career. She had no idea what she was missing. Jack could have been a more faithful husband, although I seriously doubted that. Some men or women if they are attractive will always face the problem of being "hit on." Their lives become a constant battle with temptation and their weaknesses are most difficult to analyze. It is easy to judge others if you have not been in their circumstances.

Jack once went to a Bronco game party with a couple that had one of the first big TV screens. One very attractive female guest was behind Jack and sitting off to the side obviously not that interested in the game. During a commercial break, Jack looked over and winked at this sexy woman, who then parted her legs and flashed her bare pussy at Jack. It was a quick "mini skirt flash," flash, but startled Jack. Had these things always been happening to Jack and he just didn't notice? During a commercial break, Jack went to the bathroom and this sexy lady had followed Jack and was waiting her turn behind Jack. When the previous user exited, Jack and the lady closed the door behind them since there was no one else waiting in line. There was another exit. The lady sat on the counter and lifted up her dress to her waist. Jack took out his cock and started fucking her with him standing and her sitting on the counter. There was no kissing, no words, and no foreplay. The lady was holding her legs up and apart with her arms behind her knees while sitting close to the edge of the counter. Her eyes were focused on the joining of their genitals. Jack got in about ten clumsy strokes while cupping her ass when there was a knock on the door. Jack zipped out, "coitus interruptus," and she quickly exited by the back door, Jack flushed the toilet and let the next guy in and left. Jack later got flashed discreetly every time his glances were safe. After the party, the lady's husband was at her side and Angela was at Jack's side. There was no conversation, no follow up contact to that event and no explanation.

At lunch a few days later, Jack told Cynthia and me what happened. He never heard from the almost quickie and Cynthia could not recognize her from Jack's description. Cynthia warned me that I better not wonder into any restrooms without her, but she thought Jack's adventure was exciting. The idea that some women might act out fantasies with little repercussions is hard to swallow. No pun intended. We discussed the possibility of catching some disease, but we assumed the lady might be somewhat discreet. Housewives and mothers are probably much safer than prostitutes or blatantly promiscuous women.

Now we have arrived back to the beginning of this book. Jack had an extra marital sex life that was as good as his pre-marital adventures and we enjoyed sharing his confidence. Our children were growing old; Jack and I were still in great physical shape as were our wives. Angela may have suspected something, but if she did she never raised any issues. Angela was happy, she could still star in tennis and golf and she was on the courts or courses frequently. She could have been a pro had she not had children, and her kids were her life's main interest. Jack was treated like a stud bull put out to pasture once completing his breeding and he was a cup winner at that. They say that a stud bull never tires unless he has to mate with the same old cow. Now that wasn't a nice thing to say.

I did not find Angela attractive and I despised her attitude. She was my best friend's wife and we did our best to be her good friends. Cynthia told me she felt sorry for Angela because she did not know what she was missing. It was all in her attitude. My Cynthia seemed to get better every time we made love and life was great. I have to admit that the two of us being Jack's closest confidants made our sex life better.

I don't think there is research or studies that evaluate a man's right to commit adultery, yet the man whose wife has lost interest in him is probably the most rationalized position. Each marriage would have to adjust to sexual attitudes, communicative skills, and mutual frustrations that plague all marriages. Whether they are serious enough to justify adultery would be a difficult study. Every situation would be different.

There is scientific evidence that hormones rise along with adrenalin and that there are mutual experiences causing those hormonal changes to cause people to have more or less sex.

For example, surviving a serious accident or being rescued from a raging flood or being forced into shelter with a stranger or a loved one can be enough to cause people to have passionate sex. Adrenalin can cause arousal with unusual circumstances.

Jack was once stranded in a serious snowstorm in the mountains. His car was buried and he had to spend the night with a widowed client. The cabin was not winterized and only had a fireplace, which had to be stoked periodically all night. They huddled on a big fuzzy rug in front of the fire with piles of blankets and as the wind howled outside, they clung to each other for warmth. This client was at least fifteen years older than Jack, but very attractive. They undressed under the covers and agreed not to have sex, but cuddle naked for warmth. Yeah, right.

She fell asleep, but in her sleep kept wiggling against Jack spoon fashion with her naked ass rubbing his penis. It kept Jack awake, but he was determined to keep the agreement. In her sleep, she climbed all over Jack and on one occasion her breast was against Jack's cheek, so he sucked on it. She did not awaken. Jack thinks she was faking sleep. Eventually she had her pussy against his face 69 style, later she claimed she was not aware of her actions. Jack began to lick her pussy and their blood ran hot and she reached several climaxes, probably faking semi-sleep. Eventually when she said she awoke, she says, she had Jack's cock in her mouth, still laying sixty-nine style. She quickly came face to face for a warming hug. Finally at sunrise, Jack left the warmth to fire the coals and when he came back she had spread her covered legs inviting Jack to fuck her, but only using body language. Jack could not get hard.

She said, "Was all that foreplay the main event?"

Jack explained, "Are you kidding me, I had a hundred perfectly good erections during the night that left poor Long John frustrated. I'd get hard with you rubbing against my cock, then you'd go away and I'd get soft only to be teased a few minutes later. Now, poor Long John Silver doesn't know whether he is coming or going, or going to come. If you suck on me for a while, he will return and we can create some early morning heat, perhaps too much heat, what do you say?"

She had lost all composure. She literally dove on Jack and brought Long John to full fucking status. They made passionate love for at least an hour often changing positions and when they finished and got dressed they could still see each other's breath. It was still cold, but their bodies were warm.

Jack had to dig for hours to free his old car. She helped. They had to spend another night waiting for snow removal crews and enjoyed another night of hot sex. The sex as a relationship was never to be repeated. What would any man do under those circumstances? There were two people not interested in sex until the emergency and then, did their adrenalin outperform their hormones? You make the call. Would they have frozen to death? They probably could have cuddled in their underwear and survived, but the wind noise sounded like they would be in danger.

Jack's adventures began to taper off and he settled down. He always had Maddie and his emotions ran high with her. He just seemed to lose interest in new adventures.

Not everyone falls in love just because of good sex. Does that mean that they should not or cannot enjoy sex? Is it not possible, under the right circumstances to have people enjoy pleasure without making a commitment? Often that depends on frequency of sexual opportunity with the same partners. Eventually, usually the woman will seek a commitment. That is according to the statistics.

Problems always occur when couples don't communicate well. Under casual sex circumstances one partner has little opportunity to gain something more than just pleasure. We are back to the theory of consenting adults, and maturity has everything to do with it. Many feel that morals degenerate with age. People get to an age where they want as much sex as they can get before they lose the ability. Does sexual pleasure fade with age? There are so many questions that simply cannot be answered using generalities. The question new partners should ask each other is," what do you hope to accomplish with this relationship?"

Why do people "fool around?" There are so many psychological reasons that it would take a book and a degree in psychology to explain. Most people fool around because they want their sexuality reconfirmed. Or, just plain curiosity; a normal urge. The question is always, how do these urges relate to love. Can one love and be loved and still enjoy sport sex out side of a marriage? Guilt and the breaking of vows is the problem. When one gets caught cheating it is usually interpreted as an act denying a love relationship. Perhaps penance and communications might save many divorces. Isn't it all about attitudes? Are reasons to cheat reasons to divorce? You can see where this argument is going. This is definitely an individual call based on levels of sophistication and communication. Sex does not have to mean that you have fallen out of love with someone you love. The hurt feelings of the cuckold partner usually reflect a sense of sexual incompetence and that is the main problem.

When a wife catches her husband cheating she assumes he no longer loves her and that is a misunderstanding in most cases. A man can cheat hoping to have some fun and reassure himself of his masculinity, and hoping not to get caught. That is immature, but probably the most common violation of marriage vows. If a man cheats and is looking for a better relationship it is unfair as a clandestine operation. If a woman fools around she may be looking for a better relationship and not likely fooling around for fun. A woman who gets laid enough at home is less apt to fool around, whereas a man can do both. Unfair? Yes, but that is the ugly truth. How a man feels when he fools around and then catches his wife doing the same thing begins to get complicated, too complicated for us amateurs.

The lesson always reverts to communication and foreplay. Human nature is what it is.

Chapter 36. Scientific Inqueery

In my opinion, Sigmund Freud (1856-1939) could not have gotten laid in a women's prison while waving a "get free" pardon. I doubt Siggy had a great sex life and his ability to communicate with women certainly would not be classified as tactful regarding seduction skills. His studies focus on dysfunctions that he thought could have been caused by early bed-wetting, or not having your diaper changed often enough. Imagine approaching a lovely lady and asking how often her diaper was changed as an introduction to seduction. "So, how often were your diapers changed?" I don't advise that approach.

Freud theorized that sexual development might be buried in your psyche with internal battles going on between your parents and how they treated each other, and how you felt about your Mother as a sex object, obviously such details were kept from kids anyway. You might say Sigmund wrote the prospectus on sexual behavior carefully outlining all of the disclaimers. I don't think Siggy was capable of teaching foreplay or the modern evolving sexual techniques promoted by the sexual revolution starting in the 1950s. We have obviously advanced without using Siggy's terminology, or philosophy.

Sexology, like nuclear physics has developed as a science during our lifetimes. There has been more technology and knowledge learned in the past 100 years than the past five thousand years and that certainly includes the evolution of sexual attitudes. Jack and I drew one conclusion that agrees with Freud and that is that our sex drives, our libido, is controlled by our egos. Our egos and our id are subsequently influenced by social conditions, peer groups, and to a large extent the establishment of religious moral guidelines.

There is also a theory that one's self esteem achieves a level then defined as the Ego. Does that mean too much confidence reflects an inflated Ego? I think the definition of an Ego is often confusing and exaggerated. Why is an Ego a bad thing? "He has such an Ego," is a demeaning phrase. How does one define or measure one's own sex appeal? Is that a result of an over developed Ego? I think the matter of evaluating one's sex life is a result of having self-confidence more than judging self-esteem or big Egos.

With men, sex appeal and success is defined as part of the Ego. Self-esteem, sex appeal and the Id are in constant conflict with each other for both sexes. Does anybody really care about the psychology of sex as long as they are getting laid? Sex appeal is a result of a successful battle between the Ego and the Id. In our opinion, it all boils down to attitude, and attitude is definitely related to maturity. Many women are satisfied by simply refusing to have sex, they derive satisfaction from being "pursued."

We think moral guidelines have also evolved with the evolution of sexology. Religion has always been behind the times, but Religious influence is justified for controlling promiscuity among the immature. We, again, refer to those conflicts during sexual maturation as the "Great Pube Wars."

We also believe that humor plays a major role in reducing inhibitions, which might be considered one of the ground rules for better sex. Certainly religion does not promote humor. And I doubt Freud had a sense of humor when researching sexology. A sense of humor about sex is sexy!

Think about this, Freud thought our egos had to mature and we had to learn to make rational judgments instead of acting out natural instincts. Wouldn't the "golden rule" of sex be more appropriate? "Do unto others as we wish they would do unto us." Is not "consideration for others" a better way to say it? Unselfish lovers of either gender are the ones that derive the most pleasure. That, once again brings us down to foreplay. I reiterate; Sex is an art form more than a science.

A humorous exchange; Dear Sigmund: What does it mean when a woman spreads her legs to entice a man? Dear Will: It means she has a split personality. I'll invoice you for my fee. (A bad joke?)

We began this fun book by defining the three basic human needs, or goals, as first, accomplishment, second, seeking the pleasure of sex and finally the good eating and drinking goals. The latter two are appetites. Alfred Adler, Freud's assistant had different views and thought that the basic human goal was to feel important. I think our use of the word "accomplishment" is equally appropriate. Adler further defined human self "importance" to include the need for friendships, respect, love, intimacy and marriage. We are driven to strive to satisfy our sex drives by striving for many other accomplishments. It is the guilt factor, lack of education, and lack of common sense that slows sexual development.

The bottom line on sex is to provide for survival of our species. That is true, but if that were God's sole objective why did God make sex so much fun? The prevailing theory is that the pain of childbirth had to be overcome with the desire for more pleasure. Otherwise if we bred only to procreate no one would have a second child because of the intense pain of childbirth. After a family was formed, sexual pleasure sometimes challenged the desire to control having too many children. It was too difficult for couples to simply abstain from the pleasure of sex. Birth control, rather "getting pregnant control" became one of mankind's problems because everyone desired having sex.

416

Next comes the debate over pleasure and whether pleasure was the real goal for having sex, or just procreation. Were we supposed to breed and then abstain from enjoying sex? The real conflict becomes a conflict over how much fun is acceptable. Or, should sex be used only as an act of love? How about love and respect, or how about just a level of affection below love? Is it not confusing that sex must be so regulated when it is a basic need? These social standards and rules have changed throughout history and makes for a really interesting study. In most early societies sex was more accepted as normal and not sinful. It is religion that first defined sex as sinful or immoral. Then came new rules as to what is immoral and what is sinful and how does God prioritize sin. The rules about sexual abuses were probably always if force. Abuses can be defined or prohibited by using common sense.

Alfred Kinsey was actually a zoologist (1894-1956) not a psychologist. Kinsey conducted surveys right after world war two and many thought his queries kinky. Kinsey focused more on unusual sexual things and I think, had this weird thing about promoting masturbation. He even offended his preacher father by interviewing the older preacher about his masturbation practices and sex with his mother. Kinsey's father eventually agreed, but was never happy about the interview. In the movie about Kinsey, and I cannot verify its authenticity, Kinsey's wife was a plain woman that was aroused sufficiently to fool around with some other interviewers and Alfred eventually interviewed her about how she felt and if there was any aftershock regarding her adulterous activity. As a result of his surveys, which the respondents were anonymous, sexologists concluded that masturbation plays an important role in sexual development. The Kinsey's stayed happily married.

The sexual revolution had many writers and psychologists that explored the evolution of sex. We were exposed to Masters and Johnson with more specific sexual techniques, but always objective and without passion. Alex Comfort offered a book with photos about sexual techniques, but they were drawings not real people. Ann Hooper, a British woman wrote and published illustrated sex and wrote more from a woman's point of view. Her writings are more appropriate for the current sexual environment. A more recent study conducted at the University of Minnesota claims that casual sex adds to one's mental health. The study emphasized attitude, which agrees with our theory. Sexual attitudes exploded from the sixties forward. This makes judging others about sexual attitudes more difficult.

Cavemen acted like wild animals for breeding purposes, but more for the quick pleasure. I'm not convinced that cavemen had getting tribal women pregnant on their minds. Love and marriage evolved separate from the evolution of sex. We don't know how specific civilizations' attitudes developed, especially before writing was invented. Ancient hieroglyphics might have looked like ancient porn. I remember seeing Aztec hieroglyphics showing people sitting in circles squatting and squeezing goatskins up their anuses. It took centuries to interpret those crude pictures, which finally revealed Aztec's having group social events getting high on strong coffee enemas. We don't hear much about that weird practice especially in mixed company where Christians probably never sponsored such parties. To the Aztecs it seemed to be just another social event. Hello Starbucks, we have a new marketing idea for you.

Ancient Egyptians, Greeks, and Romans seemed to be orgy oriented with no real moral codes. It was like anything goes, especially for the ruling classes. Women's bodies were simply tools made for male gratification. The Crusades brought eastern and western moral codes to a conflict, or many thought lessons to be learned by enemies. The winners often took women and raped them as part of the spoils of war. Women expected that treatment and may not have considered it rape, just submission. Orientals had written early sex books and their codes evolved back and forth between strict and liberal codes.

Pacific islanders simply did not understand sex. It was more a pleasurable appetite to be satisfied. The Victorians made sex taboo and went to the extreme with rules and morals. The twentieth century began the real psychological growth especially after each world war. Pornography grew during the Victorian age and evolved into more acceptable sex practices for those seeking more pleasure.

Disease was the primary mitigating factor raising more cautious approaches to sex until the development of condoms.

Playing with one's self (masturbation) is important in spite of the social pressures against it. For women it starts the process of self-awareness and should begin during puberty. Forget self awareness for men, it is all about feeling pleasure and boys masturbate as a natural phase of development. Sexologists now do write books about the best ways to masturbate.

All of our experiences grew during the advent of women's liberation from the distasteful positions they held throughout history. Women were chattels. They were property with no rights as they are today in Islam. I doubt there is a Muslim word for foreplay and I doubt Muslims would have any idea about courting women. There is also little written about their sexual prowess. I would wager that Muslims masturbate. I have no idea whether or how Muslim women masturbate. Without such self-pleasure they don't seem to have much enjoyment in life. But then Islam means "submission" and all human rights and pleasure are subjugated to the religious leaders. Most Ayatollahs preach and practice pedophilia. They believe only prepubescent girls are pure.

In the Muslim faith, a Muslim man can marry a baby girl starting at one year old. They can consummate the marriage at age nine. An abused Muslim woman has no recourse in a divorce court. Husbands can beat their wives at will, but recent amendments do not allow men to beat pregnant wives. Radical Muslims want to impose Islamic law on the rest of the world. I don't think American or European women would ever go for that deal, especially after the sexual revolution.

I doubt these young Muslim women have any self-awareness and considering the Muslim sometimes practice of mutilating the genitalia of young girls, I wonder if they can masturbate. I wonder what they wear under those Burkas and I wonder if they shave their legs. Nah; who cares? Studying Islamic sex seems like a waste of time to we modern day sexual athletes.

It was probably unusual that Jack Callahan's relationship with Amy and her exceptional admission to masturbating every morning of her life upon awakening interested us so much. We don't know where that fits in a survey, or how many women are like that, but it certainly had an impact on her sex life and ours. The lucky girl was unbelievably orgasmic and upon that we made our observation. Did she cause harm to herself with her masturbation practice? Amy's masturbation was for pure pleasure and served as a daily stimulant. We got the impression that Amy's masturbation was not fueled by fantasy, but simple pleasures. At the outset, I suspect she was too young to be concerned about self-awareness. We felt Amy had very low self-esteem and did not place the proper value on the use of her body. That sounds like a nice attitude adjustment to men, but definitely not for women. It could mean that excessive masturbation might lead to promiscuity. I don't think we really encountered women that we would classify as promiscuous, except Amy, but immaturity played a major role in her life. Obviously such cause and effect exists between the use of self-pleasuring and maturing attitudes.

But masturbation usually and eventually involves fantasies with the opposite sex, even with faceless partners. Fantasizing during masturbation is a form of growing self-awareness. It is only after more recent advances in the sexual revolution are women's masturbation practices discussed in detail. There are even scientifically designed vibrators, which every woman should own. The obvious problem is women having vibrators when discovered might make a man feel inadequate. That provides a whole new controversy.

Cynthia McMaster's claimed to have never masturbated during the "Great Pube Wars." I don't believe her. I suspect that with many women masturbation remains in a state of denial. (The first Queen of denial is supposedly Cleopatra, but that makes no sense since she was promiscuous). (That's a joke) It means that Women's efforts while in denial accomplished little regarding future orgasms. The basic rule is "use it or lose it." Unused clitorises may have difficulty rising to future occasions. I have heard of women who can masturbate without touching themselves. They climax in their mind and claim good pleasure. Orgasms in the mind only are commonplace among men. They are called "Nocturnal Emissions," or "wet dreams," and are a result of dreaming about sex. Most of these dreams occur during deep sleep and again alludes to the raging hormones of men. If a man has a healthy sex life and finds himself abandoned, wet dreams become more prevalent. Some men are not aware of this and simply awake with their genitals glued to the bed sheet. Ouch!

Guilt played too big a role in the sexual revolution and I suspect that was a sign of the times during the evolution. Remember the sexual revolution started with the "pill" and advanced birth control methods, which actually contributed to women's liberation. Why not? It was women's changing attitudes that made sex more normal, pleasurable and acceptable. There is an English study published in the British medical journal made from a survey conducted over four decades that women having used birth controls pills live longer. In that study the women tested only took the pill for four years or more.

Carol Mason was ahead of her time. She said she masturbated early in life and as a result she concludes she developed a big sexual appetite. She was one horny lady and thank God for that experience. My relationship with her surely made me a better lover and husband. Carol raised our level of understanding and curiosity to exceptionally high levels. She was by far the most interesting woman we met and we often wonder how many other women shared her attitude. These are some of the limitations of our experiences. Our sample is limited even if you think these experiences were that frequent. Remember, they are spread over as many as fifty years and were selected because they may reveal beneficial lessons.

The primary issue raised in this book is the rationalization regarding Jack Callahan's adultery.

Nobody's feelings were hurt. All parties benefited, yet how serious of a sin was afforded Jack. Did he not actually pleasure many women?

After the VW sex Jack had a wonderful relationship with Sue, who was married. They never were caught and in retrospect contributed much more than just sex to their lives. They traded advice on raising children and enjoyed much laughter and good times. I don't think that relationship ever ended. The sex may have faded, but they remained the best of friends. It is difficult to dismiss that relationship as anything but worthy.

Sheila's experience with Jack definitely enhanced her life. Her attitude changed and she learned to enjoy sex. She moved away a new person. We lost track of her future. What judgments could one make about that single event that also served a lesson in my marriage? My wife gained confidence in her ability to sympathize and offer constructive advice to Sheila that was advising the commission of a sin. How did that happen? Did it not reflect a broadening of attitudes? Measuring our sexual maturity from that point forward for us was significant.

My wife performing a blowjob on my best friend was shocking. Yet was it not an indication of normal curiosity? I was turned on at the time it happened because we had just experienced a beautiful voyeuristic experience. Our sexual curiosity was running high that week. Was that a battle of egos? I don't think so. It was more a moment of an enjoyable loss of control motivated by the previous sexual experiences. I was actually proud and I felt I was showing off something that was my privilege. After all, I did teach her the technique and that was an isolated opportunity to show her off. I can imagine how many readers will not agree with my reaction.

The fun and games that followed were wonderful and caused no problems. We were adults fooling around with the dangers of sin. It changed our sex lives. There was no need to repeat the lesson because the first time is always the most pleasurable moment. Repetitions of couples sharing sex would not have been productive. That was our mutual adult decision.

The college experience with Carol Mason was extremely unusual. I doubt that happens to many guys, but I guarantee you many men would love such a lesson. I never imagined getting into a female's mind with the same depth and frequency I entered her body. That sharing of both was monumental. I wish I knew what happened to Carol. Did she ever marry and have children? I'd like to think so because she had such control over her life.

Jack Callahan was amazing. His relationships with Josie, Heather, Dorothy and Maddie are true treasures. Such experiences are rare for the vast majority of men.

Jack's relationship with Maddie was almost a combination of Josie and Heather. I think Maddie was Jack's most worthwhile relationship. It was too bad that Maddie was sterile because she would have been the perfect wife for Jack, at least in my opinion and Cynthia agrees. Cynthia was a pillar of strength absorbing these immoralities and not passing judgment. Cynthia agreed that Jack was entitled to his lifestyle. It sounds too good to be true to other men, but in retrospect, who do you think suffered most? Who do you think benefited most? Or rather who do you think came in second place to Jack?

All of Jack's experiences were valuable lessons in understanding sex and women. I don't think we covered all possibilities, but enough to serve our purposes, which were truly beneficial to all involved. I believe we have reported and analyzed these rare circumstances, and they are true. That makes this story subjective, certainly more worthwhile than many scientific studies and surveys.

Here is another important conclusion: practically all men can enjoy sex without love. We can too often separate the two, but few women can separate sex from love. Sporty sex is difficult for women to swallow (no pun intended). Perhaps that is society's wisdom that women protect their gender with this moral code. But think about this, what if a woman knew she could get away with sex for sexual pleasure alone? Would not the newness and variety reaffirm her sexuality and trade that for orgasms? Few women can adjust to this anti-social rule, but I believe they fantasize about more sex than they admit. I think their risk of being exposed is greater because of the guilt factor. Why men can love one woman deeply and yet fuck another will always be a mystery to women. Can you separate sex from love?

Chapter 37. Aisle Of View

Interpreting God's purpose regarding sexual morals is beyond our pay grade. I believe, according to Saint Thomas Aquinas, God was motivated to create mankind in his own image for a good logical reason, so there could be love. Without love nothing has a purpose. Saint Thomas theorized that we are all created as a blank page and our life's free choices fill that page to be recorded in the eyes of God. We modernize that theory and say that we are all created as a blank videotape to record our lives. Then all eternal souls can view these tapes and walk in our shoes, so to speak, and learn other lessons by reviewing each other's videotapes. Isn't that the same as walking a lifetime in someone else's shoes? Think about how many lessons you learned about life and how you would benefit it you learned the lessons taught others by their different circumstances?

God's purpose for the creation was to create love, which is the fundamental reason for creating spirits or souls. During infinity, at some point in time, which technically doesn't exist for God, but nevertheless without creating something, God was theoretically alone. By creating the first souls, or spirits He had created "company." But the problem was that the souls created could only be in awe of God. God wanted to love and be loved and love only exists when offered freely. Therefore, love only occurs with a free will. A soul cannot be programmed to love you, right?

Love only existed after the first souls were given a free will; better said the ability to make choices. But there were few choices for spirits because there were no conflicts. Some angels fell from grace by not exercising their free wills to love or honor God, but what does that mean? A free will reacting into a void of nothing? What knowledge could these souls gain in heaven? There can't be much happening there. Their lessons would have to be vicarious. Perhaps angels are merely meant to be voyeurs of mankind unless they get awarded a lifetime. We really don't know the degree of angel intervention in our lives and if they watch us have sex, how do they know what it feels like?

The problem with all these newly created souls is that they were not individuals. They were all cut from the same cloth, so to speak. They were all created from "parts" of God. Therefore all new souls are created as "conformists." The logical step was for God to create the universe and the finite, a creation that has a beginning and an end. The finite created a time frame that resembles a test or gamut, or a maze of tests called a lifetime. Souls in heaven had no controversies, or even challenges that could be used in developing a personality. Every soul was essentially the same, a blank tape. Therefore, each soul was offered a lifetime to develop the soul. You begin in a womb and enter life programmed to learn and develop a free will.

So starting with Adam and Eve, God created a lifetime for each soul and provided each soul a body and mind equipped to face the challenges of life. Therefore, the sole purpose of life is to enhance and grow the soul. Bodies with souls could learn courage from feeling fear, and learning to love by knowing hate, or dislike, or disrespect. Humans had to deal with relationships with other people, competition, success and failures, happiness and sadness, tragedies and recovery, climate change, war and peace, and to fight diseases to learn to cope with life's challenges. God put these many forces (Mother Nature) into play and then allows them to exist without interference. The term describing God's creating these terms is called "existentialism." "These birthed bodies with souls were challenged by temptation as well as life's trials and tribulations. "Lead us not into temptation, but deliver us from evil."

Therefore the purpose of creation was to give each soul a chance to develop a personality, or individuality. We have free wills and we are responsible for our choices. Better said, the purpose of the Creation is to develop the souls so when they returned to heaven they would be accomplished individuals having participated in the test of life and could learn how to offer love freely. They had personalities and could love God and be awed at the same time. It is a two way street, meaning that God could love individuals with personalities that were freely developed.

The souls that were living finite lives were sent a message through the teachings of Jesus Christ that established some guidelines as to how to love God and earn your way to life everlasting. We are to love and respect each other. We learn goodness and righteousness, honor and how to love and be loved. These lifetime instructions are written in a manual for Christians called "The Bible." Each soul could better understand love because of Christ's teachings.

God allows the Devil to exist to represent the opposition, to represent "non-conformity." The Devil's influence is to serve as the opposition so mankind could comprehend the negatives as well as appreciate the acquisition of virtues. To reiterate, the most important lesson to be learned was "how to love and be loved."

God's Judgment involves the prioritizing of sin. Does every crime fit the punishment? Does every sin require the highest court of judgment? Appetites involve pleasure, therefore gluttony, greed, and selfishness, how we handle those who trespass against us and so forth are earthly choices. Should abuse of all earthly appetites be a Federal case and suffer the same repercussions? One theory is that we experience some punishment during one's lifetime that might work in our favor at judgment day. That is called "karma." How that lesson carries over into life everlasting is an unanswered question and yet is the most often discussed problem.

This holds true for all sins. Do you think a merciful forgiving God who wants to love and be loved would condemn a soul to eternal damnation for a lesser sin? This makes a strong case for purgatory and the possible rehabilitation of souls. Does Hitler, Stalin or Muslims deserve a second chance? I include Muslims because Islam is for complete submission and eliminates free will, as Christians understand it. Islam does not convert by persuasion; rather by force or intimidation and that type of submission leaves little room for love. I don't think, "love, love thy neighbor, world peace, brotherly love, or love and respect of women are ever mentioned in the Koran. However, the punishment of the condemned sinners for an eternity is hard to comprehend when enforced by a loving God. Should a Catholic school guy who does not confess to the sin of masturbation suffer an eternity in hell with serial killers?

God must certainly prioritize sins, it is logical. Our question is how serious are sexual sins? Do you really think consenting adults having sex will be considered as serious or as grievous sins deserving eternal punishment from a loving God? I wonder what level of sexual sins would qualify for serious punishment. I suspect each sin is qualified by how many people's feelings were hurt and whether or how such sins affected children. Or is sex only supposed to be an act of love? If we are God's children and you had to mete out punishment to your children, how would you prioritize such sins? Would two adults committing adultery deserve to burn in hell forever? I believe this rationalization is what is used by all sinners, albeit exaggerated.

Hell is defined as a place to be tortured for an eternity. What about torture? Today, Americans debate the use of torture while our enemies never hesitated to torture us. Torture is obviously immoral, but if that's the case why do so many believe that a loving God will use torture as a form of punishment? And, should that include everlasting suffering for moral misjudgments?

This raises a serious problem seldom discussed by Christians. What kind of punishment exists in purgatory? Should one suffer in purgatory as retaliation for causing another soul to suffer during a lifetime? If so, how is the punishment inflicted? Does that mean that purgatory is an interim torture chamber? The most common belief about hell is that it is merely the absence of God. That means boredom or self-analysis might cause the suffering. How boring would it be to spend an eternity reliving one's own life? Maybe that could be a lesson for being in purgatory. Keep living your own life over again until you get it right. It is like writing on a blackboard a hundred times, "I shall not sin." There is a lesson here, true, but how can the lesson be applied if the soul is not released to return to God's presence? I just have a hard time accepting painful burning in hell as a punishment for any sin imposed by a loving merciful God.

I believe that a soul being isolated from God and friends is how a sinner might suffer. Who decides who needs to suffer and who is forgiven raises another serious religious debate. People don't get to debate these things. The guilt is meted out against all sinners and individual consciences should be a determining factor. Doesn't this again come down to attitude, maturity and communication? If people engage in mutual pleasure, the seriousness of the sin, if there is one, has to do with who ended up suffering. Or maybe you can stretch the theory and say that sex is a reward for those who deserve it because they didn't hurt others feelings. And maybe the hurt feelings could serve as a lesson to that hurt person. Perhaps being hurt could even contribute to one's soul growth. Can you see that there is no end in such rationalization? Forgive me.

Now, think about the size of the creation. Is a universe and zillions of uncountable stars and planets necessary to test souls on just one place, earth? God is the first cause uncaused and there is logical proof that the universe is organized and has intelligent design. The force that allows all to continue to exist is called "existentialism." God exerts a continuous force that keeps the universe evolving. But all for one planet? That is not logical. I think there must be many other planets like earth where God created other creatures in his own image to test and develop souls. If in the same image, then they must be humans. If we are all created in His image, I doubt there are little green people with one eye living on other planets. The number of souls that exist universally must also be uncountable and exist infinitely. Sins and judgments must exist on a scale or in a courtroom that is incredible or incomprehensible. My point being, how do we prioritize sins in a universe that may be infinite and must contain uncountable numbers of other developing souls? It is incomprehensible and only God is capable of this organization. If you think all this organization is random, you are crazy.

Relating this universal scenario to people's sex lives is a challenge because we are not really sure what God intended with the lessons to be derived from sexual appetites. Are we to learn to control the appetite? Or should we be thanking God for these many pleasures and not abuse the benefits. If people abuse the joy of eating food they become overweight, is being obese the punishment suffered by our bodies? We don't take our bodies to heaven. Remember, we leave our bodies behind when we advance to life everlasting, we become recognizable personalities, perhaps visions. We will recognize many loved ones, yet they will have no bodies. That means we also leave our sexual appetites behind. Rationalizing too much sex, alcohol abuse, and eating abuses during our lifetimes creates many earthly problems and that relates to more than just good health. It has to do with how others see us, how others judge us.

This also raises the issue of people judging each other when maybe that is not our privilege. I think God lets us have puppies as pets to illustrate how we can be loved without compromise or judgments. Our desire for love will last a lifetime, but our desire to enjoy sex may increase in spite of physical limitations as we age. I think the intent or desire to have sex with someone has some complimentary merit between men and women. Sharing sex creates intimacy at any age. If old people can't have children, then why make rules against enjoying the pleasures of sex? There may be other mitigating circumstances like being only partially dressed, or feeling each other in the dark. That's because the older we get the more inhibited we become. So why not find some way to have sex without exposing old unshapely bodies? How about just eye contact? Like, hey, don't look at me, just feel what I'm doing and stay focused of my face. Oral sex can also involve limited exposure.

Old people might lose interest in sex for pleasure because they don't want to expose their bodies as being unattractive. I have a solution. When I made love to my wife closing in on age fifty I wondered about other people whose bodies might not be as attractive as Cynthia. When Cynthia wore the garter belt her legs were more appealing. Why don't old people who get wrinkles and blue lines on their bodies wear body tights with openings for their genitals? Even panty hose with a hole in them might make an older woman sexier. How about open shirts partially exposing breasts or men wearing T shirts during sex. If everybody smells good and they are freshly showered, then sex "uniforms" would enhance the pleasure. I think special pajamas designed to increase sex appeal is a good idea. Old people would have better sex lives if they could wear skin-covering tights for fucking. Memories might kick in for married couples and enhance those acts. I noticed Ice skaters often wear body tights and you can hardly tell they are wearing them. Body tights are designed to make skin appear tighter. I think there is a market for sexual attire for the elderly. Go figure.

At the other end of the age spectrum there may be stronger desires for pleasure, yet therein lies most of the rules of morality that have changed and may no longer be applicable. Is it possible that rules about sexual behavior are more necessary for the immature? Men reach their sexual desire peaks around age eighteen, and women a few years later. That helps to keep morality in force. But our desires grow or decline with age but we grow and vary our attitudes on an individual basis. That again reflects on our personal maturity, attitudes, and our ability to communicate with each other. That surely contributes to our soul development. Sexual adjustments are part of God's plan for soul growth even though heavenly souls may not have sex. I wonder what pleasures souls can feel. Perhaps love is the only pleasure.

In my opinion, as people get older their attitudes change and the desire to have sex overrides many moral codes. The rationalization for the adult maturation of sexual attitudes absolutely broadens with age. As people get older they have a stronger desire to prove their sexuality as well as a desire to be loved. Many older people change their attitudes regarding sex and diminish the moral values. They do so because if sex still feels good, they hope to enjoy sex as much as possible before they die. Women do enjoy sex after menopause, should they be denied that pleasure? I doubt that. There should be some major scientific studies regarding the fewer restrictions on adult sex and whether they should be justified or not. The conflicts grow with age because older people become more inhibited in spite of past experiences. It is natural that we feel we lose sex appeal with age, yet the desire grows. This may be the more serious challenge for older people that requires better communication. How do elderly negotiate sex?

There are many older people beginning around age forty, that don't think sex is something that is anybody else's business, certainly not to make rules against surviving life with pleasures they feel they have earned. Then these same older people have to deal with aging bodies that don't look so sexy anymore. The need to reassure each other that one's sexuality increases with age. True, inhibitions grow with age, because we are not physically as attractive as we age. This, again, makes another strong case for eye contact and maybe making love partially dressed or more in the dark as I just suggested. The eye contact is certainly more mature and intimate. Older lovers should be better able to talk about these things. I wonder how many old people will read this book?

The moral question is always raised when religious values interfere. Procreation is no longer a requirement for the elderly. Therefore, what role should sex play in mature relationships? Are the lessons to be learned related to life everlasting or finite gratification? Is sex a reward for a life's goals well accomplished? Can sex be more casual without fears of pregnancy? Is the emphasis shifting to pure pleasure? Can adults complement each other with sexual gratification? After all, the need for sex has changed. Should adults forget about sex? Is sex more therapeutic for older people? Is it healthier for old people to avoid stress with fornication? Sex relieves stress doesn't it? That has been proven. Can sex be recreational as well as healthy for older lovers? These many unanswered questions are very difficult to answer. We believe each set of circumstances need not be judged with generalities. Perhaps God intervenes by allowing the spreading of sexually transmitted diseases. That is certainly a control factor and a consideration for safe sex at any age.

It is a fact that men who ejaculate at least weekly will live longer. And there are statistics about ejaculating often keeps one free from prostate cancer. I would think that women might be more relaxed and have less stress if they could still have orgasms at an older age. Ladies, consider cutting a hole in your panty hose, clean up, add a small dose of perfume on your pubic hair, and request a good licking. If you get lucky you will know how a man feels during his entire lifetime always being on the begging side. If you find a "player," tell him what your plan is all about and give him the opportunity to prepare himself according to the same rules of foreplay.

These many considerations increase the need for communication among adults. It is difficult to make a comparison between adulterous young people, who are adventurous, perhaps more abusive of the privilege. Older people can be adulterous for reaffirmation of their fading appeal. Many want to enjoy sex as much as possible before they die and I guess that includes the other appetites such as eating and drinking. It seems unrealistic to prevent adults from enjoying any pleasures because society attempts to regulate pleasures. Is it not a matter of responsible choices? I think the underlying issue is what harm is caused to others. I think excessive drinking, drugs and sex abuses are not productive to soul growth. They may be productive lessons to those who must witness abuses. These abuses may seem unimportant to the participants, but works toward the destruction of sexual pleasures and these appetite abuses are never considered a good thing.

One further question that bothers Jack and I is what the heck are our souls supposed to do for an eternity? It could get pretty boring sitting around on clouds enjoying tea daily and talking about the "before after," rather than the "hereafter." We have a theory. Since we are to learn about brotherly love, why not review each other's lifetimes. Why not view every other's soul's videotapes? That could last an eternity because the creation of new souls will exist for an eternity. If a soul existed for an eternity then we have the extended duration to live each other's lives to learn to better love and understand each other.

Witnessing another's lifetime may also be considered a form of judgment by committee. Does that not include experiencing every soul's finite love life? Would that not increase each soul's wisdom as well as their capability to love and forgive everybody? What better way to praise God than to view his works and be awed. We become an infinite jury or audience that sees all that has happened to every soul. Now that would be infinitely interesting. Praise God!

There is another view that our souls become one with the universe; we become the wind; the waves, and we become part of Mother Nature. I'm not sure I understand the intellectual value of defining soul growth to become part of the wind, or even join our future spirits with Eagles or other creatures. It is logical that our individualities continue and rather than become one with the universe we continue to participate with the creation on a more intellectual level. Should not the lessons of soul growth continue as long as there is an eternity to grow? Being loved by God and loving God is greatly enhanced by this continuation of growth as another reason to be in awe of God and His works.

I don't like the idea of witnessing Hitler's exploits and morals. But, should we not learn from the negatives? I know many interesting historical figures could teach me some lessons about life and love. I wouldn't mind walking in their shoes for a lifetime; after all, I would have an eternity to spend witnessing some really interesting lives. Abe Lincoln comes to mind, or Mother Theresa. What about the Marquis de Sade? And we would learn who went to purgatory and who made the grade and advanced to heaven. I wonder if we have the option to "fast forward?"

Maybe the souls in purgatory are punished by having to view the biggest sinners first. As for the lost souls that didn't make it to the infinite audience level, I believe they eventually are forgiven and their lifetimes can serve as even more valuable lessons. I admit this is a simplistic view, but I had to present that view of love to make a case about the relative importance of sinning with sex. I don't think the actual act is the sin, but the intention of the sex act is to be judged. Remember I said that!

I wonder how Thomas Jefferson was judged since he wrote about humanity and individual rights, wrote the declaration of independence, became one of our greatest Presidents, yet he had sex with his slaves and fathered many bastards. I wonder how great people's lives are judged if we include their sex lives. Hmm, that is a conundrum.

During our lifetime we struggle to learn about the life experience of Jesus. Will we ever cease to learn how great His sacrifice was? God had to become man in order to feel what it would be like to better identify with mankind. His understanding was enhanced by becoming man because an all powerful God might be intimidating to some men. I am reminded of the late Paul Harvey's story about a man who did not understand why God had to become man in the form of Jesus. He denied the necessity for God to waste his time with a suffering lifetime. After all, God was omnipotent and having created man would certainly understand and empathize with mankind's thoughts and feelings.

This man believed in God, but did not believe that God had to become man to better understand mankind. This denier stayed home one Christmas Eve while his family went to church to celebrate the birth of Christ. There was a horrible blizzard that night and while this man was home alone he noticed six little bluebirds huddled against his rear window. The wind was rustling their feathers and they appeared extremely cold. Feeling compassionate, he bundled up and went outside and opened a nearby shed door exposing a closed in warm environment. His problem was he couldn't show the birds the opportunity for warmth. By trying to "herd" them into the warm shed he intimidated the birds and they flew away only to return to his warm window when he went back inside his warm house. It was then he understood that he so intimidated the birds that they feared him even though he meant well. He concluded that he wished he could become a bluebird for a few moments so he could lead them to shelter. Jesus came to show us the way to life everlasting. How else could God accomplish the lesson?

We believe people make too much of an issue about sex. Common sense should prevail. Two lonely adults meeting and having sex obviously isn't as big a sin as murder. Jesus actually had very little to say about sex. Jesus never married and there is nothing written about his interest in sex. There were a few generalized statements and parables about sex as a sin, but is fornication the most frequently committed sin? Perhaps that question should be rephrased; the most common sin is probably the sin of "pride." But, I was categorizing sin by physical acts and sexual intercourse outside of a blessed marriage is probably the most frequently committed physical sin.

The more I think about sin and guilt I conclude that the biggest sin is not telling the truth. All sins begin with a lie, and that immediately adds guilt to the equation. Breaking a vow is basically a lie and when a person allows their natural sex drive to take charge it becomes a lie if it breaks a vow or commitment. What if no one else learns about the lie? Sex that occurs that does not break a vow may also be more common with individuals who mutually agree to enjoy sex while not restricted by vows or commitments. Why is that a sin? It is a free choice to engage in mutual pleasure. How should we judge the relationship Jack and I had with Carol Mason? In retrospect it was a period of psychological growth that happened to involve using our bodies as well as our minds. We made no vows. What does that do to prioritize fornication? This is getting to be a deep discussion, is it not? (no pun intended).

That brings to mind the week that transformed Cynthia. We were adults that were playing games with the understanding that we wanted to explore or learn things about physical pleasures. The results were worthy and caused no harm. The person lied to was

Angela but she was not aware of the sin. Was it still a lie? Did any harm come to Angela? Her problem was in her own attitude and how responsible was Jack for changing her attitude?

The next step for any relationship is whether guilt follows the sin as a normal reaction. Does that not conclude that communication might avoid guilt? You would think that God knowing the future would have delivered more rules or explanations regarding the pleasures of sex. Most parables are lessons about love, love of mankind, world peace, and the social harmony created by love. Comparing the sin of fornication with murder is an exaggerated example, but you get the idea. Jesus did not prioritize sins, He forgave them.

In summary, is the challenge of sex supposed to be a test about controlling appetites, or a wonderful opportunity for two people to reward each other by sharing pleasure? The problem is dealing with the hurt feelings of others. To whom should that lesson apply? Promiscuity by children should be controlled, or influenced by logic and common sense. The existentialistic negative factors are diseases and conflicts between humans of the same sex or opposites. These conflicts are part of the big test of growing the soul. Relationships are essential to soul growth, are they not? Jealousy and pride come to mind as examples of how to deal with sex and love. So why not include lessons about sex as a means of personality development?

The question is who among the living should judge the intentions of all those who fornicate, or make love, or experiment with sex? "Who should cast the first stone?" How big a part should guilt play and who among the living enforces guilt? Surely guilt is counterproductive to good sex and could it not be self-induced? Therefore guilt should be replaced by other more positive influences. Knowledge comes to mind. Our leading conclusion is people's love lives are enhanced through better communications. If a person feels too much guilt, you don't have to challenge their guilt, pass them by and let them grow on their own. We all have the freedom to make choices and there are sufficient souls to interface with that we need not jeopardize another's feelings by causing stress.

We should avoid having sex with those with serious emotional problems unless love is the main factor. Many people pass on sex because they are in love with someone else and sex outside of love is hard to deal with. They should explain those circumstances and move the conversation in a different direction unless the denier asks for clarification. Love is the most valid case for rejecting sex with someone you don't love. The question remains as to whether one can enjoy sex just for the pleasure and not be responsible for another's judgment.

Adults agreeing to sex with a clear understanding of the consequences should be acceptable. That is how we learn. We learn to deal with people in all other ways and if sex plays a positive role in knowing other people intimately, so be it. There is an old saying that practice makes perfect. Should premarital partners practice sex? That seems to be today's style for couples testing future marriages. Are the rules about sex generalized? They should not be generalized. Should morals apply to every situation and every two people regardless of the circumstances? God loves us. The rules about governing human relationships have evolved over centuries, as has civilization.

The history of sexual attitudes and morals has also evolved. In my opinion, the sins of sex are over stated. How much regulation is necessary depends on the maturity of the sinner. The negative term should be sexual abuse. Who should decide who abuses sex, or who abuses eating food or alcohol? Appetites and temptation are subjective and punishment cannot be generalized.

It has taken Jack and me a lifetime to analyze our sex lives. One measurement, or judgment, is to evaluate how many people's feelings were hurt, damaged, or unnatural? We often worried about sinning and rehabilitation, or God's judgment. But our goal was to learn how to treat women and that seemed acceptable to us. Our lesson was simple. The better we treated women, the better they treated us. Because of our communicative skills we were taught, no matter how subtly, that foreplay and taking one's time was essential. That does not mean we could not enjoy quickies or therapeutic sex as long as it was not our only mode of operation. The single most important thing we learned was cunnilingus. Such a skill guaranteed reciprocity beyond expectations. Discussing sex with women also earned us many attitude points. We hope we presented you with some ideas and thoughts for your sex lives and your attitudes.

Please allow me one poll question, which I'll never see your answer. From what have you derived the most pleasure in life, sex, food or accomplishments?

Remember the old saying that love creates stress and sex relieves stress? Our general conclusion is that mature sex is healthy. The rules against adult sex actually create stress. We have presented a case to justify or rationalize sexual pleasure. Use your free will and you decide for yourself.

This may be the point of this dissertation: The actual act may not be the sin, but the intention of the act will be judged! Remember I said that!